Marital Imagery in the Bible

An Exploration of Genesis 2:24 and its Significance for the Understanding of New Testament Divorce and Remarriage Teaching

Colin Hamer

WIPF & STOCK · Eugene, Oregon

Wipf and Stock Publishers
199 W 8th Ave, Suite 3
Eugene, OR 97401

Marital Imagery in the Bible
An Exploration of Genesis 2:24 and its Significance for the Understanding of New Testament Divorce and Remarriage Teaching
By Hamer, Colin
Copyright©2015 Apostolos
ISBN 13: 978-1-5326-6920-0
Publication date 9/23/2018
Previously published by Apostolos, 2015

More Books from Apostolos

Romans: Hope for the Nations

The Emergence of Pentecostalism in Wales

The Role of the Holy Spirit in Biblical Hermeneutics

For details of all our publications visit www.apostolos-publishing.com

Comments on *Marital Imagery in the Bible*

'In this book Hamer presents a fresh and persuasive new perspective on the Old Testament roots of New Testament teaching on marriage, with great significance for contemporary debates on the nature of Christian marriage. It deserves to be widely read.' - *David Clough, Professor of Theological Ethics, Department of Theology and Religious Studies, University of Chester*

'Hamer incorporates a holistic view of Scripture that produces surprisingly enlightening insights. Regular summaries guide the reader through a detailed analysis using modern metaphor theory to arrive at a valuable conclusion.' - *Dr David Instone-Brewer, Senior Research Fellow, Tyndale House, Cambridge*

'This book makes a crucial contribution to understanding the Bible's teaching on marriage, divorce, and remarriage. Dr Hamer shows how the Divine marriage (God's relationship with his people, Israel; and Christ's relationship to the Church) relates to volitional human marriage in Gen 2:24. He then uses a brilliantly logical and clear cross-mapping methodology to grapple with the whole of the Bible's teaching on marriage, divorce, and remarriage—the result is an exegesis solidly grounded in the text of the New Testament that is a strong challenge to traditional views on divorce and remarriage.' - *Hugh Davis, Pastor, Wetherden Baptist Church*

'A ground-breaking, scholarly work that challenges our interpretation of biblical marriage. Well researched, compellingly argued, and clearly written—a must read for all in Church leadership.' - *Dr Roy Kunar, Gospel Expressions*

'This book is an in-depth study based on Hamer's PhD thesis. He maintains that biblical teaching on marriage is rooted in Genesis 2:24, which clearly indicates the establishment of a 'one flesh' relationship based on a volitional, conditional covenant relationship between man and wife. Such a relationship always included the possibility of divorce and remarriage. If we incline towards an absolutist position, it is because we are thinking of a more literal 'one flesh' relationship (unique to Adam and Eve in Gen 2:23), rooted in coitus rather than covenant. As a consequence we are importing mystical categories to sexual union which are not intended in the text of Scripture. Hamer's conclusion is that the covenant of marriage may end in divorce (with the potential for remarriage) for sexual immorality and desertion, but that the wife also has protections against abuse. This is a scholarly work, rigorous in both its scope and style, and is a very important contribution to the debate. There is a glowing tribute to the value of this volume in the Foreword by William Heth who was once absolutist but now takes a more moderate position.' - *Bill James, Pastor, Emmanuel Church, Leamington Spa*

'In this important and thoroughly researched thesis, Dr Hamer has resolved the conundrum of God's concern for marriage and the texts of scripture that appear to give conflicting instructions about people who are divorced. It provides a vitally important insight into God's healing solution for those who, like Himself, have experienced the rejection of their love.' - *Rev Dr Tom Holland, Senior Research Fellow, Wales Evangelical School of Theology*

'This is a remarkable study. Hamer's analysis of Genesis 2:24 both in its original context, and of its employment in the New Testament, is insightful, and as far as I am aware, unique in biblical scholarship. The analysis shows, among other things, that Paul in Ephesians 5:31-32 believes Genesis 2:24 to be a *protoevangelium* and a foreshadowing of the inclusion of the Gentiles in God's plan of salvation—placed in the scriptural record before the Fall. The logic of Hamer's analysis is followed through to a consistent, and to my mind, convincing exegesis of New Testament divorce and remarriage teaching.' - *Rev Trevor Baker, Albania Evangelical Mission*

'Sometimes in scholarship certain works appear that are groundbreaking, programmatic, and game-changing—Dr Hamer's study is exactly such a work. The writer's style is concise, smooth, and readable. His argument is very scholarly but expressed in a way that makes it understandable to the average Christian. I hope the book gets the attention it deserves by scholars and church leaders alike.' - *Florenc Mene, Albanian writer and theologian*

Acknowledgments

This book is based on the thesis I submitted to the University of Chester for the degree of Doctor of Philosophy in June 2015. My examiners were David Clough, Professor of Theological Ethics, Department of Theology and Religious Studies, University of Chester, and David Instone-Brewer, Senior Research Fellow, Tyndale House, Cambridge. My supervisors were Tom Holland, Senior Research Fellow, Wales Evangelical School of Theology, Bridgend, and Rich Cozart, Professor at College of Biblical Studies, Houston, Texas.

From my first mention of the subject Tom was convinced it was worthy of a PhD thesis. He never lost faith in the subject or my ability to deliver it—without him it would never have happened. Praise received at the viva was in no small part due to Rich's many effective suggestions and his detailed work on the manuscript.

I have also been supported throughout by many friends who read various drafts of the manuscript and both challenged and encouraged me on the way. I wish to mention in particular Trevor Baker, Ian Fairclough, Roy Kunar, and Florenc Mene.

But perhaps above all, my debt is to Stuart Olyott. His inspirational exegesis of Scripture at Belvidere Road Church each Sunday in the early 1970s has formed the basis of both my understanding of the Bible and my subsequent Christian life.

Foreword by William A. Heth

The biblical teaching on divorce and remarriage is clouded by the question of whether or not a duly covenanted and consummated marriage results in a mystical, ontological, indissoluble union which is permanent this side of death. Something close to that conception is the prism through which I once read the biblical passages on marriage, divorce, and remarriage, as have many others.

For me, the genesis of the assumption that marriage creates a near-indissoluble union came early in my seminary studies when an author I was reading made a statement to this effect. I found evidence for this in the kinship laws in Leviticus 18 which are rooted in the Genesis 2:24 concept that husband and wife become 'one flesh' or related kin. I argued that marriage creates vertical blood relationships in the form of children and horizontal 'one flesh' relationships between spouses that are just as permanent. Further, the Levitical prohibitions seemed to endure the death of one of the links in the relationship.

I saw further evidence for marriage permanence in Jesus's teaching in Matthew and Mark when, after quoting Genesis 2:24, Jesus repeated so as to stress 'So they are no longer two but one flesh.' Neither Mark, Luke, nor Paul seemed to be aware of the Matthean exception permitting remarriage after divorce for adultery, and when Paul did specifically address the possibility of a second marriage, in both contexts he connected it to the death of one of the spouses (1 Cor 7:39; Rom 7:2–3).

But twenty years into my ongoing study I was confronted with concepts that undermined what I thought was a tight case. I had to admit that when a man marries a woman they do not *literally* become 'one flesh'. The point of ancient Near Eastern covenants was to establish a relationship through a volitional commitment that included obligations with someone who was *not* a relative. Covenants were the vehicle for extending the loyalties that attended kinship relationships to unrelated entities. Thus the one flesh marriage relationship does *not* make husbands and wives as closely related as they will be to their own flesh and blood children.

Though still debated, I also came to the conclusion that covenants could be broken when the responsibilities pledged were not forthcoming. Adultery was such a serious violation of the marriage covenant throughout the ancient Near East and in the Old Testament that it could be punished by death. If adultery was not only an offense committed against an injured husband, but also an offense committed against God (Gen 20:6-10; Psalm 51:4), then I had to admit that Jesus, the Son of God, may have made an exception for the permanence of marriage in the face of this sin.

I also somehow missed that Paul's statement in 1 Corinthians 7:15, 'the brother or sister is not bound in such circumstances' (NIV), is a virtual negative restatement of the essential formula in the Jewish bill of divorce 'You are free to marry any man' (*m. Git.* 9:3). I can now sympathize with the candid point made by one New Testament background specialist when he said if Paul wanted to say that remarriage was not permitted, he said precisely the opposite of what he meant. And since Paul envisioned another situation that admitted of remarriage, this also meant that the unqualified version of Jesus's divorce sayings were never meant to be understood as exceptionless absolutes.

Finally, with David Instone-Brewer and others, I concluded that the only way to make sense of Jesus's teaching that the one who remarries after divorce commits adultery is to assume that the divorce was invalid. Matthew's account makes this assumption explicit and essentially endorses the Shammaite reading Deuteronomy 24:1 that divorce is permitted—not commanded—in such situations.

But how can we be sure? And what about 1 Corinthians 6:16 where Paul cites a portion of Genesis 2:24: 'Or do you not know that he who is joined to a prostitute becomes one body with her? For, as it is written, "The two will become one flesh"' (ESV). Some recent studies argue that Paul's citation of Genesis 2:24 means he believed sexual relations with a literal prostitute create an ontological union. How do we address these and other questions that still cloud the skies of how to responsibly understand and apply the biblical teaching on marriage, divorce, and remarriage today?

This is where Colin Hamer's amazing study enters in. This conceptually integrative study on *Marital Imagery in the Bible* uses both traditional metaphor theory and more recent developments in concept mapping to engage the considerable corpus of published material that considers marital imagery in

Scripture. Hamer shows there is no evidence that Jewish or Christian marriage teaching is rooted in the Genesis 2:23 *literal* flesh and blood connection of the primal couple. This neoplatonic model of indissoluble marriage patterned after the original couple first appears in the intertestamental period, and even there the evidence is scanty; nor is the primal couple marriage model a part of the implied readership of the New Testament. Rather, Hamer shows that the conceptual domain for marital imagery in the Bible is sourced in the Genesis 2:24 teaching that a woman becomes the wife of a man in a *metaphoric* one-flesh union formed by means of a volitional, conditional covenant. Hamer cross-maps this through the Pentateuch and the Prophets to *Yahweh: the Husband of Israel* and in the Gospels and Apocalypse to *Jesus: The Bridegroom of the Church* and more.

In short, the teaching of Jesus and Paul is rooted in and informed by marital imagery found throughout Scripture, and this imagery can be used as a hermeneutical tool to help sort out disputed New Testament texts. Marital imagery, according to metaphor theory, must have a source domain that is rooted in the experience of the intended audience if it is going to mean anything, and any exegesis of the New Testament teaching on mundane marriage should cohere with the marital imagery it employs. Hamer points out that as divorce and remarriage is central to all the Bible's marital imagery, it would be expected that both concepts will be evidenced in contemporary marriage practice and New Testament teaching.

The reader is in for a surprise, too, when Hamer addresses a common assumption by those who hold more restrictive views of divorce and remarriage, namely that gender reciprocity in New Testament divorce teaching can be assumed. Actually, Hamer argues this is an ill-founded assumption given the social milieu, relies on two improbable assumptions about the one and only statement in the Gospels addressing the matter from the wife's perspective (Mark 10:12), is incongruent with the New Testament's own marital imagery, and ultimately curtails a wife's freedom of action. Hamer's comprehensive study reveals that under the Old Testament economy, a wife already had divorce grounds more broadly based than those of her husband. The logic of Exodus 21:10–11 not only granted this, but also reveals that 1

Corinthians 7:15 is neither a 'Pauline privilege' nor an additional ground for divorce introduced by Paul, as I once argued. Paul is merely articulating Old Testament principles.

Hamer's appeal to marital imagery throughout Scripture and how it informs our understanding of the New Testament teaching on divorce and remarriage is brilliant. There are pastoral implications as well, though not directly addressed in this study. Simply put, at issue is how does one become 'one flesh' with another? Is it by a sexual act or be means of a conditional, volitional covenant? Hamer shows that it is the latter. So a woman becomes one flesh with her husband—a member of his family; a believer becomes one flesh with Christ—a member of Christ's body; and an unbeliever is one flesh with a 'prostitute'—which Hamer explains represents membership of the unbelieving world (as in Rev 17–21)—all by means of a covenant. This clarifies in particular the marriage relationship. To say, for example, Jesus teaches that marriage is 'more binding' than his contemporaries taught should not focus our attention on the impossibility of 'breaking' a near indissoluble bond formed by sexual union. Instead, our focus should be on covenant commitments, on loyal love, on mutual responsibilities, on integrity, on ethical living, and on the maintenance and care of spouses and children (cf. Exod 21:10–11; Eph 5:25–29) in accordance with the character of a life lived with the desire to please God.

This study builds on the work of Instone-Brewer and, in my view, confirms it. At a time when the Church of Rome is re-thinking its understanding of divorce and remarriage perhaps those of us not within that faith community should be doing the same. Hamer only briefly touches on the pastoral issues raised, so it is for those with pastoral responsibilities to work out in practice the implications of the exegesis of the New Testament divorce and remarriage passages contained here. I hope it is widely read.

William A. Heth
Professor of Greek and New Testament
Taylor University, Upland, IN

Preface by the Author

It can only be imagined that when the New Testament writers made their (albeit brief) comments on divorce and remarriage that they assumed they would be understood. So what has gone wrong?

In the years after the destruction of Jerusalem in 70 CE, when Graeco-Roman culture was at its height, the Jewish perspective of marriage and divorce, and thus the context of those brief New Testament comments was lost. The Christian church of that era was influenced by the neoplatonic ideas of the day, and an idealised concept of marriage developed from Adam and Eve's marriage recorded in Genesis 2:23—it was love at first sight, a marriage made in heaven. These concepts frame an understanding of marriage in much of Western culture even today.

However, that was never the understanding of ancient Israel. Instead they looked to Genesis 2:24: 'Therefore a man shall leave his father and his mother and hold fast to his wife, and they shall become one flesh'—so a naturally born man chooses a wife for himself, and their union was based on a 'covenant'—in other words an agreement. The Old Testament makes it clear what the basis of that agreement was. Furthermore, it is clear, if that agreement was broken, there could be a divorce and a remarriage. All the Bible's marital imagery (where the Hebrew and Christian Scriptures *imagine* that God is married to his people) is based on that understanding of human marriage.

But so strong is our concept of marriage, that when Genesis 2:24 is referred to in the New Testament, it is thought that the reference is to Adam and Eve's marriage. It is a paradigmatic marriage that for many excludes (or greatly restricts) the possibility of divorce and remarriage.

This study looks to challenge that paradigm—and to suggest that the New Testament writers would not have employed an imagery which had at its centre divorce and remarriage, only to deny the possibility of such in their own human marriage teaching.

Colin Hamer

Contents

Introduction 21

Summary 24

Chapter 1: Cross-Domain Mapping and Genesis 2:24 26

1.1 Cross-Domain Mapping 26

1.1.1 Metaphor Theory 26

1.1.2 Large-Scale Conceptual Metaphors 30

1.1.3 Cross-Domain Mapping and Theology Today 34

1.2 The One-Flesh Unions of Genesis 2:23 and 2:24 34

1.3 The Cross-Domain Mapping of Genesis 2:24 in the Old Testament 41

1.3.1 Yahweh: The Husband of Israel 41

1.4 Cross-Domain Mapping of Genesis 2:24 in the New Testament 43

1.4.1 Jesus: The Bridegroom of the Church 43

1.4.2 Sin: The Husband of Unredeemed Humanity 45

1.4.3 The Body of Christ 46

1.4.4 The Body of a Prostitute 48

1.5 Reverse Cross-Domain Mapping 58

1.6 Genesis 2:24 and the People of God 59

1.7 Summary: Cross-Domain Mapping and Genesis 2:24 60

Chapter 2: Literature Review 62

2.1 Marital Imagery in the Old Testament 62

2.1.1 Reverse Cross-Domain Mapping in the Old Testament 64

2.2 Marital Imagery in the New Testament 65

2.2.1 Reverse Cross-Domain Mapping in the New Testament 66

2.3 Divorce and Remarriage Teaching in the New Testament 67

2.4 Summary: Literature Review 68

Chapter 3: Methodology 70

3.1 Introduction 70

3.2 An Approach to the Biblical Text 70

3.3 Metaphor versus Other Literary Forms 72

3.3.1 Simile, Typology, and Allegory 72

3.3.2 *Sensus Plenior,* Intertextuality, Allusions, and Echoes 73

3.4 The Social and Literary Context 78

3.5 Cross-Domain Mapping as a Hermeneutical Tool 79

3.6 Summary: Methodology 81

Chapter 4: Marriage and Divorce in the Ancient Near East 82

4.1 Introduction 82

4.2 Ancient Near East Principal Relevant Source Materials 83

4.3 Specific Marital Practices in the Ancient Near East 85

4.3.1 Prohibited Marriages 85

4.3.2 Betrothal 85

4.3.3 The Marriage Contract 87

4.3.4 Marital Obligations 88

4.3.5 Adultery 88

4.3.6 Divorce 89

4.3.7 Divorce Initiated by the Wife 89

4.4 Provision and Protection for the Woman 91

4.5 Summary: Marriage and Divorce in the Ancient Near East 92

Chapter 5: Marriage and Divorce in the Old Testament 94

5.1 Introduction 94

5.2 Marriage in the Early Narrative Accounts 97

5.3 Mundane Marriage—Contract or Covenant? 98

5.4 The Importance of Virginity 100

5.5 Betrothal Arrangements 100

5.6 Forbidden Marriages 102

5.7 Polygyny and Concubinage 103

5.8 Marital Obligations 104

5.9 Adultery 105

5.10 Divorce 106

5.11 A Husband's Right to Divorce 107

5.11.1 Deuteronomy 107

5.11.2 Ezra 10:11 111

5.11.3 Malachi 2:14–16 111

5.12 A Wife's Right to Divorce 112

5.12.1 Exodus 21:7–11 112

5.12.2 Exodus 21:26–27 113

5.12.3 Deuteronomy 21:10–14 114

5.13 Other Divorces 115

5.14 Summary: Marriage and Divorce in the Old Testament 115

Chapter 6: Marital Imagery in the Old Testament 117

6.1 Introduction 117

6.2 Some Definitions 119

6.3 The Ancient Near East Background to Old Testament Marital Imagery .. 120

6.4 The Marriage at Sinai 122

6.5 The Sinaitic Covenant and Genesis 2:24 124

6.6 Betrothal Arrangements 125

6.7 Marital Obligations 126

6.8 Adultery 127

6.8.1 Adultery in Hosea 127

6.8.2 Adultery in Jeremiah 128

6.8.3 Adultery in Ezekiel 128

6.9 Divorce 130

6.9.1 Divorce in Hosea 130

6.9.2 Divorce in Isaiah 131

6.9.3 Divorce in Jeremiah 132

6.9.4 Divorce in Malachi 134

6.10 Remarriage 137

6.10.1 Remarriage at Sinai 137

6.10.2 Remarriage in Hosea 138

6.10.3 Remarriage in Isaiah 138

6.10.4 Remarriage in Jeremiah 139

6.10.5 Remarriage in Ezekiel 140

6.11 Inferred Cross-Mapping 140

6.11.1 Inferred Cross-Mapping: Punishments for Adultery 141

6.11.2 Inferred Cross-Mapping: Deuteronomy 24:1–4 141

6.11.3 Inferred Cross-Mapping: Covenant or Contract? 142

6.12 Marital Imagery in Eden 144

6.13 Summary: Marital Imagery in the Old Testament 145

Chapter 7: The Literature of the Second Temple Period 149

7.1 Introduction 149

7.2 The Old Testament Pseudepigrapha 151

7.2.1 Introduction 151

7.2.2 The Edenic Marriage in the Old Testament Pseudepigrapha 151

7.2.3 Contra-Indications of an Edenic Marriage in the Old Testament Pseudepigrapha 153

7.2.4 Summary: The Old Testament Pseudepigrapha 154

7.3 The Old Testament Apocrypha 154

7.3.1 Introduction 154

7.3.2 The Edenic Marriage in the Old Testament Apocrypha 155

7.3.3 Contra-Indications of an Edenic Marriage in the Old Testament Apocrypha 155

7.3.4 Summary: The Old Testament Apocrypha 156

7.4 Qumran 156

7.4.1 Introduction 156

7.4.2 The Edenic Marriage at Qumran 156

7.4.3 Contra-Indications of an Edenic Marriage at Qumran 158

7.4.4 Summary: Qumran 159

7.5 Rabbinic Writings 159

7.5.1 Introduction 159

7.5.2 The Edenic Marriage in Rabbinic Writings 160

7.5.3 Contra-Indications of an Edenic Marriage in Rabbinic Writings 161

7.5.4 Summary: Rabbinic Writings 163

7.6 Philo and Josephus 163

7.6.1 Introduction 163

7.6.2 The Edenic Marriage in Philo and Josephus 164

7.6.3 Contra-Indications of an Edenic Marriage in Philo and Josephus......... 167

7.6.4 Summary: Philo and Josephus.. 169

7.7 Summary: The Literature of the Second Temple Period 169

Chapter 8: The Documents of the Second Temple Period........................ 170

8.1 Introduction 170

8.2 The Elephantine Documents.. 171

8.2.1 Introduction 171

8.2.2 Relevance of the Elephantine Documents.. 171

8.2.3 Betrothal and Marriage Payments 173

8.2.4 Divorce and Remarriage... 174

8.2.5 Summary: The Elephantine Documents 174

8.3 The Judaean Desert Documents 175

8.3.1 Introduction 175

8.3.2 Background to the Judaean Desert Documents 176

8.3.3 The Relevance of Written Marriage Contracts 177

8.3.4 The Significance of Greek Language and Legal Instruments................ 178

8.3.5 Betrothal and Marriage Payments 179

8.3.6 The Groom's Maintenance Clause.. 181

8.3.7 Divorce and Remarriage... 184

8.3.8 Summary: The Judaean Desert Documents 187

8.4 The Graeco-Roman Documents 188

8.4.1 Introduction 188

8.4.2 The Dowry and the Groom's Maintenance Clause 189

8.4.3 Divorce and Remarriage... 190

8.4.4 Summary: The Graeco-Roman Documents 192

8.5 Summary: The Documents of the Second Temple Period 192

Chapter 9: Marital Imagery in the New Testament 194

9.1 Introduction 194

9.2 Marital Imagery in the Gospels 197

9.2.1 The Wedding at Cana 198

9.2.2 The Bridegroom Introduced 198

9.2.3 The Woman from Samaria 199

9.2.4 The Sons of the Bride Chamber 200

9.2.5 The Ten Virgins 201

9.2.6 The Wedding Banquet 201

9.2.7 The Last Supper 202

9.2.8 The Bridegroom Prepares a Place 202

9.2.9 The Cross 202

9.3 Marital Imagery in the Apocalypse 202

9.4 Marital Imagery in the Pauline Corpus 204

9.4.1 Ephesians 5:31–32 204

9.4.2 Romans 7:1–6 205

9.4.3 First Corinthians 6:15–16: The Body of Christ 212

9.4.4 First Corinthians 6:15–16: The Body of a Prostitute 215

9.4.5 First Corinthians 6:19–20: Bought With a Price 218

9.4.6 Second Corinthians 11:2: Betrothed to Christ 219

9.4.7 Second Timothy 2:10–13: The Betrothal Period 220

9.4.8 Ephesians 5:22–33 221

9.5 A Second Divorce 227

9.6 Adam and Eve as Types in the New Testament 228

9.7 Summary: Marital Imagery in the New Testament 229

9.8 New Testament Marital Imagery and Traditional Teaching 230

9.9 Some Implications for New Testament Exegesis 231

Chapter 10: Divorce and Remarriage in the New Testament 234

10.1 Introduction 234

10.2 Marriage in the New Testament 235

10.3 Divorce and Remarriage in the Gospels 238

10.3.1 Matthew 19:3–9 and Mark 10:2–12 238

10.3.2 The Question 239

10.3.3 The Digression 240

10.3.4 Moses's Teaching 240

10.3.5 Other Gospel Divorce and Remarriage Teaching 241

10.3.6 Answering the Question 242

10.3.7 Answering the Question: πορνεία 244

10.3.8 Other Grounds for Divorce 245

10.3.9 Summary: Divorce and Remarriage in the Gospels 249

10.4 Separation, Divorce, and Remarriage in First Corinthians 7 250

10.4.1 Introduction 250

10.4.2 Separation and Divorce 251

10.4.3 Not Enslaved 255

10.4.4 For God Has Called You to Peace 256

10.4.5 Remarriage after Widowhood or Divorce 257

10.4.6 Summary: Separation, Divorce, and Remarriage in First Corinthians 7 258

10.5 Adam and Eve 260

10.6 Summary: Divorce and Remarriage in the New Testament 262

Conclusion 265

Appendix A: Cross-Domain Mapping Diagrams 273

Appendix B: Judaean Desert Documents Chart 279

Appendix C: Judaean Desert Documents Translations 280

Judaean Desert Documents Select Bibliography 302

Abbreviations 306

Bibliography 310

Introduction

For millennia scholarship has sought to solve the enigmatic difficulties of Judeo-Christian divorce and remarriage teaching with little consensus.[1] This study investigates the possibility that the metaphoric marital imagery employed in the Jewish and Christian Scriptures—where Yahweh is portrayed as the husband of Israel, and Jesus as the bridegroom of the church—may provide paradigmatic and hermeneutic guidelines for a better understanding of the New Testament's teaching concerning divorce and remarriage.

It will be suggested in the course of the study that mundane marriage (i.e. non-miraculous human marriage) in those Scriptures is demonstrated to be a volitional, conditional, covenantal union and that such is underpinned by the aetiology of marriage outlined in Genesis 2:24, which was understood in ancient Israel to delineate marriage as a metaphoric (i.e. non-literal) one-flesh union of a naturally born man and woman: 'Therefore a man shall leave his father and his mother and hold fast to his wife, and they shall become one flesh.'[2]

It will be seen that this aetiology of mundane marriage—which embraced the possibility of divorce and remarriage—was exploited by the Old Testament prophets to explain the relationship between Yahweh and Israel, and by the writers of the New Testament to explain the relationship between Christ and the church.[3] Both the Jewish and Christian Scriptures see that those things which characterise mundane marriage (the source domain) also characterise the relationship between God and his people (the target domain): in metaphoric terms the source domain is 'mapped' to the target domain.

In contrast, the non-volitional, literal, one-flesh marriage union of the miraculous primal couple (Adam and Eve) described in Genesis 2:23—'Then the man said, "This at last is bone of my bones and flesh of my flesh; she shall

---

[1] See: John Jr. Witte, *From Sacrament to Contract: Marriage, Religion, and Law in the Western Tradition*, 2nd ed. (Louisville, KY: Westminster John Knox, 2012), 2–15; also: David Instone-Brewer, *Divorce and Remarriage in the Bible: The Social and Literary Context* (Grand Rapids, MI: Eerdmans, 2002), 238–67

[2] Unless otherwise stated all Bible quotations are from the anglicized ESV (London: Collins, 2002).

[3] In the main *Old Testament* will be the preferred terminology for the Jewish Scriptures rather than Hebrew Bible unless the reference is to the Masoretic Text.

be called Woman, because she was taken out of Man'"—does not appear to be employed in the metaphoric marital imagery of those Scriptures, or as a model for mundane marriage.

In chapter 1 I outline cross-domain mapping principles, where concepts from a source domain are attributed to a target domain. It will be seen that in order for metaphoric imagery to be meaningful to its intended audience, the source domain has to be rooted in a social reality. The chapter considers the different conceptual domains of Genesis 2:23 and Genesis 2:24, and suggests that it was the Genesis 2:24 marriage which underpinned not only the marital practices of ancient Israel, but it is that marriage which forms the source domain of the cross-mapping, and so Genesis 2:24 forms the basis of all the Bible's marital imagery.

In chapter 2 I will review the literature on Old Testament and New Testament marital imagery, and divorce and remarriage teaching in the New Testament. Here it is noteworthy that while the analysis of metaphoric imagery in the Old Testament is well-served in the literature, there is only a limited amount of published material addressing the New Testament imagery.

In addition, my literature review will show that New Testament scholars in their exegesis of the New Testament marriage and divorce pericopae (on the basis of a literal understanding of 1 Corinthians 6:15–16), have redefined the Genesis 2:24 one-flesh marriage as an irreversible ontological union, formed by coitus, not by covenant. This in turn appears to have led, in the literature, to the aetiology of the two marriages in Genesis 2:23 and Genesis 2:24 being conflated. It follows from this that the New Testament, when referencing Genesis 2:24, is seen as affirming the miraculous primal couple as the marriage model for marriage; a model that is seen to preclude, or at least greatly restrict, the possibility of divorce and/or remarriage.

In chapter 3 I shall outline my methodology for handling the biblical text.

To understand biblical marital imagery it is necessary to understand the source domain that has been cross-mapped. Since there is no systematic teaching in the Old Testament on marriage or divorce, I will in chapter 4 examine other texts relating to marriage and divorce from the ANE in order to elucidate the marital practices of ancient Israel.

Then in chapter 5 I will examine legislation and narratives concerning marriage and divorce in the Old Testament itself. It will be demonstrated that mundane marriage in ancient Israel embraced the concept of divorce and remarriage—few exegetes would disagree.

My reflection on Old Testament marital imagery in chapter 6 will reveal (as metaphor theory would suggest) that the social reality of mundane marriage—as practised and understood in ancient Israel—was mapped on to a target domain of *Yahweh: The Husband of Israel*. It follows that the divine marriage closely mirrors marital practice in ancient Israel, and that both embrace the concept of divorce and remarriage.

Next, in chapter 7, I survey the literature of the Second Temple period to see if there was a concept of a primal couple marriage aetiology in New Testament times. It will be suggested such a marriage model gives rise to the distinctive teaching that in mundane marriage there should be no polygyny or divorce; coitus is considered to be primarily for procreation; celibacy and holiness are linked; and each mundane marriage is believed to have a supernatural dimension. The chapter will demonstrate that there is only limited evidence of discussion in the Second Temple literature of such a marriage.

I continue my survey of the Second Temple period in chapter 8—this time focusing principally on the Judaean Desert Documents (JDD) which were published in the second half of the 20th century. It is believed by several scholars that these accurately reflect marital practices at a time contemporary with the redaction of the New Testament. Yet evidence is lacking for a primal couple marriage model in either the Jewish or the Graeco-Roman world of the day. The limited theorising about Adam and Eve's marriage forming an *archetype* for mundane marriage (which is found in the Second Temple literature) seems to have been confined to that: the marital practices of Palestine in the first century CE appear to be similar to those of ancient Israel.

The evidence presented in chapters 7 and 8 militates against an understanding that Adam and Eve's marriage forms the source domain of New Testament marital imagery—such a marriage was not part of the social reality which was available to be cross-mapped in the metaphoric marital imagery.

Chapter 9 discusses New Testament marital imagery and demonstrates how the focus of the divine marital imagery in the Gospels and Apocalypse is on a new conceptual domain: *Jesus: The Bridegroom of the Church*. In the imagery Jesus offers a marriage betrothal both to the Gentiles and divorced Israel. This adds further weight to the understanding that the primal couple's marriage cannot form the source domain of New Testament imagery: Adam and Eve's marriage does not have the characteristics required to achieve cross-mapping to such a target—for example, they had no betrothal period and neither of them were divorcees. Instead, the imagery of the Gospels and Apocalypse utilises contemporary mundane marriage—the social reality evidenced in the JDD—as its source domain. Indeed, it may be observed that if a primal couple marriage model is thought to undergird the New Testament's teaching on marriage and divorce (which many exegetes see as precluding the possibility of divorce and/or remarriage), then we encounter the problem of the New Testament authors employing marriage imagery which embraces concepts that are repudiated by their own mundane marriage teaching.

Finally in chapter 10 I will seek to find an exegesis of the New Testament marriage and divorce pericopae consistent with the analysis of the imagery in chapter 9. In other words, I will seek an exegesis of the New Testament's mundane marriage teaching concerning divorce and remarriage that is congruent with the New Testament's own marital imagery.

Summary

It is suggested that the marital imagery in both the Jewish and Christian Scriptures employs the same covenantal, metaphoric one-flesh marital principles found in Genesis 2:24. This 'source domain' then populates both Jewish and Christian ideas of the divine marriage—two 'target domains.' Metaphoric principles would imply that those Scriptures would teach an aetiology of mundane marriage congruent with their own imagery—an imagery which embraces the concept of divorce and remarriage—and hence it should be possible to find an exegesis of the disputed New Testament divorce and remarriage pericopae which is consonant with such a proposition.

It does not appear that such a study has been attempted previously. Furthermore, no published study appears to have challenged the widely assumed primal couple marriage model; or explored how the conceptual domains of Genesis 2:23 and Genesis 2:24 differ and the significance of that difference; or examined New Testament marital imagery in light of either traditional metaphor theory or the more recent developments in structure-mapping theory; or in light of that structure-mapping theory, how Genesis 2:24—with its metaphoric, covenantal concepts—is cross-mapped in both the Jewish and Christian Scriptures.

Chapter 1: Cross-Domain Mapping and Genesis 2:24

1.1 Cross-Domain Mapping

1.1.1 Metaphor Theory

Cross-domain mapping is a development of metaphor theory. A metaphor is when 'A' is declared to be 'B' when this is not literally true—a New Testament example is Jesus' claim recorded in John's gospel: 'I am the door' (John 10:9). Lakoff and Johnson say 'The essence of metaphor is understanding and experiencing one kind of thing in terms of another.'[4] Kennedy believes that metaphor is the '*greatest resource for the forceful expression of original thought*'; and Caird that, 'All, or almost all, of the language used by the Bible to refer to God is metaphor' and that comparison 'comprises ... almost all the language of theology.'[5]

Aristotle is perceived to have been the first to recognise that metaphors are a cognitive linguistic instrument but his insights were not re-visited until Richards, who identified a metaphor as consisting of a 'tenor' and a 'vehicle.'[6] The vehicle 'carries over' characteristics (hence μεταφέρω from the Greek 'to carry over') to the tenor (from the Latin *teneo* 'to hold'); thus in 'I am the door' the vehicle is the door that carries over characteristics to Jesus, the tenor, the complete statement forming the metaphor. Although not literally true a metaphor seeks to convey a truth, often such being left to the reader to surmise.

An Old Testament example of the metaphoric A is B statement is in Psalm 23:1: 'The LORD is my shepherd'—the 'LORD' is the tenor, the 'shepherd' is the

---

[4] George Lakoff and Mark Johnson, *Metaphors We Live By* (Chicago, IL: University of Chicago, 1980), 5
[5] George A. Kennedy, *New Testament Interpretation through Rhetorical Criticism* (Chapel Hill, NC: University of North Carolina, 1984), 26; George B. Caird, *The Language and Imagery of the Bible* (London: Duckworth, 1980), 18, 144. Emphasis/italics will be as per the original in all quotes.
[6] Thus: Mary Gerhart and Allan Melvin Russell, *Metaphoric Process: The Creation of Scientific and Religious Understanding* (Fort Worth, TX: Texas Christian University, 1984), 97-101; also: Macky, 'Richards ... provided the impetus to the modern study of metaphor' in Peter Macky, *The Centrality of Metaphors to Biblical Thought: A Method for Interpreting the Bible* (Lewiston, NY: Edwin Mellen, 1990), 5; I. A. Richards, *The Philosophy of Rhetoric* (New York, NY: Oxford University Press, 1936), 96-97

vehicle that accomplishes the transfer. It can be seen that the vehicle has to be a known entity to achieve a meaningful transfer: thus in the metaphoric A is B, 'A' (the tenor) is often a more abstract concept that is declared to be 'B' (the vehicle), a tangible entity employed to illustrate the tenor. Kennedy posits that: 'much can be learned about a speaker's assumptions and about his understanding of his audience from his choice and use of [the vehicle of the] metaphor.'[7]

McFague states: 'metaphorical thinking constitutes the basis of human thought and language. From the time we are infants we construct our world through metaphor'; and that, *metaphorical theology* is indigenous to Christianity.'[8] She continues: 'some metaphors gain wide appeal and become major ways of structuring and ordering experience' and from them emerge 'models' which:

> are similar to metaphors in that they are images which retain the tension of the "is and is not" ... "God the father" ... is a metaphor which has become a model. As a model it not only retains characteristics of metaphor but also reaches towards qualities of conceptual thought. It suggests a comprehensive, ordering structure with impressive interpretive potential. As a rich model with many associated commonplaces as well as a host of supporting metaphors, an entire theology can be worked out from this model.[9]

Macky suggests that Black's work on metaphor is seminal, in that it embraces what he calls an 'interaction' view, whereby the vehicle not only organises the reader's view of the tenor, but has the potential to change their view of both. He points out that metaphors can be used as models which facilitate the observation of new connections. He gives specific examples of their use in science (for example, how electricity can be metaphorically portrayed as a fluid), and considers how they 'were conceived to be more than expository or heuristic devices.'[10] *Contra* Davidson who—whilst acknowledging that he is

---

[7] Kennedy, *New Testament Interpretation*, 26
[8] Sallie McFague, *Metaphorical Theology: Models of God in Religious Language* (Philadelphia: Fortress, 1982), 14–15
[9] McFague, *Metaphorical Theology*, 23

arguing against the contemporary consensus, and accepting that metaphors might 'lead us to notice what might not otherwise be noticed'—claims that 'metaphors mean what the words, in their most literal interpretation mean, and nothing more.'[11]

To this, Black replies:

> To think of God as love and to take the further step of identifying the two is emphatically to do something more than to *compare* them as merely being alike in certain respects. But what that "something more" is remains tantalizingly elusive: we lack an adequate account of metaphorical thought.[12]

Similarly Glucksberg—exploring the difference between simile and metaphor—suggests that when a metaphor is converted to a simile ('the LORD is like my shepherd'), the conceptual process is changed, albeit in an intangible way, and so comments that the 'issue is as yet unresolved.'[13] Thus there is an element of mystery in every metaphor in that it is not clear how the mind processes them. But what is clear is that the process effects a change, not in the elements of the metaphor, but in our perception; and if Black's 'interaction' theory is correct, it has the potential to change our perception of both vehicle and tenor. Consequently that perception, as Lakoff and Johnson point out, becomes our new, albeit subjective, reality.[14]

Hence although the metaphoric 'electricity is a fluid' describes a way in which electricity can be conceived, it does not alter the way in which electricity functions; it is only our perception of electricity that has been changed by the metaphoric concept. In the metaphoric 'I am the door' (John 10:9), and 'this [bread] is my body' (Matt 26:26; Luke 22:19), an ordinary door and ordinary

---

[10] Macky, *The Centrality of Metaphors*, 1; Max Black, *Models and Metaphors: Studies in Language and Philosophy* (Ithaca, NY: Cornell University, 1962), 30–47, 226–29

[11] Donald Davidson, 'What Metaphors Mean,' in *On Metaphor*, ed. Sheldon Sacks (Chicago, IL: University of Chicago, 1978), 30, 39

[12] Max Black, 'How Metaphors Work: A Reply to Donald Davidson,' in *On Metaphor*, ed. Sheldon Sacks (Chicago, IL: University of Chicago, 1978), 192

[13] Sam Glucksberg, 'How Metaphors Create Categories - Quickly,' in *The Cambridge Handbook of Metaphor and Thought*, ed. Raymond W. Gibbs Jr. (Cambridge: Cambridge University Press, 2008), 80–81

[14] Lakoff and Johnson, *Metaphors*, 146

bread are employed as vehicles to illustrate the nature of Jesus' mission and body respectively; these mundane metaphoric vehicles each illustrate a more abstract and mysterious tenor. Notwithstanding any Christian confessional position, metaphor theory does not postulate an actual change in the properties of the metaphoric vehicle or tenor—the metaphor's aim is to illustrate, to make new connections, to change the reader's perception.

But metaphors, instead of elucidating meaning, can sometimes obscure it. The 'I am the door' of John 10:9 is part of an explanation following a series of metaphoric expressions about a shepherd and a sheepfold, used by Jesus in a discourse with the Jews. The Gospel writer comments, 'This figure of speech Jesus used with them, but they did not understand what he was saying to them' (John 10:6). The use of additional metaphoric expressions to explain the original ones in the pericope serves to underline Caird's point (noted earlier) about the ubiquity of metaphors in theological language.

Notice also Jesus' instruction to 'Watch and beware of the leaven of the Pharisees and Sadducees' (Matt 16:6), which from the explanation in v. 12 seems to portray the teaching of the Pharisees and Sadducees as having the potential to insidiously pervade one's mind. Here again a tangible and familiar element (how leaven permeates bread) is employed as the vehicle to illustrate a more abstract concept and heighten the disciples' awareness of it. Even so, such is the opacity of the metaphor that Jesus' warning brought only the confused response from the disciples: 'we brought no bread' (Matt 16:7). It can be seen how the understanding of a metaphor can lead to a difference of opinion for subsequent exegetes, as history demonstrates has happened with Jesus' 'this [bread] is my body.'

In addition, metaphors can lose the tension of their false literalism, and the metaphoric statement is then thought of as a literal statement. As an example of this, Gerhart and Russell cite, 'our Father in heaven' (Matt 6:9), claiming that the 'death' of this metaphor has given rise to an unwarranted patriarchalism.[15] Hence identifying a metaphor and its constituent parts is a

---

[15] Gerhart and Russell, *Metaphoric Process*, 116–17

process vital to the unravelling of the author's meaning, even if uncertainties remain.

1.1.2 Large-Scale Conceptual Metaphors

Fauconnier and Turner suggest that metaphor theory has previously focused on 'pair-wise bindings' (where 'A' is said to be 'B') but since the 1970s some metaphor theorists, for example Gentner and Bowdle, would describe large-scale conceptual metaphors (which McFague, Black, et al. might describe as models) as structure-mapping, and which Masson describes as cross-domain mapping.[16] Structure-mapping theorists, rather than employing the traditional terminology of vehicle and tenor, prefer to speak of cross-mapping from one conceptual domain to another. Thus Gerhart and Russell see that the pair-wise metaphoric statement, which Ricoeur described as the *root metaphor*, creates a new conceptual domain.[17] Their illustration of a root metaphor is a person in their unlit attic looking for a stored item when a flash of lightning reveals the whereabouts of not just the item but everything stored there—thus they describe the root metaphor as an 'ontological flash.'[18]

An example of such source to target cross-domain mapping is found in Psalm 23. The *root metaphor* which opens the new conceptual domain is 'the LORD is my shepherd.' The consequent new field of meaning—that God is like a shepherd to his people—allows the Psalmist to cross-map consequent metaphoric expressions from source to target. For example: 'he makes me lie down by green pastures ... your rod and staff they comfort me.'

Masson points out because of advances in metaphor research in the last two decades the details of theoretical schemes developed will inevitably change; it

---

[16] Gilles Fauconnier and Mark Turner, 'Rethinking Metaphor,' in *The Cambridge Handbook of Metaphor and Thought*, ed. Raymond W. Gibbs Jr. (Cambridge: Cambridge University Press, 2008), 53; Dedre Gentner and Brian Bowdle, 'Metaphor as Structure-Mapping,' in *The Cambridge Handbook of Metaphor and Thought*, ed. Raymond W. Gibbs Jr. (Cambridge: Cambridge University Press, 2008), 109. Robert Masson, *Without Metaphor, No Saving God: Theology after Cognitive Linguistics,* SPT 54 (Leuven: Peeters, 2014), 111

[17] Ricoeur says, 'root metaphors ... have the ability to engender conceptual diversity ... an unlimited number of potential interpretations at a conceptual level ... They are the dominant metaphors capable of both engendering and organizing a network': Paul Ricoeur, *Interpretation Theory: Discourse and the Surplus of Meaning* (Fort Worth, TX: Texas Christian University, 1976), 64

[18] Gerhart and Russell, *Metaphoric Process*, 113–14

seems one symptom of this is that linguists are not agreed on the distinction between metaphor and analogy.[19] This present study will follow Gerhart and Russell who see that analogies transfer the properties from one thing to another (as in a scale model) but leave the world of meanings undistorted:

> There is a sense in which analogies are found—they do exist or do not exist. Metaphors, by contrast, are created.... The metaphoric act distorts a world of meanings in such a way as to make possible an analogical relationship between one known and another known, an analogical relationship that was not possible before the metaphoric distortion took place.... The discovery of an analogy between two knowns is not an epistemological act that changes either knowledge or the world of meanings.[20]

---

[19] Masson, *Without Metaphor*, 111, 129–61
[20] Gerhart and Russell, *Metaphoric Process*, 113, 119–20

The root metaphor: 'The LORD is my shepherd,' with some example analogies consequent on its employment, might be diagrammatically imagined like this:

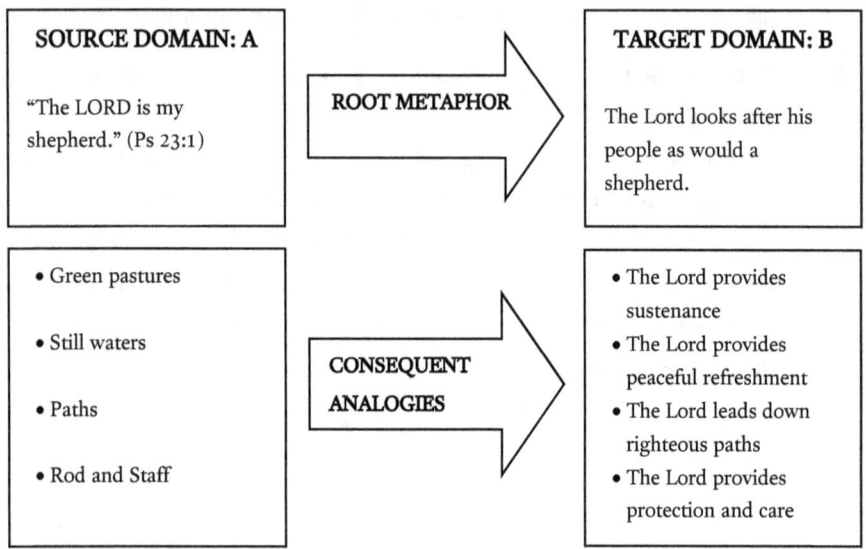

Gentner and Bowdle describe the process as an extended analogical structure-mapping between domains: 'Once the alignment is made, further candidate inferences are spontaneously projected from base to target.'[21] It is possible that some analogies are not articulated—an example is Psalm 23 where the reader is expected to understand that God's people are (metaphorically) sheep even though this is not referenced.

Masson points out that cross-mapping can be from a source domain to a new target domain (as in Psalm 23), or that two existing conceptual domains can be mapped on to each other by means of the pair-wise metaphoric statement; the consequent merging of the two domains giving rise to a third concept that leaves behind the original two in a 'tectonic reconfiguration.' His analogy is that of two tectonic plates colliding which results in a change in the landscape, and cites as an example, 'Jesus is the Messiah,' where a victorious king of Israel and a crucified son of a carpenter become one in 'Jesus Christ,' having been

---

[21] Gentner and Bowdle, 'Metaphor,' 109–10

merged in a 'forced equivalence'—making possible 'logical moves otherwise unavailable.'[22]

Diagrammatically, such a forced-equivalence cross-mapping between two existing conceptual domains to create a new third domain might be perceived thus:

CONCEPTUAL DOMAIN: A
A Messiah (Christ) King to Restore Jerusalem

The LORD swore to David a sure oath from which he will not turn back: "One of the sons of your body I will set on your throne..." (Ps 132:11)

Know therefore and understand that from the going out of the word to restore and build Jerusalem to the coming of an anointed one, a prince, there shall be seven weeks. (Dan 9:25)

CONCEPTUAL DOMAIN: B
Jesus: Crucified Son of Mary

"Is not this the carpenter, the son of Mary and brother of James and Joses and Judas and Simon? And are not his sisters here with us?" And they took offence at him. (Mark 6:3)

And the Son of Man will be delivered over to the chief priests and scribes, and they will condemn him to death and deliver him over to the Gentiles to be mocked and flogged and crucified, and he will be raised on the third day. (Matt 20:18–19)

F. E.

F.E. = Forced Equivalence

NEW CONCEPTUAL DOMAIN: C
Jesus Christ

---

[22] Masson, *Without Metaphor*, 59–68, 186; also: Mary Gerhart and Allan Melvin Russell, *New Maps for Old: Explorations in Science and Religion* (London: Continuum, 2001), 45–60

1.1.3 Cross-Domain Mapping and Theology Today

Since the 1970s cognitive mapping has emerged as a distinct interdisciplinary field of study and there is now a rapidly expanding corpus of literature exploring and applying the concepts of metaphor theory and the associated cross-domain mapping to a wide range of academic disciplines.[23]

However, Masson's perception is that:

> Recent developments in understanding ... in the interdisciplinary field of cognitive linguistics provide fresh ground for rethinking how God and religious beliefs are conceptualized.... While research groups of the Society of Biblical Literature in recent years have devoted some attention to the implications of metaphor theory in cognitive linguistics for the interpretation of ancient texts, this research has only just begun to reach the broader public.... These challenges of cognitive linguistics' to standard accounts of metaphor and figurative language have not been seriously addressed in theology and religious studies—indeed, have hardly been noted except for some recent work in biblical hermeneutics.[24]

His observation appears to be supported by the fact that although *The Cambridge Handbook of Metaphor and Thought* has 28 articles from 'distinguished scholars from different academic fields'—including science, law, mathematics, psychoanalysis, music, and art—theology is not represented.[25]

1.2 The One-Flesh Unions of Genesis 2:23 and 2:24

It will be suggested in this present study that the one-flesh union described in Genesis 2:24 is employed in the Bible's marital imagery, and in its associated corporate body imagery, to build five large-scale conceptual metaphors. Although as we shall see, in the literature review of chapter 2, it appears that the two one-flesh unions described in Genesis 2:23 and 2:24 respectively have

---

[23] Masson, *Without Metaphor*, 10–11; Fauconnier and Turner, 'Rethinking,' in Gibbs, *The Cambridge Handbook*, 53; Raymond W. Gibbs Jr., in Gibbs, *The Cambridge Handbook*, 5
[24] Masson, *Without Metaphor*, 4, 7, 16
[25] Gibbs, *The Cambridge Handbook*, 5

been conflated in the minds of many scholars, the two verses nevertheless underpin two quite distinct conceptual domains.

Genesis 2:23–24 states:

[23] וַיֹּאמֶר הָאָדָם זֹאת הַפַּעַם עֶצֶם מֵעֲצָמַי וּבָשָׂר מִבְּשָׂרִי לְזֹאת יִקָּרֵא אִשָּׁה כִּי מֵאִישׁ לֻקֳחָה־זֹּאת

[24] עַל־כֵּן יַעֲזָב־אִישׁ אֶת־אָבִיו וְאֶת־אִמּוֹ וְדָבַק בְּאִשְׁתּוֹ וְהָיוּ לְבָשָׂר אֶחָד

[23] Then the man said, "This at last is bone of my bones and flesh of my flesh; she shall be called Woman, because she was taken out of Man."

[24] Therefore a man shall leave his father and his mother and hold fast to his wife, and they shall become one flesh.

In v. 23 it seems that Adam is expressing satisfaction that—after being presented with all the animals, and yet still not finding a suitable helper (vv. 18–20)—he at last has another human with whom he can relate (vv. 21–23). But in the expression, 'This at last (זֹאת הַפַּעַם) is bone of my bones and flesh of my flesh,' Anderson sees the use of the article ה (which has the force of a demonstrative pronoun) as significant, since another demonstrative pronoun זֹאת ('this') is also appended to the phrase, emphasising the uniqueness of the occasion. He states: 'Targum Neophyti and Ps-Jonathan clarify what is so emphatically important and novel about this occasion. "This time *and never again will a woman be created from a man as this one was created from me*" (italics = midrashic explanation).' Anderson goes on to cite the Abot de Rabbi Nathan, which states: 'This one time God acted as groomsman for Adam; from now on he must get one himself.'[26] Whatever the strength of the grammatical argument, the Old Testament does not record any further miraculous unions and the pattern of marriage subsequently was that the man and woman were born naturally of their own parents and not miraculously formed by God.

---

[26] Gary Anderson, 'Celibacy or Consummation in the Garden? Reflections on Early Jewish and Christian Interpretations of the Garden of Eden,' *HTR* 82/2 (1989), 125–26.

Verse 24 is either a comment by the author introduced into the story or a later editorial gloss;[27] Kaye commenting that rabbinic interest centred on whether or not it reflected a matrilocal family structure in Jewish history.[28] But having reviewed the evidence for the idea that Hebrew patriarchy was preceded by a more remote matriarchal regime, Mace concludes, 'such a view is now entirely out of the question.'[29] It is more probable that, as Loader observes, the 'leaving' of father and mother indicates a 'new social reality, the beginning of a new household.'[30]

It is suggested the nature of the Genesis 2:24 one-flesh union is key to understanding the aetiology of mundane marriage and the Bible's marital imagery. It seems clear that the union of Genesis 2:24, unlike that of Genesis 2:23, is not a literal one-flesh union—there is no miraculous (or mystical) union of the flesh suggested in the verse, nor any evidence in the Old Testament record that this was how mundane marriage was later understood. We are told that the couple 'shall become one flesh' (וְהָיוּ לְבָשָׂר אֶחָד) thus, unlike Adam and Eve, their 'one flesh' status is a construct of their union, not a pre-existing state. This concept appears to be underpinned by the Hebrew. Verse 23 has the phrase בָּשָׂר מִבְּשָׂרִי employing the inseparable preposition מ ('from') and thus might be translated as 'flesh from my flesh' as per the ISV (even though most Bible versions opt for 'flesh of my flesh' which would normally require a construct phrase). This can be contrasted with v. 24 where the inseparable preposition ל ('into') is used (לְבָשָׂר)—thus Eve was formed *from* Adam (v. 23), whereas the mundane marriage couple come *into* their one-flesh union (v. 24).[31]

---

[27] Tosato sees it as a postexilic gloss: Angelo Tosato, 'On Genesis 2:24,' *CBQ* 52 no. 3 (1990), 406
[28] Bruce Kaye, '"One Flesh" and Marriage,' *Colloq* 2 (May 1990), 49
[29] David. R. Mace, *Hebrew Marriage: A Sociological Study* (London: Epworth, 1953), 76–82
[30] William R. G. Loader, *Making Sense of Sex: Attitudes towards Sexuality in Early Jewish and Christian Literature* (Grand Rapids, MI: Eerdmans, 2013), 12; Gehring suggests the husband 'forsakes' rather than leaves: René Gehring, *The Biblical "One Flesh" Theology of Marriage as Constituted in Genesis 2: 24* (Eugene, OR: Wipf and Stock, 2013), 22–24; also: Gordon J. Wenham, *Genesis 1-15* (Nashville, TN: Word, 1987), 70
[31] I am grateful to David Instone-Brewer for drawing my attention to this aspect of the Hebrew grammar of Gen 2:23-24.

Loader suggests: בשר ('flesh') can be used metaphorically in the Hebrew for one's own kin or family.'[32] Similarly, Instone-Brewer comments that in ancient Israel: '"they shall be one flesh" would probably have been interpreted to mean "they shall be one family."'[33] Skinner points out that in both Hebrew and Arabic, the word 'flesh' is synonymous with clan or kindred group, and he references Leviticus 25:49 where ESV translates בָּשָׂר ('flesh') as 'clan.'[34]

Kaye states:

> The term "flesh and bone" occurs only eight times in the Old Testament apart from Genesis 2:23. In Genesis 29:14 and 37:27 it directly and clearly means someone who is a close blood relation.... In general terms, the phrase has the immediate and direct sense of blood relation but, as well, is used figuratively of a close relationship.[35]

McCarthy clarifies the situation when he says a covenant was 'the means the ancient world took to extend relationships beyond the natural unity by blood.'[36] Holland considers the various understandings of בָּשָׂר in the Hebrew Bible and sees that a covenantal concept is contained in its semantic field: 'Here [Gen 2:24] "flesh," implies the covenant relationship a man has with his wife.'[37] Thus the one-flesh union of Genesis 2:24 is a covenantal *one-family* union: husband and wife are now perceived to be 'kin'—the family is a cohesive unit.

---

[32] William R. G. Loader, *The New Testament on Sexuality* (Grand Rapids, MI: Eerdmans, 2012), 278

[33] Instone-Brewer, *Divorce and Remarriage*, 22

[34] John Skinner, *A Critical and Exegetical Commentary on Genesis*, ICC (Edinburgh: T&T Clark, 1930), 70

[35] Kaye, 'One Flesh,' 48–49; he cites: Gen 29:14; 37:27; 2 Sam 5:1; 19:12, 13; 1 Chr 11:1; Neh 5:5 and Job 2:5.

[36] Dennis J. McCarthy, *Treaty and Covenant: A Study in Form in the Ancient Oriental Documents and in the Old Testament* (AB 21; Rome: Biblical Institute, 1963), 175. Hugenberger sees the predominant meaning of covenant (בְּרִית) in biblical Hebrew is 'an elected, as opposed to natural, relationship of obligation established under divine sanction.' The marriage agreement is often referred to as a 'covenant' by New Testament scholars, and this study will use that same terminology, but in so doing it is not intended to endorse any later connotations of such, or an understanding (*contra* Hugenberger), that it was deemed a contract endorsed or witnessed under divine sanction (see §5.3): Gordon P. Hugenberger, *Marriage as a Covenant: Biblical Law and Ethics as Developed from Malachi* (Grand Rapids, MI: Baker, 1994), 171, 216–79

[37] Tom Holland, *Romans: The Divine Marriage* (Eugene, OR: Wipf and Stock, 2011), 203; for further discussion: §1.4.3 and §1.4.4.

It will be seen in the course of this study that marriages in ancient Israel were formed by means of a volitional, conditional covenant, such being either understood—or articulated orally, or in writing. When the agreement was made, the bride, usually after a betrothal period, would leave her family and become part of her husband's family;[38] the process is symbolised in the West today when the bride takes her husband's family name.

The difference in a family with two birth children between the husband and wife relationship and that of the child/sibling relationships can be diagrammatically represented thus:

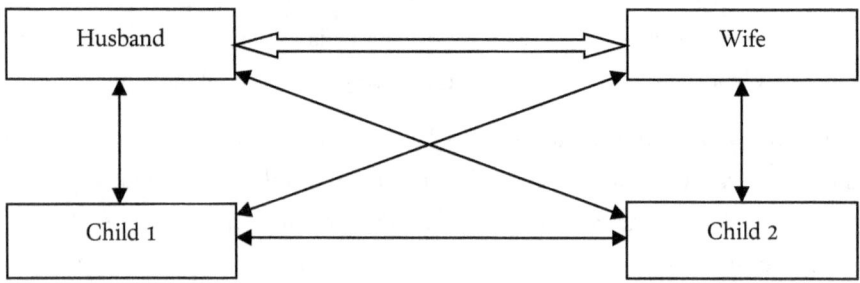

The parent/child/sibling relationships are blood relationships (i.e. consanguineous) and occupy the same conceptual domain as that of Adam and Eve, in that these relationships are (and always were) one flesh—they are non-volitional, non-covenantal, and permanent—a reality, not a construct. In contrast, the Genesis 2:24 one-flesh relationship between the husband and wife is a construct of a volitional, covenantal union; a construct which nevertheless brings the Old Testament prohibited degrees of affinity into force—that is, certain sexual relationships are now forbidden to the new family, as outlined in Leviticus chapters 18 and 20 (§5.6).

The 'they shall become one flesh' of Genesis 2:24 displays the false literalism of a metaphor and is capable of being analysed as such: two entities are said to equate—A (the couple) 'is' (or rather becomes) B (a one-flesh union), generating the tension that arises from the metaphoric distortion Gerhart and

---

[38] Daniel I. Block, 'Marriage and Family in Ancient Israel,' in *Marriage and Family in the Biblical World,* ed. Ken M. Campbell (Downers Grove, IL: InterVarsity, 2003), 58

Russell allude to. It seems that the consanguineous familial one-flesh unions and the literal one-flesh union of the primal couple form the source domain of the metaphor that illustrates the target—the metaphoric mundane one-flesh marriage union. Thus the concept of a literal/consanguineous one-flesh relationship is *carried over* in the Genesis 2:24 metaphor to the husband and wife, and it is this metaphoric one-flesh/one-family covenantal relationship which underpins the aetiology of mundane marriage.

However, it will be seen that a widely held view by New Testament scholars is that Genesis 2:24 refers to a relationship created by a sexual union that has an ontological and/or mystical dimension.[39] This seems to be based on a literal understanding of 1 Corinthians 6:15–16 where it is believed that Paul is referencing sexual intercourse with a prostitute.[40] It will be suggested that such an interpretation fails to identify Paul's metaphoric imagery. Whatever the validity of this literal view of the Corinthians pericope it will be seen in the course of this study that the marital imagery of the Jewish and Christian Scriptures cross-maps the conceptual domain of Genesis 2:24 as understood in ancient Israel.

It might be argued that the Genesis author was not familiar with metaphoric concepts; however, Genesis 3:15 states:

> I will put enmity between you and the woman, and between your offspring and her offspring; he shall bruise your head, and you shall bruise his heel.

In this metaphor, human conflict that results in physical injury is the vehicle illustrating the tenor of the imagery that portrays some future spiritual conflict. Similarly Genesis 4:7 utilises an animal as the vehicle to illustrate the nature of sin (the tenor): 'if you do not do well, sin is crouching at the door. Its desire is for you, but you must rule over it.'

---

[39] For example: Loader, *The New Testament on Sexuality*, 170, 172; Holland references others: Tom Holland, *Contours of Pauline Theology* (Fearn: Christian Focus, 2004), 124–39

[40] The authorship of the Pauline epistles is not significant for this study (§3.2) and so an assumption of Pauline authorship will usually be made.

Thus it is suggested that the one-flesh union outlined in Genesis 2:24 is cross-mapped from the conceptual domain occupied by the primal couple, the Genesis 2:24 relationship being a metaphoric restatement of that union. And rather than the literal (and therefore permanent) one-flesh union of the primal couple, it was the Genesis 2:24 metaphoric one-flesh union that was understood to be the basis of mundane marriage in the Old Testament. This metaphoric one-flesh union meant that the couple were now considered to be members of the same family, bringing relationships created by that union (which today in much of the English-speaking world would be described as 'in-law' and 'step') within the scope of prohibited sexual relationships.

The differences between the conceptual domains of the literal one-flesh relationship of the primal couple, and the one-flesh construct of mundane marriage, can be set out as below:

Genesis 2:23	Genesis 2:24
1. A miraculous man and woman.	1. A naturally born man and woman.
2. Remain as they are.	2. Become what they were not.
3. In a literal one-flesh union.	3. In a metaphoric one-flesh union.
4. Without the need for a covenant.	4. By a volitional, conditional covenant.

Wenham, reflecting the academic consensus and the conflation of the aetiology of marriage in the two verses, states that Genesis 2:24 'is a comment by the narrator applying the principles of the first marriage to every marriage';[41] however, it can be seen that the four principles of Genesis 2:24 outlined above are mutually exclusive to the principles underlying Genesis 2:23 and the first marriage described there. As articulated above, it will be seen that the Old Testament demonstrates that in ancient Israel the principles of Genesis 2:24, not those of Genesis 2:23, underpin the understanding of mundane marriage within that people group. This study will explore how these four principles of Genesis 2:24 are exploited in biblical marital imagery to show how naturally born men and women can become what they were not previously—part of a covenant community that in the imagery is the 'wife'/'bride' of God—

---

[41] Wenham, *Genesis*, 70

and how such might impact the understanding of New Testament teaching about divorce and remarriage.

1.3 The Cross-Domain Mapping of Genesis 2:24 in the Old Testament

It will be seen that the Old Testament marital imagery has many manifestations but that they are all part of one large-scale conceptual metaphor based on mundane marriage (the source domain), as outlined in Genesis 2:24, cross-mapped to a new conceptual domain: a defined people group being 'married' to their God.

1.3.1 Yahweh: The Husband of Israel

The root metaphor in Old Testament marital imagery is: *Yahweh: The Husband of Israel*. This root metaphor, it is suggested, is underpinned by the four principles of Genesis 2:24—Israel could become what they were not, the 'wife' of Yahweh, in a metaphoric union with him by means of a covenant. This 'ontological flash' opens a new conceptual domain which gives rise to many analogical inferences which are exploited in the Old Testament. McCarthy points out that the various rituals at Sinai signified that the two parties, Yahweh and Israel, were now 'considered to be' in a kinship relationship.[42] Lunn states:

> the use of the phrase "my people" on the lips of God before the Sinai encounter ... cannot then mean "my covenant people". Rather it must be understood proleptically ... [and] must be taken as shorthand for "Let go the people who shall be mine."[43]

Therefore Lunn and McCarthy believe it was by means of the Sinaitic covenant that Israel became what they were not—the people of God, Cohen suggesting it was at Sinai that 'the house of Israel was given the Torah as its "marriage-

---

[42] McCarthy, *Treaty and Covenant*, 173
[43] Nicholas P. Lunn, 'Let My people Go! The Exodus as Israel's Metaphorical Divorce from Egypt,' *EvQ* LXXXVI No. 3 (July 2014), 239–51

ring.'"[44] Thus the concepts of Genesis 2:24 are cross-domain mapped to a divine marriage (the marriage of God and his people), and the Old Testament prophets (notably Hosea) follow on by cross-mapping mundane marriage features on to this new target domain, employing concepts analogically from the source domain such as betrothal, asymmetrical marital obligations, adultery, divorce, and remarriage.

This root metaphor, with some example analogies consequent on its employment, might be diagrammatically imagined like this:

MAP 1 *Yahweh: The Husband of Israel* (Conceptual domain 'A' is created)

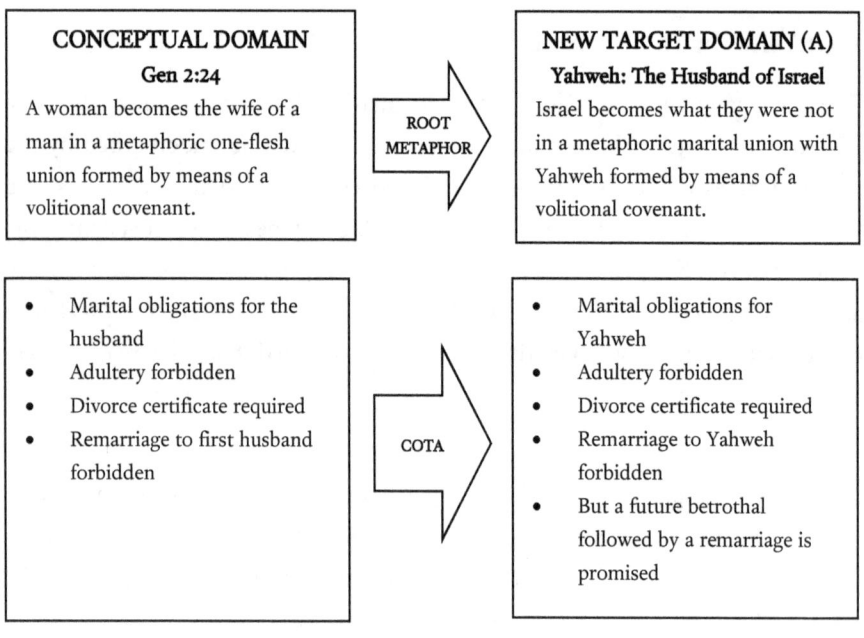

COTA = Consequent Old Testament Analogies

---

[44] Gerson Cohen, 'The Song of Songs and the Jewish Religious Mentality,' in *The Samuel Friedland Lectures 1960–1966,* ed. Louis Finkelstein (New York, NY: Jewish Theological Seminary of America, 1966), 12

1.4 Cross-Domain Mapping of Genesis 2:24 in the New Testament

The New Testament exploits the metaphoric one-flesh union of Genesis 2:24 in innovative ways to create four further large-scale conceptual metaphors (to be represented diagrammatically by MAPS 2–5).

The New Testament marital imagery employs the same source domain as the Old Testament imagery (mundane marriage as outlined in Gen 2:24) as the basis for two new marital target domains:

MAP 2 *Jesus: The Bridegroom of the Church* (creating conceptual domain 'B')

MAP 3 *Sin: The Husband of Unredeemed Humanity* (creating conceptual domain 'C')

And two new corporate body conceptual domains are created, not by means of a source to target mapping, but by a forced equivalence cross-mapping of the one-flesh/one-family concept of Genesis 2:24 with the two conceptual domains formed by the New Testament marital imagery ('B' and 'C'):

MAP 4 *The Body of Christ* (creating conceptual domain 'D')

MAP 5 *The Body of a Prostitute* (creating conceptual domain 'E')

1.4.1 Jesus: The Bridegroom of the Church

The root metaphor that arises from the Genesis 2:24 mundane marriage in the Gospels and Apocalypse, is not *Yahweh: The Husband of Israel*, but rather, *Jesus: The Bridegroom of the Church*. This new *ontological flash* gives rise to a new conceptual domain ('B' in the structure map, MAP 2, as below) and a different set of analogies related to the betrothal practices of contemporary mundane marriage, many of which are exploited in the Gospels and the Apocalypse in their imagery.

This root metaphor, with some example analogies consequent on its employment, might be diagrammatically imagined like this:

MAP 2 *Jesus: The Bridegroom of the Church* (New conceptual domain 'B' is created)

CONCEPTUAL DOMAIN Gen 2:24		NEW TARGET DOMAIN (B) Jesus: The Bridegroom of the Church
A woman becomes the wife of a man in a metaphoric one-flesh union formed by means of a volitional covenant.	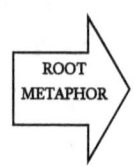 ROOT METAPHOR	Men and women are invited to become what they were not: members of the covenant community that is the metaphoric bride of Christ.
• Betrothal • Wedding feast • Invitations to guests • Groom prepares a place for his bride • Groom pays a *mohar* for his bride • Groom promises to care for his bride • Bride waits for groom • Groom comes for his bride • Groom takes his bride to his own home	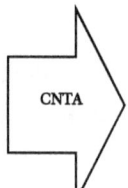 CNTA	• Betrothal • Wedding feast • Invitations to guests • Jesus prepares a place for the church • Jesus pays a *mohar* for the church • Christ cares for the church • The church waits for Jesus • Jesus comes for the church • Jesus takes the church to his own home

CNTA = Consequent New Testament Analogies

The Pauline corpus shares the same understanding of the imagery as the Gospels and the Apocalypse, thus 2 Corinthians 11:2 reads, 'I feel a divine jealousy for you, for I betrothed you to one husband, to present you as a pure virgin to Christ'—and specifically articulates the source and target domains of this New Testament marital imagery in Ephesians 5:31–32 as being Genesis 2:24/mundane marriage and the Christ/church relationship respectively:

> "Therefore a man shall leave his father and mother and hold fast to his wife, and the two shall become one flesh." This mystery is profound, and I am saying that it refers to Christ and the church. (Eph 5:31–32)

1.4.2 Sin: The Husband of Unredeemed Humanity

The Pauline corpus develops the imagery based on Genesis 2:24 to create three further large-scale conceptual metaphors, to be diagrammatically represented by structure MAPS 3–5. MAP 3 represents the mundane marriage source domain being mapped to a new target domain: *Sin: The Husband of Unredeemed Humanity.* It will be seen (§9.4.2) that Paul portrays Adam, in Eden, as having turned his back on God and taken humanity with him in a new covenantal relationship with Satan (i.e. 'Sin')—Holland suggesting that the 'body of sin' and the 'body of death' in Romans 6 and 7 are references to this community.[45] Just as the redeemed are portrayed as the wife of Yahweh/the bride of Christ bound to their husband by biblical marriage law, unredeemed humanity is portrayed as their antithesis: the 'wife' of Satan to whom she is bound by that same marriage law. Thus a new conceptual domain is articulated ('C' in the structure map, MAP 3, as below)—unredeemed humanity in a marriage to Satan.

The situation can be portrayed diagrammatically like this:

---

[45] Holland, *Contours*, 129–39

MAP 3 *Sin: The Husband of Unredeemed Humanity* (New conceptual domain 'C' is created)

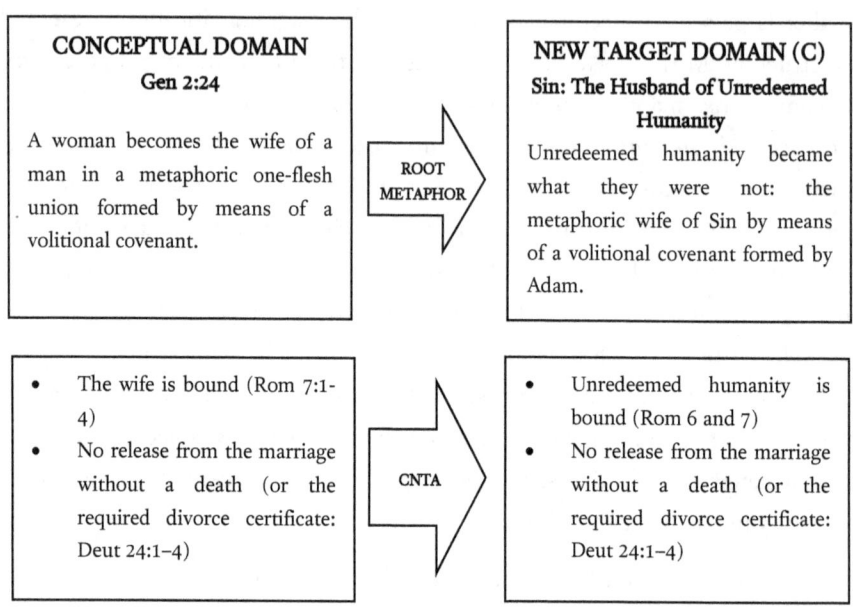

CNTA = Consequent New Testament Analogies

1.4.3 The Body of Christ

The fourth of the Bible's large-scale conceptual metaphors based on Genesis 2:24 is formed in the Pauline corpus by exploiting the fact that a new kinship group (a new family) is created by the Genesis 2:24 one-flesh union. In his first letter to the church at Corinth Paul maps that concept on to all believers to form a corporate body imagery, an imagery new to Scripture:

> Do you not know that your bodies are members of Christ?... For, as it is written, "The two will become one flesh." (1 Cor 6:15–16)

It has been pointed out (§1.2) that the בָּשָׂר (flesh) concept of Genesis 2:24 is employed in the Hebrew Bible to reference various kinship groups, for example, a clan (Lev 25:49). It can be seen from 2 Samuel 5:1 that Israel considered themselves to be united in a one-flesh union: 'Then all the tribes of Israel came to David at Hebron and said, "Behold, we are your bone and flesh."' Israel believed that they were in a 'vertical' metaphoric marital relationship with Yahweh, but it is clear they also perceived themselves to be in a 'horizontal' one-flesh/one-family relationship with each other.

Dunn and Holland believe that Paul's understanding of *flesh* includes this Hebraic concept; that is, *flesh* signified 'a corporate or national identity.'[46] It will be suggested in this present study that Paul takes the concept of the corporate one-flesh identity from Genesis 2:24, and 'overlays' it on to all believers. In other words, he transfers the kinship identity that Israel had, whereby they considered themselves to be one family, on to the conceptual domain of Christian believers: all now are perceived to be 'brothers' and 'sisters' in Christ, a new family group—in effect, a new Israel.[47]

Paul articulates the imagery in this Corinthians pericope, where, in metaphoric structure-mapping terminology, he performs a forced equivalence cross-mapping, from the kinship understanding of the one-flesh union of Genesis 2:24 on to all believers. Whereas in a source-to-target metaphor, a source domain is employed to generate a new conceptual target domain, for example, 'the LORD is my shepherd,' in this cross-mapping, Genesis 2:24 (a one-flesh horizontal metaphoric kinship identity) is cross-mapped with the pre-existing conceptual domain of all believers—a domain created by the marital imagery—to produce a new conceptual domain.

The resulting 'tectonic reconfiguration' (as Masson would describe it[48]) gives rise to the concept of a metaphoric body of Christ that has 'members' (i.e. believers)—thus Paul gives the church a new one-family/one-flesh identity. He elsewhere further develops the imagery into a functioning body of Christ and employs that concept extensively in the Pauline corpus.

---

[46] James D. G. Dunn, *The Theology of Paul the Apostle* (Edinburgh: T&T Clark, 1998), 70; Holland, *Romans*, 209

[47] Carmichael argues that the bread of the Passover meal was seen in Jewish culture to represent the nation Israel: D. B. Carmichael, 'David Daube on the Eucharist and the Passover Seder,' *JSNT* 42 (1997), 49; Evans endorses Daube: Craig A. Evans, *Mark 8:27–16:20*, WBC 34B (Nashville, TN: Nelson, 2001), 390–91; thus Jesus's comment 'this is my body' recorded in the Gospels (e.g. Matt 26:26) and in 1 Cor 11:24 might reflect a similar understanding by the New Testament writers: that is, Jesus's body represents a new Israel.

[48] Masson, *Without Metaphor*, 59–68, 186

Diagrammatically, this forced equivalence cross-mapping might be imagined thus:

MAP 4 The Corporate *Body of Christ* (New conceptual domain 'D' is created)

CONCEPTUAL DOMAIN Gen 2:24	CONCEPTUAL DOMAIN Jesus: The Bridegroom of the Church
A woman becomes the wife of a man by means of a volitional covenant forming a new kinship group.	Believers at Corinth had become what they were not: members of the covenant community that is the metaphoric bride of Christ.

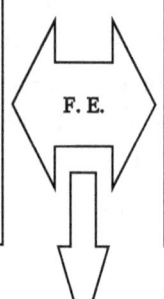

F.E. = Forced Equivalence

NEW CONCEPTUAL DOMAIN (D)
A New 'Horizontal' Identity: The Body of Christ
Do you not know that your bodies are members of Christ?... For, as it is written, "The two will become one flesh." (1 Cor 6:15–16)
For just as the body is one and has many members, and all the members of the body, though many, are one body, so it is with Christ. (1 Cor 12:12)

1.4.4 The Body of a Prostitute

It has been posited that the antithesis of the concept that the people of God are the wife of Yahweh (MAP 1) and the bride of Christ (MAP 2), is that unredeemed humanity is the wife of Satan (MAP 3). It will be seen (§9.4) that for Paul, just as the bride of Christ is the body of Christ (MAP 4), the wife of 'Sin'/Satan is the 'body of sin' (Rom 6:6), which, it is contended, is synonymous with both the 'body of death' (Rom 7:24) and the 'body of a prostitute' (1 Cor 6:15-16).[49]

Paul goes again to Genesis 2:24 to form this corporate body imagery (the fifth and last of the Bible's large-scale conceptual metaphors based on Gen 2:24), using it to portray unredeemed humanity as the antithesis to the body of Christ: the body of a 'prostitute'—a community with a 'horizontal' family identity to mirror the church's own family identity:

> Do you not know that your bodies are members of Christ? Shall I then take the members of Christ and make them members of a prostitute? Never! Or do you not know that he who is joined to a prostitute becomes one body with her? For, as it is written, "The two will become one flesh." (1 Cor 6:15-16)

Paul tells the members of the church at Corinth that, because of their immoral behaviour, they are identifying themselves with the wrong corporate body; that is, they are in effect becoming one body with a 'prostitute'—exchanging metaphoric membership of one corporate body (the church 'family') for the metaphoric membership of another (the 'family' of the unbelieving world). Thus, it is suggested, that Paul employs *prostitute* in a way that reflects its use in the Old Testament marital imagery where it refers to Israel's apostasy away from Yahweh. Huber sees that such a concept is exploited in the imagery of Revelation 17–21:

> the images of harlot and bride depict two possible forms of existence for the Christian community. The community can live in idolatry, as a prostitute, or the community can live in faithfulness to God, as a bride.[50]

---

[49] Thus: Holland, *Contours*, 137; Holland, *Romans*, 245

[50] Lynn R. Huber, *Like a Bride Adorned: Reading Metaphor in John's Apocalypse* (New York, NY: T&T Clark, 2007), 32; similarly Beale, pointing out the parallel between Rev 17:1-3 and Rev 21:9-10 states: 'Just as Babylon symbolizes socio-economic and religious culture arrayed in antagonism to God, so the bride, portrayed as the new Jerusalem, represents the redeemed community': G. K. Beale, 'The Book of Revelation' in NIGTC (Grand Rapids, MI: Eerdmans, 1999), 1064

Thus Paul forms his *prostitute* imagery in the Corinthians pericope by cross-mapping the concept that the lost are in a marriage to 'Sin' (a marriage based on the principles of Gen 2:24), with the concept that the volitional, covenantal union of Genesis 2:24 creates a new kinship group. The cross-mapping gives rise to a new corporate body identity for unredeemed humanity. Diagrammatically, this forced equivalence cross-mapping might be imagined thus:

MAP 5 The Corporate *Body of a Prostitute* (New conceptual domain 'E' is created)

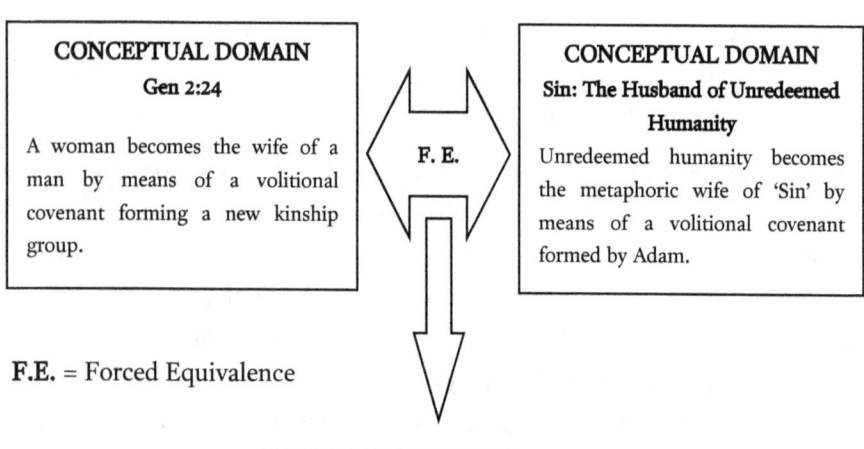

F.E. = Forced Equivalence

However, the scholarly consensus is that Genesis 2:24 is understood differently in the New Testament from the way it is understood in the Hebrew Bible. This new understanding appears, at least in part, to be based on a literal reading of 1 Corinthians 6:15–16.[51] It is considered Paul is saying that sexual intercourse with a literal prostitute creates an ontological union.[52] Commenting on this passage Loader says:

> Sexual intercourse leads to people becoming "one flesh".... Again we have to draw on Gen. 2:24. I make myself a member of a prostitute by having sexual intercourse with her.[53]

Thus Loader believes that one act of sexual intercourse with a prostitute creates a new reality and precludes a believer from communion with Christ, as the two realities created by sexual intercourse are 'mutually exclusive.'[54]

Loader gives a linguistic justification for this consensus view:

> when the man leaves his home and is joined to his wife, the two become one. How would this have been understood? It certainly includes sexual union. Again the LXX gives greater support to this. The Hebrew word, בשר ("flesh") in the expression "become one flesh" has its primary focus on creation of kin, whereas the word used in the LXX, σάρξ ("flesh"), puts the emphasis more on sexual union. Whereas בשר can be used metaphorically in the Hebrew for one's own kin or family, σάρξ ("flesh") is rarely used this way in the LXX. In the

---

[51] Holland points out the literal understanding of the prostitute that many scholars hold: Holland, *Contours*, 124–39; other examples apart from those that will be cited in §9.4.3 include Grosheide, despite him seeing that 1 Cor 6:19 might reference the corporate body of believers: F. W. Grosheide, *Commentary on The First Epistle to the Corinthians: The English Text with Introduction, Exposition and Notes* (Grand Rapids, MI: Eerdmans, 1953), 148–52. Gehring similarly comments that a corporate interpretation in 1 Cor 6:19-20 is possible: 'thus "leaving" the world behind, "joining" Jesus Christ (v. 17), becoming ... "one body" (vv. 17, 19) with him' but does not apply the concept to the 'prostitute': Gehring, *The Biblical "One Flesh,"* 266–67. Sampley also sees a literal prostitute being referenced in the pericope: J. Paul Sampley, 'The First Letter to the Corinthians,' in *Acts Introduction to Epistolary Literature Romans 1 Corinthians*, Vol. X of The New Interpreter's Bible: A Commentary in Twelve Volumes, ed. Leander E. Keck (Nashville, TN: Abingdon, 2002), 862–63

[52] Chapter 10 will consider the Gospel pericopae that deal with divorce and remarriage where a similar exegetical deduction about the nature of the Gen 2:24 one-flesh union appears to have been made: that is, it is an irreversible ontological and/or mystical union.

[53] Loader, *The New Testament on Sexuality*, 170, 172

[54] Loader, *The New Testament on Sexuality*, 177; similarly: Aaron S. Son, 'Implications of Paul's "One Flesh" Concept for His Understanding of the Nature of Man,' *BR* 11 (2001), 108

> Hebrew the sexual is more likely to be located in the word דָּבַק ("join to/stick to"), whereas in the LXX both προσκολλάω ("join to") and σάρξ ("flesh") are capable of including sexual connotations.... It allows Paul ... to apply Gen. 2:24 to sexual intercourse with a prostitute (1 Cor. 6:16).[55]

Dunn considers Paul's extensive and varied use of σάρξ and the related term σῶμά (body), Paul seemingly using the words interchangeably in this Corinthians pericope. However, Dunn cautions against reading too much into the LXX use of σῶμά as there was no equivalent Hebrew term for it, and points out that the dominant view has been that Paul's use of σάρξ reflects a combination of both Jewish and Hellenistic features.[56]

Holland surveys the use of בָּשָׂר and σάρξ in the Jewish and Christian Scriptures, pointing out that Paul's use of σάρξ in the New Testament reflects the varied understanding of בָּשָׂר that the Hebrew Bible demonstrates.[57] Holland contrasts those Hebraic understandings with the Hellenist concept of σάρξ, which he sees as bound up with the concept of the individual sinful human body. He then suggests that the early church, although using the LXX, would have known the Hebraic concept of σάρξ, and would have understood when Paul employed the term in a Hebraic way.[58]

Thus Holland believes Paul employs σάρξ in Philippians 3 in a typical Hebraic way to mean the 'covenant people of God':

> For we are the real circumcision, who worship by the Spirit of God and glory in Christ Jesus and put no confidence in the flesh— though I myself have reason for confidence in the flesh also. If anyone else thinks he has reason for confidence in the flesh, I have more: circumcised on the eighth day, of the people of Israel, of the tribe of

---

[55] Loader, *The New Testament on Sexuality*, 278. Loader elsewhere states when commenting on Gen 2:24: 'The [LXX] translator used the word προσκολληθήσεται ("shall be joined/shall join") to translate the Qal, דָּבַק ("join to/stick to"). The range of meaning of both verbs is similar, including "cleave" and "stick". It need not be a sexual reference': William R. G. Loader, *The Septuagint, Sexuality, and the New Testament: Case Studies on the Impact of the LXX on Philo and the New Testament* (Grand Rapids, MI: Eerdmans, 2004), 41

[56] Dunn, *Theology of Paul*, 56, 62

[57] Holland, *Romans*, 203–25

[58] Holland, *Romans*, 207

Benjamin, a Hebrew of Hebrews; as to the law, a Pharisee; as to zeal, a persecutor of the church; as to righteousness, under the law blameless. (Phil 3:3–6)

Dunn agrees with Holland:

> The problem was that this confidence was understood in classic Reformation terms as confidence in human ability to keep the law.... What had been lost sight of, however, was the fact that in the immediate context, "confidence in the flesh" for Paul was confidence in belonging to the people of Israel.... It follows then that it is *sarx* as denoting membership of Israel.[59]

Thiselton similarly sees that the New Testament has an emphasis on 'a people' rather than individuals and cites the work of Holland and Robinson in support—the latter, like Holland, emphasising the corporate understanding of σῶμά.[60]

Robinson comments:

> Now, if we ask why it was that the Jews here made do with one word (basar) where the Greeks required two (σάρξ and σῶμά), we come up against some of the most fundamental assumptions of Hebraic thinking about man. Our contention will be that the Pauline use of σάρξ and σῶμά is to be understood only in the light of these assumptions, and, consequently, that the Greek presuppositions, which necessarily demanded two words instead of one, are simply misleading if made the starting point in interpreting Paul's meaning. When it is remembered that our modern use of the terms "body" and "flesh" is almost wholly conditioned by these Hellenic presuppositions, it is clear that great care must be observed if we are not to read into Paul's thought ideas which are foreign to him.[61]

---

[59] Dunn, *Theology of Paul*, 69
[60] Anthony C. Thiselton, *The Hermeneutics of Doctrine* (Grand Rapids, MI: Eerdmans, 2007), 187, 480
[61] A. T. Robinson, *The Body: A Study in Pauline Theology*, SBT 5 (London: SCM, 1952), 11–12

This present study suggests, based on an understanding of metaphoric cross-mapping principles, that in 1 Corinthians 6:15–16, as in Philippians 3, σάρξ is used in a Hebraic way with a meaning within the same semantic domain as in the Philippians pericope, which in turn reflects the kinship meaning of בָּשָׂר in Genesis 2:24. That is, it is a relational term that Paul uses to posit a new metaphoric kinship group. Thus believers in Corinth were being told that their behaviour indicated to which metaphoric kinship group they now belonged: the body of Christ, the church family, God's new covenant people—or its antithesis, the body of a prostitute.

As Loader continues his argument he demonstrates how his understanding of 1 Corinthians 6:15–16—that the 'two becoming one' references sexual intercourse with a prostitute, a physical act which forms a permanent, non-covenantal, ontological union—facilitates the conflation of the primal couple marriage with that of Genesis 2:24. He writes:

> The notion of the two becoming one has many complexities, especially when Gen. 2:24 and 1:27 are placed side by side as here [Mark 10:6-8]. The assumptions behind this use of scripture and the saying about not undoing the yokes is that this coming together is an irreversible procedure: the oneness is no more to be reversed than a body is to be split in two.[62]

Loader, reflecting the academic consensus, links the primal couple (in this case Genesis 1:27) with Genesis 2:24, and deduces that the mundane marriage relationship (or, as he more precisely articulates, a relationship formed by coitus) is modelled on Adam and Eve's relationship; for Loader this makes mundane marriage 'irreversible.'[63] When the one-flesh union of Genesis 2:24 is understood in the way Loader et al. suggest (i.e. representing a union formed by sexual intercourse), it will be seen in the course of this present study that it does not have the properties to be effectively cross-mapped in either the New

---

[62] Loader, *The New Testament on Sexuality*, 278

[63] Commenting on 1 Cor 6 Loader states: 'sexual intercourse actually changes people by creating a new reality: oneness with another person, as Paul understands Gen 2:24' and that 'sexual union creates permanent union and severs any previous union.... Juxtaposing Gen 1:27 and Gen 2:24 leads to the conclusion ... that they are no longer two but one flesh': Loader, *The New Testament on Sexuality*, 176, 277, 290

Testament body imagery, or the New Testament marital imagery, where it is so employed.⁶⁴

Loader posits that in 1 Corinthians 6:15–16:

> While Paul applies the literal engagement with a prostitute on the basis of Gen. 2:24 to becoming one flesh with her (6:16-17 [*sic*]), he employs it metaphorically in relation to the believer's previous relationship, that is, not with his wife, but with Christ.⁶⁵

Thus he believes (as does this present study) that the *one-flesh* union of Genesis 2:24 is the basis in the pericope of an individual becoming either one body with Christ or one body with a prostitute. Metaphoric conceptual mapping brings two conceptual domains together by means of a pair-wise metaphoric statement. The pericope makes two cross mappings: Genesis 2:24 = the body of Christ, and Genesis 2:24 = the body of a prostitute.

1 Corinthians 6:15–16 can be diagrammatically represented as per MAP 6:

---

⁶⁴ Gehring shares Loader's perspective, quoting Blomberg (1990) he states: "'becoming one flesh" then focuses on the sexual union of marriage'; then Gehring states, citing Gen 4:1, 17, 25: 'Becoming "one flesh" in the sense of having sexual intercourse ... it is through ידע that man and woman become "one flesh"'; on 1 Cor 6:15–16 he states, 'two individualities become one new unity ... implying "that the man and the prostitute are wedded together even though there are no wedding vows"'.... As the texts demonstrate [quoting Son (2001)], "Paul conceives the union with Christ to be as real as the physical union created by sexual intercourse".... While even cleaving to a prostitute results in an (inferior) "one flesh" union (1 Cor 6:16) ... [again quoting Son (2001)] "Adam/Eve (sexual union) = husband/wife (sexual union) = Christ/church (spiritual union)"': Gehring, *The Biblical "One Flesh,"* 30, 52, 152, 265, 276, 296–97, 312

⁶⁵ William R. G. Loader, 'Did Adultery Mandate Divorce? A Reassessment of Jesus' Divorce Logia,' *NTS* 61.1 (January 2015), 76

MAP 6 Structure Map of First Corinthians 6:15–16

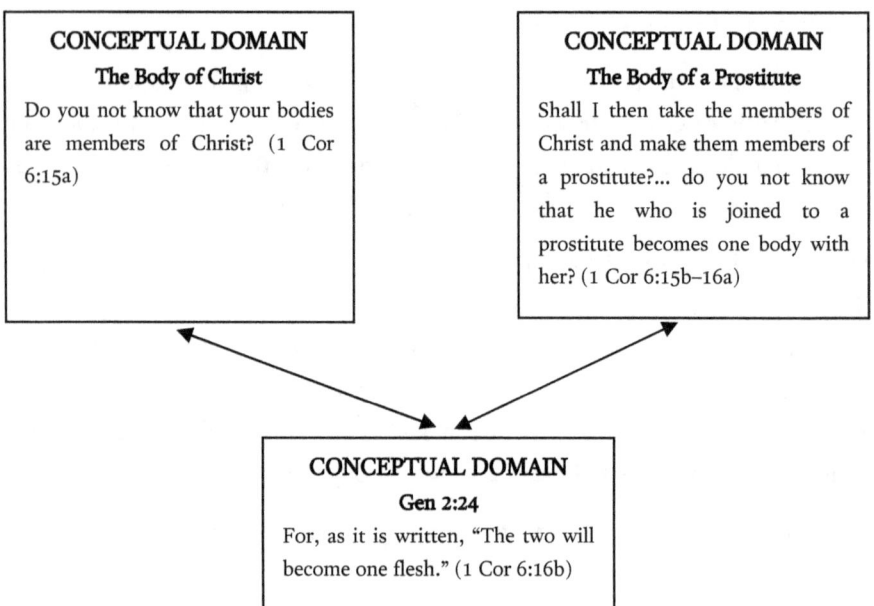

The first cross-mapping, Genesis 2:24 = the body of Christ, might be expressed as: 'the one-flesh union of Genesis 2:24 is the believer's relationship in the body of Christ.' However, if Genesis 2:24 were to be understood as a relationship formed by sexual intercourse, as posited elsewhere by Loader, the cross-mapping would be 'the one-flesh union formed by coitus is the believer's relationship in the body of Christ.' It has been proposed in this present study (as above) that the New Testament *body of Christ* imagery is based on a metaphoric kinship formed by a covenant whereby believers are considered to be brothers and sisters—this imagery cannot be meaningfully cross-mapped from a sexual act. Loader seems to suggest (as above) that Genesis 2:24 is employed in this first cross-mapping with its metaphoric, kinship understanding of בָּשָׂר—if this is the case, he is surely correct.[66]

---

[66] Loader points out elsewhere that metaphoric kinship is a Hebraic understanding 'flesh': Loader, *The New Testament on Sexuality*, 278

With such a covenantal, kinship understanding of Genesis 2:24, the Genesis 2:24 = the body of Christ mapping of 1 Corinthians 6:15–16 becomes: 'a volitional, covenantal, metaphoric, family relationship is the believer's relationship in the body of Christ.' This is consonant with metaphoric cross-mapping principles whereby concepts from one domain are cross-mapped to another—in this case the concept cross-mapped is the covenantal, kinship union of Genesis 2:24.

The second cross-mapping in vv. 15–16 is Genesis 2:24 = the body of a prostitute. A consistent exegesis would be to apply the same understanding of Genesis 2:24 as in the first cross-mapping. Thus you become a member of a prostitute's body in the same way you become a member of Christ's body—by means of a volitional covenant, not a sexual act. Such a covenantal understanding of the union undermines an exegesis of the pericope as referencing a literal prostitute—an exegesis which requires us to understand Genesis 2:24 to be firstly cross-mapped as a kinship, covenantal, metaphoric relationship, and then secondly as an ontological relationship formed by coitus.

As outlined above, the New Testament corporate body imagery is based on the New Testament marital imagery (this will be further explored in chapter 9). Both the marital and corporate body imagery, it will be suggested, are cross-mapped from the covenantal understanding of the Genesis 2:24 one-flesh union. While the marital imagery exploits the marital union of the verse, the corporate body imagery exploits the concept that a new kinship group, a new family, is created by mundane marriage—but neither the marital imagery nor the body imagery is cross-mapped from an understanding of the one-flesh union as representing a sexual act. Thus in the marital imagery the focus is on the new affinity relationship formed by the marriage covenant. Indeed, the root metaphor of the marital imagery, *Jesus: The Bridegroom of the Church* cross-maps an inchoate (i.e. as yet unconsummated) marriage-union with Christ based on a betrothal covenant—a distinctive feature of such being that coitus has not taken place.

1.5 Reverse Cross-Domain Mapping

Caird suggests:

> metaphors derived from human relationships have a special interest and importance, because they lend themselves to a two-way traffic in ideas. When the Bible calls God judge, king, father or husband it is, in the first instance, using the human known to throw light on the divine unknown, and particularly on God's attitude to his worshippers. But no sooner has the metaphor travelled from earth to heaven than it begins the return journey to earth, bearing with it an ideal standard by which the conduct of human judges, kings, fathers and husbands is to be assessed.... Husbands must love their wives as Christ loved the church (Eph 5:25).[67]

Various expressions are employed in the literature to describe how the target domain is mapped back on to the source domain—Black calling it 'interaction' (§1.1.1), and Baumann 'reverse action' (§2.1.1); however, this study will describe such as reverse (or dual-direction) cross-mapping. Inferred cross-domain mapping is the terminology that will be used to indicate inferred consequent analogies: that is, when an aspect of marriage from one conceptual domain, although not articulated as being cross-mapped, might be seen to be implied in the other conceptual domain, or perhaps influence the perception of the other conceptual domain. It can be seen from Caird (as above) that he is positing an inferred reverse cross-mapping from target to source in some of the Bible's metaphoric imagery. By way of contrast, Ephesians 5:25 (cited by Caird) is an example of articulated reverse cross-mapping, that is, the Christ/church relationship is declared to be a model for human marriage.

This present study seeks to use the Bible's marital imagery as a demonstrably valid hermeneutical tool to aid an understanding of the disputed New Testament divorce and remarriage pericopae—in effect, positing that it is valid to employ reverse cross-mapping to help elucidate a disputed pericope.[68]

---

[67] Caird, *Language and Imagery*, 19

[68] Instone-Brewer demonstrates the use of inferred reverse cross-mapping as a hermeneutical tool, in that he points out in the Old Testament imagery God divorces Israel, and that this should be taken into account to help

However, an aspect of the imagery will only be employed to such an end if the resulting exegesis is consonant with either Old Testament or New Testament teaching, or is evidenced in contemporary marriage practice.

1.6 Genesis 2:24 and the People of God

Gerhart and Russell claim:

> The Bible remains the premier challenge in linguistic interpretation ... there is no larger, more overarching problem than that posed by the changes that take place in the relationship between God and the people of Israel.[69]

This present study suggests that once the one-flesh union of Genesis 2:24 is understood as a metaphoric one-flesh covenantal relationship then it can be seen that Genesis 2:23 and Genesis 2:24 underpin two different conceptual domains. It seems that the conceptual domain of Genesis 2:23 and its literal/consanguineous one-flesh union underpinned Israel's perception of its own identity. Block states:

> the biblical texts from Genesis to Malachi assume that common descent from an eponymous ancestor provides the basis for Israel's ethnic unity and that the Israelites perceived themselves as one large extended kinship group.[70]

Thus Israel's identity relied on a consanguineous one-flesh ancestral union going back to Jacob, and in turn, to Abraham, to whom God had made the covenantal promises (e.g. Gen 12:7; 15:1–21; 17:1–21). Israel's hope was in the conceptual domain of Genesis 2:23 in that they came *from* Abraham—just as Eve came *from* Adam (בָּשָׂר מִבְּשָׂרִי). In contrast the Gentile hope lies in Genesis 2:24 in that they can come *into* a one-flesh union (לְבָשָׂר) with Christ. This, it will be argued, is the profound mystery of Ephesians 5:31–32 where Paul

---

reach an understanding of Old Testament mundane divorce teaching: David Instone-Brewer, 'How Do We Read Malachi in the Light Of God's Divorce? Interview with Dr. Instone-Brewer on Divorce in Cases of Abuse and Neglect in the Old Testament,' <https://www.youtube.com/watch?v=zNtvV7NAaFs> [Accessed: 1/25/2015]

[69] Gerhart and Russell, *New Maps for Old*, 61–62
[70] Block, 'Marriage and Family', 35

specifically links Genesis 2:24 with the Gentiles' union with Christ (see analysis in §9.4.8). It can be seen that the New Testament consistently pursues this theme. Thus familial blood relationships are not employed as a concept to describe a person's relationship to Christ, but instead it is the metaphoric family concepts of Genesis 2:24 that define the church—the bride and body of Christ—and the New Testament claims that believers are a metaphoric family, the metaphoric offspring of Abraham (Gal 3:29) and considered to be 'brothers' (e.g. 1 Cor 1:10).

1.7 Summary: Cross-Domain Mapping and Genesis 2:24

This study will seek to explore the marital imagery of the Jewish and Christian Scriptures and consider its significance for the understanding of divorce and remarriage teaching in the New Testament. It will be seen that there are three source-to-target large-scale conceptual marital metaphors in those Scriptures. All of them employ the volitional, covenantal, marital, one-flesh understanding of Genesis 2:24 to create three new conceptual domains—and it will be seen that all three conceptual domains embrace the concept of divorce and remarriage

MAP 1 *Yahweh: The Husband of Israel* (creating conceptual domain 'A')

MAP 2 *Jesus: The Bridegroom of the Church* (creating conceptual domain 'B')

MAP 3 *Sin: The Husband of Unredeemed Humanity* (creating conceptual domain 'C')

It will also be seen that two further large-scale conceptual metaphors, based on a forced equivalence cross-mapping of the volitional, covenantal, one-family understanding of Genesis 2:24 with the two conceptual domains formed by the New Testament marital imagery ('B' and 'C'), create two new corporate body conceptual domains:

MAP 4 *The Body of Christ* (creating conceptual domain 'D')

MAP 5 *The Body of a Prostitute* (creating conceptual domain 'E')

Lakoff and Johnson consider that, 'The most fundamental values in a culture will be coherent with the metaphorical structure of the most fundamental concepts in the culture.'[71] Thus it will be argued in this present study that the Jewish and Christian Scriptures would not employ an imagery that did not reflect a social reality—nor would they repudiate in their own mundane marriage teaching the principles they employ in their marital imagery.

---

[71] Lakoff and Johnson, *Metaphors*, 22

Chapter 2: Literature Review

2.1 Marital Imagery in the Old Testament

There is a considerable corpus of published material that considers marital imagery in the Old Testament and engages with metaphor theory, but no published work appears to have considered the imagery in light of the more recent structure-mapping concepts.

Adler's unpublished PhD dissertation, frequently cited by academic authors in the field, remains one of the most comprehensive treatments of Old Testament marital imagery.[72] Although she does not reference metaphor theory she points out the unique nature of the imagery compared with other ANE cultures, its pervasive use in the Old Testament, and the extent to which the Yahweh/Israel relationship mirrors Israelite marriage legislation and practice. Stienstra, in her study, does reference metaphor theory and comments:

> It is regrettable, to put it mildly, that so many translators have shown themselves insensitive to a number of manifestations of the marriage metaphor. This is mainly due to the fact they are not aware of the way these many manifestations are all linked up into one large system.[73]

She believes that the metaphor can be recognised in texts where it is not overtly present and makes the point that to understand the metaphor it is necessary to understand Israelite marriage.[74] Thus, although not referencing cross-mapping principles, she believes that the marital imagery is a large-scale structural metaphor such as Gentner and Bowdle describe, involving many metaphoric expressions (expressions that Gerhart and Russell call inferred analogies—see §1.1.2). Similarly Bauman, who suggests a key indicator for marital imagery when the relationship of Israel and Yahweh is referenced, is

---

[72] Elaine J. Adler, 'The Background for the Metaphor of Covenant as Marriage in the Hebrew Bible' (Ph.D diss., University of California, Berkeley, 1989).

[73] Nelly Stienstra, *YHWH is the Husband of His People: Analysis of a Biblical Metaphor with Special Reference to Translation* (Kampen: Kok Pharos, 1996), 7

[74] Stienstra, *YHWH is the Husband*, 39–40

not the concept of *love*, but rather the appearance of זָנָה (harlotry) and נָאַף (adultery).⁷⁵

Abma—who makes a detailed study of the prophetic marriage imagery in passages from Hosea, Isaiah, and Jeremiah—while seeing that marital imagery is 'an umbrella for various sub-forms of metaphorical speech' that embraces divorce, adultery, promiscuity, and love—argues that if Israel is not personified as a woman and the concept of marriage explicitly articulated, it is not strictly marriage imagery.⁷⁶ This present study will follow Baumann and Stienstra's broader criteria for identifying marital imagery (in both Old and New Testaments), as it appears to be more consonant with the concept of analogical structure mapping between domains based on the root metaphor having opened a new target domain (§1.1.2).

Abma points out the flexibility in the imagery in that Jeremiah 3:8 speaks of Yahweh divorcing Israel (not Judah), but in Jeremiah 3:18–22 the reuniting of the nation seems to be a remarriage, even though such is forbidden in mundane marriage according to the Deuteronomy 24 pericope cited in Jeremiah 3:1.⁷⁷ However, Instone-Brewer points out that Yahweh's new marriage is:

> described as though it were the first marriage of a virgin bride, as though the new united nation was a completely new individual without the murky past of either of her component nations.⁷⁸

Although it will be suggested in this present study that the target and source domains have a high degree of congruence (§3.5), the very nature of metaphoric concepts means that the two domains are not identical—this allows both the Jewish and Christian Scriptures to employ the imagery creatively. Lunn demonstrates the flexibility of the imagery in that he argues (it

---

⁷⁵ Gerlinde Baumann, *Love and Violence: Marriage as Metaphor for the Relationship between YHWH and Israel in the Prophetic Books*, trans. Linda M. Maloney (Stuttgart: Verlag Katholisches Biblewerk, 2000; Repr. Collegeville, MN: Liturgical Press, 2003), 41

⁷⁶ Richtsje Abma, *Bonds of Love: Methodic Studies of Prophetic Texts with Marriage Imagery (Isaiah 50:1-3 and 54:1–10, Hosea 1–3, Jeremiah 2–3)* (Assen, Netherlands: Van Gorcum, 1999), 3

⁷⁷ Abma, *Bonds of Love*, 12–13

⁷⁸ Instone-Brewer, *Divorce and Remarriage*, 53

seems uniquely), based on the marital terminology employed, that the exodus from Egypt was consciously portrayed as a divorce of Israel from Pharaoh and the Egyptian gods, and thus the 'marriage' of Israel at Sinai was the marriage of a divorcee;[79] this article will be referenced again in chapter 6.

2.1.1 Reverse Cross-Domain Mapping in the Old Testament

The aim of this study is to seek a harmonisation of the Bible's marital imagery with New Testament divorce and remarriage teaching. Thus any consideration of reverse cross-mapping of the imagery is of interest as it would illuminate any congruency to be found between the two conceptual domains.

Bauman points out the 'reverse action' of Old Testament marriage imagery and that it can influence our understanding of 'women, men, God, and marriage ... even today.'[80] Weems believes that: 'Metaphorical language is at the center of how ancient prophets conceived of and understood the world, themselves, and God,' and considers the impact of Old Testament marital imagery on the Old Testament audience and a contemporary audience today.[81] O'Brien believes that prophetic metaphors have a role in forming a worldview—a worldview considered so obvious that no conscious thought is given to it. She articulates what she sees as the consequence of the interaction between tenor and vehicle:

> When the Prophetic Books call God King, Father, and Husband, they reveal the privilege granted to human kings, fathers and husbands.... In a loop of cause and effect, the human roles in which God is depicted also take on greater power.[82]

Moughtin-Mumby comments on the concern of some feminist scholars (who see dangers in inferred reverse cross-mapping) that the imagery can have potentially negative consequences, an issue Day also reflects on.[83]

---

[79] Lunn, 'Let My people Go!', 239–51

[80] Baumann, *Love and Violence*, 22–26, 35–36

[81] Renita Weems, *Battered Love: Marriage, Sex, and Violence in the Hebrew Prophets* (Minneapolis, MN: Augsburg Fortress, 1995), 33

[82] Julia M. O'Brien, *Challenging Prophetic Metaphor: Theology and Ideology in the Prophets* (Louisville, KY: Westminster John Knox, 2008), xvii–xviii

[83] Sharon Moughtin-Mumby, *Sexual and Marital Metaphors in Hosea, Jeremiah, Isaiah, and Ezekiel* (Oxford:

This present study will demonstrate that the Old Testament marriage metaphor is used creatively, thus any analogies postulated when reverse cross-mapping the two domains have to be treated with caution (§6.11). But it is clear that it is perceived in the literature that the marital imagery is consonant with ancient Israel's understanding of mundane marriage teaching.

2.2 Marital Imagery in the New Testament

There appears to be no published systematic treatment of New Testament marital imagery in English that engages with metaphor theory. Chavasse[84] and Batey[85] consider New Testament marital imagery but neither reference metaphor theory. Yet Smolarz suggests that the Old Testament marriage metaphor 'constituted part of the Jewish beliefs in first century CE' (despite Satlow pointing out its absence in the literature—§7.1).[86] McFague considers the concept of a relational God is pervasive in the New Testament:

> The dominant model in the Judeo-Christian tradition is that of a personal God relating to responsible and responsive beings.... The content of the root-metaphor of Christianity, then, is a mode of personal relationship.[87]

McWhirter claims that before her own study there had been no comprehensive analysis of the allusions to marital imagery in John's gospel;[88] like Long,[89] and

---

Oxford University Press, 2008), 1–46; Peggy L. Day, 'The Bitch Had It Coming To Her: Rhetoric and Interpretation in Ezekiel 16,' *Biblical Interpretation* 8 (2000), 231–53; Peggy L. Day, 'Yahweh's Broken Marriages as Metaphoric Vehicle in the Hebrew Bible Prophets,' in *Sacred Marriages: The Divine-Human Sexual Metaphor from Sumer to Early Christianity,* ed. Marti Nissinen and Risto Uro (Winona Lake, IN: Eisenbraums, 2008), 219–41

[84] Claude Chavasse, *The Bride of Christ: An Enquiry into the Nuptial Element in Early Christianity* (London: Faber & Faber, 1940)

[85] Richard A. Batey, *New Testament Nuptial Imagery* (Leiden: Brill, 1971)

[86] Smolarz points out that Israel's hope for a future restoration at this time was bound up with the marital imagery: Sebastian R. Smolarz, *Covenant and the Metaphor of Divine Marriage in Biblical Thought* (Eugene, OR: Wipf and Stock, 2011), 183

[87] McFague, *Metaphorical Theology*, 106, 108

[88] Jocelyn McWhirter, *The Bridegroom Messiah and the People of God: Marriage in the Fourth Gospel,* SNTSMS (Cambridge: Cambridge University Press, 2006), 11

[89] Phillip J. Long, *Jesus the Bridegroom: The Origin of the Eschatological Feast as a Wedding Banquet in the Synoptic Gospels* (Eugene, OR: Pickwick, 2013)

Pitre,[90] she sees that the Gospel writers portray Jesus as self-consciously adopting the role of a bridegroom to his people and that they rely heavily on Jewish mundane marriage customs to that end. However, none of these publications engage with metaphor theory.

The portrayal of Jesus as a bridegroom has Christological implications—cognitive mapping concepts would seem to indicate that the root metaphor (Jesus 'is' the bridegroom to the church) opens a conceptual domain comparable to that employed in the Old Testament imagery, and gives rise to the potential deduction that Jesus 'is' Yahweh.[91] Christology is the focus of Tait's[92] consideration of New Testament marital imagery, as it is for several German scholars (who do engage with metaphor theory) as in Frey et al.[93] Similarly the German scholar Zimmermann[94] considers marital imagery in the Gospels and the Apocalypse and refers to some of the underlying metaphoric concepts involved.

2.2.1 Reverse Cross-Domain Mapping in the New Testament

Although Old Testament scholarship addresses the subject of reverse cross-mapping and its implications, this is not the case in New Testament studies despite the articulation of such, for example, in Ephesians 5:25, which will be considered in §9.4.8.[95]

---

[90] Brant Pitre, *Jesus the Bridegroom: The Greatest Love Story Ever Told* (New York, NY: Crown, 2014)

[91] Long, 'It goes beyond the evidence to claim that the image of a bridegroom was a metaphor for the Messiah. Rather, the bridegroom is in fact God as he reconciles with his bride, Israel': Long, *Jesus the Bridegroom,* 239

[92] Michael Tait, *Jesus, the Divine Bridegroom, in Mark 2:18–22: Mark's Christology Upgraded,* Analecta Biblica 185 (Rome: Pontificio Istituto Biblico, 2012)

[93] Jörg Frey, Jan Rohls and Ruben Zimmermann, eds., *Metaphorik Und Christologie, Theologische Bibliothek Tapelmann* (Berlin: Walter de Gruyter, 2003)

[94] Ruben Zimmermann, 'Das Hochzeitsritual im Jungfrauengleichnis: Sozialgeschichtliche Hintergrunde zu Mt 25.1–13,' *New Testament Studies* 48 (2002), 48–70. Also: Zimmermann, *Geschlechtermetaphorik Und Gotteseverhaltnis* (Tübingen: Mohr Siebeck, 2001) and 'Nuptial Imagery in the Revelation of John,' *Biblica* 84 (2003), 153–83

[95] Knight reflects on Eph 5 and the relevance of Paul's teaching for mundane marriage but he does not reference metaphor theory: George W. Knight, 'Husbands and Wives as Analogues of Christ and the Church: Ephesians 5:21–33 Colossians 3:18–19,' in *Recovering Biblical Manhood and Womanhood: A Response to Evangelical Feminism,* ed. John Piper and Wayne A. Grudem (Wheaton, IL: Crossway, 2012), 165–78; the subject is addressed (but again without reference to metaphor theory and the associated cross-mapping principles) in: Elisabeth Elliot, *Let Me be a Woman* (London: Tyndale, 1976); Colin Hamer, *Being a Christian Husband: A Biblical Perspective* (Darlington: Evangelical Press, 2005); Colin Hamer, *Divorce and the Bible: A Systematic*

2.3 Divorce and Remarriage Teaching in the New Testament

No published work this study is aware of explores the difference between the marriages in Genesis 2:23 and Genesis 2:24. Instead, 1 Corinthians 6:15–16 is used to teach that mundane marriage—or more precisely sexual intercourse—creates an ontological and/or mystical union, and that this is the meaning of the Genesis 2:24 one-flesh union; *contra* the Old Testament understanding that the Genesis 2:24 one-flesh union refers to a union of kinship formed by a volitional covenant (§1.2). The conceptual domains of Genesis 2:23 and Genesis 2:24 are thus conflated and the primal couple assumed to be the subject of references to Genesis 2:24 within the New Testament.[96] The academic consensus is that Matthew 19:3–9 and Mark 10:2–12, with their reference to 'in the beginning' and to Genesis 2:24, affirm, or re-affirm, that the aetiology of mundane marriage lies in the primal couple—an Edenic ideal that the Gospel writers seek to apply to the Christian era. Thus Adam and Eve's marriage is utilised as the model to exegete the Bible's divorce and remarriage teaching.

It is this perspective that forms the basis of Gehring's *The Biblical "One Flesh" Theology of Marriage as Constituted in Genesis 2:24*[97] and underpins Loader's 500 page study *The New Testament on Sexuality*.[98] Other studies either specifically articulate the same idea, or at least appear to have assumed a primal couple marriage model. Examples from the last twenty years include: Loader,[99] MacArthur,[100] Davidson,[101] Wenham,[102] Clark,[103] Köstenberger and

---

Exegesis to Challenge the Traditional Views (Bloomington, IN: Author House, 2006)

[96] For example: Loader, *The New Testament on Sexuality*, 278

[97] René Gehring, *The Biblical "One Flesh" Theology of Marriage as Constituted in Genesis 2:24* (Eugene, OR: Wipf and Stock, 2013), 30, 52, 152, 265, 276, 296-97, 312; see further details in n. 64 in §1.4.4 of this present study.

[98] Loader, *The New Testament on Sexuality*, 176, 277, 290; see further details in n. 63 in §1.4.4 of this present study.

[99] William R. G. Loader, *Making Sense of Sex: Attitudes towards Sexuality in Early Jewish and Christian Literature* (Grand Rapids, MI: Eerdmans, 2013)

[100] John MacArthur, *The Divorce Dilemma: God's Last Word on Lasting Commitment* (Leominster: Day One, 2009)

[101] Richard M. Davidson, *The Flame of Yahweh: Sexuality in the Old Testament* (Peabody, MA: Hendrickson, 2007)

Jones,[104] Taylor and Clendenen,[105] France,[106] Son,[107] Deasley,[108] and Hugenberger.[109]

Although Instone-Brewer's *Divorce and Remarriage in the Bible*[110] does not look to challenge a paradigmatic primal couple model, or address metaphor theory, his focus on the 'social and literary context' of Jesus and Paul's day causes him to question the way the relevant New Testament pericopae have been treated in the past—the result is an exegesis which is largely congruent with the Bible's marital imagery—an imagery that metaphoric principles dictate will be based on a social reality.

2.4 Summary: Literature Review

A review of the literature indicates that Old Testament marital imagery has a considerable body of published material devoted to it, the majority of which engages with metaphor theory, although not the more recent structure-mapping concepts. However, New Testament marital imagery is only sparsely represented in New Testament studies, and only the German scholars seem to engage with metaphor theory.

It appears this lack of engagement by New Testament scholars with metaphor theory, and with structure-mapping concepts in particular, has inhibited an effective analysis of the New Testament marital and corporate body imagery.

---

[102] Gordon J. Wenham, 'No Remarriage After Divorce,' in *Remarriage after Divorce in Today's Church: 3 Views*, ed. Paul E. Engle and Mark L. Strauss (Grand Rapids, MI: Zondervan, 2006), 19–42

[103] Stephen Clark, *Putting Asunder: Divorce and Remarriage in Biblical and Pastoral Perspective* (Bridgend: Bryntirion, 1999)

[104] Andreas J. Köstenberger and David J. Jones, *God, Marriage, and Family: Rebuilding the Biblical Foundation* (Wheaton, IL: Crossway, 2004)

[105] Richard A. Taylor and Ray E. Clendenen, *Haggai Malachi*, The New American Commentary: An Exegetical and Theological Exegesis of Holy Scripture Vol 21A (Nashville, TN: Broadman & Holman, 2004)

[106] R. T. France, *The Gospel of Mark*, NIGTC (Grand Rapids, MI: Eerdmans, 2002)

[107] Aaron S. Son, 'Implications of Paul's "One Flesh" Concept for His Understanding of the Nature of Man,' *Biblical Research* 11 (2001), 107–22

[108] Alex R. G. Deasley, *Marriage and Divorce in the Bible and the Church* (Kansas City, MO: Beacon Hill, 2000)

[109] Gordon P. Hugenberger, *Marriage as a Covenant: Biblical Law and Ethics as Developed from Malachi* (Grand Rapids, MI: Baker, 1994)

[110] David Instone-Brewer, *Divorce and Remarriage in the Bible: The Social and Literary Context* (Grand Rapids, MI: Eerdmans, 2002)

This, it is suggested, has resulted in a failure by many to correctly identify the imagery employed by the New Testament writers, and has given rise to some of the conflicting views on New Testament divorce and remarriage teaching as referenced in the Study Outline.

Chapter 3: Methodology

3.1 Introduction

Several scholars believe that Israelite marriage practice 'mirrored,' at least to a measure, the perceived relationship of Yahweh and Israel;[111] in other words, the two conceptual domains had a high degree of congruence, Stienstra believing that they were so closely tied together in the Israelite mind that it was a metaphor Israelites 'lived by.'[112] It will be pointed out in this present study that the marital imagery of the New Testament appears to be a continuation of the imagery found in the Hebrew Bible, and thus it would be expected, as metaphoric principles dictate, that the imagery of the New Testament would similarly reflect the contemporary understanding of marriage. It is further posited that the New Testament writers would not repudiate mundane marital practices they employ in their own marital imagery. Thus this present study will explore the possibility of using the metaphoric divine marriage model as a hermeneutical tool to help elucidate the teaching of the disputed divorce and remarriage pericopae of the New Testament.

3.2 An Approach to the Biblical Text

It is the intention in this study to adopt a text-centred approach as outlined by Postell where (with reference to the Hebrew Bible) he considers the text in the final form 'embodies the intentionality of a historical author'; such an author being the person or persons responsible for the final text. He posits: 'texts have meaning because an author meant them to.... There are many indications ... [that] compositional strategy is synonymous with authorial intention'; he suggests that by focusing on the final form of the text that it is possible to detect 'literary coherence and authorial strategy.'[113] Skinner writes:

---

[111] For example: Instone-Brewer, *Divorce and Remarriage*, 53; Michael L. Satlow, *Jewish Marriage in Antiquity* (Princeton, NJ: Princeton University Press, 2001), 43–44

[112] Stienstra, *YHWH is the Husband of His People*, 39

[113] Seth D. Postell, *Adam as Israel: Genesis 1-3 as the Introduction to the Torah and Tanakh* (Eugene, OR: Pickwick, 2011), 26, 44, 49–50

> The understanding of texts, I have sought to insist, presupposes the grasp both of what they were intended to mean, and how this meaning was intended to be taken. It follows from this that to understand a text must be to understand both the intention to be understood, and the intention that this intention should be understood, which the text itself as an intended act of communication must at least have embodied.[114]

Kennedy's description of this approach is 'rhetorical criticism':

> Rhetorical criticism takes the text as we have it, whether the work of a single author or the product of editing, and looks at it from the point of view of the author's or editor's intent, the unified results, and how it would be perceived by an audience of near contemporaries.[115]

Kennedy sees the essence of rhetoric as the intention to convey a message, to persuade, and contrasts this approach with form and redaction criticism and its focus on the sources of the text; or literary criticism which he sees as focusing on how the Bible was received by 'literary geniuses of other times.'[116] Abma believes that seeing the text 'as a reality in itself rather than as a reflection of other realities is central to all synchronic approaches.'[117] Satlow describes a diachronic approach (when talking of rabbinic texts) as interpreting texts 'in line with interpretive traditions ... that have crystallized around them over the course of centuries,' and contrasts this with his own synchronic approach of evaluating the text against other contemporaneous evidence, whereby he ignores 'how this evidence was read by later interpreters.'[118]

With this text-centred approach, the question of ontological truth or historical factual accuracy will not be addressed—for the purposes of this study such details as to whether Hosea married Gomer or not, or whether the account is

---

[114] Skinner, *Genesis*, 48

[115] Kennedy, *New Testament Interpretation*, 4

[116] Kennedy, *New Testament Interpretation*, 4–5

[117] Abma, *Bonds of Love*, 33

[118] Michael L. Satlow, *Tasting the Dish: Rabbinic Rhetorics of Sexuality* (Atlanta, GA: Brown Judaic Studies, 1995), 11–12

entirely allegorical are irrelevant. As Abma states: 'The text presents certain events as real and it is this perspective ... that is our main point of concern';[119] or as Walton suggests: 'Yahweh was real [to the Israelites].... The significance and nature of the literature are not dependent on *our* assessment of their reality.'[120]

Thus in this present study the text will be considered an entity in its own right; how it was put together, or the identity of the author is not relevant, and it will be assumed that the marital imagery pericopae demonstrate intentionality in the final redaction—the New Testament claiming for itself that it is a final authoritative revelation to the church (e.g. Jude 1:3; Rev 22:18-19).

3.3 Metaphor versus Other Literary Forms

3.3.1 Simile, Typology, and Allegory

Glucksberg points out that a metaphor (A is B) is different to a simile because a metaphor demonstrates a false literalism (§1.1.1).[121] Typology differs from metaphor in that an earlier event is seen as 'a veiled reference to some new theological reality, usually Christological';[122] thus 'A' in the past symbolises 'B' in the future, whereas in a metaphor A 'is' B and has a present and/or continuing aspect to it. As regards allegory Fairbairn sees that:

> An allegory is a narrative ... for the purpose of representing certain higher truths ... [that] have had no foundation in fact ... [or] even if wearing the appearance of a real transaction, is considered incapable as it stands of yielding any adequate or satisfactory sense, and is consequently employed ... to convey some meaning of quite diverse and higher kind.[123]

---

[119] So: Abma, *Bonds of Love*, 119

[120] John H. Walton, *Ancient Near Eastern Thought and the Old Testament: Introducing the Conceptual World of the Hebrew Bible* (Nottingham: Apollos, 2007), 44

[121] But the differences are debated, for example Glucksberg, while maintaining the distinction points out that some similes are built on metaphorical concepts: Glucksberg, 'How Metaphors,' in Gibbs, *The Cambridge Handbook*, 67-81

[122] Long, *Jesus the Bridegroom*, 35

[123] Patrick Fairbairn, *The Typology of Scripture: Viewed in Connection with the Whole Series of the Divine*

And Foulkes states:

> We may call that method of interpretation allegorical which is concerned not with the interpretation of history, but simply of words that are believed to be inspired symbols.[124]

Some describe Ezekiel 16 and Ezekiel 23 as allegory, others as extended metaphor.[125] However, the prophet seems to be exploiting the analogical inferences between the source domain (actual mundane marriage as practised in Israel) and a target domain as a means of interpreting the history of the relationship between Yahweh and Israel, thus these chapters will not be considered to be allegorical in this study.

3.3.2 *Sensus Plenior,* Intertextuality, Allusions, and Echoes

Hays points out that in the New Testament Paul engages with the Old Testament 'with great imaginative freedom, without the characteristic modernist anxiety about factuality and authorial intention.'[126] An example would be the citation of Genesis 2:24 in Ephesians 5:31–32 where the author says 'it [i.e. Gen 2:24] refers to Christ and the church.' This study (§9.4.8) will argue a *sensus plenior* is read into that Pentateuchal verse beyond which, it is suggested, could have been intended by the original author.

Beale does not deny that the New Testament writers exercised 'imaginative freedom' but he points out that such was contained within a framework of a 'broad redemptive-historical perspective' and suggests:

> there are no clear examples where they [New Testament writers] have developed a meaning from the Old Testament which is inconsistent or

---

Dispensations (New York, NY: Funk & Wagnalls, 1900), 2

[124] Francis Foulkes, 'The Acts of God: A Study of the Basis of Typology in the Old Testament,' in *The Right Doctrine from the Wrong Texts?,* ed. G. K. Beale (Grand Rapids, MI: Baker, 1994), 367

[125] See discussion in: Julie Galambush, *Jerusalem in the Book of Ezekiel: The City as Yahweh's Wife,* SBL Dissertation Series 130 (Atlanta, GA: Scholars, 1992), 10–11

[126] Richard B Hays, *The Conversion of the Imagination* (Grand Rapids, MI: Eerdmans, 2005), ix; similarly Lindars, who argues that the New Testament writers used the Old Testament texts creatively to elucidate their own *kerygma*: Barnabas Lindars, 'The Place of the Old Testament in the Formation of New Testament Theology: Prolegomena,' in Beale, *The Right Doctrine,* 143

contradictory to some aspect of the original Old Testament intention.[127]

Beale further suggests, when discussing the New Testament use of the Old Testament, that it is valid for the contemporary church to use the apostolic method of exegesis, whereby it is possible to see a *sensus plenior* in Old Testament texts when such is consonant with the Christian *kerygma*.[128] *Contra* Kaiser, who rejects any reading by a post-apostolic exegete that involves the notion of a *sensus plenior* in addition to the 'human writers' supposed nominal or prosaic meanings'; he further explains his exegetical principles by stating that for him the original meaning is important, which he defines as the meaning the text had in its original context.[129]

Postell defines intertextuality as the 'relationship between one text and some other text(s) whereby its historical author *intended* it [i.e. the relationship] to be *recognized* by the reader' and that a text's literary allusions are either implicit (i.e. echoes or allusions) or explicit (i.e. citations).[130] Accepting that definition, and that *sensus plenior* is reading a meaning into an earlier text beyond the original author's intent, *sensus plenior* and intertextuality are different, and this present study sees that marital imagery in both the Jewish and Christian Scriptures employs the latter but not the former, notwithstanding the *sensus plenior* understanding of Genesis 2:24 in Ephesians 5:31–32.[131]

---

[127] G. K. Beale, 'Positive Answer to the Question: Did Jesus and His Followers Preach the Right Doctrine from the Wrong Texts? An Examination of the Presuppositions of Jesus' and the Apostles' Exegetical Method,' in Beale, *The Right Doctrine*, 394, 398; similarly: C. H. Dodd, *According to the Scriptures* (London: Nisbet, 1952), 130

[128] Beale, 'Positive Answer to the Question,' in Beale, *The Right Doctrine*, 399–404

[129] Walter C. Jr. Kaiser, 'The Single Intent of Scripture, in Beale, *The Right Doctrine*, 65, 67

[130] Postell, *Adam as Israel*, 65, 73. Hays uses the term metalepsis and sees it as 'a literary echo [that] links the text in which it occurs to an earlier text, the figurative effect of the echo can lie in the unstated or suppressed … points of resonance between the two texts'; thus text 'B' is understood in the light of text 'A'—'encompassing aspects of A beyond those explicitly echoed': Richard B Hays, *Echoes of Scripture in the Letters of Paul* (New Haven, CT: Yale University Press, 1989), 20. Thus metaphoric principles underlie metalepsis in that text 'A' can be equated to the vehicle of a metaphor, but metalepsis does not embrace a false literalism and in a metaphor the posited equivalence is in the control of the author not the suggestion of a later exegete.

[131] It is argued in §9.4.8 that the *sensus plenior* of Gen 2:24 is found in a fusion of the New Testament marital imagery with its body of Christ imagery.

Marital imagery in the Hebrew Bible and the New Testament is explicit. Thus, Isaiah describes Yahweh as the husband of Israel (Isa 54:5); John the Baptist describes Jesus as the bridegroom (John 3:29); the Apostle Paul sees the church as a bride betrothed to Christ (2 Cor 11:2); and the New Testament climaxes with the marriage supper of the Lamb (Rev 19:6–10).

However, many see marital imagery elsewhere. That is, although not specifically articulated in the text, many scholars see that the writer intended the reader to understand that he was alluding to a divine marriage. Thus the covenant giving at Sinai is seen by many as marital imagery, based on both the language and the event: a 'jealous' God wanting no rivals tells Israel he is entering into a covenant with them whereby they will be a special people to him—the justification for seeing marital imagery there is further strengthened by later references that appear to describe the event as a marriage (e.g. Jer 31:31–32). However, Lunn's argument that the exodus from Egypt (§2.1), and McWhirter's et al. belief that the encounter with the Samaritan woman in John 4 (§9.2.3) are referencing marital imagery, are based on rather more subtle allusions.

Two principal questions arise from the concept of such allusions: firstly, how valid is it to read such into a text—and secondly, why would an author want an allusion to be implicit rather than explicit? The latter question appears to have received less scholarly attention than the former. It could be that what seems implicit to the 21st century reader was explicit to the contemporary audience. Hays argues that in 1 Corinthians 5—with allusions to Old Testament concepts—Paul either believes his emissary is going to explain his argument, or he assumes the readers of the letter have sufficient knowledge of Scripture to understand his allusions.[132] If the latter is correct then intertextuality might serve as a form of stylistic short-hand. Conversely, France suggests that even if Matthew knew that not all his readers would grasp his seemingly obscure Old

---

[132] Hays, *Conversion of the Imagination*, 23; McWhirter posits that the first-century audience were better acquainted with the Jewish Scriptures than many in a Christian audience of the 21st century might be: McWhirter, *The Bridegroom Messiah*, 134–35; Holland similarly argues that many first-century Christians were familiar with the Old Testament and it was the Jewish Scriptures and Jewish concepts (not Hellenistic concepts) that formed the background to Christian Scripture: Holland, *Romans*, 1–6

Testament references (in Matt 2), he was writing in a style comparable to that of:

> many of the most successful writers of all ages, whose work has an immediate impact without extensive academic analysis, but is not exhausted on a first reading and continues to delight and reward in successive encounters over the years.[133]

As regards the first question—whether or not posited implicit allusions are illusory—Postell, citing the work of Sommer,[134] believes that despite the element of subjectivity in identifying echoes and allusions, the likelihood of such grows with cumulative evidence. Postell posits that such evidence includes the presence of stylistic or thematic patterns, and the probability that the author would allude to such a source, and believes his understanding reflects the scholarly consensus.[135]

It will be seen in the consideration of New Testament marital imagery in chapter 9 that several scholars see intentional implicit imagery. For example, Long believes Jesus' earthly ministry is consciously portrayed in the Gospels as his bridal week, mirroring the practice of Jewish bridegrooms.[136] Similarly, McWhirter believes the account of Jesus and the woman from Samaria in John 4 describes an encounter between a potential bridegroom and bride—the Samaritan woman fulfilling the role of the bride both for herself, and as a symbol for the Samaritan people.[137] Both Long and McWhirter give detailed justifications for their methodologies, and both rely extensively on intertextuality for identifying the imagery, specifically citing the work of Hays (as does Postell) and the concept of allusions and echoes.[138] Hays suggests seven tests for identifying an intentional echo or allusion to another text:

---

[133] R. T. France, 'The Formula-Quotations of Matthew 2 and the Problem of Communication,' in Beale, *The Right Doctrine*, 133

[134] Benjamin D. Sommer, *A Prophet Reads Scripture: Allusion in Isaiah 40–66* (Stanford, CA: Stanford University Press, 1998)

[135] Postell, *Adam as Israel*, 65–66

[136] Long, *Jesus the Bridegroom*, 194

[137] McWhirter, *The Bridegroom Messiah*, 58–76

[138] For example: Long, *Jesus the Bridegroom*, 16–35; McWhirter, *The Bridegroom Messiah*, 21–36; Postell, *Adam as Israel*, 65–66

1. Availability: whether or not the author and/or original reader had access to the source of the echo.

2. Volume: the degree of explicit repetition of words or syntactical patterns.

3. Recurrence: the frequency with which the author cites the same text.

4. Thematic coherence: how the alleged echo fits into the context.

5. Historical plausibility: the probability that the author intended the allusion and that his readers would have understood it.

6. History of interpretation: whether or not such echoes have been seen before.

7. Satisfaction: whether or not the proposed reading makes sense.[139]

With the caveat that New Testament marital imagery is seemingly a neglected field, and thus does not have a 'history of interpretation' (Hays' sixth criterion) to support it, this present study will adopt the approach of Hays (an approach endorsed by Long, McWhirter, and Pitre) when identifying marital imagery in either the Jewish or Christian Scriptures. For example, in the case of the exchange with the woman from Samaria in John 4, it is the author's placing of the meeting in the Gospel story after the wedding at Cana (John 2) and the Baptist's description of Jesus as the bridegroom (John 3) which suggests intentional marital imagery. In addition, the intertextual links to marital themes, and Jesus' comments about the woman's marital history (which on a nominal reading, do not appear to fit the redemptive theme of the conversation), and the event itself (a meeting at a well, where Isaac, Jacob, and Moses all encountered their future brides), all strongly indicate that the Gospel writer was intentionally alluding to a divine marriage theme. Such a deduction is supported by the contention in this present study that marital imagery is a persistent theme of Jewish Scripture and it is that Scripture which forms the background to the New Testament.

The writers of both the Jewish and Christian Scriptures use a wide range of literary genres. These include allegories, metaphors, and parables, all of which

---

[139] Hays, *Echoes of Scripture*, 29–32.

have implicit meanings, not all of which are fully explained in the scriptural texts. It is certainly the case with metaphors: to only allow a 'nominal' meaning (an exegetical method Kaiser seems to suggest) would lead to nonsensical deductions (e.g. the ubiquitous but unexplained metaphoric 'Son of God'), or to miss the point (e.g. the leaven of the Pharisees and Sadducees in Matthew 16:6). Nonetheless, it is suggested that this present study's exegesis will be consonant with an understanding of the 'original meaning,' in that the exegesis will endeavour to be congruent with the original meaning of the pericope in its original context—it is simply that any allusions, as France implies, and McWhirter et al. claim, have not always been detected by subsequent exegetes.

3.4 The Social and Literary Context

Metaphor theory dictates that any metaphoric statement must contain at least one known entity to achieve a meaningful cross-mapping. In the case of the Bible's marital imagery it is how the intended audience understood marriage that forms the source domain of the metaphor. It follows that an understanding of the social and literary context of the Jewish and Christian Scriptures is key to an understanding of their marital imagery. Thus this study will consider wider ANE marriage practices to provide some context for ancient Israel's understanding of marriage (chapter 4), and the literature and documents of the Second Temple period (chapters 7 and 8) to help give some context to the marital practices of the New Testament era.

There is an increasing awareness in recent years of the Jewish context of New Testament authorship; as Sanders puts it, 'There is today virtually unanimous consent ... [that] Jesus lived as a Jew.'[140] And Dodd points out that Paul could argue in Acts 26:22: 'I stand here ... saying nothing but what the prophets and Moses said would come to pass.'[141]

---

[140] E. P. Sanders, *Jesus and Judaism* (London: SCM, 1985), 19; a literature review of material published in the last 100 years on the historical Jesus is contained in: James H. Charlesworth, *The Historical Jesus* (Nashville, TN: Abingdon, 2008), 6-12

[141] Dodd, *According to the Scriptures*, 16; however, Hengel points out the linguistic and cultural complexities of the Jewish-Hellenistic mix of the New Testament era and cautions against a simplistic analysis: Martin Hengel, *The 'Hellenization' of Judaea in the First Century after Christ,* trans. John Bowden (London: SCM, 1989)

Nonetheless, it appears, particularly in literature addressed to the Christian church, as Skinner says on a different but related matter, that there has been an:

> unconscious application of paradigms whose familiarity to the historian disguises an essential inapplicability to the past ... it seems clear that at least a part of [any] understanding must lie in grasping what sort of society the given author was writing for and trying to persuade.[142]

Skinner's point seems self-evident, and yet Hays suggests that 'Christian tradition early on lost its vital connection with the Jewish interpretative matrix in which Paul had lived and moved.'[143] It is a point Meyers repeatedly makes:

> The attitudes engendered by the Judeo-Christian tradition are so well entrenched in contemporary religion that they constitute powerful barriers to an understanding of the antecedent functions of certain texts in Israelite life.[144]

3.5 Cross-Domain Mapping as a Hermeneutical Tool

It seems clear that the source domain of mundane marriage as understood in ancient Israel has been cross-mapped to the relationship of Yahweh and Israel in all Old Testament marital imagery—this study is only aware of one contrary view in the literature;[145] the target domain has been populated from the mundane marriage source domain and it is this cross-mapping that gives rise to the congruence between the two domains. Thus it is suggested that any exegesis that results in a divergence between the two conceptual domains, even

---

[142] Quentin Skinner, 'Meaning and Understanding in the History of Ideas,' *History and Theory* 8:1 (1969), 7, 40

[143] Hays, *Conversion of the Imagination*, 43

[144] Carol Meyers, *Discovering Eve: Ancient Israelite Women in Context* (New York, NY: Oxford University Press, 1988), 73

[145] Kelle, 'the marriage metaphor in the Hebrew Bible expresses not the covenant relationship between Yahweh and the people of Israel but the religious, social, and political activities of those rulers who held office in the seats of power': Brad E. Kelle, *Hosea 2: Metaphor and Rhetoric in Historical Perspective* (Atlanta, GA: Society of Biblical Literature, 2005), 90. Galambush sees that in the prophetic corpus the 'wife' in the imagery is predominantly represented by a personified city, but in the extra-prophetic texts she is represented by the nation Israel (§6.8.3): Galambush, *Jerusalem*, 35–38

in an area when their congruence has not been specifically articulated, needs to be treated with caution.

For example, it is not specifically articulated in the Old Testament that a free-born wife in ancient Israel was able to divorce her husband. Yet it is clear in the imagery that Israel could leave Yahweh, Joshua pleading with them not to do so (e.g. Josh 24:15). Exegetes from within the Christian community have more recently seen that the freedom of a slave-wife to divorce her husband, belonged also to the free-born wife (§5.12), as is now also seemingly evidenced in recent archaeological discoveries (§8.3.7), but a consideration of the imagery might have led to such a conclusion earlier.

Poythress discusses the use of analogies and models in biblical interpretation and makes the point that a particular view in any disputed exegesis is 'made plausible partly by the use of a governing analogy' and suggests that they can be 'used as a key element in a theological or hermeneutical system.'[146] However, this present study, in suggesting that marital imagery can be used as a hermeneutical tool, does not intend to adopt a radical deconstructionist view where the reader's perception overrides any other consideration, and the text, as Vanhoozer cautions, is allowed to go '*another* way.'[147]

Thus, as articulated in §1.5, an aspect of the imagery will only be employed to help elucidate any disputed New Testament pericope on mundane marriage or divorce teaching if the resulting exegesis is consonant with either Old Testament or New Testament teaching, or is evidenced in contemporary New Testament marriage practice.

---

[146] Vern S. Poythress, 'Science and Hermeneutics,' in *Foundations of Contemporary Interpretation: Implications of Scientific Method for Biblical Interpretation* Vol. 5, ed. Moisés Silva (Grand Rapids, MI: Zondervan, 1996), 489, 491

[147] Vanhoozer sees that Jacques Derrida's approach allows words to go the way the reader determines, the original context no longer defining their meaning—'By reading texts in light of other texts and contexts, the reader forces the words to go *another* way': Kevin J. Vanhoozer, *Is There Meaning in this Text?* (Grand Rapids, MI: Zondervan, 1998), 163

3.6 Summary: Methodology

This study seeks to understand the mundane marriage and divorce teaching and marital imagery of the Jewish Scriptures, and the marital imagery of the Christian Scriptures, to inform an exegesis of the New Testament divorce and remarriage pericopae. Although the imagery will be used as a hermeneutical tool there will be no attempt to force the text away from its original meaning, which will be taken to be the original meaning of the pericope in its original context. To that end the study will adopt a synchronic text-based approach where it will be assumed that the text in the final form embodies the intention of its author. It will be accepted that although the marital imagery of the Bible is often explicit, some imagery is to be found in intentional intertextual allusions, and to detect such Hays' criteria will be adopted. There will be no attempt to read a *sensus plenior* into a text except where it is believed it is articulated: it appears the only example of such in the imagery is to be found in Ephesians 5:31–32.

Chapter 4: Marriage and Divorce in the Ancient Near East

4.1 Introduction

Chapter 5 will explore the source domain of Old Testament marital imagery, that is, mundane marriage in ancient Israel. However, there is no systematic teaching in the Old Testament concerning marriage or divorce—there are law codes (e.g. 'You shall not commit adultery' Exod 20:14) that explain which sexual relationships are forbidden, but other parts of the Pentateuch are in effect case law framed with a protasis and apodosis to outline what is to be done if, for example, a slave woman—or a woman taken in battle—is taken as a wife (Exod 21; Deut 21); or there is sexual immorality (Deut 22); or a husband divorces his wife (Deut 24); or a brother dies without children (Deut 25). Thus much of the text concerns what is forbidden or what is to be done in exceptional cases. Neufeld goes as far as to suggest that 'the Old Testament in its existing form is incomplete.... Several Books are manifestly lacking.'[148]

The background to Old Testament marriage legislation can be partially filled out from the scattered references in the Old Testament narrative accounts, although Neufeld suggests it is necessary:

> to consider as carefully as possible whether such narratives possess the features which clearly show that they reflect general customs or in some cases definite laws known to, and observed by, the Hebrew people.[149]

Another possible source of reference is the wider cultural milieu of the ANE, Neufeld suggesting that 'Biblical laws are, generally speaking, in harmony with these other Semitic systems.'[150] An example might be the Pentateuchal consanguinity codes that contain no law to forbid a sexual relationship

---

[148] He sees references to the 'missing' books in: Num 21:14-15; 2 Sam 1:18-27; Josh 10:12-13; 1 Kgs 14:19, 29: E. Neufeld, *Ancient Hebrew Marriage Laws: With Special References to General Semitic Laws and Customs* (London: Longmans, Green & Co, 1945), 1

[149] Neufeld, *Ancient Hebrew Marriage Laws*, v

[150] Neufeld, *Ancient Hebrew Marriage Laws*, 10

between a father and daughter (although incest is forbidden in wider family relationships e.g. Lev 18); ANE laws explicitly forbid a father/daughter sexual relationship and it seems, as Greengus argues, that against this background ('societal norm') there was no reason to explicitly articulate such a ban.[151]

While Stienstra advises caution in any attempt to extrapolate from the wider ANE into Israelite culture, Pritchard says that in the last 150 years many documents have been excavated in the ANE that have 'sharpened considerably' an understanding of the Old Testament.[152] Moreover Greengus states: 'we cannot assume that the Israelites were uniquely insulated and separated from their neighbours,' and sees the existence of cultural dialogue evidenced in several biblical passages (e.g. Deut 4:6–8; 1 Kgs 9:20–21; Ps 147:19–20; Ezek 5:7; Ezek 16:3, 45; Ezra 9:1).[153] Thus ancient Israel, despite its distinctive religious beliefs, did not live in a cultural vacuum. But if parallels are found between these ANE cultures and those of ancient Israel the object is not to seek which beliefs might have been derivative—Walton makes the point that comparative studies do not need to consider whether any particular aspect of a culture or belief system was or was not based on another to be valid.[154] Instead this chapter will look at some key features of marriage and divorce practice in the ANE and determine if these might help inform an understanding of marriage in ancient Israel where other direct Old Testament evidence is lacking.

4.2 Ancient Near East Principal Relevant Source Materials

The principal sources are listed below:

---

[151] Samuel Greengus, *Laws in the Bible and in Early Rabbinic Collections: The Legal Legacy of the Ancient Near East* (Eugene, OR: Cascade, 2011), 12. He further states, 'the biblical law collections as we have them, even when considered in total, fall short of including the full range of procedures, statutes, and regulations that governed ancient Israelite society': Samuel Greengus, 'Filling Gaps: Laws Found in Babylonia and in the Mishnah but Absent in the Hebrew Bible,' *Maarav* 7 (1991), 171

[152] Stienstra, *YHWH is the Husband of His People*, 72; James B. Pritchard, ed., *Ancient Near Eastern Texts Relating to the Old Testament,* with supplement, 3rd ed. (Princeton, NJ: Princeton University Press, 1969), xix

[153] Greengus, *Laws in the Bible*, 5–6

[154] Walton, *Ancient Near Eastern Thought*, 21–22

- The Mesopotamian Laws of Ur-Nammu (King of Ur 2112–2095 BCE) are the earliest extant law codes known from scribal documents dated ca. 1800 BCE.

- The Laws of Eshnunna (LE) inscribed on two cuneiform tablets are from the kingdom of Eshnunna (just east of Babylon) that flourished ca. 2000 BCE.

- The Laws of Hammurabi (LH), a Babylonian king ruling from 1792 BCE, are a set of law codes whose function has been debated. The 282 statements contained therein might represent examples of what were considered a model for others to follow rather than a set of actual laws. Notwithstanding this Mieroop considers the codes provide insight into Babylonian society at the time.[155]

- The Hittite Laws (HL) represent legal thinking in the Hittite empire (with its capital in Hattusa situated in modern day Turkey) between 1650 and 1200 BCE.[156]

- The Nuzi archive from Akkadia was discovered in 1925 and dates from 1480–1355 BCE.[157]

- The references to family life in Ugarit (on the Mediterranean coast in modern day Syria) are based on the 14th century BCE literature found in archaeological digs that began there in 1929—but no systematic law-code has been found.

- The Middle Assyrian Law (MAL) was developed during the reign of Tiglath-Pileser 1 (1114–1076 BCE).[158]

- Roth has collected together and published marriage agreements dating from the Neo-Babylonian period.[159]

---

[155] Marc Van De Mieroop, *A History of the Ancient Near East ca. 3000–323 BC,* 2nd ed. (Malden, MA: Blackwell, 2007), 114; Walton, quoting Jean Bottéro, sees them as a model that 'inspires': Walton, *Ancient Near Eastern Thought,* 288

[156] Victor H. Matthews and Don C. Benjamin, *Old Testament Parallels: Laws from the Ancient Near East* (Mahwah, NJ: Paulist Press, 2006), 115

[157] John Walton, *Ancient Israelite Literature in Its Cultural Context: A Survey of Parallels Between Biblical and Ancient Near Eastern Texts* (Grand Rapids, MI: Zondervan, 1989), 50

[158] Matthews and Benjamin, *Old Testament Parallels,* 120

Unless otherwise stated these sources have been accessed via Pritchard's *Ancient Near Eastern Texts Relating to the Old Testament.*[160]

4.3 Specific Marital Practices in the Ancient Near East

4.3.1 Prohibited Marriages

Although there is no extant record of an Assyrian law on incest, LH 154 to LH 158 prohibit sexual relations between a man and his daughter, his son's betrothed or married wife, his mother, or his father's wife. Thus it can be seen that the wider ANE had a concept of incest that embraced consanguinity and affinity, the latter relationships being created by marriage; it follows that marriage was believed to create a union comparable to a blood relationship.

4.3.2 Betrothal

Matthews suggests that patriarchal extended families were common in the ANE and it was the father or eldest brother of the groom who arranged the marriage with the bride's parents; rites and procedures were determined by custom, formal written contracts being the exception.[161] Selms points out that it is not clear from the Ugaritic literature whether or not marriages were usually arranged, but the purpose of marriage was to have sons and that romantic and emotional considerations did not figure.[162] Usually a sum of money would be agreed between the two families which would be paid to the bride's family by the groom's family. Prenuptial agreements would state what would happen in case of divorce by either party, and the inheritance rights of any children might be specified, along with clarification of any rights if it was

---

[159] Martha Roth, *Babylonian Marriage Agreements: 7th-3rd Centuries B.C.*, Alter Orient und Altes Testament (Kevelaer: Butzon & Bercker, 1989)

[160] James B. Pritchard, ed., *Ancient Near Eastern Texts Relating to the Old Testament,* with supplement, 3rd ed. (Princeton, NJ: Princeton University Press, 1969)

[161] Victor H. Matthews, 'Marriage and Family in the Ancient Near East,' in Cambell, *Marriage and Family,* 1, 2, 7; Greengus comments that in Old Babylonia written contracts were for 'abnormal family situations': Samuel Greengus, 'The Old Babylonian Marriage Contract,' *JAOS* 89 (1969), 512–15

[162] Adrianus van Selms, *Marriage and Family Life in Ugaritic Literature* (London: Luzac, 1954), 13–15

to be a polygynous marriage.[163] Greengus commenting on UET 5636 (Ur Excavations, Texts: I Royal Inscriptions) says:

> We know of pre-nuptial agreements in the Ur III period [2100-2000 BCE], which consisted of a promise to marry made between the "guardians" of the future bride and groom. The pre-nuptial agreement created a binding relationship that required a full "divorce" for its abrogation. However, we have no indication from the evidence that all marriages in Ur III Sumer required this preliminary agreement, nor do we at present have any clear indication of such formally binding pre-nuptial agreements in the Old Babylonian period.[164]

Other examples include LE 17 and LE 18 which describe the groom bringing the 'bride-money' and generally outline principles similar to those found in rabbinic teaching if there is a breach of contract.[165]

LH 139, LH 159–LH 161, and LH 163 all mention 'marriage-price' and some refer to 'betrothal-gift'; LH 162 states: '[if the wife] has gone to (her) fate, her father may not lay claim to her dowry, since her dowry belongs to her children.' Lemos suggests that gifts from the groom to the father of the bride were, at least on occasion, passed on to the couple, becoming an 'indirect dowry' (as inferred from LH 138 and LH 139), and that in Old Babylonia the dowry was a 'premortem inheritance passed down from a father to his daughter and her children, his grandchildren, that may be managed by her husband but never becomes his property.'[166] HL 29, HL 30, and HL 34 similarly refer to a 'bride-price.'

Walton says the Nuzi documents demonstrate that 'the father either gives the bride part of the bride price or reserves it for her use in case her husband dies or deserts her';[167] Nuzi Akkadian §3 has: 'If ... Shennima takes another wife,

---

[163] Matthews, 'Marriage and Family,' in Campbell, *Marriage and Family*, 8
[164] Samuel Greengus, 'Old Babylonian Marriage Ceremonies and Rites,' *JCS* 20/2 (1966), 59
[165] Thus: Greengus, *Laws in the Bible*, 42
[166] T. M. Lemos, *Marriage Gifts and Social Change in Ancient Palestine: 1200 BCE to 200 CE* (New York, NY: Cambridge University Press, 2010), 144, 151
[167] Walton, *Ancient Israelite Literature in Its Cultural Context*, 55

she may *take* her dowry and leave.'[168] Grosz, from those same documents, believes that a wife could take the dowry with her if divorced before any children were born, after that the dowry was assimilated into the marital assets and divorce was 'impossible, or at least very difficult.' But by then, Grosz argues, the wife had earned the right to lifelong support in the conjugal household and her dowry would be included in the property eventually inherited by her children from their father.[169]

In Ugarit, Selms suggests that a sum of money is paid to the bride's parents—Korpel pointing out that even the gods were not exempt from such payments when they took a wife.[170] It seems that although the husband does not take ownership of the dowry he is allowed use of it provided he does not divorce his wife.[171] Once the payments had been made the betrothal period started and the woman was considered to belong to the prospective groom—this was in effect a marriage awaiting consummation, which usually happened when the bride finally entered the groom's home.[172]

MAL A.30 and MAL A.38 reference 'betrothal-gift' and 'marriage-price' respectively. In Neo-Babylonia Roth suggests that the dowry was considered part of the daughter's share of the family estate.[173]

4.3.3 The Marriage Contract

Yamauchi points out that in Mesopotamia and Egypt marriage was a civil affair which required no religious sanctions.[174] Selms believes that in Ugarit, as elsewhere in the ANE, there were not written marriage contracts, nor written acts of repudiation of the marriage; the ceremonial act of bringing the bride

---

[168] Pritchard, *Ancient Near Eastern Texts*, 220

[169] Katarzyna Grosz, 'Bride Wealth and Dowry in Nuzi,' in *Images of Women in Antiquity*, ed. Avril Cameron and Amélie Kuhrt (Detroit, MI: Wayne State University, 1983), 203

[170] Selms, *Marriage and Family Life*, 22; Marjo Christina Annette Korpel, *A Rift In the Clouds: Ugaritic and Hebrew Descriptions of the Divine* (Munster: Ugarit-Verlag, 1990), 226; for further discussion on marriage-gifts at Ugarit see: Lemos, *Marriage Gifts*, 38–39

[171] Selms, *Marriage and Family Life*, 33

[172] Selms, *Marriage and Family Life*, 28, 35

[173] Roth, *Babylonian Marriage Agreements: 7th-3rd Centuries B.C.*, 9; for further discussion of ANE dowry gifts see: Neufeld, *Ancient Hebrew Marriage Laws*, 110–17

[174] Edwin Yamauchi M, 'Cultural Aspects of Marriage in the Ancient World,' *BSac* 135 (1978), 246–47

into the husband's house or sending her away took the place of any written documents.[175] Greengus believes that it was only in rabbinic times (perhaps under the influence of Roman practice) that signed documents were seen as effecting a legal transaction rather than being merely a witness to them.[176] LH 128 does suggest that a woman is not a wife without 'contracts' and MAL A.36 refers to 'the marriage-contract,' but Greengus argues that in Babylonia the contract did not have to be in writing to have legal validity, and that the marriage documents ('contracts') extant are not a record of the marriage but were created to record transactions in relation to it.[177]

4.3.4 Marital Obligations

LH 133–LH 135, LH 148, MAL A.36, MAL A.45, and MAL A.46 demonstrate that the husband was responsible for his wife's food and clothing. Neufeld, commenting on both ancient Israel and the ANE, states: 'Maintenance and the performance of marital duties seem everywhere to be the main obligations of the husband towards his wife.'[178]

4.3.5 Adultery

Matthews states that all the major law codes of the ANE contain statutes regarding adultery, which is seen as violating the marriage, being grounds for divorce, and justifying the punishment of the guilty parties—adultery being understood as a wife having sexual intercourse with a man not her husband.[179] Westbrook comments: 'adultery in the ancient near East was ... an offence against the husband, for which he could claim certain remedies, and a sin, which might bring down divine punishment.'[180] The Ur-Nammu law B §1 defines the death penalty for the wife but not her paramour. In LH 132 (also MAL A.17) if a wife is accused of adultery, but there are no witnesses, she was to be thrown into the river—it was deemed that the river-god would protect

---

[175] Selms, *Marriage and Family Life*, 49

[176] Greengus, *Laws in the Bible*, 39

[177] Greengus, 'The Old Babylonian Marriage Contract,' 505, 512. Neufeld suggests the Babylonians and Assyrians favoured written records in contrast to the Hebrews in Palestine: Neufeld, *Ancient Hebrew Marriage Laws*, 161–62

[178] Neufeld, *Ancient Hebrew Marriage Laws*, 249

[179] Matthews, 'Marriage and Family,' in Campbell, *Marriage and Family*, 27–30

[180] Raymond Westbrook, 'Adultery in Ancient Near Eastern Law,' *RB* 97 (1990), 576

her if she was innocent, if not, she would drown.[181] HL 197–HL 198 and MAL A.13 provide for the execution of both guilty parties for adultery; in both codes the husband is allowed to spare his adulteress wife but in that case the adulterer is also to be spared (MAL A.15 and HL 198).

4.3.6 Divorce

Neufeld states that divorce was known in Babylonia, Assyria, Arabia, Nuzi, and among the Hittites, but Greengus comments that in light of the oral nature of most contracts in the ANE divorce documents are rare.[182] Matthews similarly points out that divorce was a fact of life in the ANE.[183] LE 59, LH 137–LH 140, and LH 142 set out various penalties and/or compensation payments incurred by the divorcing husband. Selms see that all the circumstantial evidence at Ugarit points to the husband having the power to repudiate his wife but there is no evidence that this was reciprocal.[184] MAL A.37 implies a husband is able to divorce his wife at will with or without a financial settlement. LH 137 suggests that a divorced woman was free to remarry.

4.3.7 Divorce Initiated by the Wife

Neufeld observes: 'The Semitic systems from the *C.H.*, *A.L.* ... allowed to the wife in a number of cases the right not to divorce her husband, but to sue for a divorce.'[185] It is suggested that this distinction is an important one, but often missed (or not articulated) by scholars when commenting on divorce. Lipiński sees widespread evidence of divorce in the ANE and, in effect, endorses Neufeld's view, in that he believes there were often equal rights to sue for divorce granted to the wife with freedom for her to remarry.[186] LH 142 appears to give the wife a right to divorce and the retention of her dowry:

---

[181] W. W. Davies, *The Codes of Hammurabi and Moses* (Stilwell: Digireads.com, 2006), 62–63

[182] Neufeld, *Ancient Hebrew Marriage Laws*, 185; Greengus, *Laws in the Bible*, 39

[183] Matthews, 'Marriage and Family,' in Campbell, *Marriage and Family*, 24–27. Westbrook lists the various penalties for divorce without grounds: Raymond Westbrook, *Old Babylonian Marriage Law* (New Haven, CT: Yale University Microfilms International, 1984), 78 n. 67

[184] Selms, *Marriage and Family Life*, 49

[185] Neufeld, *Ancient Hebrew Marriage Laws*, 182

[186] Edward Lipiński, 'Divorce in the Light of an Ancient Near Eastern Tradition,' in B.S. Jackson, ed., *The Jewish Law Annual* Vol. 4 (Leiden: Brill, 1981), 9–27

> If a woman so hated her husband that she has declared, "You may not have me," her record shall be investigated at her city council, and if she was careful and was not at fault, even though her husband has been going out and disparaging her greatly, that woman, without incurring any blame at all, may take her dowry and go off to her father's house.

But Matthews sees a problem with this interpretation of LH 142 in that the husband is not required to make a financial settlement to the wife he has mistreated. He cites Westbrook's solution that it is referencing an inchoate marriage—a view not shared by Neufeld or Greengus.[187]

Lipiński quotes an Old Assyrian contract from the 19th century BCE that gives the wife the same right to divorce as the husband, but the financial penalty payable for initiating the divorce is identical in both cases—'five minas of silver.'[188] He also sees evidence of this in some Old Babylonian marriage contracts, but points out that they all involve the wife successfully attaching some 'serious blame' to her husband.[189] Another example is found in LH 148 and LH 149 which suggest if the wife is ill and the husband marries another woman the first wife may leave taking her dowry with her. MAL A.36 and MAL A.45 appear to grant a wife divorce rights based on the failure of the husband to provide for her, either by his neglect, or his capture by an enemy. But Lipiński cautions against drawing too many conclusions from such laws, pointing out the judges were not involved in divorce procedures unless there was a legal problem and therefore they might be exceptional cases.[190]

Greengus comments that in the ANE:

> Both wife and husband, at least in theory, seem to have had equivalent legal power to divorce the other partner, although ... measures were

---

[187] Matthews, 'Marriage and Family,' in Campbell, *Marriage and Family*, 27; Westbrook, 'Adultery in Ancient Near Eastern Law,' 570; Neufeld, *Ancient Hebrew Marriage Laws*, 186; Greengus, 'Filling Gaps,' 167–68
[188] Lipiński, 'Divorce in the Light of an Ancient Near Eastern Tradition,' 14; the document is published in: Pritchard, *Ancient Near Eastern Texts*, 543
[189] Lipiński, 'Divorce,' in Jackson, *The Jewish Law Annual*, 14–16
[190] Lipiński, 'Divorce,' in Jackson, *The Jewish Law Annual*, 11

anciently often instituted to suppress the ability of wives to divorce their husbands.[191]

4.4 Provision and Protection for the Woman

To modern sensibilities the ANE law codes seem harsh to women, but Hugenberger says when commenting on Genesis 2 and Malachi 2:

> What is especially striking ... is the fact that the primary obligation of marriage ... is not that of the wife toward her husband, as might be expected from their ancient context, but that of the husband toward his wife.[192]

However, the ANE context clearly demonstrates a similar gender-based asymmetry.[193] Many of the provisions in the law codes and prenuptial agreements that have survived are, in the main, to protect women in that they specify the material support and security they could expect both in their husband's lifetime, and on his death. It is clear that the marriage payments (whether from the groom or the bride's father) referenced in §4.3.2 were to give the wife a measure of financial security. Westbrook comments: 'The duty of a husband to provide his wife with sustenance was so self-evident that it went virtually unmentioned in ancient Near Eastern sources.'[194]

An analysis of the law codes referenced in this chapter demonstrate this gender-based asymmetry, for example, in protection from or after divorce in Ur-Nammu §6 and §7, LE 59, LH 138, LH 139, LH 140, and MAL A.34;[195] protection for a wife's dowry or marriage-price in LH 150, LH 162, LH 163, LH 167, MAL A.27, MAL A.38, HL 30, and Neo Babylonian Laws 10–13; the right

---

[191] Greengus, *Laws in the Bible*, 40

[192] Hugenberger, *Marriage as a Covenant*, 182

[193] This is not to deny that in one notable area—the power to enact a divorce—the asymmetry is to the benefit of the man, see for example MAL A.37.

[194] Raymond Westbrook, 'The Female Slave,' in *Gender and Law in the Hebrew Bible and the Ancient Near East*, ed. Victor H. Matthews, Bernard M. Levinson, and Tikva Frymer-Kensky, (Sheffield: Sheffield Academic, 1998; Repr. London: T&T Clark, 2004), 236

[195] Commenting on LH 138 and LH 139, Lemos says that 'Clauses prescribing such a divorce penalty [payable by the husband] abound in the [Old Babylonian] marriage documents': Lemos, *Marriage Gifts*, 147

of a wife/widow (or daughter) to material provision in LH 178, MAL A.36, MAL A.45, and MAL A.46; the freedom of a wife (or daughter) to dispose of her own inheritance in LH 179–LH 182, and LH 184; and levirate clauses to give protection in widowhood in MAL A.30, MAL A.33, and HL 193.

4.5 Summary: Marriage and Divorce in the Ancient Near East

The ANE is not a homogenous cultural entity, spanning as it does several millennia, people groups, and languages—undoubtedly marital practices varied widely;[196] but it seems in ANE marriage that there is widespread evidence of commonality. For example, marriage to close relations, both by blood and affinity (i.e. relationships created by marriage) was forbidden in the LH, and Mace believes that although such are not articulated in the Assyrian laws, the LH was assumed as a background.[197] Marriage created a new set of forbidden incestuous relationships—on marriage people became what they were not previously in a metaphoric one-flesh union; that is, they were considered as blood relations.

Furthermore, marriages (often arranged) were perceived as contractual with mutual obligations. These obligations were sometimes outlined in a document, but any such document was not the essence of the contract. Marriage was considered to be functional, and that function was in the main the rearing of children in a new family unit. To that end the husband's role was to provide material security for his wife and family, and for the wife to bear his (and not another man's) children. The law codes and prenuptial agreements that have survived emphasise those asymmetrical gender specific roles. Divorce rights seemed to be mutual, indicating the volitional, conditional nature of the relationship—but the husband's freedom of action greatly exceeded that of the wife.

---

[196] A point made by Lemos and illustrated with 20th century anthropological studies showing wide variations in people groups in close geographic proximity: Lemos, *Marriage Gifts*, 16

[197] Mace, *Hebrew Marriage*, 151

Chapter 1 posited that the aetiology of mundane marriage in ancient Israel will be seen to be underpinned by the four principles found in Genesis 2:24:

1. A naturally born man and woman.
2. Become what they were not.
3. In a metaphoric one-flesh union.
4. By means of a volitional, conditional covenant.

It is suggested, broadly speaking, that the four principles evidenced in Genesis 2:24 can be seen in ANE mundane marital practice outside of Israel.

Chapter 5: Marriage and Divorce in the Old Testament

5.1 Introduction

There is a lack of documentary evidence to indicate the marital practices of ancient Israel. The Elephantine marriage contracts dating from the fifth century BCE are considered in chapter 8, but it is debated how accurately they reflect life in main-stream Judaism. The JDD (also considered in chapter 8) belong to the first and second century CE, and while it might be considered they accurately reflect life in ancient Israel they considerably post-date that era. Thus the most reliable source material available to date is to be found in the Old Testament legislation and narratives.[198] Block however, cautions against seeking a social reality behind its text:

> Not only do many of these texts [in the Hebrew Bible] derive from a much later time than the events they describe, but they also provide inconsistent pictures. The frankness of the accounts of people's behavior often flies in the face of ideals promulgated elsewhere ... we must always ask ourselves whether the texts we are reading present a normative picture, or whether the authors have consciously described a deviation from the norm.[199]

Meyers makes a similar observation from the converse point of view:

> The biblical scholar does not have the methodological option of observing behavior. Only the ideology is available. Hence there is danger in equating ideology with daily reality, which can diverge from the normative expression contained in the biblical text.[200]

---

[198] 'For information on the family we depend primarily on the biblical texts. Relevant archaeological data are not abundant': John Blenkinsopp, 'The Family in First Temple Israel,' in Leo G. Perdue et al., eds., *Families in Ancient Israel* (Louisville, KY: Westminster John Knox, 1997), 48

[199] Block, 'Marriage and Family,' in Campbell, *Marriage and Family*, 34

[200] Meyers, *Discovering Eve*, 13

Furthermore, Blenkinsopp commenting on the formulation of laws in the Pentateuch points out the lack of a comprehensive code for marriage and marital dissolution.[201]

However, as Westbrook states:

> If God's relationship with Israel is to be explained by a metaphor drawing upon the everyday life of the audience then that metaphor, to be effective, must reflect accurately the reality known to the audience. If the narrator were to invent the legal rules on which the metaphor is based, it would cease to be a valid metaphor.[202]

This observation accords with the metaphoric principles which Lakoff and Johnson elucidate: 'The most fundamental values in a culture will be coherent with the metaphorical structure of the most fundamental concepts in the culture.'[203] Thus it is argued in this present study that the Old Testament would not employ an imagery that did not reflect a social reality; nor would it contradict the imagery it employed in its own legislative teaching and narrative accounts of mundane marriage. The aim of this chapter is to explore the nature of that social reality, to determine whether mundane marriage is underpinned by the conceptual domain of Genesis 2:24 (as posited in §1.2–§1.3.1), or that of Genesis 2:23 (the primal couple).

Satlow, Collins, and Gafni suggest that distinctive teaching arises from a primal couple marriage model:

1. God ordains each marriage and joins the 'two into one' (Gafni).[204]

2. Marriage is a sacrament (Gafni).[205]

3. The prohibition of polygyny and divorce (Satlow).[206]

---

[201] John Blenkinsopp, 'The Family in First Temple Israel,' in Perdue et al., *Families in Ancient Israel*, 48, 58–59
[202] Westbrook, 'Adultery in Ancient Near Eastern Law,' 577
[203] Lakoff and Johnson, *Metaphors*, 22
[204] Isaiah M. Gafni, 'The Institution of Marriage in Rabbinic Times,' in *The Jewish Family: Metaphor and Memory*, ed. David Kraemer (Oxford: Oxford University Press, 1989), 13–15
[205] Gafni, 'The Institution of Marriage,' in Kraemer, *The Jewish Family*, 13–15
[206] Satlow, *Jewish Marriage*, 60–61

4. Sexual intercourse is deemed primarily for procreation (Collins).[207]

5. Celibacy and holiness are linked (Collins).[208]

The understanding that God forms, or at least ordains, each marriage can be traced directly to Genesis 2:23, and it seems that a sacramental concept logically follows from this (taking *sacrament* to mean that each mundane marriage union is perceived to have an ontological dimension, in other words, something is thought to have transpired in heaven to form the union). Also, teaching about monogamy and divorce within the Christian community (so scholars argue) specifically references Adam and Eve.[209] However, the teaching that sexual intercourse should be primarily for procreation, and that celibacy and holiness are linked, is difficult to trace directly to Genesis 2:23 and the primary couple model. But it will be demonstrated in the course of this study that such a model only emerged in the early Christian era, coinciding with the development of all the five key teachings outlined above.[210] Furthermore, it seems clear that many in the literature (e.g. Collins, Gafni, and Satlow) see that the distinctive teachings as above are linked with v. 23 and the primal couple marriage.

Thus, if the Old Testament legislation and narratives demonstrate that mundane marriage was considered to be a volitional, conditional, covenantal union, as it has been posited that v. 24 outlines (§1.2), and no evidence is found of the five distinctive teachings that are widely believed to originate from an understanding of the marriage in v. 23, it will be considered that this reinforces the argument that ancient Israel understood that it is the conceptual domain of v. 24 that underpinned the aetiology of mundane marriage.

The focus in this chapter will be on those matters that might be seen to inform an understanding of the underlying model of Old Testament mundane marriage; or that elucidate aspects of mundane marriage that are cross-mapped

---

[207] John J. Collins, 'Marriage, Divorce, and Family in Second Temple Judaism,' in Perdue et al., *Families in Ancient Israel* (Louisville, Ky.: Westminster John Knox, 1997), 147
[208] Collins, 'Marriage, Divorce, and Family,' in Perdue et al., *Families in Ancient Israel*, 147
[209] For example: Andrew Cornes, *Divorce and Remarriage: Biblical Principles & Pastoral Practice* (London: Hodder & Stoughton, 1993), 185
[210] These developments are considered in detail in: Witte, *From Sacrament to Contract*, 1–112

to the target domain in either Old Testament or New Testament marital imagery (e.g. betrothal, divorce, remarriage); or are thought to be significant for the exegesis of New Testament mundane marriage which will be undertaken in chapter 10 (e.g. Deut 24:1–4).

5.2 Marriage in the Early Narrative Accounts

There is no specific term for marriage in biblical Hebrew;[211] a man 'takes' (לְקַח) a wife or is 'given' (נָתַן) a wife by his parents;[212] Block commenting that Hebrew expressions for marriage and sexual intercourse reflect male initiative.[213] The word employed for husband is often בַּעַל 'lord,' but Meyers considers that this does not imply 'absolute sovereignty' of one person over another 'because it involves an intimate relationship, a limit to power.'[214]

After Eden the first marriage referenced is in Genesis 4:17 where Cain's wife (אִשָּׁה) is mentioned without further elaboration as to her origin or any associated marital procedure. It is not until Genesis 24 that some record is found of a process or custom attached to the marriage union, where Abraham seeks a wife for his son Isaac from 'my kindred' (Gen 24:4). The concept of love (אָהֵב) as a basis for mundane marriage is not articulated in the Old Testament, but the narratives comment that Jacob loved Rachel (Gen 29:18) and that Michal loved David (1 Sam 18:20); Samson's love for Delilah is also mentioned (Judg 16:4) but it is not known if they married.

Although the Old Testament does not specifically mandate parentally arranged marriages, Block sees that some texts infer it (citing Deut 7:3);[215] he points out that the tribes in ancient Israel were sub-divided into clans, and although marriage did occur between the different clans, for the most part, Israelite

---

[211] Selms, *Marriage and Family Life*, 13

[212] See analysis of Hebrew marriage terms in: Seock-Tae Sohn, *YHWH, The Husband of Israel* (Eugene, OR: Wipf and Stock, 2002), 5–21

[213] Block, 'Marriage and Family,' in Campbell, *Marriage and Family*, 46

[214] Meyers, *Discovering Eve*, 182; also discussion in: Block, 'Marriage and Family,' in Campbell, *Marriage and Family*, 62

[215] Block, 'Marriage and Family in Ancient Israel,' in Campbell, *Marriage and Family*, 56; another inferred example might be Gen 24:4 as above.

marriages were endogamous.[216] These clans were further sub-divided into local households which would be large extended families headed by a single living male ancestor, the family structure being patrilineal, patrilocal, and patriarchal. Block describes such a family:

> These families were made up of a single living male ancestor, his wife/wives, the man's sons and their wives, grandsons and their wives, and conceivably even great grandchildren; any unmarried male or female descendants ... and unrelated dependents.[217]

5.3 Mundane Marriage—Contract or Covenant?

Hugenberger outlines the debate around the meaning of *covenant*, the usual translation in English Bibles of בְּרִית (occurring more than 280 times in the Hebrew Bible), and *contract*—and whether marriage can be described as the former.[218] Although Hugenberger argues for a distinct covenantal understanding for marriage there is no evidence that בְּרִית in the Hebrew Bible meant any more than might be implied by *contract;* that is, an agreement between parties that is both volitional and conditional.[219] Hugenberger sees that a key indicator of a marriage covenant is that it is undertaken 'under divine sanction.'[220] He looks for evidence of an 'oath,' or declaration (*verba solemnia*) confirming a marriage in the: ANE, Elephantine papyri, JDD, talmudic, and Hebrew Bible texts.[221]

However, he can only point to three possible references to mundane marriage in the Hebrew Bible where בְּרִית is used: Proverbs 2:17, Ezekiel 16:8, 59–62, and Malachi 2:14. Proverbs 2:17 is a possible reference to Yahweh's Sinaitic

---

[216] Block, 'Marriage and Family,' in Campbell, *Marriage and Family*, 37; also: Blenkinsopp, 'The Family in First Temple Israel,' in Perdue et al., *Families in Ancient Israel*, 49–57

[217] Block, 'Marriage and Family,' in Campbell, *Marriage and Family*, 38–40; Patai, *Sex and Family*, 19; also: Leo G. Perdue, 'The Israelite and Early Jewish Family: Summary and Conclusions,' in Perdue et al., *Families in Ancient Israel*, 174–79

[218] Hugenberger, *Marriage as a Covenant*, 1–12

[219] Thus: Instone-Brewer, *Divorce and Remarriage*, 15–19

[220] Hugenberger, *Marriage as a Covenant*, 171; the analysis above is not to imply that a covenant cannot be made under divine sanction—an example of such is in Gen 17:1–14.

[221] Hugenberger, *Marriage as a Covenant*, 216–79

covenant with Israel; the focus of Ezekiel 16 is certainly marital imagery—leaving Malachi 2:14 where the Hebrew text is unclear, ESV has:

> Because the LORD was witness between you and the wife of your youth, to whom you have been faithless, though she is your companion and your wife by covenant. (Mal 2:14)

Even if this translation is accepted it will be seen (§6.9.4) that it is not clear whether this is a reference to mundane marriage or a reference to Yahweh's relationship to his people—thus all three references to a marital *covenant* might belong in the target domain of the imagery.

His most convincing argument for a set verbal declaration is found where it is clear that the reference is in the target domain of the imagery. Thus in Hosea 2:2 Yahweh is seen to declare, 'Plead with your mother, plead—for she is not my wife, and I am not her husband'—a form of words similar to that found at Elephantine to declare the marriage ('she is my wife and I am her husband').[222] In effect, in his argument, Hugenberger sees it is possible to infer reverse cross-mapping from the target to the source domain and posit a set verbal formula in mundane marriage to enact a marriage (and conversely a divorce). But this present study suggests that the paucity of evidence makes it difficult to deduce that such a formula indicated that marriage (or divorce) was believed to be formed under divine sanction.

Collins posits that marriage in Second Temple Judaism was evidenced to be of a 'pragmatic, contractual character' and Instone-Brewer argues persuasively that marriage 'contract' better conveys the Old Testament meaning.[223] However, this present study uses *covenant* without implying any later theological concepts that have become associated with the word.

Although not specifically articulated in the Old Testament, the volitional nature of the marriage agreement is clear. There is no evidence of marriages being conducted against the will of the bride (except in the cases of a slave

---

[222] Hugenberger, *Marriage as a Covenant*, 231–34, 239
[223] Collins, 'Marriage, Divorce, and Family,' in Perdue et al., *Families in Ancient Israel*, 149; Instone-Brewer, *Divorce and Remarriage*, 18

wife, Exod 21:7–11, or a woman taken in a battle, Deut 21:10–14), or against the will of the groom, in any of the narrative accounts, and Friedman argues that mutual consent is fundamental to Jewish marriage law codes.[224] The divorce rights of a wife (§5.12) pre-suppose that if she did not want to maintain the marriage she need not.

5.4 The Importance of Virginity

Davidson argues convincingly that the term בְּתוּלָה in the Hebrew Bible references a virgin, not a young woman of marriageable age.[225] The sexual purity of a woman before a first marriage was significant in the Old Testament law codes. If any husband accuses his (previously unmarried) bride of not being a virgin on marriage and he is not believed he is punished and never allowed to divorce her (Deut 22:13–19). The high priest could only marry a virgin (Lev 21:13–14) and a rapist had to pay compensation to his victim's father for any loss of virginity (Deut 22:28–29; Exod 22:16–17). However, virginity is not held in the Old Testament as a permanent virtue—for example Jephthah's daughter when facing death wanted two months to 'weep for my virginity' (Judg 11:37).[226]

5.5 Betrothal Arrangements

Some form of monetary exchange appears to have been the means by which a marriage agreement was formalised.

Satlow posits:

> The Hebrew Bible describes a single primary marriage payment, the *mohar*. This is a sum of money to be paid by the groom to the father or family of his prospective wife.[227]

---

[224] Mordechai A. Friedman, *Jewish Marriage in Palestine: The* Ketubba *Traditions,* A Cairo Geniza Study Vol 1 (Tel Aviv: The Jewish Theological Seminary of America, 1980), 133

[225] Davidson, *The Flame of Yahweh*, 339–40

[226] For further examples and discussion: Davidson, *The Flame of Yahweh*, 341–42

[227] Satlow, *Jewish Marriage*, 200

Archer suggests that the *mohar* is not a specific amount and cites Genesis 29:27 and Deuteronomy 22:29 as examples of varying *mohar* payments.[228] Lemos makes a detailed analysis of Hebrew Bible marital payments and sees examples in Exodus 22:16-17, and in 1 Samuel 18:25 where Saul told David that he would accept as a 'bride price' for his daughter Michal a hundred foreskins of the Philistines.[229] Wasserstein and Archer distinguish the *mohar* payment from a dowry which traditionally means a gift from the bride's father to the bride.[230] Bickerman suggests that the LXX translators of the Hebrew text confused the *mohar* with a dowry;[231] nonetheless Lemos sees possible oblique references to dowry gifts in several narrative accounts but concludes that it was not a widespread custom.[232]

Although Neufeld considers that no rules are given about the betrothal process, he suggests that on payment of the *mohar* the marriage became legally effective but inchoate until consummated;[233] he further suggests that the *mohar* was passed on to the bride on her marriage (such an indirect dowry is evidenced in the ANE (§4.3.2) but Lemos comments on the lack of evidence for such in the Old Testament.[234] It is not difficult to see the possible wider ANE origins of the Hebrew *mohar* payment but there is some debate about its significance.

Bickerman sees it as a compensation payment:

> whatever the nature of the *mohar* or its interpretation by the Hebrew groom was, he had to give a compensation for his wife to the latter's father. Such compensation was required because in the agricultural

---

[228] Léonie J. Archer, *Her Price is Beyond Rubies: The Jewish Woman in Graeco-Roman Palestine*, Journal for the Study of the Old Testament Supplement 60 (Sheffield: Sheffield Academic, 1990), 159

[229] Lemos, *Marriage Gifts*, 20-61

[230] 'Dowry does not exist as a legal institution in the Bible': A. Wasserstein, 'A Marriage Contract from the Province of Arabia Nova: Notes on Papyrus Yadin 18,' *JQR* 80 No.1/2 (Jul-Oct 1989), 126. Archer concurs: 'biblical law contained no stipulations about dowries (indeed there is not even a word in the Old Testament for "dowry")': Archer, *Her Price is Beyond Rubies*, 166

[231] Elias Joseph Bickerman, 'Two Legal Interpretations of the Septuagint,' in *Studies in Jewish and Christian History: Ancient Judaism and Early Christianity*, ed. Amram Tropper (Leiden: Brill, 1976), 203-204

[232] Lemos, *Marriage Gifts*, 51-59, 231

[233] Neufeld, *Ancient Hebrew Marriage Laws*, 94-95, 142-43; a view endorsed in: Lemos, *Marriage Gifts*, 230-31

[234] Neufeld, *Ancient Hebrew Marriage Laws*, 105; Lemos, *Marriage Gifts*, 10

economy the bride leaving her family deprived the latter of a worker and transferred her operational force to her husband's family.[235]

However, Archer et al. believe that the *mohar* was not considered a payment for the woman herself.[236]

5.6 Forbidden Marriages

Deuteronomy 27:20, 22, and 23 forbid sexual relations between a man and his father's wife, his sister or half-sister, or his mother-in-law respectively, and Ezekiel 22:10–11 forbids such with a father's wife, a daughter-in-law, and a half-sister; but it is in Leviticus 18 and 20 that a systematic code of forbidden relationships is given. Mace makes a detailed analysis of the code and states:

> Incest is based primarily upon *consanguinity*—that is, it applies to those of the opposite sex to whom one is related by blood. But in many societies [including Israel] it operates too in regard to *affinity*— that is, relationship through marriage is regarded in the same light as relationship through blood.[237]

The Levitical affinity codes reinforce the analysis of §1.2 that a marriage covenant creates a relationship that was considered to be comparable to a blood relationship, and that this was the understanding of the Genesis 2:24 'becoming one flesh.'

It is of interest, however, that Leviticus 20:21—'If a man takes his brother's wife, it is impurity. He has uncovered his brother's nakedness; they shall be childless'—appears to contradict Deuteronomy 25:5—'If brothers dwell together, and one of them dies and has no son, the wife of the dead man shall not be married outside the family to a stranger. Her husband's brother shall go

---

[235] Bickerman, 'Two Legal Interpretations of the Septuagint,' in Tropper, *Studies in Jewish and Christian History*, 196

[236] Archer, *Her Price is Beyond Rubies*, 164–65; Lemos, *Marriage Gifts*, 3–11; Perdue, 'The Israelite and Early Jewish Family,' in Perdue et al., *Families in Ancient Israel*, 184; see also: Weiss, David H., 'The Use of קנה in Connection with Marriage,' *Harvard Theological Review* Vol. 57, No. 3 (July 1964), 244–48

[237] Mace, *Hebrew Marriage*, 151–64; other forbidden marriages based on ethnicity and the priesthood are analysed in: David Chapman, 'Marriage and Family in Second Temple Judaism,' in Campbell, *Marriage and Family*, 198–204

in to her and take her as his wife and perform the duty of a husband's brother to her.'

Haley believes that the reference in Leviticus 20:21 is to the divorced brother's wife.[238] If correct, two factors might indicate that divorce in ancient Israel was not unusual: firstly, there was specific legislation for the posited situation; and secondly, the Pentateuchal author did not see the need to specifically reference divorce, which suggests he believed his readership would have assumed his meaning.

5.7 Polygyny and Concubinage

Genesis 4 records the first example of polygyny when Lamech takes two wives. Genesis 16 records the childless Sarai giving Hagar her servant to Abram as a wife to produce offspring; a practice Walton sees as evidenced in the Nuzi archives.[239] Davidson sees in this passage intentional intertextual echoes of Genesis 3, which he takes as evidence of divine disapproval, but there is no specific legislation against the practice in the Old Testament.[240] Epstein sees that in the Hebrew Bible, 'There was no anti-sexual or ascetic tradition' and that polygyny in ancient Israel was, at least in part, to ensure every woman could belong to a family structure.[241] As the Old Testament narratives unfold there are several examples of polygyny including Jacob, Gideon, David, and Solomon.[242] 1 Chronicles 1:32 describes the woman Abraham married after Sarai's death as his 'concubine' (פִּילֶגֶשׁ); it is not always clear what this signifies—the term is never applied to a man's first wife but seems at times to be used interchangeably with 'wife' (אִשָּׁה). For example, Bilhah is described as Jacob's concubine in Genesis 35:22, but as his wife in Genesis 37:2.[243] Epstein

---

[238] John W. Haley, *Alleged Discrepancies of the Bible* (New Kensington, PA: Whittaker, 1992), 292

[239] Walton, *Ancient Israelite Literature in Its Cultural Context*, 54–55

[240] Davidson, *The Flame of Yahweh*, 184–86

[241] Louis M. Epstein, *Sex Laws and Customs in Judaism* (Jersey City, NY: Ktav, 1967), VII-VIII

[242] For a more comprehensive list of examples and discussion: Davidson, *The Flame of Yahweh*, 177–212

[243] For discussion of terminology concerning wife/concubine: Davidson, *The Flame of Yahweh*, 186; also: Louis M. Epstein, *Marriage Laws in the Bible and the Talmud*, HSS 12; 1942 (repr. New York, NY: Johnson Reprint Company, 1968), 34–76; Epstein elsewhere claims, 'The Bible nowhere confuses the slave-wife with the concubine, except in one instance where Bilhah, the maid-servant of Rachel, is called *Pillegesh* [concubine]':

claims that there is 'strong evidence' that the concubine is under full legal marriage bond to her husband.[244]

5.8 Marital Obligations

Hugenberger comments that the primary obligation of marriage is that of the husband toward his wife;[245] her marital obligations are not specifically outlined in the law codes (except for sexual faithfulness) and it was only later rabbinical Judaism that looked to codify them. The narrative accounts appear to portray the typical wife in ancient Israel as the bearer of children and homemaker who acknowledges her husband's authority (e.g. 1 Pet 3:5–6), but Proverbs 31:10–31 does not confine her role to that.

The case law in Exodus 21:7–11 appears to outline the situation where a father sells his daughter into slavery with the expectation that her new master will marry her, and describes the 'triad' of obligations of the master as a husband to this woman, even if he takes a second wife; however, the marital status of the slave is debated.[246] There has been a similar debate about the precise nature of the obligations, but most opt for the food, clothing, and marital rights of ESV, Instone-Brewer commenting that, 'there was virtual unanimity even for the difficult third term "conjugal rights," among early and later Jewish interpreters.'[247] This issue is addressed further in §5.12.1.

Louis M. Epstein, 'The Institution of Concubinage among the Jews,' *PAAJR* 6 (1934–1935), 161; Mace suggests that the children of concubines could inherit together with wives but this was discretionary: Mace, *Hebrew Marriage*, 133–34

[244] Epstein, 'Institution of Concubinage,' 167

[245] Hugenberger, *Marriage as a Covenant*, 182

[246] It seems the academic consensus endorses the fact that the slave becomes the master's wife (or concubine or slave wife), ESV translating Exod 21:10 as, 'If he takes another wife to himself,' as do many English Bible translations; scholars who concur include Block, Instone-Brewer, and Pressler: Block, 'Marriage and Family in Ancient Israel,' in Campbell, *Marriage and Family*, 48; Instone-Brewer, *Divorce and Remarriage*, 99; Carolyn Pressler, 'Wives and Daughters, Bond and Free: Views of Women in the Slave Laws of Exodus 21:2-11,' in Matthews, Levinson, and Frymer-Kensky, *Gender and Law*, 159; co*ntra* Westbrook: 'the slave is assigned and taken, but never specifically as a wife, and the relationship is ended by sale or manumission, not by divorce': Westbrook, 'The Female Slave,' in Matthews, Levinson, and Frymer-Kensky, *Gender and Law*, 218

[247] Instone-Brewer, *Divorce and Remarriage*, 99–100; Bible translations opting for the triad as per ESV include: KJV, NASB, NIV, and RSV. Paul disagrees: he argues from ancient documents found at Nuzi that the triad of provision found in Exod 21:10 is 'a reflex—albeit a very modified one' of those documents and should be read as 'food, clothing, and oil': Shalom M. Paul, 'Exod 21.10: A Threefold Maintenance Clause,' *JNES* 28 (January 1969),

5.9 Adultery

The law code explicitly forbids adultery (Exod 20:14), understood in the Old Testament as a married woman having sexual intercourse with a man who is not her husband.[248] Deuteronomy 22:23–27 puts consensual sex involving a betrothed virgin and a male who was not her fiancé on a par with adultery and prescribes the death penalty; if it was deemed non-consensual only the male offender would die. Westbrook considers the death penalty for adultery was a maximum penalty and Mace points out that there is no record of its enactment in the Old Testament.[249]

Some see that adultery in the Old Testament is principally an offence against a husband's property, partly because of the placing of its prohibition in the second table of the Decalogue where property offences dominate.[250] But Epstein comments:

> The biblical law of adultery has gone beyond these more ancient [ANE] laws in making adultery a moral crime rather than an injury to the husband.[251]

And Philips states: 'in Israel adultery was regarded as a sin against God ... a distinctive principle found nowhere else in the ancient Near East.'[252] Davidson points out that in Numbers 5, the test for adultery where there are no witnesses:

49, 52; those that agree with Paul appear to be in a minority, but include Pressler—who finds Paul's argument 'impressive' but the issue, she says, is 'uncertain': Pressler, 'Wives and Daughters,' in Matthews, Levinson, and Frymer-Kensky, *Gender and Law*, 160; Block finds Paul 'convincing': Block, 'Marriage and Family,' in Campbell, *Marriage and Family*, 48 n. 69; and Kaiser, like Paul, rejects the concept of marital rights: Walter C. Jr. Kaiser, *Toward Old Testament Ethics* (Grand Rapids, MI: Zondervan, 1983), 185; Davidson opts for 'normal food, clothing, and ... lodging': Davidson, *The Flame of Yahweh*, 193

[248] Hugenberger, *Marriage as a Covenant*, 313-14

[249] Westbrook, 'Adultery in Ancient Near Eastern Law,' 565; Mace, *Hebrew Marriage*, 249; also: Epstein, *Sex Laws and Customs*, 199

[250] For example Neufeld: 'The wife is considered as the property of her husband (Exod 20:17)': Neufeld, *Ancient Hebrew Marriage Laws*, 231; and: Blenkinsopp, 'The Family in First Temple Israel,' in Perdue et al., *Families in Ancient Israel*, 62; *contra*: Block, 'Marriage and Family,' in Campbell, *Marriage and Family*, 63-64

[251] Epstein, *Sex Laws and Customs*, 199

[252] Anthony Phillips, 'Another Look at Adultery,' *JSOT* 20 (1981), 3

> is performed by a priest ... in the sanctuary ... and is associated with various ritual offerings ... thus this is a *sanctuary* ritual, conducted in the presence, and under the direct control, of Yahweh himself.... This is the only biblical law where the outcome depends upon a miracle.[253]

In contrast, within ANE cultures, although adultery was considered an offence that could result in divine punishment, the principal offence appears to have been against the husband, as he was able to spare his wife the death penalty (§4.3.5).

5.10 Divorce

The conditional nature of the marriage agreement is evidenced by the ability to break the union by means of a divorce. The verbs (and their cognates) used for divorce, or where the context appears to be divorce, are: כָּרַת (to 'cut off') in Deuteronomy 24:1, 3, Isaiah 50:1, Jeremiah 3:8; גָּרַשׁ ('to cast out') in Genesis 21:10, Leviticus 21:7, 14; 22:13, Numbers 30:9, Ezekiel 44:22; שָׁלַח ('to send' or 'to let go') in Genesis 21:14, Deuteronomy 21:14; 22:19, 29; 24:4, Jeremiah 3:1, 8, Malachi 2:16; יָצָא (to 'go' or 'come out') in Ezra 10:3, 19; בָּדַל ('to separate') in Ezra 10:11; בָּגַד ('to deal treacherously') in Malachi 2:14.

Block argues that divorce in ancient Israel belonged to the realm of internal family law;[254] but Deuteronomy 21:18–21 implies that Meyers is correct in suggesting not everything was settled by the family themselves.[255] Leviticus 22:13 considers the rights of a priest's childless daughter who is divorced, and Numbers 30:9 makes a divorced woman accountable for her own vows. Nowhere in the Pentateuch is divorce condemned: Abraham sends Hagar away (Gen 21:10–14) seemingly with divine approval; but Leviticus 21:7, 14 forbids a priest or high priest to marry a divorced woman (also Ezekiel 44:22). Perdue

---

[253] Davidson, *The Flame of Yahweh*, 351–52

[254] Block, 'Marriage and Family,' in Campbell, *Marriage and Family*, 49; see also: Christopher J. H. Wright, *God's People in God's Land* (Grand Rapids., MI: Eerdmans, 1990; Repr. Carlisle: Paternoster, 1997), 216–17

[255] 'Only when internal family redress failed to control tensions among members of the household might there be recourse to a suprafamily judicial body—perhaps a group of elders drawn from each household': Carol Meyers, 'The Family in Early Israel,' in Perdue et al., *Families in Ancient Israel*, 31

points out that the purpose of divorce was to remarry, and Instone-Brewer considers that to be the reason for the written certificate of Deuteronomy 24.[256]

5.11 A Husband's Right to Divorce

5.11.1 Deuteronomy

5.11.1.1 Prohibition of Divorce in Deuteronomy 22

Deuteronomy 22 prohibits divorce in two cases: where a husband has falsely accused his wife of not being a virgin on marriage (vv. 13–19); and where the husband has been compelled to marry the unbetrothed virgin he raped (vv. 28–30). In the former case Mace points out that if a husband under Old Testament legislation could divorce his wife at will (as Hillel's followers claimed that Deut 24 taught—§10.3.2) there would appear to be no point in attempting a false accusation and risking the consequent restriction. Mace speculates (and Patai agrees, albeit basing his view on the Mishnah and modern Middle Eastern parallels) that there was perhaps a financial penalty for unjustified divorce, such as LH 137 and LH 138 imply; a penalty that rabbinic Judaism codified.[257] Deuteronomy 24:1–4 prohibits remarriage after divorce to the original husband—this will be considered separately below.

5.11.1.2 Divorce in Deuteronomy 24:1–4

Greengus comments that he finds no examples in ANE collections of the prohibition of a wife returning to her husband after a divorce as in Deuteronomy 24.[258] Laney argues that Deuteronomy 24:1–4 is case law with a protasis-apodosis sequence that elsewhere in Deuteronomy does not imply approval of the situation, and argues the pericope neither gives grounds for, nor approves of, divorce—but simply states if a wife was divorced and issued

---

[256] Perdue, 'The Israelite and Early Jewish Family,' in Perdue et al., *Families in Ancient Israel*, 171; Instone-Brewer, *Divorce and Remarriage*, 28

[257] Mace, *Hebrew Marriage*, 252–53; Raphael Patai, *Sex and Family in the Bible and the Middle East* (Garden City, NY: Doubleday, 1959), 119; the Mishnah *Ketubbot* outlines when the husband is to pay the *ketubah* to the wife he is divorcing and when he is free from that obligation—for example, he had no obligation to pay her when she had transgressed the 'Law of Moses and Jewish Custom' (*m. Ketub.* 6:6).

[258] Greengus, *Laws in the Bible*, 36

with a certificate she could not remarry the first husband.[259] This view, however, does not appear to carry the current scholarly consensus. Warren, in a detailed grammatical analysis, argues that Moses issued a specific directive on divorce, but points out it could be read as either permission or a command (hence the clarification required as recorded in the Matthew 19 and Mark 10 pericopae).[260] There are three aspects of this passage to consider: the reason for the two divorces, the certificate itself, and the prohibition of remarriage.

5.11.1.3 The Reasons for the Two Divorces in Deuteronomy 24

The passage has generated much academic interest on account of the ambiguity of the reason given in v. 1 for the divorce certificate, ESV opting for 'some indecency' for the disputed expression עֶרְוַת דָּבָר. Neufeld suggests it literally means 'the nakedness of a matter' but that the phrase was deliberately 'elastic' in meaning, as the husband had 'purchased' his wife and saw his rights over her as being 'absolute,' and therefore he would not accept unreasonable restrictions on divorcing her; despite this, Neufeld still considers the phrase denoted some 'gross indecency.'[261] Isaksson argues persuasively that it was some form of indecent exposure.[262]

As regards the second divorce in v. 3 ('and the latter man hates her and writes her a certificate of divorce') Davidson suggests that it is probably 'summarizing the same situation as the first divorce ... not as positing a distinction between two different types of divorce.'[263] Instone-Brewer points out that *hate* was a common word for divorce in the ancient Near East and did not indicate

---

[259] Carl J. Laney, 'Deuteronomy 24:1-4 and the Issue of Divorce,' *BSac* 149 (1992), 6–7

[260] Andrew Warren, 'Did Moses Permit Divorce? Modal *wĕqāṭal* as Key to New Testament Readings of Deuteronomy 24:1–4,' *TynBul* 49 (1998), 39, 41; Neufeld speculates that previously no grounds were needed for a husband to divorce his wife: Neufeld, *Ancient Hebrew Marriage Laws*, 176

[261] Neufeld, *Ancient Hebrew Marriage Laws*, 178–79; Zakovitch also sees that the issue is sexual impurity because, as Mace also points out, if divorce was possible for some arbitrary misdemeanour by the wife a husband would not risk claiming she was not a virgin and risking the penalties outlined in Deut 22:13–18: Yair Zakovitch, 'The Woman's Rights in the Biblical Law of Divorce,' in B.S. Jackson, ed., *The Jewish Law Annual* Vol. 4 (Leiden: Brill, 1981), 29; Mace, *Hebrew Marriage*, 252–53

[262] Abel Isaksson, *Marriage and Ministry in the New Temple* (Gleerup: Lund, 1965), 26–27; a view endorsed by Davidson, *The Flame of Yahweh*, 391–92; also: Patai 'When the reference is to the genitals of either a male or a female ... the term used is "nakedness" (*erwāh*)': Patai, *Sex and Family*, 157

[263] Davidson, *The Flame of Yahweh*, 394

revulsion.²⁶⁴ Westbrook argues that *hate* references a divorce without valid grounds and thus sees that the second divorce was unjustified, and as a consequence, the wife would have been entitled to take with her any marital gifts received by the couple on the occasion of the marriage.²⁶⁵ However, the New Testament debate around this pericope does not suggest there was any understanding that v. 3 gave valid and different grounds for divorce from v. 1, so either the grounds were the same for both (as per Davidson), or the divorce in v. 3 was invalid as Westbrook argues.

5.11.1.4 The Deuteronomy 24 Certificate

Instone-Brewer comments that the provision of the certificate to allow the woman to remarry does not appear in ANE culture;²⁶⁶ and Sprinkle that the certificate gives legal permission to remarry without the woman being accused of the capital offence of adultery;²⁶⁷ Davidson thinks it possibly contained the later rabbinic formula found in *m. Git.* 9:3: 'thou art free to marry any man.'²⁶⁸ Only the wife required the certificate as polygyny was permitted in ancient Israel, leading some to surmise that only the husband could divorce;²⁶⁹ however, it is suggested below (§5.12) that a wife in ancient Israel could initiate a divorce.

5.11.1.5 The Deuteronomy 24 Prohibition of Remarriage

The import of the pericope is that a wife may not return to her husband once she had been divorced and subsequently married to another man. The literature is replete with speculation as to why this might be the case, Sprinkle commenting that none of the alternatives are entirely convincing.²⁷⁰

---

²⁶⁴ Instone-Brewer, *Divorce and Remarriage*, 78

²⁶⁵ Raymond Westbrook, 'The Prohibition on the Restoration of Marriage in Deuteronomy 24:1-4,' in Sarah Japhet, ed., *Scripta Hierosolymitana: Studies in Bible: 31* (Jerusalem: Magnes, 1986), 399-404

²⁶⁶ Instone-Brewer, *Divorce and Remarriage*, 32

²⁶⁷ Sprinkle, 'Old Testament Perspectives,' 530

²⁶⁸ Davidson, *The Flame of Yahweh*, 392

²⁶⁹ For example, Murray: 'In the Old Testament there is no provision for divorce by the woman': John Murray, *Divorce* (Phillipsburg, NJ: Presbyterian and Reformed, 1961), 54

²⁷⁰ Joe M. Sprinkle, 'Old Testament Perspectives on Divorce and Remarriage,' *JETS* 40 (Dec 1997), 531; Satlow points out that rabbinic sources do not attempt to explain the reason for the prohibition: Satlow, *Tasting the Dish*, 170-71

Hugenberger summarises ten different views before apparently favouring a view espoused by Westbrook (and endorsed by Instone-Brewer) that the problem lies in the husband unjustly benefiting financially from remarrying his wife after the intervening marriage.[271]

However, Stienstra and Isaksson both point out that the divorced woman would have been forbidden a return to her husband once there had been a sexual relationship with another man even if there had been no subsequent marriage. A betrothed or married woman who had been sexually unfaithful was technically subject to the death penalty and therefore denied a return to her fiancé/husband (Deut 22)—thus they see this Deuteronomic pericope is in effect applying the same outcome for a divorced woman.[272]

There was nothing to prevent the divorced woman of Deuteronomy 24 going on to a relationship with a third man, or a widow having many subsequent husbands (as Luke 20:27–36 suggests)—the divorced woman of Deuteronomy 24 had for some reason become 'defiled' only to her original husband. Laney points out the unusual reflexive passive conjugation of טָמָא (defiled) here, which Luck claims is unique in the Hebrew Bible.[273] Davidson, pursuing a grammatical analysis, suggests that the phrase is best rendered as 'she "*has been caused* to defile herself"';[274] it seems the woman had become defiled by having legitimate intercourse with another man, but only to her first husband, thus it seems that it is the first husband's purity that is being protected. It will be seen that it is possible that this aspect of mundane divorce is cross-mapped to the target domain of the marital imagery (God's relationship to his people) to portray Adam's permanent exclusion from Eden (Gen 3:24) as consequent on God's 'divorce' of him (§6.12).

---

[271] Hugenberger, *Marriage as a Covenant*, 76 n. 144, 79–81; Westbrook, 'The Prohibition,' in Japhet, *Scripta Hierosolymitana*, 404–05; Instone-Brewer, *Divorce and Remarriage*, 7; for further analysis: David Instone-Brewer, 'Deuteronomy 24:1-4 and the Origin of the Jewish Divorce Certificate,' *Journal of Jewish Studies* 49 (1998), 230–42; Carl J. Laney, 'Deuteronomy 24:1-4,' 3–15

[272] Stienstra, *YHWH is the Husband*, 88–89; Isaksson, *Marriage and Ministry*, 23

[273] William F. Luck, *Divorce & Re-Marriage: Recovering the Biblical View*, 2nd. edition (Richardson, TX: Biblical Studies, 2009), 60; Laney, 'Deuteronomy 24:1-4,' 8

[274] Davidson, *The Flame of Yahweh*, 396–97

5.11.2 Ezra 10:11

Deuteronomy forbids marriage to foreign women (Deut 7:1–7), and Deuteronomy 23:2 has:

> No one born of a forbidden union may enter the assembly of the LORD. Even to the tenth generation, none of his descendants may enter the assembly of the LORD.

Thus Ezra (Ezra 10:11) gives an instruction to the men of Judah to separate from their foreign wives. But Davidson believes that these are not divorces *per se* but dissolutions of invalid marriages;[275] certainly the separations seemed to have circumvented any procedures of the law codes. Satlow points out that Ezra appeared less concerned with the risk of apostasy than he was about such marriages being 'unclean'—doubt is cast on the purity of any offspring;[276] he argues that Ezra had the concept that all Jewish men had holy seed and comments: 'The mingling of this [Jewish male] holy seed with the impurity of Gentile women ... was seen as a true abomination.'[277]

5.11.3 Malachi 2:14–16

Kaiser comments: 'Almost every commentator has taken his/her turn bemoaning the difficulties found in Malachi 2:10–16,' and in Malachi 2:15 he sees the Hebrew as being particularly difficult.[278] Hugenberger points out that others see Malachi 2:16 as being 'hopelessly corrupt' and identifies nine major interpretive approaches to the verse;[279] he cites Westbrook's analysis of the word *hate* in ANE marriage documents as an abbreviation for 'hate and divorce'—terminology thought to reference a divorce without justification (§5.11.1.3).[280]

---

[275] Davidson, *The Flame of Yahweh*, 417; Satlow has an extensive consideration of Jewish mixed marriages and the status of the offspring: Satlow, *Jewish Marriage*, 133–61

[276] Satlow, *Jewish Marriage*, 137; however, Nehemiah did appear to express concern about the risk of apostasy from non-Jewish wives (Neh 13:23–27) so it seems his concern was not just about the purity of offspring.

[277] Satlow, *Jewish Marriage*, 259–60

[278] Walter C. Kaiser Jr., 'Divorce in Malachi 2:10–16,' *CTR* 2.1 (1987), 73

[279] Hugenberger, *Marriage as a Covenant*, 51, 82

[280] Hugenberger, *Marriage as a Covenant*, 71, 83; Westbrook, 'Prohibition of Restoration of Marriage,' in Japhet,

Thus Hugenberger suggests the following paraphrase of Malachi 2:16, which sees unjust divorce condemned but not divorce *per se*:

> If one hates and divorces [that is, if one divorces merely on the grounds of aversion], says Yahweh, God of Israel, he covers his garment with violence [i.e., such a man visibly defiles himself with violence], says Yahweh of hosts. Therefore, take heed to yourselves and do not be faithless [against your wife].[281]

But Davidson takes issue with both Westbrook and Hugenberger and defends what he describes as the 'traditional Christian interpretation,' believing that the majority of modern commentators see Malachi 2:16 as an unconditional condemnation of divorce.[282]

Even though the contemporary scholarly consensus is that it is mundane divorce that is being referenced, several commentators persuasively argue that Malachi 2:14–16 forms part of Old Testament marital imagery and references Yahweh's threatened divorce of Judah (§6.9.4).

5.12 A Wife's Right to Divorce

5.12.1 Exodus 21:7–11

Although this Exodus passage had been considered by others in the context of divorce, Clark believes that it was Instone-Brewer's treatment of it in *Divorce and Remarriage in the Bible* that brought it to the fore of the debate within the Christian community.[283] Some are not convinced that the woman becomes the master's wife which would mean that there is no divorce (§5.8); however others, including Instone-Brewer, think it is a marriage and what applied to the

---

Studies in Bible, 400–403

[281] Hugenberger, *Marriage as a Covenant*, 76; Instone-Brewer endorses Hugenberger's view: Instone-Brewer, *Divorce and Remarriage*, 56–57

[282] Davidson, *The Flame of Yahweh*, 418–22; an example is Zehnder, who believes that Mal 2:10–16 references mundane divorce and can be 'understood as a basis for a fundamental questioning of the acceptability of divorce ... the marriage covenant is not to be dissolved': Markus Zehnder, 'A Fresh Look at Malachi II 13–16,' *VT* 53 (2003), 259

[283] Clark, *Putting Asunder*, 230; Instone-Brewer notes others who had previously considered the pericope: David Instone-Brewer, 'Jewish Women Divorcing Their Husbands in Early Judaism: The Background to Papyrus Se'elim 13,' *HTR* 92:3 (July 1999), 352 n. 9

slave wife must apply to the free wife, so she would be entitled to leave the marriage if she had not received her entitlement.[284]

Zakovitch expresses a similar view:

> One can expect a free woman's rights to be not inferior to those of a maidservant's, so that she too may leave her husband if her basic needs are not supplied by him. Our right to make such an inference here [Exod 21:10–11] is derived from the expressed equality between the maidservant and the free woman within this very law: "And if he have betrothed her unto his son, he shall deal with her after *the manner of the daughters*" (v. 9).[285]

It will be seen (§8.3.6) that all eight marriage documents (forming part of the JDD) published in the second half of the 20th century from the Wadi Murabba'at and Naḥal Ḥever dating from the first and second centuries of the CE appear to give wives a contractual right to the Exodus 21:10 triad of provision and, by implication, grounds for divorce if they failed to receive their due.

5.12.2 Exodus 21:26–27

Davidson sees a woman's right to divorce is also found in Exodus 21:26–27:

> When a man strikes the eye of his slave, male or female, and destroys it, he shall let the slave go free because of his eye. If he knocks out the tooth of his slave, male or female, he shall let the slave go free because of his tooth.

Davidson believes this principle applies to a servant married to her master and that the verb שָׁלַח 'seems to imply both sending her away from the marriage (i.e., the right to a divorce) and sending her away from servitude (i.e., the right to be set free).'[286] But despite the use of שָׁלַח the pericope does not appear to address the issue of divorce, although it is possible to infer the right to a

---

[284] Instone-Brewer, *Divorce and Remarriage*, 99–105
[285] Zakovitch, 'The Woman's Rights,' in Jackson, *The Jewish Law Annual*, 36; Mace also sees a free woman's right to divorce implied in the passage: Mace, *Hebrew Marriage*, 258
[286] Davidson, *The Flame of Yahweh*, 407–08

divorce if a wife was ill-treated in this way based on the *qal wahomer* argument; what applied to a slave should apply to a wife.

5.12.3 Deuteronomy 21:10–14

> When you go out to war against your enemies, and the LORD your God gives them into your hand and you take them captive, and you notice among the captives a beautiful woman, and you desire to take her to be your wife, and you bring her home to your house, she shall shave her head and pare her nails. And she shall take off the clothes in which she was captured and shall remain in your house and lament her father and her mother for a full month. After that you may go in to her and be her husband, and she shall be your wife. But if you no longer delight in her, you shall let her go where she wants. But you shall not sell her for money, nor shall you treat her as a slave, since you have humiliated her. (Deut 21:10–14)

Luck speculates that there was no consummation so there was no divorce;[287] but a consummated marriage appears to be the academic consensus.[288] Block sees parallels between Exodus 21:10–11 and Deuteronomy 21:10–14: 'releasing a slave-wife or captive woman whom an Israelite warrior has married is preferable to the man's refusing in either case to fulfil his marital duties.'[289] Clark similarly sees parallels and states: 'while not possessing a right to divorce her husband, she would have the right to initiate the process whereby the husband would have to divorce her.'[290] In both cases the woman is to be given her freedom but not to be sold—Exodus 21:11 cf. Deuteronomy 21:14. The apparent link between these two pericopae, and the fact that Exodus 21:10 has וְעֹנָתָהּ (ESV: 'marital rights') and Deuteronomy 21:14 has עִנִּיתָהּ (ESV: 'humiliated her'), both derived from the root עָנָה reinforces the argument that the Exodus pericope is referencing a marital entitlement (§5.8).[291]

---

[287] Luck, *Divorce & Re-Marriage*, 49

[288] Thus: Clark, *Putting Asunder*, 31–32; Davidson, *The Flame of Yahweh*, 408; Sprinkle, 'Old Testament Perspectives,' 534–35

[289] Block, 'Marriage and Family,' in Campbell, *Marriage and Family*, 50

[290] Clark, *Putting Asunder*, 32

[291] I am grateful to Florenc Mene for pointing out to me the common Hebrew root in the two verses in

5.13 Other Divorces

Hosea 2 and Jeremiah 3 clearly relate to marital imagery so will be considered in chapter 6. Judges 14:20–15:2 records the fact that Samson's father-in-law had given his daughter, Samson's wife, to another—it seems he had presumed a divorce on the grounds of Samson's 'hatred' (§5.11.1.3 and §5.11.3). 1 Samuel 25:44 records Saul giving his daughter Michal (David's wife) to Palti as if he presumed she and David were divorced, and yet David subsequently took her back (2 Sam 3:14–16) seemingly in contradiction to Deuteronomy 24:1-4. But there is no mention of a divorce from David, and Westbrook suggests that the situation reflects ANE practice: when a husband has been forcibly detained abroad, a wife is free to remarry, but if the husband returns he can reclaim her.[292]

5.14 Summary: Marriage and Divorce in the Old Testament

After the primal couple there are no further miraculous, literal, one-flesh marital unions in the Old Testament record, nor, it is suggested, is there any evidence of an Edenic marriage model. It seems marriages were arranged (or at least agreed) by the families of the bride and groom. There was no understanding of an ontological or mystical dimension to the relationship, but each marriage did create what was considered to be a one-flesh union: that is, the couple were accepted as being in a family relationship—thus on marriage the couple had become what they were not previously and as a consequence there was a new set of forbidden sexual relationships.

It is possible that there was an agreed *verba solemnia,* but not necessarily any written agreement to formalise the marriage—there was nonetheless a volitional contract implied. Thus it appears (as in the ANE) that marriage

---

conversation about the two pericopae in December 2014.

[292] Westbrook, 'The Prohibition,' in Japhet, *Scripta Hierosolymitana*, 392; for further discussion see: Zafira Ben-Barak, 'The Legal Background to the Restoration of Michal to David,' in *Telling Queen Michal's Story: An Experiment in Comparative Interpretation,* Journal for the Study of the Old Testament Supplement 119, ed. David J. A. Clines and Tamara C. Eskenazi (Sheffield: Sheffield Academic, 1991), 74–93; also: Ellen White, 'Michal the Misinterpreted,' *JSOT* 31 (2007), 451–64

carried mutual, asymmetrical, gender-based obligations for husband and wife. The husband's responsibility was to provide for his wife and, although not articulated, sexual faithfulness by the wife was presumed, as adultery was forbidden in the Decalogue and divorce was permitted if a wife engaged in sexually impure behaviour (Deut 24).

Although the wife's freedom to divorce her husband is less clear, both Exodus 21:10–11 and Deuteronomy 21:10–14 appear to show that if the husband failed in his marital obligations then the wife should be released from the marriage, and as these wives were slaves, or captive women, it is not unrealistic to suppose that a free-born woman would have had the same rights.[293] Divorce pre-supposed a freedom to re-marry; however, a divorced woman needed a certificate, and could not re-marry her first husband after a subsequent marriage (Deut 24), nor could she marry a high priest (Lev 21:10–14). As in the ANE, these divorce provisions indicate a volitional, conditional marriage covenant.

None of the five markers of an Edenic marriage model as outlined in §5.1 appear to be reflected in the Old Testament mundane marriage teaching and practice—rather, it is suggested, it is the conceptual domain of Genesis 2:24 that underpins mundane marriage in ancient Israel. Metaphoric principles articulated, for example, by Lakoff and Johnson, therefore dictate that it is the marriage of Genesis 2:24 that forms the source domain of the Old Testament imagery.[294] Chapter 6 will explore Old Testament marital imagery to analyse the cross-mapping from this source domain to the target domain of Yahweh 'married' to his people.

---

[293] Sexual faithfulness of the husband is not the essence of the Old Testament marriage contract as polygyny was culturally acceptable in ancient Israel (§5.7) but, in effect, Exod 21:10-11 gives the wife the right to a divorce if he took another wife, and some surviving marriage contracts specify that a husband should not take another wife (§4.3.2; §8.4.3).

[294] Lakoff and Johnson, *Metaphors*, 22

Chapter 6: Marital Imagery in the Old Testament

6.1 Introduction

Brettler claims that, 'God is king' is, 'the predominant relational metaphor used of God in the Bible.'[295] However, if it is accepted that many metaphoric expressions are derived from the marital root metaphor, then Adler's claim that, 'many more continuous verses in the prophetic books are devoted to depicting YHWH's "marriage" to Israel than to any of the other personal metaphors' seems more realistic.[296] Satlow states that 'a reader—modern or ancient—who approaches the Hebrew Bible looking for the marriage metaphor will not be disappointed.'[297]

I have suggested—in the analysis of chapter 5—that mundane marriage in ancient Israel was underpinned by the conceptual domain of Genesis 2:24:

1. A naturally born man and woman.

2. Become what they were not.

3. In a metaphoric one-flesh union.

4. By means of a volitional, conditional covenant.

In this chapter I shall demonstrate how these four principles, carried over in the root metaphor, allowed Israel to believe that they had become what they were not previously: the 'wife' of Yahweh—in a metaphoric union with him by means of a covenant. The resulting new conceptual domain, with its many consequent analogies, was exploited by the Old Testament authors. It allowed the prophets to explain Israel's perceived relationship with Yahweh and its history in a way that other familial blood relational metaphors (e.g. father, son, brother, daughter, etc.) or kingship would not.

---

[295] Marc Zvi Brettler, *God is King: Understanding an Israelite Metaphor* (Sheffield: Sheffield Academic, 1989), 160
[296] Adler, 'The Metaphor of Covenant in the Hebrew Bible', 380
[297] Satlow, *Jewish Marriage*, 43; similarly: Stienstra, *YHWH is the Husband*, 134

You will recall that the structure map of Old Testament marital imagery in §1.3.1 with example consequent analogies was as follows:

MAP 1 *Yahweh: The Husband of Israel* (Conceptual Domain 'A' is created)

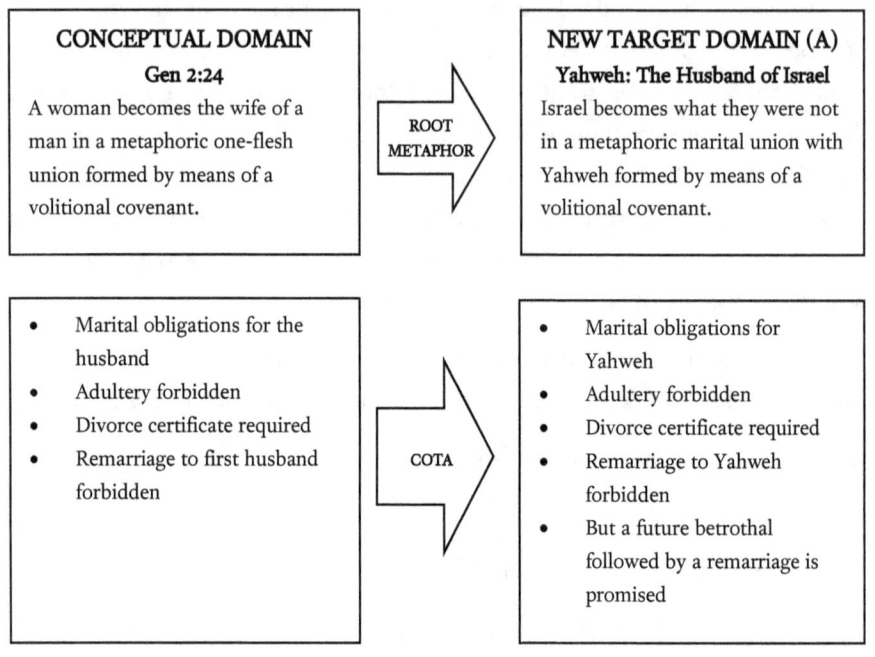

COTA = Consequent Old Testament Analogies

Adler states:

> Israelite marriage and YHWH's bond with Israel have three common traits: (a) they are both legal and artificial relationships; (b) both oblige exclusive fidelity from one party in particular, i.e., Israel and the mundane wife; (c) the element of choice or election; (d) the range of emotions expressed in the Bible regarding YHWH's relationship with Israel (love, jealousy, and passionate longing) is applicable to human relationships.[298]

Weems comments:

---

[298] Adler, 'The Metaphor of Covenant in the Hebrew Bible,' Abstract, 1

The point of prophetic metaphors was to shed light ultimately on divine activity. And while they were never at a loss to explain what motivated Israel to act in certain ways, the prophets (and audiences) were frequently hard pressed to explain why God did what God did or failed to do what Israel expected. Imagining Israel as the promiscuous wife and God as the dishonored, outraged husband became a way for prophet and audience to contemplate and explain Israel's experience with a God whom the people perceived at times to be actively engaged in their history and at other times to be deafly silent to their pleas.[299]

Marital imagery is extensively referenced in the prophetic corpus and there is a considerable body of published material devoted to it—however, the aim of this chapter is not to undertake a comprehensive analysis of the imagery, but to seek to identify any cross-mapping from the source to the target domain that might help illuminate the New Testament imagery, and thus in turn illuminate the divorce and remarriage teaching of the New Testament.

6.2 Some Definitions

As articulated in §2.1, an approach will be adopted close to that of Baumann and Stienstra: a text will be considered to embrace marital imagery if it includes metaphoric expressions related to the root metaphor (*Yahweh: The Husband of Israel*) even if Israel is not personified as a woman or the concept of marriage explicitly articulated. Baumann, in her consideration of marital imagery in the prophetic books, suggests that נָאַף (adultery) and זָנָה (harlotry) are key to identifying marital imagery and includes in her definition a wide range of texts.[300]

However, נָאַף and its derivatives rarely appear in connection with Old Testament marital imagery. Abma comments that the metaphoric use of זָנָה predominates, but this is 'only intelligible in light of the covenant relationship

---

[299] Weems, *Battered Love*, 69–70
[300] Baumann cites: Isa 1:21; 50:1; 54:1–6; 57:6–13; 62:4–5; Jer 2:1–3, 13; 4:1–31; 13:20–27; Lam 1:1–22; Ezek 16; Ezek 23; Hos 2:1–23; 9:1; Mic 1:6–7; Nah 3:4–7; Mal 2:10–16 and 'less explicit' texts: Isa 49:15–23; 51:17–52:2; Jer 30–31; Mic 1:4; Zeph 3:4–17 'among others': Baumann, *Love and Violence*, 41

between Yhwh and Israel ... [and] has the special connotation of "breaking away from an existing relationship"'; she cites its use in Exodus 34:14-16 in support of her argument, that in the context of marital imagery, it is used to denote Israel's lack of faithfulness to Yahweh and is synonymous with adultery.[301] Bird sees that זָנָה can refer to a common prostitute or a promiscuous daughter or wife, and that the activity has, in itself, no cultic connotations, and its metaphorical employment to denote apostasy of the general population is unique to the Hebrew Bible.[302]

There is not always agreement as to whether the sexual immorality depicted in any one text is immorality on the social level, metaphorical adultery/harlotry on the national level, or sexual practices performed on the cultic level.[303] For example, Davidson sees Jeremiah 3:2 as reference to cultic sexual practices by individual Israelites, whereas Baumann sees the passage as part of marital imagery and that the reference is to the worship of foreign deities.[304] It is suggested in this present study that the context usually makes it clear, and the context in Jeremiah 3 lends weight to Baumann's analysis.

6.3 The Ancient Near East Background to Old Testament Marital Imagery

There appears to be a broad consensus on the unique nature of Old Testament marital imagery, Abma pointing out that:

> the correspondence between the marriage patterns of gods in the cultures surrounding Israel and biblical marriage imagery is only of a general and superficial kind. While it is phenomenologically true that the people as marriage partner of Yhwh take over the role of the goddess, the whole idea of marriage is considerably different and far more developed in the relation between Yhwh and Israel than with

---

[301] Abma, *Bonds of Love*, 138-40

[302] Phyllis Bird, 'To Play the Harlot: An Enquiry into Old Testament Metaphor,' in *Gender Difference in Ancient Israel*, ed. Peggy L. Day (Minneapolis, MN: Fortress, 1989), 76, 88-89

[303] Bird however, casts doubt on the concept of the sacred prostitute in Canaanite religions: Bird, 'To Play the Harlot,' in Day, *Gender Difference*, 75-76

[304] Davidson, *The Flame of Yahweh*, 110; Baumann, *Love and Violence*, 115

> respect to the deities in the surrounding cultures. In the biblical metaphor there is an emphasis on the analogy with human marriage, on the long-lasting character of the relationship and on the exclusive nature of the relationship. The love affair between Yhwh and Israel is not just one among many but a special and enduring relationship.... The connections between the biblical marriage imagery and the patterns of intimate relations between deities in the surrounding cultures are indirect and superficial while the distinctions between both phenomena seem to preponderate.[305]

However, Korpel in her study (which appears to be the only detailed consideration of the use of metaphors in extra-biblical ANE literature), points out that Ugaritic literature was laden with self-conscious metaphorical language about their gods which she believes influenced later Old Testament writers. She cites Numbers 6:25: 'the LORD make his face to shine upon you and be gracious to you' as an example of a metaphoric concept present in Ugaritic literature.[306]

Korpel references three possible instances in the Ugaritic literature of divine/human relations: Ilu seduces two women; 'Anatu proposes to a human prince; and a king declares he will dedicate his daughter to Ba'lu.[307] However, although there are examples of gods marrying each other, she affirms that 'the texts of Ugarit do not contain an explicit reference to a marriage between a deity and a human being.'[308]

Nonetheless, she considers that Old Testament marital imagery had its origin in Ugaritic literature:

> the love life and marriages of the Canaanite gods was deliberately and consistently transferred to the relation between YHWH and his chosen people. This must have happened at a relatively early date, possibly even before the ministry of Hosea.... Whereas in the texts of the Ugarit

---

[305] Abma, *Bonds of Love*, 19–20
[306] Korpel, *A Rift In the Clouds*, 2–3
[307] Korpel, *A Rift In the Clouds*, 214–15
[308] Korpel, *A Rift In the Clouds*, 214, 228

the emphasis was on the sexual pleasure of the gods, the Old Testament rather stresses conjugal fidelity, faithfulness and loving care as characteristics of a sound relation between the divine "Husband" and his "wife" Israel.[309]

Galambush argues that Old Testament metaphorical marital imagery was developed from the ANE personification of cities as women (i.e. goddesses) but notes what she describes as three significant differences: in the Old Testament the city is mortal; its image is not positive but negative; and in the Old Testament the metaphor is extended to include the concept of a city's infidelity.[310] Patterson also sees differences: in Mesopotamia there was no communion between the deity and the people; and although some divine-human relations were expressed in ancient Egypt, and that many Mesopotamian kings claimed to be the son of a particular deity, the 'concept of a nation being the wife of a deity is foreign to the extrabiblical world in general.'[311]

Furthermore, Abma agrees with Adler (against Wolf et al.) that there is no clear evidence that Hosea's marital imagery originated in the Canaanite concept of a relationship between Baal and an earth goddess.[312] Thus it seems that Adler is correct to refer to the 'singularity' of the biblical marriage metaphor within the ANE.[313]

6.4 The Marriage at Sinai

McCarthy et al. believe that it is Hosea who introduced and developed the marriage analogy, Baumann suggesting this is the view of most scholars.[314] But

---

[309] Korpel, *A Rift In the Clouds*, 231
[310] Galambush, *Jerusalem in the Book of Ezekiel*, 20, 25–27
[311] Richard D. Patterson, 'Metaphors of Marriage as Expressions of Divine-Human Relations,' *JETS* 5 (December 2008), 690–91
[312] Abma, *Bonds of Love*, 14–15
[313] Adler, 'The Metaphor of Covenant in the Hebrew Bible,' 2
[314] Dennis J. McCarthy, 'Covenant in the Old Testament: The Present State of Enquiry,' *CBQ* 27 (1965), 234–35 Baumann states: 'most scholars believe—Hosea is to be regarded as the "inventor" or first exemplar of the prophetic marriage imagery': Baumann, *Love and Violence*, 65 n. 37; also Moughtin-Mumby: '[Hosea] is likely to be the earliest text in the Hebrew canon to use sexual and metaphorical marital language' in Moughtin-Mumby, *Sexual and Marital Metaphors*, 49; Leith says that, 'Hosea ... has also imaginatively modified the [creation of

Abma concludes that it is difficult not to see that 'an existing covenant relation between Yhwh and Israel, together with blessing-and-curse implications, serves as a background for much that is found in the book of Hosea.'[315] Similarly Instone-Brewer, who suggests that Hosea's marital imagery was not developed in a vacuum and that the 'whole language of "jealousy," which is central to the picture of God in the Pentateuch, has the connotation of marriage' and that Sinai can be seen as the point at which God marries his people.[316]

Davidson agrees and cites several scholars who see inferences of marital imagery in the Pentateuch in Exodus 34:15–16; Leviticus 17:7; 20:5–6; Numbers 25:1; Deuteronomy 31:16, and 33:3.[317] Sohn points out that marriage is often expressed with the verb לָקַח in the Hebrew Bible and the Semitic root *lqḥ* is used extensively in the ANE for such, and considers the use of לָקַח in Exodus 6:7 ('I will take you to be my people') to express Yahweh's choice of Israel links that relationship to the concept of a marriage. Sousan comments that the 'hold fast' (וְדָבַק) in Genesis 2:24 and Yahweh's commendation of those who similarly 'held fast' (הַדְּבֵקִים) to him in Deuteronomy 4:4 is a possible allusion to the Old Testament marriage metaphor;[318] furthermore, based on Jeremiah 31:31–33, Sohn considers that Jeremiah understood the Sinaitic covenant to be a marriage between Yahweh and Israel.[319] Similarly Lunn suggests that Exodus 6:7 is a reference to a marriage at Sinai, and that the account of the golden calf being ground to powder and the people being forced to drink it (Exod 32:20) is a reference to the Numbers 5:12–31 ordeal for the

---

Israel] myth ... so that Israel metaphorically becomes a woman' in: Mary Joan Winn Leith, 'Verse and Reverse: The Transformation of the Woman, Israel, in Hosea 1–3,' in Day, *Gender Difference*, 95

[315] Abma, *Bonds of Love*, 113

[316] Instone-Brewer, *Divorce and Remarriage*, 34–35; also: Block, 'Marriage and Family,' in Campbell, *Marriage and Family*, 30–51. Although Adler sees no explicit early reference to the husband-wife metaphor she suggests the concept was familiar to a pre-Hoseanic audience: Adler, 'The Metaphor of Covenant in the Hebrew Bible,' 94

[317] Davidson, *The Flame of Yahweh*, 113–15; also Cohen, 'The Song of Songs,' in Finkelstein, *The Samuel Friedland Lectures*, 5–12

[318] André Sousan, 'The Woman in the Garden of Eden: A Rhetorical-Critical Study of Genesis 2:4b–3:24,' (Ph.D. diss., Graduate School of Vanderbilt University, 2006), 203

[319] Seock-Tae Sohn, '"I Will Be Your God and You Will Be My People": The Origin and Background of the Covenant Formula,' in *Ki Baruch Hu: Ancient Near Eastern, Biblical, and Judaic Studies in Honor of Baruch A. Levin*, ed. Robert Chazan, William W. Hallo, and Lawrence H. Schiffman (Winona Lake, IN: Eisenbrauns, 1999), 358, 364–68

suspected adulteress. If such a view is valid, then clearly Israel had been unfaithful on her wedding night.[320] In addition, it can be seen that both Hosea 2:14–15 and Jeremiah 2:2–3 look back to the desert wanderings after Sinai as the 'honeymoon' period in Yahweh's relationship with Israel.

6.5 The Sinaitic Covenant and Genesis 2:24

There are several covenants or covenant-like relationships between God and his people in the Old Testament which carry theological significance, among them the Edenic (Gen 1:26–30; 2:15–17); Adamic (Gen 3:14–19); Noahic (Gen 9:1–17); Abrahamic (Gen 12:1–3, 7; 13:14–17; 15:1–21; 17:1–21); Sinaitic (Exod 19–24); and Davidic (2 Sam 7:5–16)—so a key to understanding Old Testament marital imagery is to understand the basis of the Sinaitic covenant.[321]

McCarthy points out that promissory (Patriarchal/Davidic) and conditional (Sinaitic) covenants are different from each other and states, 'the attempt to make the Davidic covenant formally identical with the Mosaic on the basis of a covenant form common to the two has failed.'[322] McCarthy believes that the Sinaitic covenant was volitional, that is, Israel had choices: both at the outset (e.g. Exod 19:3–8; Exod 24:3–8; Deut 30:11–20) and later (e.g. Josh 24:1–28)—Joshua's speech seemingly containing real options for Israel many years after Sinai: 'the people are asked, never compelled, to enter into the relationship.'[323] Thus the Sinaitic covenant is articulated as a conditional, contractual covenant based on Israel's obedience and her own desire to remain in the covenant. McCarthy points out that Jeremiah developed the marital imagery of Hosea, and that 'the image of the husband-wife relationship between Yahweh and Israel ... is, of course, a contractual relationship.'[324] Thus an understanding of a

---

[320] Lunn, 'Let My People Go,' 241–42

[321] Beckwith delineates five covenants between God and Israel in: Roger T. Beckwith, 'The Unity and Diversity of God's Covenants,' *TynBul* 38 (1987), 100–101

[322] Dennis J. McCarthy, *Old Testament Covenant: A Survey of Current Opinions* (Stuttgart: Verlag Katholisches Bibelwerk, 1967; Repr. Oxford: Blackwell, 1972), 46–52, 58

[323] McCarthy sees that Israel's realisation of the implications of its failure to maintain the Sinaitic covenant gives rise to a post-exilic de-emphasis on that covenant and in its place the prospect of a Davidic covenant is developed in (exilic) second Isaiah: McCarthy, *Old Testament Covenant*, 46–48, 55

[324] McCarthy, 'Covenant in the Old Testament,' 235

divine marriage based on the Sinaitic covenant is consistent with the concept that the marriage has been mapped from the volitional, conditional, covenantal mundane marriage of Genesis 2:24.

6.6 Betrothal Arrangements

There does not seem to have been a betrothal period associated with the Sinaitic marriage, and Baumann considers that Hosea is unique in the prophetic corpus in speaking of a betrothal.[325] Moreover, it is a betrothal that lies in the future:

> And I will betroth you to me forever. I will betroth you to me in righteousness and in justice, in steadfast love and in mercy. I will betroth you to me in faithfulness. And you shall know the LORD. (Hos 2:19–20)

Similarly, Hosea 3:2–5 states:

> So I bought her for fifteen shekels of silver and a homer and a lethech of barley. And I said to her, "You must dwell as mine for many days. You shall not play the whore, or belong to another man; so will I also be to you." For the children of Israel shall dwell many days without king or prince, without sacrifice or pillar, without ephod or household gods. Afterward the children of Israel shall return and seek the LORD their God, and David their king, and they shall come in fear to the LORD and to his goodness in the latter days.

Lemos sees Hosea 3:2 is a possible allusion to a marriage payment;[326] thus it is possible that the period of isolation that follows (v. 4) marks the betrothal period before a (re)marriage in v. 5. Mackay posits that during the time referenced in v. 4 Hosea's new wife (Mackay takes that to be Gomer) would not be available to any man, not even to Hosea himself.[327]

---

[325] Baumann, *Love and Violence*, 93

[326] Lemos, *Marriage Gifts*, 48–50

[327] John L. MacKay, *Hosea: A Mentor Commentary* (Fearn: Christian Focus, 2012), 116

6.7 Marital Obligations

Galambush comments:

> the husband was required to protect the wife (in this case provide food and clothing) and the wife was to obey the husband and to refrain from sexual relationships with other men.... The Israelite covenant with Yahweh shares this basic shape.[328]

Thus the thrust of the covenant made at Sinai is asymmetrical: Yahweh would protect and provide for Israel and in return they were to be faithful to him and his commands (e.g. Exod 19:4-6; Deut 30:1-10). This care and provision by Yahweh is seen in the desert wanderings in the guidance by day and night (Exod 13:21-22), and the provision of manna (Exod 16) and water (Exod 17:1-7), as well as in the abundant provision in the Promised Land (e.g. Deut 8:7-10).

Instone-Brewer believes that Psalm 132:13-16 is set in the context of a marriage covenant where Yahweh will clothe and feed his bride based on the three-fold duty of a husband described in Exodus 21:10;[329] and in the imagery of Hosea he points out that Gomer looked to her lovers for the support that Yahweh had withdrawn from her (Hos 2:7-8); imagery which is 'described in terms of the marriage vows of Exodus 21:10-11.'[330] He further comments: 'The description of the breakdown of the marriages [in Ezek 16 and 23] is inspired both by Hosea and the divorce law of Exodus 21:10-11'—Israel is portrayed as giving to her lovers the clothing and food Yahweh had provided.[331]

---

[328] Galambush, *Jerusalem in the Book of Ezekiel*, 33

[329] David Instone-Brewer, 'Three Weddings and a Divorce: God's Covenant with Israel, Judah and the Church,' *TynBul* 47.1 (1996), 8-9

[330] Instone-Brewer, *Divorce and Remarriage*, 37-38

[331] Instone-Brewer, *Divorce and Remarriage*, 45; Sherwood points out that Hosea portrays Baal as an imposter who has taken Yahweh's role as a provider: Yvonne Sherwood, *The Prostitute and the Prophet: Reading Hosea in the Late Twentieth Century* (Sheffield: Sheffield Academic, 1996; Repr. London: T&T Clark, 2004), 215

6.8 Adultery

6.8.1 Adultery in Hosea

Galambush points out that the tenor of the imagery is virtually impossible to follow as it has several different referents. For example, Gomer herself acts as a vehicle for the tenor of the land (Hos 1:2);[332] and although the land functions as a synonym for Israel, and Gomer personifies the people and shares in their whoredom, it is not always clear whether the use of זָנָה refers to actual sexual activity on the behalf of Gomer or is a term for the spiritual unfaithfulness of Israel.[333] Wolf suggests it is a combination of both, but Abma and Adler suggest the reference is to the latter.[334] Abma comments that in this milieu the source and target domain of the metaphor almost blend into one.[335] Although Cohen looks to delineate the vehicle by suggesting that in the imagery the mother/wife figure equates to Israel as a nation (whereas individual Israelites are represented by the children), Abma sees that Hosea's children are just another aspect of the vehicle put on stage in order to embody the harlotry of

---

[332] Moughtin-Mumby in her 'resistant' reading of Hosea suggests the prophet, 'sign-acts YHWH's relationship with the land through sexual liaison with Gomer ... Hosea does not represent YHWH, nor does Gomer represent Israel' nevertheless she sees that the sign-act 'conveys the horror of Israel's "prostitution" away from YHWH': Moughtin-Mumby, *Sexual and Marital Metaphors*, 221. Commenting on Hos 1:2, Galambush suggests the land that commits 'whoredom' is like the land that sins in Deut 24:4 (also Lev 19:29) and that the land is personified and has been made to prostitute itself as a result of the sin of its inhabitants: Galambush, *Jerusalem in the Book of Ezekiel*, 44–46, 46 n. 56, 51 52.

[333] Thus: Abma, *Bonds of Love*, 141–42

[334] Wolff: 'Instead of a realistic interpretation—which has become traditional—or a metaphorical one, we suggest a metaphorical-ritual explanation: she was a young Israelite woman, ready for marriage, who had demonstrably taken part in the Canaanite bridal rite of initiation that had become customary': Hans Walter Wolff, *Hosea*, translated by Paul D. Hanson (Pensylvania: Fortress, 1974), 15. Also: Abma, *Bonds of Love*, 137–138; Adler, 'The Metaphor of Covenant in the Hebrew Bible,' 398–411. Bird suggests that the noun זְנוּנִים in Hos 1:2 refers to fornication not specifically harlotry, although she points out that Hos 2:12 portrays the action of a prostitute: Bird, 'To Play the Harlot,' in Day, *Gender Difference*, 80, 82

[335] Abma, *Bonds of Love*, 120; so concurs: Baumann, *Love and Violence*, 88

Israel;³³⁶ a view with which Bird concurs.³³⁷ These difficulties are not aided by the northern dialect of the Hebrew text of Hosea.³³⁸

Despite this the broad scope of the source domain (mundane marriage and adultery) is unambiguous—Bird claiming that ultimately the imagery is clear: 'the land (people) has relations with other lovers in place of ... Yahweh' that is, these are 'affairs' with other gods.³³⁹

6.8.2 Adultery in Jeremiah

Abma sees the primary audience of Jeremiah as being Judah and makes a detailed linguistic analysis of 'The movement away from Yhwh' in Jeremiah 2 and 3.³⁴⁰ But Instone-Brewer succinctly summarises the nations 'adultery' as portrayed in the imagery:

> Jeremiah addresses chiefly Judah, reminding her of the honeymoon period after Sinai (2:2), and then describing at length the pitiful state she has fallen into. She is like a wild animal lusting after many mates (2:23–25; 5:8). She has forgotten her husband (2:32–37) and has been unfaithful to him by whoring after other gods (2:27–28; 5:7) and by allegiances with other nations (2:36–37). She will be shamed like a harlot (13:26), and she is threatened with divorce like her sister Israel (3:1–20). Yet in the end Israel will be restored as though she were a virgin bride once more (31:1–7), and Judah will be restored with her as one united nation (31:31–34).³⁴¹

6.8.3 Adultery in Ezekiel

Galambush states:

---

[336] Cohen, 'The Song of Songs,' in Finkelstein, *The Samuel Friedland Lectures*, 9; Abma, *Bonds of Love*, 141

[337] 'the author intended to claim for the children the same nature as their mother.... Thus mother and children should not be sharply differentiated': Bird, 'To Play the Harlot,' in Day, *Gender Difference*, 80–81

[338] Instone-Brewer, *Divorce and Remarriage*, 36

[339] Bird, 'To Play the Harlot,' in Day, *Gender Difference*, 81

[340] Abma sees the whole of Jer 2:1–4:2 as referencing Judah: Abma, *Bonds of Love*, 235–37, 239–41, 250; Dumbrell comments: 'When in the book of Jeremiah the term Israel specifically refers to the old northern kingdom, the context always makes that reference clear': William J. Dumbrell, *Covenant and Creation: An Old Testament Covenant Theology* (Milton Keynes: Paternoster, 2013), 257

[341] Instone-Brewer, *Divorce and Remarriage*, 40

> In these two chapters [Ezek 16 and 23] Jerusalem is depicted metaphorically as a wife who is unfaithful and is therefore punished at the behest of the husband, but at the hands of her lovers. Ezekiel uses the metaphor of the woman's misbehaviour to portray two related actions on the part of Jerusalem, both of which he describes as "infidelity" (*tznwt*), and both of which result in "uncleanness" (*tm'*), the defilement of the city and its temple: idolatry (and possibly other improprieties within the cult) and alliances with foreign nations. The husband's vengeance on the unfaithful wife metaphorically depicts Yahweh's instigation of the destruction of Jerusalem by Nebuchadrezzar.[342]

Galambush takes 'Jerusalem' in both Ezekiel 16 and 23 to be the city and its temple and not a metonym for Judah.[343] Moughtin-Mumby discusses this issue and concludes that 'prophetic sexual and marital metaphorical language cannot be limited to such a hypothetical "etymology"' and accepts Jerusalem could represent Judah;[344] Baumann in a similar vein points out that Ezekiel introduces a great many 'facts' and 'persons' in its marital imagery which cannot be equated with the historical texts of the Old Testament.[345] Instone-Brewer accepts that Jerusalem is Judah (this view seems most persuasive) and points out that the marriage of Yahweh to her is explicit in Ezekiel 16:8—it is described as a covenant and Judah's 'husband' had provided her with food clothes and oil (Ezek 16:9-13) reflecting the provision described in Exodus 21:10.[346] But (as in Hos 2:8) Yahweh's provision was used in Judah's harlotry (Ezek 16:15-19). Baumann sees that a feature unique to Ezekiel's marital imagery is that Yahweh's 'wife' is portrayed as 'whoring' with foreign powers as

---

[342] Galambush describes the two chapters as extended metaphor and not allegory: Galambush, *Jerusalem*, 1-2, 10-11

[343] She further states that 'If the city is a woman, then the temple is her vagina, and the offense of Jerusalem's granting illicit "access" to foreign men and competing gods becomes plain': Galambush, *Jerusalem*, 86-88, 111 n. 58

[344] Moughtin-Mumby, *Sexual and Marital Metaphors*, 158-59 n. 9

[345] Baumann, *Love and Violence*, 142

[346] Instone-Brewer, *Divorce and Remarriage*, 45-48

well as foreign deities (Ezek 16:26–29);[347] but vv. 60–63 make it clear that there is to be a better future.

Although Ezekiel 23 has similar imagery to Ezekiel 16 there are differences: Ezekiel 16 tells the story of Jerusalem as a baby girl rescued by Yahweh, but after being taken as a wife, proves unfaithful; in Ezekiel 23 the sisters (Instone-Brewer takes them to be Israel and Judah) are prostitutes before the marriage; Ezekiel 23 starts the story in Egypt, whilst Ezekiel 16 starts in the wilderness.[348] Baumann suggests that in Ezekiel 23 Jerusalem's guilt is intensified in comparison to Ezekiel 16, and that she has learned nothing from the bad example of her 'sister.'[349]

6.9 Divorce

6.9.1 Divorce in Hosea

Abma believes that Jezreel (Hos 1:4) and Israel—with their strong sound correspondence—are synonymous; whatever judgement is passed on Jezreel relates also to Israel. The 'bow of Israel' (Hos 1:5) being broken indicates that she will cease to exist as a national state.[350] The second child's name, 'No Mercy' (Hos 1:6), highlights the fact that Israel will be judged but Judah spared, although not, apparently, by military intervention (v. 7b).[351] The last child ('Not My People' v. 9) is seen by Abma as symbolising the fact that the 'covenant relation between Yhwh and Israel is cancelled' and that Israel here is probably the northern kingdom.[352] Moughtin-Mumby is equally emphatic in declaring that here, 'we are presented with the end of YHWH's relationship with the people of Israel.'[353] This perspective is in harmony with Hosea 2:2 and is also consistent with the way the marital imagery is developed by Jeremiah and Ezekiel.

---

[347] Baumann, *Love and Violence*, 141, 146; however Jer 2:36–37 does refer disapprovingly to Israel's alliances with Egypt and Assyria in the context of marital imagery.

[348] Instone-Brewer, *Divorce and Remarriage*, 44

[349] Baumann, *Love and Violence*, 143

[350] Abma, *Bonds of Love*, 133, 146

[351] Abma, *Bonds of Love*, 147

[352] Abma, *Bonds of Love*, 151

[353] Moughtin-Mumby, *Sexual and Marital Metaphors*, 228

However, Mackay argues that there is no divorce in the target or the source domain of the metaphor, only threats.[354] Westbrook, on the other hand, believes that Hosea 2:2, 'she is not my wife, and I am not her husband,' is a divorce declaration originating in the ANE; by considering the arguments for and against Hosea actually divorcing Gomer, he concludes that there is 'no overwhelming difficulty interpreting the events of chapter 2 in the light of a divorce at its inception.'[355]

Instone-Brewer's analysis that Israel (the northern kingdom) is portrayed as suffering a divorce is the most persuasive, as he points out that she herself accepts the fact (Hos 2:7); and that she would no longer receive the grain, wine, and oil (vv. 8–9) which she had been entitled to as Yahweh's wife (as outlined in Exod 21:10).[356] Abma suggests Israel's return depicted in v. 7 is 'a fantasy of Yhwh ... a future possibility.'[357]

6.9.2 Divorce in Isaiah

Instone-Brewer points out the difficulty of identifying 'Israel,' suggesting that such references before Isaiah 40 might refer to the 10 tribes, whilst from chapter 40 onwards the names Israel, Jacob, Jerusalem, and Zion are used interchangeably to represent Judah. He sees that the imagery is rooted in the historical situation, in that Isaiah portrays Judah as having suffered a period of separation, but not a divorce.[358] Isaiah 50:1 states:

> Thus says the LORD: "Where is your mother's certificate of divorce, with which I sent her away? Or which of my creditors is it to whom I have sold you? Behold, for your iniquities you were sold, and for your transgressions your mother was sent away."

---

[354] MacKay, *Hosea*, 75-78; Perdue sees that Gomer is not divorced: Perdue, 'The Israelite and Early Jewish Family,' in Perdue et al., *Families in Ancient Israel*, 195

[355] Westbrook believes the words used are a formula for divorce found throughout the ANE including Elephantine: Westbrook, 'Adultery in Ancient Near Eastern Law,' 561, 577–80

[356] Instone-Brewer also draws attention to the presence of the verb שָׂנֵא ('hate') in Hos 9:15 which is associated with divorce (for *hate* see §5.11.1.3 and §5.11.3): Instone-Brewer, *Divorce and Remarriage*, 37-38

[357] Abma, *Bonds of Love*, 175

[358] 'We must ... assume everything referring to "Israel" or "Jacob" in Second Isaiah is addressed to Judah, unless it is clearly indicated otherwise': Instone-Brewer, *Divorce and Remarriage*, 48

Yahweh challenges Israel to produce their certificate of divorce. Moughtin-Mumby understands the phrase 'which of my creditors is it to whom I have sold you?' to be a rhetorical question addressed to Judah, and believes such represents the scholarly consensus.[359] Similarly Instone-Brewer, who points out the improbability of Yahweh selling his people to creditors underlines the force of the rhetorical nature of the question—that is, there is no divorce of Judah.[360] This is a persuasive analysis—and implies there is a difference between Judah's situation and that of Israel, and if a divorce certificate had been issued it would imply Judah could then not come back to Yahweh.

6.9.3 Divorce in Jeremiah

> If a man divorces his wife and she goes from him and becomes another man's wife, will he return to her? Would not that land be greatly polluted? You have played the whore with many lovers; and would you return to me? declares the LORD.... The LORD said to me in the days of King Josiah: "Have you seen what she did, that faithless one, Israel, how she went up on every high hill and under every green tree, and there played the whore? And I thought, 'After she has done all this she will return to me', but she did not return, and her treacherous sister Judah saw it. She saw that for all the adulteries of that faithless one, Israel, I had sent her away with a decree of divorce. Yet her treacherous sister Judah did not fear, but she too went and played the whore. (Jer 3:1, 6–8)

Instone-Brewer considers the divorced party to be Israel and that Judah is being warned by means of Israel's example:

> It has been suggested here that the whole of chapter 3 can be read as an exposition of Hosea's prophecy and as a single argument that developed sequentially. First Jeremiah outlines the problem of the law in Deuteronomy 24 as applied to Israel's divorce and reconciliation

---

[359] Moughtin-Mumby, *Sexual and Marital Metaphors*, 140–41
[360] Instone-Brewer, *Divorce and Remarriage*, 48–51

(vv. 1–5); then he uses their dire situation to warn Judah, who is being even more faithless (vv. 6–11).[361]

The dilemma Jeremiah 3:1 presents is how can Israel come back to Yahweh after their divorce in light of Deuteronomy 24:1–4? The impossibility is further emphasised by the fact the Deuteronomic legislation applies to a divorced woman who had had just one further partner (Jer 3:1 'becomes another man's wife'), and yet Israel had had 'many lovers,' giving what Abma sees as a *qal wahomer* effect.[362] Furthermore, Abma believes that Jeremiah 3:6–10 constitutes a parable: Israel has been sent away with a letter of divorce (having already suffered her exile), but Judah is not to follow the negative example set by her sister Israel, and still has a chance to repent, even though there is no evidence of such yet (Jer 3:10). Although describing Jeremiah 3:11–18 as 'complex,' Abma sees that the motif continues, and notwithstanding the obstacles the text implies that 'against all odds, Yhwh *will* take Israel back.'[363] Thus Jeremiah 31:31–32 speaks of a new covenant:

> Behold, the days are coming, declares the LORD, when I will make a new covenant with the house of Israel and the house of Judah, not like the covenant that I made with their fathers on the day when I took them by the hand to bring them out of the land of Egypt, my covenant that they broke, though I was their husband, declares the LORD.

The above analysis suggests Jeremiah employs Deuteronomy 24:1–4 from the source map of the imagery to portray the exile of the northern kingdom as a divorce from Yahweh, and that Judah, unlike Israel, had not been divorced, but should take note lest she suffer the same fate. However, despite the restrictions of Deuteronomy 24:1–4, a future reconciliation is spoken of which is portrayed in a marital imagery that embraces both kingdoms.

---

[361] Instone-Brewer, *Divorce and Remarriage*, 42–43
[362] Abma, *Bonds of Love*, 248
[363] Abma, *Bonds of Love*, 249–51

6.9.4 Divorce in Malachi

> Have we not all one Father? Has not one God created us? Why then are we faithless to one another, profaning the covenant of our fathers? Judah has been faithless, and abomination has been committed in Israel and in Jerusalem. For Judah has profaned the sanctuary of the LORD, which he loves, and has married the daughter of a foreign god. May the LORD cut off from the tents of Jacob any descendant of the man who does this, who brings an offering to the LORD of hosts! And this second thing you do. You cover the LORD's altar with tears, with weeping and groaning because he no longer regards the offering or accepts it with favour from your hand. But you say, "Why does he not?" Because the LORD was witness between you and the wife of your youth, to whom you have been faithless, though she is your companion and your wife by covenant. Did he not make them one, with a portion of the Spirit in their union? And what was the one God seeking? Godly offspring. So guard yourselves in your spirit, and let none of you be faithless to the wife of your youth. "For the man who hates and divorces, says the LORD, the God of Israel, covers his garment with violence, says the LORD of hosts. So guard yourselves in your spirit, and do not be faithless. (Mal 2:10–16)[364]

Malachi is not generally included in a consideration of Old Testament marital imagery, despite Abma pointing out that the books from Hosea to Malachi can be seen as a unit, and that the first three chapters of Hosea function as the opening section not only of the book of Hosea but also of the Book of the Twelve.[365] Hugenberger gives extensive consideration to the interpretative context of Mal 2:10–16 and comments:

> Although the evidence does not allow us to be sure whether Malachi preceded, followed, or was a contemporary of Ezra and Nehemiah,

---

[364] This translation is from ESV (London: Collins, 2002); however, ESV has produced different translations of this pericope, for example ESV 2001 has v. 16 state: "'For I hate divorce,' says the LORD, the God of Israel, "and him who covers his garment with wrong," says the LORD of hosts. "So take heed to your spirit, that you do not deal treacherously'"—thus demonstrating the difficulties in the Hebrew text.

[365] Abma, *Bonds of Love*, 117–18

that he preached in the same general period is assured; this is significant for the interpretation of the text.[366]

Hugenberger sees this contemporary situation as supporting his exegesis that Malachi 2 is referencing literal divorce; however, the body of scholars who believe the passage is dealing with marital imagery see no reason to dispute the dating, only the inference that is drawn from it, that Malachi was condemning literal divorce from the mixed marriages that Ezra and Nehemiah condemn (Ezra 9 and 10; Neh 13:23-31).

O'Brien challenges the academic consensus (that Malachi is addressing the current social situation) and argues for a figurative reading.[367] Petersen adopts such a reading and argues that the 'daughter of a foreign god' relates not to a mundane wife but to an alien cult—that the 'abomination has been committed' of Malachi 2:11 is a reflection of the term in the Deuteronomistic corpus and that, 'To perform an abomination is to perform some non-Yahwistic religious practice, as Deut 17:3 makes especially clear.'[368]

Isaksson similarly suggests the covenant in v. 14 must be the same as the covenant in v. 10 and that the 'daughter of a foreign god' (v. 11) is a goddess—not 'daughters of a foreign people'; this metaphoric interpretation means that the 'wife of your youth' (v. 14) is a reference to Yahweh—the covenant partner of Judah, Isaksson suggesting the unusual portrayal of Yahweh as feminine was to enable Malachi to continue the imagery from v. 11.[369]

---

[366] Hugenberger, *Marriage as a Covenant*, 17

[367] Julia M. O'Brien, 'Judah as Wife and Husband: Deconstructing Gender in Malachi,' *JBL* 115 (1996), 244-45, 249; also: Howard Eilberg-Schwartz, *God's Phallus and Other Problems for Men and Monotheism* (Boston, MA: Beacon, 1994), 129-30

[368] David L. Petersen, *Zechariah 9-14 and Malachi* (Louisville, KY: Westminster John Knox, 1995), 198-99; similarly Hvidberg who sees that the 'daughter of a foreign god' is: 'a deity of the Anat-Astarte type': Flemming F. Hvidberg, *Weeping and Laughter in the Old Testament: A Study of Canaanite-Israelite* (Leiden: Brill, 1962), 122-23

[369] Isaksson, *Marriage and Ministry*, 27-34; Ackerman refers to gender flexibility in the imagery employed by Hosea, for example, in Hos 3:1 the prophet is commanded to take a wife, but where Gomer stands for Israel, in the text Israel takes the male gender: Susan Ackerman, 'The Personal is Political: Covenantal and Affectionate Love (*'āhēb, 'ahăbâ*) in the Hebrew Bible,' *VT* 52 (October 2002), 450-51; Brettler sees that although seemingly contradictory such gender constructs still work in their metaphorical settings: Marc Zvi Brettler, 'Incompatible Metaphors for Yhwh in Isaiah 40-66,' *JSOT* 78 (1998), 110-11; Baumann references other feminine imagery of

Torrey sees vv. 10–16 as a unity and the 'wife of your youth' and 'your wife by covenant' in v. 14 is the same entity and the latter cannot mean 'wife of thy marriage vows'; that is, the pericope is uniformly figurative in its language and in Torrey's view the 'wife' is the 'covenant religion' itself:

> Judah ... has betrayed the wife of his youth, the covenant religion, by espousing the daughter of a strange god, *i.e.* a foreign cult ... [this] necessarily involved 'divorce' from the covenant religion.[370]

Ogden also argues persuasively for a figurative interpretation seeing that the divorce God hates is his dismissal of his own 'wife'; for Ogden she is represented by the Levitical priests (Mal 2:1, 4–7, 10) who had failed in their duties.[371]

Isaksson suggests that in failing to see the imagery many scholars have read a later view of divorce into the Malachi pericope that is not compatible with its social context:

> A really quite decisive argument against interpreting these verses as dealing with marriage and divorce is that the Old Testament concept ברית is quite incompatible with what marriage meant at this period. Marriage was not a compact entered into by man and wife with Yahweh as witness but a matter of commercial negotiation between two men.[372]

Glazier-McDonald demonstrates the strength of various arguments for a literal interpretation, but then argues for the cultic perspectives of Hvidberg, Isaksson, and Torrey, finally suggesting that both cultic and literal interpretations are correct: that is, Malachi was addressing the social problem of intermarriage which had given rise to the religious apostasy—the daughter of a foreign god representing literal women and religious apostasy.[373]

Yahweh, for example: Isa 42:14b: Baumann, *Love and Violence*, 200

[370] C. C. Torrey, 'The Prophecy of "Malachi",' *JBL* 17 (1, 1898), 8–10; Torrey also considers in the article the argument that Malachi would not have to address the issue of foreign cults so soon after the restoration.

[371] Graham S. Ogden, 'The Use of Figurative Language in Malachi 2.10–16,' *BT* 39 (1988), 229–30

[372] Isaksson, *Marriage and Ministry*, 31

[373] Beth Glazier-McDonald, 'Intermarriage, Divorce and the Bat-'él Nékar: Insights into Mal. 2:10–16,' *JBL* 106 (1987), 609–10

I would suggest that the arguments articulated above are sufficient cause to question the assumption that the pericope references divorces by Jewish men. The interpretation that Israel (i.e. Judah at this stage) has been unfaithful to Yahweh, or at least unfaithful to the covenant religion, and as a consequence is now at risk of suffering a divorce appears to have some validity. Such a perspective is reinforced when it is considered that the book opens with an address proclaiming Yahweh's love for his collective people: 'The oracle of the word of the LORD to Israel by Malachi. "I have loved you," says the LORD' (Mal 1:1-2a); and concludes in Malachi 4 with an appeal, and a warning, to the nation:

> Remember the law of my servant Moses, the statutes and rules that I commanded him at Horeb for all Israel. Behold, I will send you Elijah the prophet before the great and awesome day of the LORD comes. And he will turn the hearts of fathers to their children and the hearts of children to their fathers, lest I come and strike the land with a decree of utter destruction. (Mal 4:4–6)

This perspective sees that the Book of the Twelve opens and closes with marital imagery portraying the unfaithfulness of Yahweh's covenant partner and the consequences of such—a divorce, but this time for Israel's 'sister,' Judah.

6.10 Remarriage

6.10.1 Remarriage at Sinai

The prophetic corpus indicates that there is a prospect of a remarriage for divorced Israel in the future and this is extensively addressed in the body of literature devoted to Old Testament marital imagery. But Lunn, it seems uniquely, but persuasively, argues that the exodus from Egypt had been in effect a divorce of Israel from Pharaoh and the Egyptian gods to prepare for the marriage to Yahweh at Sinai. He references Ezekiel 23:3: 'They played the whore in Egypt; they played the whore in their youth'; and sees the gifts taken from the Egyptians (Exod 3:22; 11:2; 12:35) represented the return of the *mohar*.[374] This present study suggests such a divorce would be justified in the imagery as the 'slave wife' Israel was being mistreated (Exod 1:8-14) and therefore would be free to go (Exod 21:7-11). If Lunn's analysis is correct Yahweh at Sinai was marrying a divorcee.

6.10.2 Remarriage in Hosea

Abma sees Hosea 1:11 as depicting a future reunion of Judah and Israel, and considers various interpretations of 'they shall go up from the land,' concluding that the most obvious interpretation is of some sort of future exodus.[375] Hosea 2:14-15 seems to represent a new entry into the land, the reference to the wilderness not representing a place of desolation but rather one of intimacy devoid of distractions. Abma suggests the text presents the reunion between Yahweh and Israel 'in terms of the pattern of exodus - wilderness - entrance into the promised land' and that vv. 16-23 focus on a new bridal time for Yahweh and Israel—not 'a return to a previously existing marriage but as a completely new beginning!'[376]

6.10.3 Remarriage in Isaiah

Isaiah 54:1-8 also looks forward to a time of reconciliation. Israel's 'widowhood' (v. 4) is probably a reference to Israel's deserted (v. 7) rather than bereaved status.[377] Moughtin-Mumby considers Isaiah 54:5 is possibly the most direct reference to Yahweh as a 'husband' in the Old Testament and a rare reference to an actual 'marriage' and suggests others have missed the potential impact of that.[378] Yet Abma sees that reference as a problem—*baal* (בַּעַל) is in the plural and although usually translated as husband, the LXX implies the reference is to 'lord'; but she points out that the commentaries consider the verb to be a *pluralis majestatis* and considers that 'husband' is the

---

[374] Lunn, 'Let My People Go,' 242-47; the return of the *mohar* is not a practice explicit in the Old Testament but evidenced in rabbinic writings (e.g. *m. Ketub.* 2:1; 4:7-12) and in the JDD, for example, Mur 20 line 6: 'And if you are divorced from me I will return the money of your *kethubah* and all that you have brought to my house' (§8.3.5).

[375] Abma, *Bonds of Love*, 162-63

[376] Abma, *Bonds of Love*, 186-87, 189, 191

[377] Thus: Instone-Brewer, *Divorce and Remarriage*, 50

[378] Moughtin-Mumby, *Sexual and Marital Metaphors*, 126, 133

correct translation.³⁷⁹ Baumann suggests that now בַּעַל was no longer important as a primary competitor of Yahweh the name can be used without any fear of awakening associations with the Canaanite god:

> Thus Isa 54:1–6 takes up the older image of YHWH as the marital "lord" of Jerusalem and reshapes it ... YHWH is to be seen now, despite all his world-dominating power, in an astonishing pose of self-renunciation towards his "wife." In Isa 54:7–9 he takes the major responsibility for the previous "crisis in the marriage," and woos her once again.... The text does not clearly indicate who the "wife" is. She is only described as the rebuilt city of Jerusalem in Isa 54:11–17.³⁸⁰

More definite marital imagery is found in Isaiah 61:10 where the text speaks of Israel, in the first person singular, being dressed like a bridegroom, and like a bride. Baumann points out that there are two other places where personified Jerusalem is again addressed by Yahweh: Isaiah 62:1–8 where in vv. 4–5 'the text speaks of a (re?)marriage of YHWH and Jerusalem'; and 66:7–13 where once again Jerusalem is a woman, but here the imagery is of a mother and childbirth. She comments: 'The only plausible construction in the context is that it [the city/land] will be married to YHWH' and she comments on the use of בעל four times in Isaiah 62:4–5 'which otherwise occurs very seldom.... It is one of the few Old Testament words that means "marry" in most contexts' and signifies that it 'was no longer necessary to set YHWH and everything that could refer to his former competitor בעל in such crass opposition.'³⁸¹

6.10.4 Remarriage in Jeremiah

Jeremiah 3:18–22 speaks of a reunited nation, and Jeremiah 31:31–32 promises a 'new covenant' which is cited in Hebrews 8:8–13 as being mediated by Christ, who is portrayed as the 'Bridegroom Messiah' in the Gospels—thus the promise is embraced within the marital imagery of the New Testament.

---

³⁷⁹ Abma, *Bonds of Love*, 87–88

³⁸⁰ Baumann further notes that in Hos 2:16 Israel is told that when the courtship is renewed: 'she shall no longer say בעל to him, but instead "husband" (איש)': Baumann, *Love and Violence*, 185–86

³⁸¹ Baumann, *Love and Violence*, 188–89; Instone-Brewer points out that 'Isaiah speaks of the reconciled bride as a "virgin" (בתולה, *bethulah*),' in Isa 62:5: Instone-Brewer, *Divorce and Remarriage*, 51

6.10.5 Remarriage in Ezekiel

Instone-Brewer sees that Ezekiel 40–44 offers hope for the people, 'but distances the new bride from the old by abandoning the city and projecting a completely new Jerusalem.'[382] The new situation is described by Galambush:

> In Ezekiel 33–39, in the aftermath of the Babylonian invasion, the woman Jerusalem is neither condemned nor forgiven, but forgotten. The only remnant of Yahweh's former wife is the abiding memory of her uncleanness. Ezekiel's vision in chaps 40–48 of the new temple city completes the cycle of the city's defilement, destruction, and restoration. The God who left in rage returns in triumph, and the city is renewed and recreated. Only Jerusalem, the chastened and forgiven wife, is absent from the scene. The new city is described as inanimate stone.[383]

6.11 Inferred Cross-Mapping

It has been suggested (§2.1.1) that there can be an inferred cross-mapping between the two conceptual domains of the imagery—Day references (in effect) inferred reverse cross-mapping and articulates this principle:

> It is my methodological practice to require corroborating evidence from nonfigurative genres of writing before positing a basis in social reality for any given aspect of figurative marriage or marital infidelity. Conversely, when a feature of figurative marriage or marital infidelity is contradicted by what we do know about Israelite laws and practices from the nonfigurative texts, I take this as evidence that the feature in question has no basis in ancient Israelite social reality.[384]

Similarly, this present study (as indicated in §1.5), will only posit inferred cross-mapping when such appears to be consonant with specific biblical teaching, or is evidenced in contemporary marriage practice.

---

[382] Instone-Brewer, *Divorce and Remarriage*, 47

[383] Galambush, *Jerusalem*, 147

[384] Peggy L. Day, 'Yahweh's Broken Marriages as Metaphoric Vehicle in the Hebrew Bible Prophets,' in Nissinen and Uro, *Sacred Marriages*, 226

6.11.1 Inferred Cross-Mapping: Punishments for Adultery

Kamionkowski commenting on Ezekiel 16 states: 'An overly simplistic reading of the marital metaphor between God and Israel may lead to the conclusion that ... God condones rape as a suitable punishment for female adultery.'[385] Day similarly points out the dangers of analysing such pericopae to find some correlation with the various punishments in mundane marriage without taking into full consideration the metaphoric nature of the imagery—a mistake she claims some scholars make.[386] One such might be Westbrook, for when analysing Jeremiah 13:26 ('I myself [Yahweh] will lift up your [i.e. Judah's] skirts over your face, and your shame will be seen') he says 'whether this gesture reflects the process of a divorce is not made clear.'[387]

But such mundane marriage practice is not taught in the Old Testament, nor is there any documentary evidence to support it, thus this present study suggests that speculation as to whether the imagery reflects such practices is, as both Day and Kamionkowski suggest, potentially unhelpful. Some aspects of the target domain do involve rhetorical language that cannot be validly reverse cross-mapped.

6.11.2 Inferred Cross-Mapping: Deuteronomy 24:1–4

The fact that Jeremiah cross-maps Deuteronomy 24:1–4 to the target domain to justify Yahweh's divorce of Israel (and to point out that she could not return) suggests that such was the understanding of the pericope—that a husband could initiate a divorce on the grounds of his wife's sexual immorality (after which she was not allowed to return)—and this reinforces the academic consensus of the correct translation of the ambiguous עֶרְוַת דָּבָר (§5.11.1.3). However, Westbrook argues that Jeremiah 3:1 and Deuteronomy 24:1–4 are not connected ('contrary to the views of most scholars'), because the

---

[385] Tamar S. Kamionkowski, 'Gender Reversal in Ezekiel 16,' in *Prophets and Daniel: A Feminist Companion to the Bible (Second Series)*, ed. Athalya Brenner (London: Sheffield Academic, 2001), 171

[386] Peggy L. Day, 'The Bitch Had It Coming To Her: Rhetoric and Interpretation in Ezekiel 16,' *Biblical Interpretation* 8 (2000), 247-53; Kamionkowski, 'Gender Reversal in Ezekiel 16,' in Brenner, *Prophets and Daniel*, 171

[387] Westbrook, 'Adultery in Ancient Near Eastern Law,' 560-61

dissolution of the second marriage is not mentioned, and 'it is the husband in the rhetorical example who is to return to the wife, whereas in marriage it would be the other way round.' Galambush considers Westbrook's arguments 'strong,' although acknowledges problems in de-linking the two verses.[388] Davidson is another dissenting voice—despite seeing that Jeremiah 3:1 accurately reflects the meaning of Deuteronomy 24:1-4, he states, 'It is important hermeneutically not to utilize this metaphorical application of the legislation to interpret Deut 24:1-4 or vice versa.'[389]

Nevertheless, the scholarly consensus that the two passages are linked is persuasive, and Instone-Brewer comments: 'Although Israel has not actually married someone else ... Jeremiah says that she has done far worse because she has had many lovers' and suggests that the problem of a future remarriage presented by Deuteronomy 24:1-4 is circumvented because the future Israel is different from the faithless Israel.[390]

6.11.3 Inferred Cross-Mapping: Covenant or Contract?

Some scholars see New Testament mundane marriage as a covenant that denotes an indissoluble union that precludes divorce and argue from their understanding of the source domain of the Old Testament imagery (mundane marriage) to the target —for example Dumbrell:

> The indivisibility, however, of the covenant from the divine point of view is referred to in [Jer 31] v. 32 by its depiction in [mundane] marriage terms. Yahweh had been 'their husband.' The use of this marriage imagery ... ought to be carefully noted in this new covenant section. It is saying by its very nature the covenant arrangement with

---

[388] Westbrook, 'The Prohibition,' in Japhet, *Scripta Hierosolymitana*, 405 n. 66; Galambush, *Jerusalem in the Book of Ezekiel*, 56 n. 93

[389] Davidson, *The Flame of Yahweh*, 415; similarly Gane, who points out that Yahweh did not divorce Israel so she could remarry—the divorce resulted in Israel's destruction and concludes: 'Thus, it is clear that Pentateuchal legal practice cannot be safely extrapolated from a theological prophetic oracle': Roy Gane, 'Old Testament Principles Relevant to Divorce and Remarriage,' *JATS* 12 (2 2001), 51

[390] Instone-Brewer, *Divorce and Remarriage*, 41–43

Israel could not be sundered. Divorce on the divine side could never be contemplated.[391]

MacKay makes a similar source to target inference:

> Marriage was divinely intended to institute an exclusive and permanent bond between a man and a woman (Gen 2:24), and so it also is a covenant relationship.... In this way the circumstances of Hosea's marriage vividly illustrated the LORD's own relationship with Israel.[392]

This perspective causes MacKay to reject any interpretation of Hosea 2 that involves a divorce.[393]

I would suggest that these comments, perhaps unwittingly, demonstrate the potential cognitive power of cross-mapping in the marriage metaphor. Thus Dumbrell and MacKay argue permanence from the mundane marriage 'covenant' to Yahweh's covenant with Israel (i.e. source to target)—but there is no unequivocal evidence in the text of the Old Testament directly linking mundane marriage with בְּרִית (§5.3); and no indication in the Old Testament record that marriages in ancient Israel were considered unbreakable.

Furthermore, the passage Dumbrell quotes appears to suggest the opposite—that is, a covenant, even with Yahweh, could be 'broken':

> Behold, the days are coming, declares the Lord, when I will make a new covenant with the house of Israel and the house of Judah, not like the covenant that I made with their fathers on the day when I took them by the hand to bring them out of the land of Egypt, my covenant that they broke, though I was their husband, declares the Lord. (Jer 31:31–32)

---

[391] Dumbrell, *Covenant and Creation*, 259; also: Block, 'Marriage and Family,' in Campbell, *Marriage and Family*, 50–51
[392] MacKay, *Hosea*, 38
[393] MacKay, *Hosea*, 75–78

6.12 Marital Imagery in Eden

It is possible to see marital imagery being utilised in the Edenic story. Postell surveys the history of the interpretation of Genesis 1–3 and points out that many scholars have seen distinct parallels between Eden and the events recorded there and the story of Israel in the Promised Land:

> Adam and Eve's relationship with God—the contingency of their enjoyment of the land, their duties in the garden, and the consequences of their disobedience—foreshadows Israel's life under the Sinai covenant.[394]

Sousan (whom Postell references) believes it was Augustine who first noticed the covenantal nature of God's relationship with Adam; Sousan sees this as an intentional metaphor for Yahweh's covenant with Israel at Sinai.[395] Postell further points out that the rabbinic commentary *Genesis Rabbah* describes Adam's exile from Eden in 'the same terms used for disannulment of a marital covenant.'[396] Although Postell draws attention to the possible marital imagery he does not develop the theme. However, the Genesis text itself employs שָׁלַח ('to send' or 'to let go') in Genesis 3:23 and גָּרַשׁ ('to cast out') in Genesis 3:24 to describe Adam's expulsion from the garden which are used elsewhere in the Hebrew Bible to describe divorce (§5.10); thus, accepting the posited narrative typology, this present study suggests that Adam's exile from Eden is consciously portrayed as a 'divorce' from Yahweh by the Genesis writer (with

---

[394] Postell, *Adam as Israel*, 114; Futato similarly sees that background to the composition of the Edenic story is the Baalism experienced by pre-exilic Israel: Mark D. Futato, 'Because It Had Rained: A Study of Gen 2:5–7 with Implications for Gen 3:4–25 and Gen 1:1–23,' *WTJ* 60 (1998), 18–21. Dumbrell comments that Gen 2 'presupposes that Adam's role, transferred to Israel and then to Christ, was to extend the contours of the garden to the whole world,' and that, 'Canaan (cf. Deut 7:12–15) was the restored garden of God, and Israel had made that connection': Dumbrell, *Covenant and Creation*, 41, 45

[395] Sousan, 'The Woman in the Garden,' 177, 185; Collins believes Hos 6:7 is a reference to a covenant that God had with Adam: John C. Collins, *Genesis 1–4: A Linguistic, Literary, and Theological Commentary* (Phillipsburg, NJ: Presbyterian and Reformed, 2006), 113; Hos 6:7 states: 'But like Adam they transgressed the covenant; there they dealt faithlessly with me'; however, the verse is a possible reference to the city Adam, as MacKay believes: MacKay, *Hosea*, 196

[396] Postell is not sure if the rabbinic comment was an intentional allusion to marriage: Postell, *Adam as Israel*, 6 n. 5

Hosea 6:7 being a possible reference to such), just as Israel's exile from the Promised Land is described as a divorce in Jeremiah 3:1–8.

Sailhamer points out that the exile from Eden implied that in some way Adam and Eve had become contaminated and so had to be dealt with in a manner that reflected the cultic regulations of Leviticus 13:1–14:57;[397] Gilchrest posits that the purpose of banishment (citing Leviticus 16 and the scapegoat ritual) is to maintain 'the boundary between what is holy and what is not. That which is not holy is sent away leaving behind a holy community with a holy God.'[398] Thus the 'flaming sword' (Gen 3:24) that prevented Adam's return (and prevented direct access to God for all his progeny), is possibly a further example of conscious marital cross-mapping from the mundane divorce rule of Deuteronomy 24:

> Then her former husband, who sent her away, may not take her again to be his wife, after she has been defiled, for that is an abomination before the LORD. And you shall not bring sin upon the land that the LORD your God is giving you for an inheritance. (Deut 24:4)

In summary, this analysis of marital imagery in Eden would suggest a compositional strategy behind the Pentateuch linking Eden and the exodus from Egypt (climaxing at Sinai) with marital imagery; the prophetic corpus developing the imagery to make sense of the Assyrian and Babylonian exiles, describing them as a divorce and a separation respectively, with an eschatological hope for the re-united nation framed, certainly for divorced Israel if not the 'estranged' Judah, as a future remarriage.

6.13 Summary: Marital Imagery in the Old Testament

Moughtin-Mumby comments in the opening of her chapter on Ezekiel:

> it is time finally to lay to rest the assumption contested throughout this exploration that in the prophetic books there is a definable entity

---

[397] John H. Sailhamer, *The Pentateuch as Narrative* (Grand Rapids, MI: Zondervan, 1992), 110

[398] Eric Gilchrest, 'For the Wages of Sin is … Banishment: An Unexplored Substitutionary Motif in Leviticus 16 and the Ritual Aspect of the Scapegoat,' *EvQ* 85.1 (2013), 45

that we can call 'the marriage metaphor', consisting of a recognizable story of YHWH's relationship with the nation, or city.[399]

But Moughtin-Mumby is referring to the varied language employed by the different prophets and the difficulty in much of the marital imagery of making a definitive identification of Yahweh's 'wife'; this is further complicated by the rhetorical nature of much of the language when referencing the target domain. But the source map of the imagery is clear, and is always the same: it is mundane marriage as practised in ancient Israel. It is this that binds together the imagery employed by the prophets giving it a common theme. It is an imagery that sees the Sinai event as a marriage, and is possibly also utilised in the Edenic story. However, it is Hosea who first articulates the metaphor precisely, and the subsequent split of the kingdoms is portrayed as Yahweh being married to two sisters. The apostasy of both kingdoms resulted in the exile ('divorce') of Israel and then the exile ('separation') of Judah, the former being seen as irrevocable (Jer 3 referencing the divorce law of Deut 24:1–4). Finally, in Malachi, Yahweh's covenant partner is still portrayed as being in a state of apostasy.

Thus the target domain of the imagery embraces the concept of a volitional, conditional covenant. Such is to be expected, as it has been seen that the target domain has been populated from a source domain (Israelite mundane marriage) which was also based on a volitional, conditional covenant—one that included the possibility of divorce and remarriage. Block sees reference to Yahweh's divorce of Israel as a 'rhetorical device'—that is, there was no divorce.[400] But the very real exile of the northern kingdom is portrayed in the marital imagery as a divorce—one based on the grounds of their idolatry ('prostitution' in the imagery); McCarthy pointing out that the Sinaitic covenant had been broken, and that 'This had to mean the end of the covenant as such.'[401]

Furthermore, despite Dumbrell's comment that the covenant with Israel, 'could not be sundered,' he nonetheless sees that the Sinai covenant was tied to

---

[399] Moughtin-Mumby, *Sexual and Marital Metaphors*, 156
[400] Block, 'Marriage and Family,' in Campbell, *Marriage and Family*, 50–51
[401] McCarthy, *Old Testament Covenant*, 46

political forms and a territorial state and that the stability of this depended upon Israel's response.[402] Yahweh's relationship with Israel in the Old Testament text seems rooted in the land (e.g. Exod 20:12; Deut 5:33), making exile and divorce appear synonymous.[403] Nonetheless, there appears to be envisaged a future restoration that Hosea, Jeremiah, and Isaiah see as a new marriage, and Ezekiel expresses as a re-built temple.

It is now possible to give example references for the key analogies in the cross-mapping chart posited in §1.3.1, including the promised future betrothal and remarriage:

MAP 1 *Yahweh: The Husband of Israel* (Conceptual Domain 'A' is created)

CONCEPTUAL DOMAIN Gen 2:24		NEW TARGET DOMAIN (A) Yahweh: The Husband of Israel
A woman becomes the wife of a man in a metaphoric one-flesh union formed by means of a volitional covenant.	ROOT METAPHOR 	Israel becomes what they were not in a metaphoric marital union with Yahweh formed by means of a volitional covenant. (Jer 31:31–32)
• Marital obligations for the husband (Exod 21:7–11) • Adultery forbidden (Exod 20:14) • Divorce certificate required (Deut 24:1–4) • Remarriage to first husband forbidden (Deut 24:1–4)	COTA 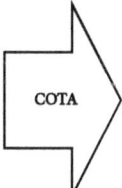	• Marital obligations for Yahweh (Ps 132:13–16) • Adultery forbidden (Ezek 23:1–9) • Divorce certificate required (Jer 3:6–8) • Remarriage to Yahweh forbidden (Jer 3:6–8) • But a future betrothal followed by a remarriage is promised (Hos 2:19–20; Isa 54:4–8)

COTA = Consequent Old Testament Analogies

---

[402] Dumbrell, *Covenant and Creation*, 129, 259
[403] Thus: Wright, *God's People*, 3–43

Our study in this chapter provides further evidence that the root metaphor *Yahweh: The Husband of Israel* was based on the principles of Genesis 2:24 and that the consequent analogies employed demonstrate that the source domain of the imagery was mundane marriage in ancient Israel—Sohn comments: 'the origin and background of the [Sinaitic] covenant were the marriage practices of the people of Israel.'[404] Both source and target domains embraced the concept of a conditional, volitional covenant that included: betrothal, asymmetrical marital obligations, adultery, divorce, and remarriage.

---

[404] Sohn, 'I Will Be Your God,' in Chazan, Hallo, and Schiffman, *Ki Baruch Hu*, 368

Chapter 7: The Literature of the Second Temple Period

7.1 Introduction

Both mundane marriage and the marital imagery of the Old Testament demonstrate that marriage in ancient Israel was not patterned on the marriage of Adam and Eve. Rather mundane marriage was itself seen as the archetype for the divine marriage of Yahweh and Israel. Satlow believes that Old Testament marriage legislation gave either partner the right to divorce, and that as a consequence the marital metaphor posed a problem for Second Temple Judaism: 'What is to prevent God from sending away His covenanted spouse, Israel?'—although Satlow does not discuss metaphor theory, he is referencing cross-mapping inferences from source to target.[405] If his analysis is correct, it might account for the apparent absence of Old Testament metaphoric imagery in intertestamental literature, he comments:

> Among Jews writing in Greek, the description of the relationship between God and Israel as a marriage was stunningly uninfluential. With the exception of Paul [the apostle] ... no Jew writing in Greek uses this metaphor.[406]

Carr and Conway specifically endorse Satlow's perception that the biblical divine-human marriage metaphor virtually disappeared in Second Temple literature, and also agree that 'when Paul uses it, he is among the first Hellenistic Jewish writers to do so.'[407]

Satlow suggests that early Christian writers adopting the marriage metaphor would, like Second Temple Judaism, have seen that any divorce teaching was a

---

[405] Satlow explores this and other potential reasons for Second Temple Judaism turning its back on the Old Testament marital imagery: Satlow, *Jewish Marriage*, 44–50; McCarthy sees a post-exilic de-emphasis on the conditional Mosaic covenant and a new focus of the Davidic unconditional covenant: McCarthy, *Old Testament Covenant*, 47–48

[406] Satlow considers other marital metaphors (e.g. Solomon's desire to make the personified Wisdom his mistress—Wis 8:2–16) but sees them as being different to the Old Testament marital metaphor: Satlow, *Jewish Marriage*, 44

[407] David M. Carr and Colleen M. Conway, 'The Divine Human Marriage Matrix and Constructions of Gender and Bodies in the Christian Bible,' in Nissinen and Uro, *Sacred Marriages*, 294

potential 'theological nightmare.' For if a husband could divorce his wife, what was to stop God divorcing his church? Satlow believes that as a consequence, the church consciously utilised the marriage of Adam and Eve to forbid divorce, and thus align mundane marriage with their perception of the divine marriage—that is, that God would never divorce his people.[408] He suggests this new primal couple model gradually emerged from the literature of the Second Temple period:

> This evidence, scattered and scanty as it may be, indicates that throughout the Hellenistic period, especially (or perhaps exclusively, depending on where Tobit was written) in Palestine, there was an increasing tendency to see contemporary marriage as patterned on the biblical primal marriage. This view was probably far from common; the elite and sectarian writers themselves do not explicitly make this link until late in the Second Temple period. The reason that the Qumran and early Christian communities do explicitly link marriage to the creation accounts appears to lie in its normative utility.[409]

Whilst recognising that the literary evidence is scant, Satlow claims the Qumran and Christian communities adopted the primal couple model to suit their own ends. Collins appears to endorse Satlow's analysis of the literature: 'The later we go in the second temple period, the more influential the text of Genesis becomes' and considers that both Philo and Josephus see that text as 'fundamental.'[410] Although Collins believes the implications of this were not always followed through, like Satlow, he sees evidence of such at Qumran.[411]

It was pointed out (§5.1) that scholars believe that an Edenic marriage model gives rise to the distinctive teaching that in mundane marriage there should be no polygyny or divorce, coitus is considered to be primarily for procreation, celibacy and holiness are linked, and each mundane marriage is believed to have a supernatural dimension.

---

[408] Satlow, *Jewish Marriage*, 48–49

[409] Satlow, *Jewish Marriage*, 60–61

[410] However, this present study sees little evidence for such a comment in the works of Josephus, whose writings do not appear to embrace a primal couple model (§7.6.2 and §7.6.3).

[411] Collins, 'Marriage, Divorce, and Family,' in Perdue et al., *Families in Ancient Israel*, 147

During the Second Temple period Diaspora Jewish communities were to be found in Egypt, Cyrene, Rome, Greece, Asia Minor, and Babylonia, and within Judaea there were several diverse groups (e.g. the Houses of Shammai and Hillel), but Chapman considers that despite such diversity a shared history and ancestral religion were unifying factors.[412] This chapter will consider the different categories of Second Temple literature extant from these communities to look for evidence of the primal couple model Collins and Satlow suggest.

In chapter 8 evidence will be sought to see if an adoption of an Edenic model in the literature influenced contemporary marriage and divorce practice, and finally in chapters 9 and 10, New Testament marital imagery and its mundane marriage and divorce teaching will be explored to determine the metaphoric marital cross-mapping and the marriage model that underpins it.

7.2 The Old Testament Pseudepigrapha

7.2.1 Introduction

The works considered in this section are those published in the two volumes edited by J. H. Charlesworth. He defines the writings as those:

> 1) that, with the exception of Ahiqar, are Jewish or Christian; 2) that are often attributed to ideal figures in Israel's past; 3) that customarily claim to contain God's word or message; 4) that frequently build upon ideas and narratives present in the Old Testament; 5) and that almost always were composed either during the period 200 B.C. to A.D. 200 or, though late, apparently preserve, albeit in an edited form, Jewish traditions that date from that period.[413]

7.2.2 The Edenic Marriage in the Old Testament Pseudepigrapha

Some of the Pseudepigrapha literature appears to consider sexual desire a consequence of the first sin and therefore possibly sinful itself. The *Sibylline*

---

[412] Chapman, 'Marriage and Family,' in Campbell, *Marriage and Family*, 183–84
[413] James H. Charlesworth, ed., *The Old Testament Pseudepigrapha Vol. 1: Apocalyptic Literature and Testaments* (Garden City, NY: Doubleday, 1983), xxv

Oracles re-work the creation story so that Adam's interest in Eve in Eden is in conversation not sex, thus *Sib. Or.* 1:26-37 has:

> But he [Adam] being alone in the luxuriant plantation of the garden desired conversation, and prayed to behold another form like his own. God himself ... made Eve ... when he saw her.... They conversed with wise words.... For they neither covered their minds with licentiousness nor felt shame, but were far removed from evil heart.[414]

It is possible the 'becoming one flesh' of Genesis 2:24 is reflected in *Jos. Asen.* 20:4 where Aseneth objects to Joseph's suggestion that another woman wash his feet: 'No, my Lord.... For your feet are my feet, and your hands are my hands, and your soul my soul.'[415]

Johnson in his introduction to the *Apocalypse of Moses* (Life of Adam and Eve) states that: 'The Greek and Latin texts ... both purport to narrate in Midrashic form some episodes in the life of the "first made" after their expulsion from Paradise'—the original composition he believes to date from between '100 B.C. and A.D. 200' and written by a Jew.[416]

Apocalypse of Moses 25:3–4 refers to the punishment of the pains of childbirth and sees that Eve equates sexual intercourse with sin: 'you [Eve] shall confess and say, "LORD, LORD, save me and I will never again turn to the sin of the flesh."'[417]

Testament of Issachar 2:3 suggests that sex for procreation is more honourable than for gratification: 'For he [the Lord] perceived that she [Leah] wanted to lie with Jacob for the sake of children and not merely for sexual

---

[414] John J. Collins, 'Sibylline Oracles: A New Translation and Introduction,' in *The Old Testament Pseudepigrapha Volume 1: Apocalyptic Literature and Testaments*, ed. James H Charlesworth (Garden City, NY: Doubleday, 1983), 335

[415] James H. Charlesworth, ed., *The Old Testament Pseudepigrapha Volume 2: Expansions of the 'Old Testament' and Legends, Wisdom and Philosophical Literature, Prayers, Psalms, and Odes, Fragments of Lost Judeo-Hellenistic Works* (Garden City, NY: Doubleday, 1985), 234

[416] M. D. Johnson, 'Life of Adam and Eve: A New Translation and Introduction,' in *The Old Testament Pseudepigrapha: Expansions of the 'Old Testament' and Legends, Wisdom and Philosophical Literature, Prayers, Psalms, and Odes, Fragments of Lost Judeo-Hellenistic Works*, ed. James H Charlesworth (Garden City, NY: Doubleday, 1985), 249, 252

[417] Johnson, 'Life of Adam and Eve,' in Charlesworth, ed., *The Old Testament Pseudepigrapha Vol. 2*, 283

gratification.'[418] And *1 En.* 15:5 seems to describe sexual intercourse as being primarily for procreation: 'On that account, I have given you wives in order that (seeds) might be sown upon them and children born by them.'[419]

Andersen believes in *2 Baruch* 56:6 the writer is suggesting coitus was not present in Eden and therefore sexual intercourse was required for the production of children only after the fall:[420]

> For when he [Adam] transgressed ... the realm of death began to ask to be renewed with the blood, the conception of children came about, the passion of parents was produced.[421]

Jubilees 2-4 (dated by Wintermute at 161-140 BCE) retells the Edenic story, and Andersen's analysis suggests that the author here follows the Levitical concept, that although sexual activity was not evil or associated with the fall, nonetheless semen emission made you ritually unclean (Lev 15:8). Thus *Jub.* 3 portrays the account of creation and the sex act as having taken place before the couple are brought into Eden, so that Eden itself, which Andersen sees as portrayed as prototype of the temple in *Jub.* 4:23-26, is kept pure.[422]

7.2.3 Contra-Indications of an Edenic Marriage in the Old Testament Pseudepigrapha

There is no specific condemnation of polygyny in the Pseudepigrapha, however, it is possible to see that *T. Reu.* 4:1 ('live in integrity of heart ... until the Lord gives you the mate whom he wills') and *T. Iss.* 7:2 ('I have not had intercourse with any woman other than my wife') assume monogamy but neither of these references is conclusive.[423] Also the 'Do not add marriage to

---

[418] Charlesworth, *The Old Testament Pseudepigrapha Vol. 1*, 802-03

[419] Charlesworth, *The Old Testament Pseudepigrapha Vol. 1*, 21

[420] Anderson, 'Celibacy or Consummation,' 123

[421] Charlesworth, *The Old Testament Pseudepigrapha Vol. 1*, 641; Loader sees *2 Baruch* as written 'in the aftermath of the destruction of the temple in 70 CE': Loader, *Making Sense of Sex*, 22

[422] O. S. Wintermute, 'Jubilees: A New Translation and Introduction,' in Charlesworth, *The Old Testament Pseudepigrapha Volume 2*, 129, 139

[423] Charlesworth, *The Old Testament Pseudepigrapha Vol. 1*, 783, 804

marriage' of Ps.-Phoc. 205 might be discouraging remarriage after divorce but it could refer to polygyny.[424]

7.2.4 Summary: The Old Testament Pseudepigrapha

There is an interest in the Edenic marriage in the Pseudepigrapha and a link is occasionally made between sin and sexual desire, and a view is expressed that the primary purpose of intercourse is perceived to be for procreation, although polygyny and divorce are not condemned.

7.3 The Old Testament Apocrypha

7.3.1 Introduction

The works considered in this section (and any translations unless otherwise stated) are those published in *The New Oxford Annotated Apocrypha*. Newsom comments:

> All of the writings in the Apocryphal/Deuterocanonical books are Jewish in origin, but it is not clear that they were collected by any particular community of Jews. Some of them (for instance Sirach) were quoted by rabbis, but for others no evidence exists that they were regarded as central to the Jewish community at any point.... Nevertheless, influences from some of these works are apparent within Judaism.[425]

Newsom further points out that although the New Testament does not quote directly from these works, she does see literary echoes (for example, from the Wisdom of Solomon in Romans and 2 Corinthians), and considers the apocryphal/deuterocanonical books do elucidate Jewish life as it developed immediately before the Common Era.[426]

---

[424] Charlesworth, *The Old Testament Pseudepigrapha Vol. 2*, 581

[425] Carol A. Newsom, 'Introduction to the Apocryphal/Deuterocanonical Books,' in *The New Oxford Annotated Apocrypha: New Revised Standard Version*, ed. Michael D. Coogan et al. (Oxford: Oxford University Press, 2010), 8

[426] Newsom, 'Introduction,' in Coogan, *New Oxford Apocrypha*, 9

7.3.2 The Edenic Marriage in the Old Testament Apocrypha

The marriage of Tobias and Sarah was sealed with a marriage contract (Tob 7:13) and there is a reference to this union being a reflection of the marriage of Adam and Eve (Tob 8:4-8). Satlow sees this pericope as 'The clearest and perhaps first extrabiblical text to link contemporary marital practice with the primal marriage of Adam and Eve,' but then comments:

> It is difficult to know to what extent Tobias's prayer reflected a common understanding of a link between Gen 2 and contemporary human marriage. Nevertheless, it is significant that Adam and Eve [in Tob 8] are invoked not as part of a regular marital liturgy, but as part of a charm.[427]

Sirach 36:29 has: 'He who acquires a wife gets his best possession, a helper fit for him and a pillar of support' which possibly references Genesis 2:18.

7.3.3 Contra-Indications of an Edenic Marriage in the Old Testament Apocrypha

Loader refers to many texts from Sirach that portray women in a negative light but they do not suggest a move away from an Old Testament understanding of marriage or an ascetic attitude to sex, for example embracing polygyny (Sir 26:5-6; 37:11).[428] Balla comments on Sirach:

> In a good marriage, desire and sex are not negative. There are even comments which refer to enjoying a wife's sexuality without making any mention of offspring.[429]

And divorce is apparently an option: 'If she [your wife] does not go as you direct, separate her from yourself.' (Sir 25:26)

---

[427] Satlow, *Jewish Marriage*, 58-59
[428] Loader, *Making Sense of Sex*, 34-35, 49
[429] Ibolya Balla, 'Ben Sira / Sirach,' in *The Pseudepigrapha on Sexuality: Attitudes towards Sexuality in Apocalypses, Testaments, Legends, Wisdom, and Related Literature*, ed. William R. G. Loader (Grand Rapids, MI: Eerdmans, 2011), 397

7.3.4 Summary: The Old Testament Apocrypha

Although the Old Testament Apocrypha references a primal couple marriage model it does not present a developed understanding of the Edenic marriage that would directly impact this present study.

7.4 Qumran

7.4.1 Introduction

Vermes believes it most probable that the Essenes were the Qumran sect and that the MSS discovered there date between 200 BCE and 70 CE[430] He considers the relationship between the Scrolls and the New Testament and concludes that while there are similarities of language, ideology, and attitude to the Old Testament, these may be due to the religious milieu of the era; however, he considers the early church modelled itself on certain aspects of the community (e.g. monarchic administration and strict discipline) but that it is 'the charismatic-eschatological aspects of the Scrolls [that] have provided the richest gleanings for comparison.'[431] However, Instone-Brewer considers: 'the Qumran documents do not say anything significant about divorce or remarriage.'[432] Satlow sees the Qumran sect were a sectarian group opposed to conventional social and power structures, and thus were against family structures, but not 'in any significant way, antimarriage.'[433]

7.4.2 The Edenic Marriage at Qumran

Satlow points out that the community's rejection of polygyny is a radical break with the Hebrew Bible tradition, and believes such rejection is based on their understanding of Genesis 1:27 ('So God created man in his own image, in the image of God he created him; male and female he created them.'); Genesis 7:9 ('two and two, male and female, went into the ark with Noah, as God had

---

[430] Geza Vermes, *The Complete Dead Sea Scrolls in English* (London: Pelican, 1962; Repr. 1998), 14, 48. Also: Jacob Neusner and William S. Green, *Dictionary of Judaism in the Biblical Period: 450 B.C.E. to 600 C.E.* (Peabody, MA: Hendrickson, 1999), 153

[431] Vermes, *Dead Sea Scrolls*, 22

[432] Instone-Brewer, *Divorce and Remarriage*, 72

[433] Satlow, *Jewish Marriage*, 21–24

commanded Noah.'); and Deuteronomy 17:17 ('And he [a king] shall not acquire many wives for himself ... ').[434]

Loader sees the reference to 'helpmate' and 'one flesh' in the book of *Instruction* as evidence of an Edenic marriage model:[435]

You have taken a wife in your poverty, take the offspring ...

from the approaching mystery

when you are joined together.

Walk with the helpmate of your flesh. (4Q416 III)[436]

... his father and his mother and he will cling [to his wife and they will become one flesh]

He made him rule over her and she ...

He did not make her father rule over her

and He separated her from her mother

and towards you [will be her longing

and she will be] one flesh for you. (4Q416 IV)[437]

It seems 4QMMT has a reference to Genesis 2:23: 'they [ta]ke [wives so as to be] {one} (4Q397 5) bone (with them).'[438]

Collins points out that Josephus, Philo, and Pliny all thought the Essenes lived a celibate life, so if they are the Qumran sect they must have been mistaken; but he considers that the Dead Sea Scrolls 'provide abundant indications of a mind-set that was conducive to sexual abstinence.'[439] Collins believes this

---

[434] Satlow, *Jewish Marriage*, 60
[435] Loader, *Making Sense of Sex*, 15
[436] Vermes notes: 'Lacunae impossible to complete with any measure of confidence are indicated by dots in the translation. Texts supplied from a different manuscript of the same document appear between { }. Hypothetical but likely constructions are placed between [ ] and glosses for fluency between ( )': Vermes, *Dead Sea Scrolls*, 93, 431
[437] Vermes, *Dead Sea Scrolls*, 431
[438] Vermes, *Dead Sea Scrolls*, 225
[439] Collins, 'Marriage, Divorce, and Family,' in Perdue et al., *Families in Ancient Israel*, 130-35

mind-set was rooted in Leviticus 15:18 which describes sexual intercourse as rendering both the man and the woman impure, seeing evidence for this in the *War Scroll*, the *Temple Scroll*, and the *Damascus Document*. However, he concludes:

> The evidence on celibacy at Qumran is not conclusive ... there was a strand of Jewish tradition, prominently represented at Qumran, that viewed sexual activity negatively, as a source of impurity, and that required abstinence on certain occasions.[440]

7.4.3 Contra-Indications of an Edenic Marriage at Qumran

Some have seen that the *Damascus Document* CD 4.20–5.2 forbids divorce. Vermes cites it as:

> The builders of the wall ... are caught in fornication twice by taking two wives *in their lifetime*, whereas the principle of creation is, "Male and female created he them" (*Gen.* 1:27). Also, those who entered the ark went in two by two (*Gen.* 7:7–9). And, concerning the prince, it is written, "He shall not multiply wives to himself" *Deut.* 17:17).[441]

He offers four possible interpretations and surveys the strength of the different scholarly positions of each but suggests, especially in light of the subsequent discovery of part of the same text at Qumran, that the safest interpretation is that the passage is forbidding polygyny.[442] Instone-Brewer considers the passage as represented in the two documents in some detail and concludes consonant with Vermes that both texts are critical of polygyny and neither prohibit divorce or remarriage.[443] This seems to be evidenced by 4Q159 2–4, 8–10 which references Deuteronomy 22:13–19 where a false accusation by a

---

[440] Collins, 'Marriage, Divorce, and Family,' in Perdue et al., *Families in Ancient Israel*, 134

[441] Geza Vermes, 'Sectarian Matrimonial Halakhah in the Damascus Rule,' *JJS* 25 (1974), 197

[442] Vermes, 'Sectarian Halakhah,' 202; in two articles post-dating Vermes' publication, Fitzmyer sees a prohibition of divorce: J. A. Fitzmyer, 'Divorce Among First-Century Palestinian Jews,' *Eretz-Israel* 14 (1978), 103–10; and Noam suggests a nuance in that the sect was endorsing divorce but only on the grounds of adultery: Vered Noam, 'Divorce in Qumran in Light of Early Halakah,' *Journal of Jewish Studies* LVI, No. 2 (Autumn 2005), 206–23

[443] Instone-Brewer, *Divorce and Remarriage*, 61–72; also: David Instone-Brewer, 'Nomological Exegesis in Qumran "Divorce Texts",' *RevQ* 18 (1998), 565, 572

husband that his bride was not a virgin forbids him ever to divorce her, suggesting that otherwise divorce was possible.

7.4.4 Summary: Qumran

Evidence for an Edenic marriage model at Qumran is mixed: they rejected polygyny but accepted divorce; sexual abstinence seems to have been considered a virtue but there is no clear teaching about celibacy.

7.5 Rabbinic Writings

7.5.1 Introduction

Neusner comments specifically on the Mishnah, (which he states was seen as the 'first statement of the oral Torah'): 'while [it] clearly addresses Israel, the Jewish people, it is remarkably indifferent to the Hebrew Scriptures.'[444] Both Ilan and Neusner comment on the difficulty of dating the source of much rabbinic material, Neusner suggesting much of it post-dates the Christian era: 'it has still to be demonstrated that rabbinic Judaism, as expressed in its principal and indicative traits ... had yet come into being in the first century.'[445] Furthermore, Greengus suggests rabbinic Judaism might reflect more a scholastic tradition rather than any operative law, Satlow believing that it 'is likely ... at least in Roman Palestine in the third century CE the rabbis had little juridical power.'[446] Satlow further suggests that much rabbinic material is more prescriptive than descriptive and that Hellenistic Jews did not have distinctive marriage laws; he sees the material as being 'rabbinic inventions ... [which] even the rabbis had trouble convincing other Jews to adopt ... until relatively late.'[447] Similarly Chapman believes that rabbinic writings concerning marriage

---

[444] Jacob Neusner, *Judaism and its Social Metaphors: Israel in the History of Jewish Thought* (Cambridge: Cambridge University Press, 1989), 4; Jacob Neusner, ed., *The Mishnah: A New Translation* (New Haven, CT: Yale University, 1988), xiii

[445] Tal Ilan, *Jewish Women in Greco-Roman Palestine: An Inquiry into Image and Status* (Peabody, MA: Hendrickson, 1995), 33; Jacob Neusner, *Rabbinic Literature and the New Testament: What We Cannot Show, We Do Not Know* (Eugene, OR: Wipf and Stock, 1994), 8

[446] Greengus, *Laws in the Bible*, 8; Michael L. Satlow, 'Rhetoric and Assumptions: Romans and Rabbis on Sex,' in *Jews in a Graeco-Roman World,* ed. Martin Goodman (Oxford: Oxford University Press, 1998), 136

[447] Satlow, *Jewish Marriage*, xix-xx, xxiv

in Judaism were written during a later era and probably present the views of a fairly cohesive group.[448]

Despite these reservations Satlow suggests the rabbinic corpus can provide a glimpse of the pre 70 CE Jewish world: 'The Rabbis may not have been the carriers of a continuous historical tradition, but neither did they arise out of a vacuum.'[449]

7.5.2 The Edenic Marriage in Rabbinic Writings

Satlow sees that the bulk of the rabbinic traditions that cite the primal couple as a model for mundane marriage are found in *Genesis Rabbah*. He points out in that rabbinic commentary that the obligations to 'your own flesh' of Isaiah 58:7 were perceived to include a divorced wife—that is, the one-flesh marriage relationship survived divorce, Satlow believing such an understanding was 'grounded in the biblical [i.e. primal couple] myth.'[450]

However, he believes that this concept was only evidenced among the Palestinian rabbis, and suggests that a primal couple marriage model was a better fit with a contemporary Hellenistic Stoic view of marriage:

> The biblical metaphor of marriage is at once more powerful and more potentially dangerous than the biblical myth of the first marriage. Use of this metaphor is rare in most of the extant Jewish literature from antiquity, and I suggest that this is because most Jews would have found the metaphor theologically and socially problematic.... Tracing early Jewish use of the biblical myth of the first marriage offers an intriguing case study of assimilation and adaption. During the Hellenistic period some Jewish groups, especially in Palestine, did allude to this myth in some of the [*sic*] their discussions of marriage. Only, however, when Jews were able to integrate this myth into a wider framework did they develop it. As Stoic understandings of

---

[448] Chapman, 'Marriage and Family,' in Campbell, *Marriage and Family*, 184
[449] Michael L. Satlow, *Creating Judaism: History, Tradition, Practice* (New York, NY: Columbia University Press, 2006), 119
[450] Satlow, *Jewish Marriage*, 61–63; Satlow cites *Gen Rab.* 8:12–13—David Instone-Brewer has pointed out to me that this rabbinic comment probably dates from the mid-second century CE at the earliest and thus is consistent with Satlow's analysis of the late development of a primal couple model articulated below.

> marriage as part of the divine order increased and were used increasingly even in Christian circles, Palestinian rabbis found in Gen. 1 and 2 a Jewish idiom for articulating the same idea. Their use of the myth of the primal marriage is an attempt to Judaize an otherwise ubiquitous ideology of marriage.[451]

Thus he sees the primal couple model within Judaism post-dates the Christian church's adoption of it.

7.5.3 Contra-Indications of an Edenic Marriage in Rabbinic Writings

Gafni contrasts the Christian concept of marriage with the rabbinic concept:

> Marriage was neither a sacrament nor supernaturally ordained. To be sure, the rabbis did not remove God from an involvement of sorts in the marriage process, and the idea that marriages, or matches, are made in heaven found its way into numerous legends and midrashim ... [but] Marriage ... was in fact contracted by individuals.[452]

Gafni compares this with what he sees as the sanctification of marriage by the Christian church and its conception that God has 'joined together ... two into one' and contrasts this 'sacramentum' idea with the contractual approach of Judaism where the:

> arrangement or contract, the conditions of which—while ascribing to certain stipulations—could ... be concluded on an individual basis by the parties concerned.... Thus, whereas the point of departure assumed certain basic requirements on the part of both parties, such as the husband's obligation to provide 'food, raiment and conjugal duties' and the wife's responsibility to perform various household chores ... all this was contracted with the understanding that precisely *because* marriage provided both parties with certain benefits, each

---

[451] Satlow, *Jewish Marriage*, 66–67
[452] Gafni, 'The Institution of Marriage,' in Kraemer, *The Jewish Family*, 13–14

party's relative interest in the agreement might determine the precise nature of the contract.[453]

Epstein points out that in ancient Judaism marriage and divorce were enacted by the husband, not the state, and in rabbinic times the *ketubah* was the key written instrument, or marriage 'contract.' However, he believes that such did not create the marriage; rather it recorded the fact of the marriage and outlined what in effect were its terms and conditions.[454]

Greengus sees the rabbinic *ketubah* as being instituted in the first century BCE and that it is:

> a written prenuptial contract required of all husbands, by which the husband pledges a certain sum of money as a stipend for his wife in the event of widowhood or divorce.[455]

The Mishnah deals with bills of divorce in the *Gittin* and includes the teaching 'The essential formula in the bill of divorce is, "Lo, thou art free to marry any man"' (*m. Git.* 9:3), although *m. Git.* 9:2 suggests restrictions on whom the woman can remarry (e.g. close relatives or the high priest) and the *Gittin* concludes with:

> The School of Shammai say: A man may not divorce his wife unless he has found unchastity in her, for it is written, *Because he hath found in her* indecency *in anything*. And the School of Hillel say: [He may divorce her] even if she spoiled a dish for him, for it is written, *Because we hath found in her indecency in* anything. R Akiba says: Even if he found another fairer than she, for it is written, *and it shall be if she found no favour in his eyes*. (*m. Git.* 9:10)[456]

---

[453] Gafni, 'The Institution of Marriage,' in Kraemer, *The Jewish Family*, 15; the husband's obligation Gafni sees as rooted in Exod 21, as does Satlow: 'The biblical text that anchors most rabbinic discussion of the sexual obligations of a husband to his wife is Exod 21:7–11': Satlow, *Tasting the Dish*, 265

[454] Louis M. Epstein, *The Jewish Marriage Contract: A Study in the Status of the Woman in Jewish Law* (New York, NY: Jewish Theological Seminary, 1927; Repr. Clark, NJ: Lawbook Exchange, 2004), 1–16

[455] Greengus, *Laws in the Bible*, 45 n. 77

[456] Translations as per: Herbert Danby, ed., *The Mishnah*, trans. Herbert Danby (Oxford: Oxford University Press, 1933); italics are Scripture quotes; square brackets embrace text not in the original.

It will be suggested in chapter 10 that the arguments presented in *m. Git.* 9:3 and *m. Git.* 9:10 underpin specific New Testament divorce teaching.

7.5.4 Summary: Rabbinic Writings

Early rabbinic material embraces a contractual view of marriage and does not appear to endorse any of the five suggested indicators of an Edenic archetype. References to the primal couple that Satlow points to are not found in the Mishnah and, it is suggested, belong to a later post-Christian Judaism.

7.6 Philo and Josephus

7.6.1 Introduction

Loader postulates that the many Jews living in Alexandria would have had access to the works of Plato, Aristotle, and treatises of Stoics, Epicureans, and Neo-Pythagoreans, and that many of their ideas would seem compatible with their own.[457]

Hengel suggests it was a 'lively interchange' and some Jewish Hellenistic writings might have actually originated in Palestine;[458] he considers the impact of the Greek language and the Septuagint:

> This special significance of the Greek language in Jerusalem in the first centuries before and after Christ is no coincidence.... Jerusalem was not only the capital of Jewish Palestine but was at the same time a metropolis of international, world-wide significance, a great "attraction" in the literal sense, the centre of the whole inhabited world. Nor was it the 'navel' only for pious Jews of the Diaspora but also an interesting place for educated Greeks, pagans, and adventurers.... In Greek speaking synagogue communities in Jerusalem the Septuagint was used, and while on the one hand there was teaching in the style of the Hellenistic Judaism of Alexandria, on the other there was an attempt to make the understanding of the law

---

[457] Loader, *Making Sense of Sex*, 107
[458] Hengel, *The Hellenization of Judaea*, 26

which was predominant among the Pharisees in Palestine known to the festival pilgrims from the Diaspora.[459]

Loader believes many Jewish writings were influenced by Hellenistic philosophy (he suggests the household codes as New Testament examples), and that Stoic thought, which embraced the concept of restricting human passions, was compatible with Jewish ideas and traditions.[460] He suggests Philo is a leading exponent of this convergence, and that the advice of the patriarchs in the *Testaments of the Twelve Patriarchs* follows this pattern.[461] Charlesworth comments: 'Philo and Josephus sought to adapt Judaism to the realities of Hellenistic culture ... [they] smoothed the boundaries between Judaism and the non-Jewish world.'[462]

Sly makes a similar point:

> By interpreting the Scripture of the Jews in terms of Platonic tradition of his day Philo of Alexandria made a profound contribution to the religious consciousness of the West ... [he] created a link between Jewish Scripture and Greek philosophy.[463]

Satlow sees weaknesses in Philo's analysis of Judaism but does not deny the influence of his ideas.[464]

7.6.2 The Edenic Marriage in Philo and Josephus

Loader believes the Genesis stories from the Septuagint appealed to the Greek mind and gave rise to a range of possible new meanings for those familiar with Plato; they would see Genesis 1:27 as being a reference to the making of an archetype, or in Platonic terms the idea of human kind.[465] He comments:

---

[459] Hengel believes that Josephus received the foundation of his Greek education in Jerusalem: Hengel, *The Hellenization of Judaea*, 11, 13

[460] Loader, *Making Sense of Sex*, 107, 109

[461] Loader, *Making Sense of Sex*, 117–19

[462] James H. Charlesworth and L. Loren Johns, eds., *Hillel and Jesus: Comparisons of Two Major Religious Leaders* (Minneapolis, MN: Fortress, 1997), 21

[463] Dorothy Sly, *Philo's Perception of Women* (BJS 209; Atlanta, GA: Scholars, 1990), v, 1

[464] Satlow, *Creating Judaism*, 101

[465] Loader, *Making Sense of Sex*, 17

> The most extensive interpretations of Greek Genesis are found in the voluminous writings of Philo. According to Philo, who was well versed in Platonic philosophy, God created the ideas or patterns for all things at the beginning of the first day of creation, and on the other days made the categories or species of each genus, including the genus, human being ... Philo takes up the Platonic notion of invisible "ideas" functioning as patterns after which the physical manifestations, the "real", are formed ... and employs it in his exposition of the Genesis stories.[466]

Philo makes many references to the sexual union of Genesis 2:24. In *Leg.* 2.49 he portrays it in a negative light:

> "On this account a man will leave his father and mother, cleave to his wife; and the two shall become one flesh." On account of the external sensation, the mind, when it has become enslaved to it, shall leave both its father, the God of the universe, and the mother of all things, namely, the virtue and wisdom of God, and cleaves to and becomes united to the external sensations, and is dissolved into external sensation, so that the two become one flesh and one passion. (*Leg.* 2.49)[467]

On the other hand in *Leg.* 2.51 Philo is more positive about the union:

> This man leaves his father and mother; that is to say, his mind and the material of his body, in order to have as his inheritance the one God; "For the Lord himself is his inheritance." (*Leg.* 2.51)

De opificio mundi 157 comments on Adam, Eve, and the serpent:

> And these things are not mere fabulous inventions, in which the race of poets and sophists delights, but are rather types shadowing forth some allegorical truth, according to some mystical explanation.[468]

---

[466] Loader, *Making Sense of Sex*, 20–21, 107

[467] Translations are from: Philo, *The Works of Philo,* trans. C. D. Yonge (Peabody, MA: Hendrickson, 1993)

[468] Evans reviews the literature on Philo's interpretation of biblical stories in light of his neoplatonic understanding (which he defines as: 'the view that what the physical senses perceive on earth below is but an

And in *Agr.* 97:

> But, in the allegorical explanations of these statements, all that bears a fabulous appearance is got rid of in a moment, and the truth is discovered in a most evident manner.

Sly comments that in Philo the drama of Eden is worked out in the experience of each individual and that:

> Primarily, all Philo's allegorical interpretation of the story is a development of that pattern ... Adam is the prototype of man as husband, Eve the prototype of woman as wife.[469]

Zimmermann points out that *On the Cherubim* develops an allegorical interpretation whereby the wives of the patriarchs are seen to be having their children by God's seed, for example:

> but Moses, who received Zipporah, that is to say, winged and sublime virtue, without any supplication or entreaty on his part, found that she conceived by no mortal man. (*Cher.* 47)

Zimmermann comments:

> In Philo's writings, transcendent metaphors of brides and marriage are clearly combined with the consequences of sexual asceticism for the first time. One who seeks to unite with wisdom and God should abstain from sensual, bodily pleasures during the earthly existence, remaining unsullied and virginal.[470]

Philo, while accepting that marriage included companionship, saw that the chief aim of intercourse was for propagation, and therefore deemed intercourse with sterile women as wasting seed and indulging sex merely for pleasure:

---

imperfect reflection of the true and perfect reality of heaven above') whereby Philo reads allegorical meanings into the narratives; he cites as an example *Sacr.* 5 where Abel represents a 'good doctrine' and Cain an 'evil doctrine': Craig A. Evans, *Ancient Texts for New Testament Studies* (Peabody, MA: Hendrickson, 2005), 168–70

[469] Sly, Philo's Perception of Women, 95

[470] Ruben Zimmermann, 'The Love Triangle of Lady Wisdom: Sacred Marriage in Jewish Wisdom Literature,' in Nissinen and Uro, *Sacred Marriages,* 256–57

> But those people deserve to be reproached who are ploughing a hard and stony soil. And who can these be but they who have connected themselves with barren women? For such men are only hunters after intemperate pleasure, and in the excess of their licentious passions they waste their seed of their own deliberate purpose. (*Spec. Laws* 3:34a)[471]

Although Josephus references the Edenic creation story (e.g. *Ant.* 1.27-51) this present study sees little evidence of a primal couple model in his writings. Loader believes that Adam's 'passionate desire to beget a family' (as he cites it) in *Ant.* 1.67 means that Josephus 'merges affirmation of sexual pleasure with affirmation of the role of sexual intercourse as propagation';[472] however, there is a clearer link made between sexual intercourse and propagation in *Ag. Ap.* 2.199:

> But then, what are our laws about marriage? That law owns no other mixture of sexes but that which nature hath appointed, of a man with his wife, and this be used only for the procreation of children.[473]

Josephus praises Antonia for not remarrying although widowed when young (*Ant.* 18.180); and expresses his admiration for the Essenes, including their supposed celibacy, but his admiration is seemingly for their dedication to their religion, not so much for their celibacy *per se* (*Ant.* 18.18–22).

7.6.3 Contra-Indications of an Edenic Marriage in Philo and Josephus

Instone-Brewer considers that by New Testament times in the Graeco-Roman world divorce was common; men and women could divorce at will without citing any grounds although there were financial penalties if adultery was

---

[471] However, Loader sees that Philo believes: 'Neither woman nor sexual intercourse with its accompanying passion and pleasure is itself evil': William R. G. Loader, *Philo, Josephus, and the Testaments on Sexuality: Attitudes Towards Sexuality in the Writings of Philo and Josephus and in the Testaments of the Twelve Patriarchs* (Grand Rapids, MI: Eerdmans, 2011), 30

[472] Loader, Making Sense of Sex, 131

[473] Flavius Josephus, *Josephus: The Complete Works,* trans. William Whiston (Nashville, TN: Thomas Nelson, 1998), 966

involved.⁴⁷⁴ Josephus states that Salome (the sister of Herod the Great) initiated her own divorce of her husband Costobarus (*Ant.* 15.259-60). Epstein believes the issue Josephus references here was that Roman law acknowledged a bill of divorce from a wife whereas the Jewish courts did not—but that there was not a problem in (talmudic) Jewish law with a wife initiating a divorce.⁴⁷⁵ Josephus himself it seems had three marriages and two divorces (*Life* 414-30)—Rabello makes the point that as Josephus always took care to present himself well it can only be assumed that he perceived that his actions were in conformity with traditional Judaism.⁴⁷⁶ Josephus reflects on the Deuteronomy 24:1-4 divorce legislation and the rabbinic debate as recorded in *m. Git.* 9:10, seemingly without disapproval of the relaxed Hillelite position (§10.3.2):

> He that desires to be divorced from his wife for any cause whatsoever (and many such courses happen among men), let him in writing give assurance that he will never use her as his wife anymore; for by this mean she may be at liberty to marry another husband, although before this bill of divorce be given, she is not permitted so to do. (*Ant.* 4.253)⁴⁷⁷

Josephus' account of Herod's wives (*Ant.* 17.19-23) is given as if it reflects Jewish custom and something to be valued; however, Loader believes polygyny declined because it was not fashionable in Hellenistic and Roman culture.⁴⁷⁸ Another contra-indication of an Edenic model and a more pragmatic approach to marriage is the levirate teaching of the Old Testament (Deut 25:5-10) which is repeated in *Ant.* 4.254-56, but Josephus adds that if the widow's brother-in-law refuses to take her in marriage she is free to marry 'whom she pleases,' reflecting the teaching as recorded in *m. Git.* 9:2-3.

This present study is not aware of any contra-indications of an Edenic marriage model in the works of Philo.

---

⁴⁷⁴ Instone-Brewer, *Divorce and Remarriage*, 72-74

⁴⁷⁵ Epstein, *The Jewish Marriage Contract*, 203

⁴⁷⁶ Alfredo Mordechai Rabello, 'Divorce of Jews in the Roman Empire,' in *The Jewish Law Annual* Vol. 4, ed. B. S. Jackson (Leiden: Brill, 1981), 95

⁴⁷⁷ Josephus, *Josephus*, 142

⁴⁷⁸ Loader, *Making Sense of Sex*, 52-53; similarly: Satlow, *Jewish Marriage*, 58-67

7.6.4 Summary: Philo and Josephus

The Hellenistic mind seems to have found the Edenic narrative and the primal couple a fruitful source of speculation, and Satlow's claim that they emerge as a human marriage archetype in Second Temple literature (§7.1) is seen to be vindicated, at least with reference to the works of Philo.

7.7 Summary: The Literature of the Second Temple Period

The review of the literature undertaken in this chapter appears to suggest, even though the evidence as Satlow comments is 'scattered and scanty,' that the Edenic model (with the five posited indicators as outlined in §5.1: God ordains each marriage; marriage is perceived to have a supernatural dimension; no polygyny or divorce; coitus primarily for procreation; celibacy linked with holiness)—had its origin in the intertestamental period in a synthesis of the Genesis story with neoplatonic concepts.

There appears to be an academic consensus that Palestinian Jews of the first century CE were acquainted with the Greek teachers and philosophers but it is unclear how much they were influenced by them. Chapter 8 will examine the available documentary evidence to see if the concept of an Edenic marriage model referenced in the literature was reflected in marital practice in the Second Temple period, either within Judaism, or in the wider Graeco-Roman world.

Chapter 8: The Documents of the Second Temple Period

8.1 Introduction

Chapter 5 considered mundane marriage and divorce teaching in the Old Testament, as it was suggested that without an understanding of this teaching, Old Testament marital imagery cannot be understood. Subsequently the analysis of Old Testament marital imagery in chapter 6 demonstrated that the target map of the imagery (the divine marriage of Yahweh and Israel) closely mirrored mundane marriage as evidenced in both the Old Testament narratives and marital legislation. In chapter 7 we looked for evidence of a primal couple model of mundane marriage in the literature of the Second Temple period and found only limited evidence for this.

Before considering marital imagery in the New Testament (chapter 9) this chapter will survey the New Testament social context as evidenced in the extant archaeological data. Metaphors rely on the utilisation of a vehicle within the experience of their intended audience. A marriage which only existed as a theoretical concept (e.g. a marriage based on an Edenic/neoplatonic model) cannot serve meaningfully as a source map for the imagery, since the source domain needs to reflect a social reality to achieve a meaningful transfer to the target domain.

Furthermore, the source domain of the metaphoric imagery has to possess the characteristics of the imagery that it seeks to portray. It will be seen that New Testament marital imagery is based on a volitional, conditional covenant embracing the concept of divorce and remarriage. Thus evidence in the Graeco-Roman world of the Second Temple period of a volitional, conditional, mundane marriage covenant, embracing the concept of divorce and remarriage, will be taken to mean that that is the source domain of the imagery—not an Edenic/neoplatonic understanding of marriage. This chapter will also look for evidence of other features in contemporary mundane marriage which are present in New Testament marital imagery, including betrothal, *mohar*, and a groom's maintenance clause, in order to identify further cross-mapping.

8.2 The Elephantine Documents

8.2.1 Introduction

In 1907 a large body of papyri was discovered at Elephantine, an island in the Nile on the southern border of Egypt, which was the location of a military colony housing Jewish mercenaries working for the Persians.[479] The documents (dating from the fifth century BCE) include a betrothal contract and seven Aramaic marriage contracts (four are fragmentary); there are no divorce certificates but there are two documents concerning payment of a divorce settlement.

8.2.2 Relevance of the Elephantine Documents

This Jewish community was remote from Jerusalem and evidenced a syncretism in their religious and social practices—they seem to have been subject to various influences including Aramean, Babylonian, Egyptian, Persian, and Greek.[480] Despite this Porten sees the community as essentially Jewish;[481] and several believe the documents do have something to contribute to an understanding of marriage and divorce in ancient Israel.[482]

The three complete marriage documents use a standard wording. Instone-Brewer believes it is safe to assume this was the norm for the Elephantine community and points out the similarities to extant ANE marriage contracts, except that they grant 'equal rights to divorce, equal inheritance rights, equal

---

[479] Bezalel Porten, *Archives from Elephantine: The Life of an Ancient Jewish Military Colony* (Berkeley: University of California, 1968), vii; Matthews and Benjamin, *Old Testament Parallels*, 210

[480] Porten, *Archives from Elephantine*, ix-x, 173-86; De Vaux claims, 'they practised a syncretistic religion which the Prophets had condemned': Roland De Vaux, *Ancient Israel: Its Life and Institutions* (London: Darton, Longman & Todd, 1961), 340; Grabbe points out they had their own temple despite such being forbidden in the Pentateuch: Lester L. Grabbe, *Introduction to Second Temple Judaism: History and Religion of the Jews in the Time of Nehemiah, the Maccabees, Hillel, and Jesus* (London: T&T Clark, 2010), 4-5

[481] Porten, *Archives from Elephantine*, 173

[482] For example: Mordechai A. Friedman, 'Termination of the Marriage upon the Wife's Request: A Palestinian *Ketubba* Stipulation,' *PAAJR* 37 (1969), 31-33, 55; 'The Elephantine Papyri and Hosea 2, 3: Evidence for the Form of the Early Jewish Divorce Writ'; Markham J. Geller, *Journal for the Study of Judaism in the Persian, Hellenistic, and Roman Periods* 8 (1977), 139-48; Tal Ilan, 'On a Newly Published Divorce Bill from the Judaean Desert,' *HTR* Vol. 89, No. 2 (April 1996), 201; Kelle, *Hosea 2*, 72-78; Lipiński, 'Divorce,' in Jackson, *The Jewish Law Annual*, 21-27

conjugal rights, and equal rights to demand monogamy from their spouse.'[483] These features are seen in the Contract of Miphtahiah's Third Marriage (Cowley, 15)[484] which states:

> Should Ashor [the husband] die tomorrow ... Miphtahiah shall be entitled to the house, chattels and all worldly goods of Ashor.... Should Miphtahiah die tomorrow ... Ashor shall inherit her property and chattels ... I [Ashor] shall have no right to say I have another wife besides Mipht<ah>iah.[485]

Instone-Brewer concludes that the documents are:

> a strange mixture of ancient Near Eastern forms and trends in the Greco-Roman world.... The rarity of documents surviving from that period makes it impossible to conclude how common these developments were.[486]

Thus Instone-Brewer believes that these marriage contracts are somewhat dissimilar to later Jewish marriage contracts and suggests that the Elephantine community had lost most of their Jewish roots.[487] Those that agree with this analysis include Archer:

> While of great interest in themselves, [they] furnish no real proof for the existence of similar deeds within Judaea. Their origin is probably to be seen in terms of Egyptian practice, and as such their history and development must be regarded as independent of any (alleged) Judaean innovation.[488]

And Bickerman:

> It is true that in the marriage contracts of Elephantine (fifth century B.C.), the effects which the bride brings into her new home are named

---

[483] Instone-Brewer, *Divorce and Remarriage*, 75–80
[484] The 'Cowley' designations are as per: A. E. Cowley, ed., *Aramaic Papyri of the Fifth Century B.C.* (Oxford: Oxford University Press, 1923)
[485] All translations of the Elephantine documents are from: James B. Pritchard, ed., *Ancient Near Eastern Texts Relating to the Old Testament*, with supplement 3rd ed. (Princeton, NJ: Princeton University Press, 1969)
[486] Instone-Brewer, *Divorce and Remarriage*, 80
[487] Instone-Brewer, *Divorce and Remarriage*, 78–80
[488] Archer, Her Price is Beyond Rubies, 172

and evaluated. These documents however, though the parties are Jewish, follow the common law of Aramaic scribes and notaries, and do not necessarily represent the development of Jewish law.[489]

Despite these difficulties Lemos considers that the documents justify a detailed study to see how they correlate with wider Judaean customs.[490] Both Geller and Kelle see the marital practices at Elephantine underpin an understanding of Hosea, Kelle commenting:

> these texts from the Jewish colony ... are an important window into the continuing application of customs that stretch back to eighth-century Israel.[491]

Although opinion is divided over the usefulness of the documents for gaining an understanding of Jewish marriage and divorce, this present study considers a brief consideration of the features relevant to this study is justified.

8.2.3 Betrothal and Marriage Payments

Greengus refers to the 'prenuptial provisions' evidenced in the papyri and in this they are similar to the JDD.[492] Lemos believes that two (possibly three) of the marriage documents refer to the *mohar,* but she sees it is a token amount outstripped by the value of the dowry, and further suggests that the money goes to the bride and so considers it an indirect dowry.[493]

In the Contract of Mibtahiah's First Marriage (Cowley, 9) the father of the wife gifts a house, on the condition that the husband:

> may not sell that house or give it as a present to others; only your children by my daughter Mibtahiah shall have power over it after you two. If ... my daughter divorces you and leaves you, you shall have no

---

[489] Bickerman, 'Two Legal Interpretations of the Septuagint,' in Tropper, *Studies in Jewish and Christian History*, 199–201

[490] Lemos, *Marriage Gifts*, 63

[491] Kelle, *Hosea 2*, 73; Markham. J. Geller, 'The Elephantine Papyri and Hosea 2, 3: Evidence for the Form of the Early Jewish Divorce Writ,' *JSJ* 8 (1977), 147

[492] Greengus, *Laws in the Bible*, 38

[493] Lemos, *Marriage Gifts*, 69

> power to take it or give it to others; only your children by Mibtahiah shall have power over it.

In Cowley, 15 the groom goes to his bride's father's house and states: 'I have given you as the bride-price of your daughter Miphtahiah (a sum of) 5 shekels.'

8.2.4 Divorce and Remarriage

The documents suggest that divorce and remarriage was accepted practice at Elephantine.[494] Instone-Brewer sees that the most unusual feature in the papyri is the right granted to the wife to enact an oral divorce.[495] Cowley, 15 has: 'Should [Miph]tahiah, tomorrow [or] another [d]ay stand up in a congregation and say, I divorce my husband Ashor, the price of divorce shall be upon her head.'

Porten comments:

> The only right of the Jewish woman at Elephantine not clearly evident in the Bible was that of divorce, but it would be hazardous to say that such a right never existed.[496]

Lipiński similarly sees this divorce right as belonging to a genuine Semitic tradition and believes that any evidence of such in the later Egyptian contracts written in Greek stem from that influence and concludes that the Jewish colony 'cannot be treated as though they were an isolated episode in the history of Oriental law.'[497]

8.2.5 Summary: The Elephantine Documents

The pragmatic contractual nature of the marriages, negotiated between the bridegroom and the bride's father, the payment of a *mohar* by the groom, and the availability of divorce as a remedy for a failed marriage, all evidenced in the papyri, support Porten's claim (§8.2.4) that, notwithstanding some

---

[494] Pritchard comments on Cowley, 14 (not a divorce certificate, but a record of the payment of a divorce settlement) that Mibtahiah's first marriage had been dissolved: Pritchard, *The Ancient Near East*, 491

[495] Instone-Brewer, *Divorce and Remarriage*, 79

[496] Porten, *Archives from Elephantine*, 261

[497] Lipiński, 'Divorce,' in Jackson, *The Jewish Law Annual*, 21–26

idiosyncrasies, they do reflect Old Testament marital practice. There is no evidence in the papyri of a neoplatonic concept of marriage.

8.3 The Judaean Desert Documents

8.3.1 Introduction

The eight marriage and two divorce papyri under consideration are listed in the table in Appendix B which includes their SBL nomenclature, their most usual former sigla, presumed date of origin, language, date discovered, and first publication date. Appendix C gives a brief description of each document and a translation. They cover a period 72 CE to 131 CE and thus are contemporaneous with the redaction of the New Testament. Cotton suggests that in the absence of the Sanhedrin the marriage contracts in the papyri endeavoured to encapsulate the Jewish understanding of marriage into civil law in the rapidly changing legal situation that existed within Judaism after the destruction of the Temple.[498]

Cotton and Eck, when speaking of the Naḥal Ḥever documents, state:

> No doubt the drastic curtailment of Jewish judicial independence—expressed *inter alia* in the dissolution of the Sanhedrin—in the wake of the suppression of the revolt of 66–70 made it all the more necessary to have recourse to a Roman court of law.[499]

Katzoff and Schaps et al. believe that:

> Here for the first time one has written evidence on events, private events, of that era as presented by private individuals ... for the history of the Jews it is if anything more compelling [than the Qumran discoveries], giving us for the first time a non-rabbinic window on the actual lives and transactions of people.[500]

---

[498] Hannah M. Cotton, 'The Languages of the Legal and Administrative Documents from the Judaean Desert,' *ZPE* 118 (1997), 230–31

[499] Hannah M. Cotton and Werner Eck, 'Roman Officials in Judaea and Arabia and Civil Jurisdiction,' in *Law in the Documents of the Judaean Desert,* ed. Ranon Katzoff and David Schaps (Leiden: Brill, 2005), 36

[500] Ranon Katzoff and David Schaps, eds., *Law in the Documents of the Judaean Desert* (Leiden: Brill, 2005), 1–2;

Cotton states:

> [XḤev/Se 69] was written in the province of Judaea and not in Arabia, but we should not overlook the essential unity of the Jewish society reflected in all the papyri from the Judaean Desert, whether they originate in Arabia or in Judaea.[501]

The place names in the documents are mainly from the eastern Judaean hill country.[502] Cotton comments:

> I maintain ... that they are representative of Jewish society as a whole in the period under discussion. They present a faithful picture of the realities of life at the time that they were written.[503]

Thus, although post-dating the Second Temple period, they are thought to accurately reflect Jewish marriage practices of that era and so are considered in this chapter.

8.3.2 Background to the Judaean Desert Documents

In November 1951 Roland De Vaux was offered fragments of papyri that he was told had come from the vicinity of Qumran. In the following January the trail led to the Wadi Murabba'at, a ravine which runs from the Judaean desert east of Bethlehem to the Dead Sea, some 25 km south east of Jerusalem and 18 km to the south of the first of the Qumran caves.[504] In the subsequent excavations at the Wadi Murabba'at, one papyrus was found that documented a divorce, and four that documented marriages. All of them dated from the first and second centuries CE. They were published in Benoit et al. in 1961 and subsequently catalogued as Mur 19, Mur 20, Mur 21, Mur 115, and Mur 116.

---

also: Satlow, *Jewish Marriage*, 100

[501] Hannah M. Cotton, 'A Cancelled Marriage Contract from the Judaean Desert,' *JRS* Vol. 84 (1994), 65

[502] Safrai analyses the geography of the documents: Ze'ev Safrai, 'Halakhic Observance in the Judaean Desert,' in Katzoff and Schaps, *Law in the Documents of the Judaean Desert*, 206–11

[503] Hannah M. Cotton, 'The Rabbis and the Documents,' in Martin Goodman, ed., *Jews in a Graeco-Roman World* (Oxford: Oxford University Press, 1998), 172–73

[504] Pierre Benoit, Jozef T. Milik, and Roland De Vaux, *Discoveries in the Judaean Desert II: Les Grottes de Murabba'at* (Oxford: Oxford University Press, 1961), 3–7

In August 1952 Bedouin handed in other papyri, including the Greek cancelled marriage document now catalogued as XḤev/Se 69 and first published in 1994. In 1956 Jozef T. Milik, an associate of De Vaux, said that he possessed a further divorce papyrus.[505] It was thought, like XḤev/Se 69, to be from Wadi Seiyal (otherwise known as Naḥal Se'elim) which is 25 km south of Wadi Murabba'at and 4 km north of Masada; this document (XḤev/Se 13) was first published by Yardeni in Hebrew in 1995, and by Cotton and Yardeni in English in 1997.[506] It is now believed that most, if not all the documents that were initially thought to have come from Naḥal Se'elim, actually originated in Naḥal Ḥever (20 km south of Wadi Murabba'at).[507]

8.3.3 The Relevance of Written Marriage Contracts

Instone-Brewer comments that most marriages in the ancient Near East were enacted by verbal ceremony without any written contract.[508] Satlow points out that the written contract did not make the marriage:

> These contracts were almost certainly not constitutive of marriage: the marriage existed with or without the document. All marriage contracts in antiquity, whether Jewish or not, focused primarily on economic relations, occasionally giving some attention to the way that spouses should treat each other. The purpose of Jewish marriage documents was not to create the marriage, but to clarify and codify economic obligations within it. A woman (and her family), for example, wanted a concrete, legally actionable guarantee that her dowry would be returned or passed to her (male) children when the marriage ended. She wanted assurance that her husband would provide her with

---

[505] Jozef T. Milik, 'Le travail d'edition des manuscript du Desert de Juda,' *VTSup* 4 (1956), 21

[506] Ada Yardeni, *Naḥal Se'elim Documents (Hebrew)* (Israel: Ben-Gurion University of the Negev Press & the Israel Exploration Society, 1995); Hannah M. Cotton and Ada Yardeni, 'Aramaic, Hebrew and Greek Documentary Texts from Naḥal Ḥever and Other Sites: With an Appendix Containing Alleged Qumran Texts The Seiyâl Collection II' in *Discoveries in the Judaean Desert* XXVII, ed. Emmanuel Tov (Oxford: Oxford University Press, 1997)

[507] Evans, *Ancient Texts*, 139; Hannah M. Cotton, 'The Archive of Salome Komaïse Daughter of Levi: Another Archive from the "Cave of Letters",' *ZPE* 105 (1995), 171

[508] Instone-Brewer, *Divorce and Remarriage*, 11

> clothing and food. The marriage contract was a civil contract that ordered these relations.[509]

Thus it cannot be assumed that written contracts were the norm, but Archer, on the basis of the written bill of divorce in Deuteronomy 24, speculates that written instruments in connection with marriage were not unusual.[510]

8.3.4 The Significance of Greek Language and Legal Instruments

Instone-Brewer comments:

> Palestinian Jews in the first two centuries used both the Greek and Aramaic languages in their marriage documentation ... both appeared to have equal standing. The most likely reason for using a Greek form of contract is greater legal respectability and perhaps enforceability.[511]

Cotton states:

> the use of Greek by Jews has no ideological implications: it should not be mistaken for the hellenization of the writer nor be taken as evidence for his political and national sentiments.[512]

And that: 'The Babatha Archive has taught us that the resort to Greek in legal documents does not reveal Hellenized Jews: their signatures and subscriptions in Aramaic prove the opposite.'[513]

While Cotton suggests that the use of the Greek language does not indicate Hellenisation she nonetheless believes that the resulting marriage contracts had non-Jewish elements, for example, the obligation in 5/6Ḥev 37 for the groom to follow Greek law and custom in providing for children to come. Thus she believes the document cannot be described as a Jewish *ketubah*;[514] she

---

[509] Satlow, *Jewish Marriage*, 84

[510] Archer, *Her Price is Beyond Rubies*, 171

[511] David Instone-Brewer, '1 Corinthians 7 in the Light of the Jewish Greek and Aramaic Marriage and Divorce Papyri,' *TynBul* 52.2 (2001), 230

[512] Cotton, 'The Languages of the Documents,' 228

[513] Cotton, 'A Cancelled Marriage Contract,' 77

[514] Cotton, 'The Archive of Salome Komaïse,' 206

makes similar comments about 5/6Hev 18: 'These Jews felt free to use legal forms which went together with the use of the Greek language.'[515]

Katzoff accepts that there was a synthesis of elements in his analysis of 5/6Hev 18 but believes that Jewish elements dominate;[516] it seems the dowry is a feature from Greek marital practices (§8.3.5) and Lewis sees evidence of it in this papyrus.[517] However, Katzoff suggests any overlapping similarities with other cultures are not necessarily a sign that Jewish families were importing other influences into their own marriage beliefs and practice.[518] Wasserstein speculates (like Cotton) that Jewish families had two contracts drawn up, a traditional Jewish *ketubah,* and a separate contract for the Greek courts;[519] however, he believes 5/6Hev 18 is a typically Greek-style contract *contra* Katzoff.[520]

8.3.5 Betrothal and Marriage Payments

Lemos comments that the giving of a *mohar* is not well evidenced in the Hellenistic period (although, like Satlow, she sees evidence of betrothal in Matt 1:18–19).[521] The financial transactions in the documents are ambiguous due in part to their fragmentary nature, it is not always clear if any payment from the groom to the bride is in the tradition of the *mohar* (§5.5); or a *ketubah*, where the payment is in effect a delayed *mohar* claimable on a dissolution of the marriage. Cotton sees evidence of a *ketubah* tradition in 5/6Hev 10, *contra* Satlow: '[in the JDD] there is not a single unambiguous reference to the *ketubah* payment.'[522] Furthermore, scholars differ over the terminology to be used: for example, Satlow calls a payment to the bride from the groom in

---

[515] Cotton, 'A Cancelled Marriage Contract,' 84
[516] Naphtali Lewis, Ranon Katzoff, and Jonas C. Greenfield, 'Papyrus Yadin 18,' *IEJ* 37 (1987), 236
[517] Lewis, Katzoff, and Greenfield, 'Papyrus Yadin 18,' 230–34
[518] Ranon Katzoff, 'Papyrus Yadin 18 Again: A Rejoinder,' *JQR* 82 (1991), 172
[519] Wasserstein, 'A Marriage Contract,' 120–21
[520] Wasserstein, 'A Marriage Contract,' 108
[521] Lemos, *Marriage Gifts*, 83, 87–88; Satlow, *Jewish Marriage*, 71–73
[522] Cotton, 'A Cancelled Marriage Contract,' 82–83; Michael L. Satlow, 'Reconsidering the Rabbinic *Ketubah* Payment,' in *The Jewish Family in Antiquity,* ed. Shaye J. D. Cohen (Atlanta, GA: Brown Judaic Studies, 1993), 137

5/6Hev 18, rather than a *mohar*, a 'dowry addition'—while Lemos calls the payment there, and in 5/6Hev 10, an 'indirect dowry.'[523]

However, what is significant for this study is the evidence of any payments made or promised by the groom to secure his bride—Cotton sees such payments as the key to determine whether or not a marriage was 'Jewish.'[524] Instone-Brewer says when referring to the Aramaic 5/6Hev 10: 'As in all Jewish Aramaic and Hebrew contracts, the main financial transaction is a gift from the groom, not from the bride's family.'[525]

In the Greek contracts Cotton suggests that four of the five reference dowries, including 5/6Hev 18. In that document, although a payment clearly goes from the groom to the bride, she seems reluctant to accept it as evidence of a Jewish *mohar* or a *ketubah* addition.[526]

The relevant section has:

> Cimber [the bridegroom] ... owes Shelamzion his wife ... three hundred denarii which he promised to give her in addition to the sum of her aforestated bridal gift, all accounted toward her dowry, pursuant to his undertaking of feeding and clothing both her and the children to come.[527]

But Yiftach-Firanko believes that this payment is not typical of a Greek contract:

> Considering the financial transactions brought about by the marriage, we find a completely different mechanism in the Judaean documents from that known in the contemporary Greek papyri from Egypt ... the Judaean documents show two crucial peculiarities. First is the husband's obligation to the bride of 150% of the value of her dowry, documented in line 13-15 of Yadin 18 [5/6Hev 18]. A contribution on

---

[523] Satlow, *Jewish Marriage*, 201–02; Lemos, *Marriage Gifts*, 87

[524] Cotton, 'A Cancelled Marriage Contract,' 82; Archer also points out that, alongside the change from *mohar* to *ketubah* rabbinic Judaism also accepted the dowry into the marriage contract: Archer, *Her Price is Beyond Rubies*, 168–70; for *ketubah* see §7.5.3.

[525] Instone-Brewer, '1 Corinthians 7 in the Light of the Jewish Papyri,' 232

[526] Cotton, 'A Cancelled Marriage Contract,' 83–84

[527] All translations of the JDD are as per Appendix C.

the part of the husband is not evident in Egypt before the fourth century CE. It seems that even in Arabia it was not a well-known institution, for the author of Yadin 18 does not seem to have been able to find an appropriate legal term for it.[528]

However, Lemos sees that a decline of the *mohar* in the Second Temple period is demonstrated in the JDD and Bickerman accepts that by the second century CE the 'alien' dowry had become an accepted fact in Jewish marriage.[529]

In summary, it can be said that although there was no clear dowry system in the Old Testament (§5.5) such a marriage payment came into Jewish marriage customs in the intertestamental period and that this is the situation reflected in the marriage papyri under consideration. In this matter the Jewish community reflected Greek practice, but it seems in some marriages the groom had also made a payment to secure his bride.

8.3.6 The Groom's Maintenance Clause

An element cross-mapped in biblical marital imagery is the mundane groom's obligation to maintain his new bride. The wording of the groom's maintenance clause obligating the groom to clothe and feed (and in some contracts provide conjugal relations for) his wife appears to originate in Exodus 21:10.[530] Instone-Brewer says of the documents: 'All of them contain a phrase referring to the obligation to clothe and feed. Like Greco-Roman contracts, these obligations are incumbent only on the man.'[531] An analysis confirms this:

> Mur 20:
>
> 3.   You shall be my wife according to the law of Mo[ses ... and me I shall feed and clothe you, from today for]

---

[528] Uri Yiftach-Firanko, 'Judaean Desert Marriage Documents and *Ekdosis* in the Greek Law of the Roman Period,' in Katzoff and Schaps, *Law in the Documents of the Judaean Desert*, 81–82

[529] Lemos, *Marriage Gifts*, 87; Bickerman, 'Two Legal Interpretations of the Septuagint,' in Tropper, *Studies in Jewish and Christian History*, 202–3

[530] Thus: Yigael Yadin et al., eds., *The Documents from the Bar Kokhba Period in the Cave of Letters: Hebrew, Aramaic and Nabatean-Aramaic Papyri* (Jerusalem: Israel Exploration Society, 2002), 134–35

[531] Instone-Brewer, *Divorce and Remarriage*, 215

4. Always, from my property and upon [me is the duty of/I am giving you the *mohar* of your virginity ...].

The reconstruction is supported by lines 9 and 10:

9. Until marriage. Or if I [go] to the house [of eternity before you, you will dwell ...]

10. And you will be nourished and clothed [all the days, in the house of our children throughout the time of].

Mur 21:

11. According to the law, th[ey a]re to live [in] my house and [be] nourished fr[om my possessions ... until]

12. To marriage [and even a]fter [me (my death) wi]th you until their marriage. [I]f you [go] to [the House of eternity] bef[ore me].

In Mur 115 Eleaios (the groom) acknowledges receipt of the dowry that will be used to help maintain his wife Salome:

8. And against (?) his goods. If [...] and of the children which she has and which she may have

9. By him, sons and daughters that [...] that she may have by him, they will be nourished and clothed with the help of

10. The goods that the same Eleaios [...] If at the same Eleaios son of Simon happens to die before the same

11. Salome or if she [... it will nourish and clothe Sa]lome with the help of the goods [...] the above.

Mur 116 has a similar groom's provision as that of Mur 20 and it seems reasonable to accept this also as evidence of a lifetime responsibility for the husband:

8. ... If Aurelios before Salo-

9. me happens to die Salome will be nourished and clothed from the

10. Fortune of Aurelios all the time that she wishes to remain a widow.

XHev/Se 69 acknowledges the dowry and states:

> 10. wedded (wife) so that Selampious is nourished and cloth[ed ... upon the security of all his posse-
>
> 11. ssions both those which he has now and those which he will acquire. And in the event of the death of
>
> 12. [ ] the male children or if heirs
>
> 13. [ ] the daughters will be nourished and clothed[
>
> 14. [ ] and if he who is mentioned before[
>
> 15. [ ] five hundred denarii.

5/6Hev 10 (italics indicate that the Aramaic is uncertain):

> 5. as a wif[e (**or:** in wife[hood) according to the la]w of Moses and the J[u]daeans. And I will [feed] you and cl[othe] you (**or:** and I will re[mit] to you, pursuant to your *mo*[*har*]), and pursuant to your *ketubba*, I will bring you into (my house).
>
> 6. And you have a binding claim on me (for) silver (in the amount of) four hundred denarii (*zuzin*), which equal one hundred T[y]rian (tetradrachms), whatever
>
> 7. she (!=you) may wish to take and to ... from the *dowry*, together with the rightful allocation of your food, and your clothing and your *bed*,

5/6Hev 18:

> Judah called Cimber acknowledged that he has received from her by hand forthwith from Judah her father and owes Shelamzion his wife together with another three hundred denarii which he promised to give her in addition to the sum of her aforestated bridal gift, all accounted toward her dowry, pursuant to his undertaking of feeding and clothing both her and the children to come.

5/6Ḥev 37:

> Yeshuʻa, acknowledged that he has received from her on the present day feminine adornment in silver and gold and clothing and other feminine articles equivalent in appraised value to the [stated sum of] money, with his undertaking to feed and clothe both her and her children to come.

It seems the husband's duty to maintain his bride in his life-time was presumed, thus much of the comment in the papyri is on the husband's liability for this after the death of either partner, possibly because such is not articulated in Exodus 21:10.

8.3.7 Divorce and Remarriage

Mur 19 is certainly a divorce certificate; XḤev/Se 13 is either a divorce certificate, or the renunciation of claims in the aftermath of a divorce; Mur 20 and Mur 21 mention what is to happen in the event of a divorce; Mur 115 is the remarriage of a couple after they had been divorced. Thus five of the ten papyri unambiguously reference divorce. Satlow, based on other documents in the Babatha archive, speculates that Salome Komaïse, the bride in 5/6Ḥev 37 had divorced her previous husband.[532] XḤev/Se 69 is a cancelled marriage contract—either cancelled on the death of one of the partners or after a divorce, and 5/6Ḥev 18 also appears to reference divorce (as below). Satlow comments:

> It is possible that the relatively numerous testimonies in these documents to divorce are a function of ancient source preservation—that is, divorce was accompanied by documents that both parties want to save—but it is also likely that divorce among these Jews was neither difficult nor uncommon.[533]

The wording of Mur 19 appears to make the right to remarriage after divorce clear: 'you [the divorced wife] are free to go and become the wife of any Jewish

---

[532] Satlow, *Jewish Marriage*, 99–100

[533] Michael L. Satlow, 'Marriage Payments and Succession Strategies in the Documents from the Judaean Desert,' in Katzoff and Schaps, *Law in the Documents of the Judaean Desert*, 60

man that you wish.' Instone-Brewer comments that the purpose of the divorce certificate was to enable the woman to remarry.[534] Epstein endorses this position.[535] As regards wife-initiated divorces there is ambiguity in 5/6Hev 18 and Katzoff comments:

> The phrase [in 5/6Hev 18], 'whenever she may demand it of him,' it has been suggested, is intended to provide the woman with a right to divorce on demand, a right, so it is claimed, recognized by the Jewish community in talmudic times ... unfortunately discussion of this issue has suffered from a lack of such clarity as might have been achieved by the use of strictly defined terms. It is necessary to distinguish between the notions of 'power' and 'right'.... In the rabbinic law of divorce, then, only the husband has the *power* to divorce. That is to say, only the action of the husband by his own will can effect a divorce, by delivering to the wife a properly written and witnessed bill of divorce. His action is both necessary and sufficient. No action on the part of the woman can effect a divorce.... On the other hand, under certain conditions, the wife may have a *right* to divorce, that is, may expect the courts on her behalf to require the husband to exercise his power to divorce her.[536]

So Katzoff is not persuaded that the wording in 5/6Hev 18 refers to a wife's power to divorce. Nonetheless his point about the difference between the 'power' and the 'right' is an important one—and one Brody endorses.[537] As regards XHev/Se 13 there are three positions:

1. The document is a renunciation of a wife's claim on her husband after he has divorced her.

---

[534] Instone-Brewer, *Divorce and Remarriage*, 28
[535] Epstein, *The Jewish Marriage Contract*, 200
[536] Lewis, Katzoff, and Greenfield, 'Papyrus Yadin 18,' 243–44
[537] Robert Brody, 'Evidence for Divorce by Jewish Women,' *JJS* L, No. 2 (Autumn 1999), 230. At the time of writing this present study neither a husband nor a wife in the UK legal system has the power to divorce, such being vested in the courts—but both have a right to a divorce.

2. The document is a renunciation of a wife's claim on her husband after she has divorced him.

3. The document is a divorce certificate issued by a wife to her husband.

The first is favoured by Brody; the second by Cotton, and the third by Instone-Brewer and Ilan.[538] Ilan is particularly persuasive in presenting her position, which takes into account the views expressed in a debate about this papyrus in the *Harvard Theological Review*.[539]

Satlow appears to agree with the thrust of Ilan's thesis in that he suggests that a wife could initiate (if not enact) a divorce in the pre-rabbinic period and that this right was removed in later rabbinic Judaism.[540] However, if Ilan's thesis about XḤev/Se 13 is accepted, would any suitor be convinced by such a certificate signed by a wife? If the certificate was subsequently repudiated by her former husband, or otherwise disputed, the new husband would *de facto* be guilty of adultery. It might be thought any prospective husband, to obviate such a risk, would seek some confirmation from the former husband of the validity of the certificate thus casting doubt on the practical usefulness of such.

If Katzoff's point about the difference between the power and the right to divorce is taken into account it means that Cotton, Ilan, Instone-Brewer, and Satlow all see that wife-initiated divorces were possible at this time and demonstrated to be so in the papyri under consideration.

---

[538] Brody, 'Evidence for Divorce by Jewish Women,' 230–34; Hannah M. Cotton and Elisha Qimron, 'XḤev/Se ar 13 of 134 or 135 C.E: A Wife's Renunciation of Claims,' *Journal of Jewish Studies* 49 (1998), 108–18; Instone-Brewer, *Divorce and Remarriage*, 88–89; Tal Ilan, *Integrating Women into Second Temple History* (Peabody, MA: Hendrickson, 2001), 253–62

[539] Ilan, *Integrating Women*, 253–62; Tal Ilan, 'The Provocative Approach Once Again: A Response to Adiel Schremer,' *HTR* Vol. 91, No. 2 (April 1998), 203–04; Tal Ilan, 'A Correction: On a Newly Published Divorce Bill from the Judaean Desert,' *HTR* Vol. 90, No. 2 (April 1997), 225; Tal Ilan, 'On a Newly Published Divorce Bill from the Judaean Desert,' *HTR* Vol. 89, No. 2 (April 1996), 195–202

[540] 'In ancient Semitic law, and among Jews in the prerabbinic period, the right of divorce was bilateral: a husband or wife could initiate a divorce. Some (most?) Jews in first-century Palestine may have also allowed a woman to initiate a divorce.... It seems probable to me that when tannaitic law deprived Jewish women of their right to initiate divorce, *it also attempted to compensate for this loss by offering the protection of the* ketubba *payment*': Satlow, *Jewish Marriage*, 214

8.3.8 Summary: The Judaean Desert Documents

Any syncretism apparent in the Greek marriage papyri that the Jewish families signed is only meaningful for the purposes of this study if it could be demonstrated that the contracts indicated they had departed from ancient Israel's marital practices in a significant way. Certainly the dowry is an alien import, but it can be seen from the papyri that the focus of the marriage documents is on the groom's material support of his bride—the marriage payments were, it seems, simply a means to that end. Although this support for the wife was not a specifically Jewish expectation, several do see that the origin of the phrasing in the Jewish marriage contract was rooted in Exodus 21:10.[541]

Although the documents do not give the reasons for the divorces referenced, it is difficult not to see that a divorce by a wife would be based on the failure of the husband to do as he had agreed in the contract (that is to provide for his wife), a contract which had been duly signed and witnessed. Although not articulated, rather it appears to be assumed, it is suggested that divorce for the husband would have been based on the Deuteronomy 24:1–4 teaching: that is, he could divorce his wife if she had been 'sexually indecent.'

It seems clear that in the period these documents cover all the distinctive features of an Old Testament Jewish marriage were still retained in practice, that is, it was seen to be a conditional, asymmetrical, contractual, non-sacramental union that allowed for divorce and remarriage.

None of the documents suggest that any of the features of the neoplatonic model were part of the marriage customs of the day.

---

[541] For example: Yadin et al., *The Documents from the Bar Kokhba Period*, 134-35; Rabinowitz, although not commenting on the JDD (his article pre-dating their publication), references Graeco-Egyptian marriage contracts and believes that the requirement for the husband to 'supply the proper necessaries to the wife' is derived from Exod 21:10, and sees such as being reflected in the Aramaic Elephantine contracts: Jacob J. Rabinowitz, 'Marriage Contracts in Ancient Egypt in the Light of Jewish Sources,' *HTR* 46. No. 2 (April 1953), 95-97

8.4 The Graeco-Roman Documents

8.4.1 Introduction

While any Graeco-Roman marriage papyri are not Jewish documents and cannot be used to aid an understanding of either Old Testament metaphoric imagery or marital practices, or Jewish marriage contemporary to the New Testament redaction, they do provide a window into the world the New Testament writers were addressing. Hunt and Edgar contrast the people that the literature of the period portrays with those who feature in the documentary evidence:

> The figures in the papyri, on the other hand, are off their guard, they are seen to be following their ordinary pursuits.... They neither make nor possess any claim to fame, and therein lies their interest.[542]

Treggiari comments on the paucity of surviving marriage contracts and the difficulty of constructing the life of any one individual from Roman times, nonetheless she believes divorce was an option for both husband and wife and claims:

> The Romans did not see each human marriage as an allegory. But each was an example of a natural animal mating. Marriage also existed on the divine plane, although the mythical adventures of gods and goddesses, with their many adulteries, were consciously rejected as models of human behavior. Nevertheless, the divine sister/wife and brother/husband, Juno and Jupiter, represented divine authority and protection for the institution of human marriage.[543]

Treggiari believes that the couple themselves enacted the marriage and that no priest, or public official, or legal or written document was required. Furthermore, she sees that both husband and wife could divorce unilaterally and that no public authority was required to ratify it. She further asserts that polygyny was not practised.[544] She quotes the Stoic Musonius Rufus (died 101

---

[542] Arthur S. Hunt and C. C. Edgar, *Select Papyri with an English Translation* (London: Heinemann, 1932), xii
[543] Susan Treggiari, 'Marriage and Family in Roman Society,' in Campbell, *Marriage and Family,* 142–43, 146
[544] Treggiari, 'Marriage and Family,' in Campbell, *Marriage and Family,* 154–69

or 102 CE) to show he thought the primary purpose of marriage was to have children and she believes that this was a widely held position;[545] this is possibly a reflection of a neoplatonic model but Treggiari comments, 'lifelong celibacy is practically unexampled. Even the six Vestal Virgins could retire after thirty years'—but there was an idealisation of the woman who had married only once.[546]

Baugh believes literary sources indicate that Greek marriage involved a betrothal arranged between the groom and the bride's father and that divorce could be initiated by either party, and this 'was usually the result of some failure to provide the basic requirements of the implicit contract; for instance, house and board or legitimate children.'[547]

The survey below of Graeco-Roman marriage and divorce documents dated between the first century BCE and the first century CE reinforces this analysis: the documents suggest a conditional, asymmetrical, contractual concept of marriage similar to that evidenced in the JDD. The emphasis is on acknowledging receipt of the dowry, the responsibility of the groom to support his wife, and the financial arrangements on divorce or death of either spouse. The pragmatic financial arrangements, in the main involving the dowry, the groom's obligation, and divorce are all counter-indicators of a neoplatonic model.

8.4.2 The Dowry and the Groom's Maintenance Clause

Llewellyn states, 'The dowry was fundamental to the husband's obligation to maintain his wife. In other words, it gave to the married woman some security and right against neglect.'[548]

P.Eleph1 1, II.1-18 (311 BCE) is a Greek marriage document from Elephantine pre-dating the period under consideration but it is consonant with the Aramaic

---

[545] Treggiari, 'Marriage and Family,' in Campbell, *Marriage and Family*, 147-48; Witte has a further analysis of views of Rufus on marriage: Witte, *From Sacrament to Contract*, 20-21

[546] Treggiari, 'Marriage and Family,' in Campbell, *Marriage and Family*, 174

[547] S. M. Baugh, 'Marriage and Family in Ancient Greek Society,' in Campbell, *Marriage and Family*, 109-10, 118

[548] S. R. Llewelyn, ed., *New Documents Illustrating Early Christianity* (NewDocs 3; North Ryde: Macquarie University, 1981), 3

papyri at Elephantine and later Graeco-Roman documents. It states: 'Heraclides shall supply to Demetria all that is proper for a freeborn wife.'[549]

Grenfell et al. comment on the fragmentary state of Oxy.II.265 (81-95 BCE Oxyrhynchus) but see that reconstruction is possible and that the formula runs on the same lines as other contracts; that is, the groom acknowledges to the bride the receipt of the dowry and there follows provision for the children and what is to happen on the death of either spouse.[550]

BGU IV 1050 BG (early first century BCE Alexandria) sates the groom 'will maintain and clothe Isadora.'[551] BGU 1052 (13 BCE Alexandria) is a marriage contract that declares the groom shall furnish his wife 'all necessaries.'[552] Amst.40 (first century CE origin unknown),[553] and Ups.Frid.2 (59-60 CE Tebtunis),[554] follow a similar pattern to these other examples.

8.4.3 Divorce and Remarriage

Divorce is prominent in the papyri. Llewellyn claims in 'Roman law divorce could be initiated by either spouse ... and remarriage was actively encouraged.'[555]

P.Eleph1 1, II.1-18 (311 BCE) has a clause to state that Heraclides was not to bring in another wife (suggesting polygyny was a possibility) nor to have children by another woman—if proved that such had happened she was entitled to a divorce and her dowry was to be returned to her.[556]

P.Tebt. 104 (92 BCE Tebtunis) makes a similar provision: 'it shall not be lawful for Philiscus to bring in another wife beside Apollonia, nor to keep a concubine or boy, nor to have children by another woman while Apollonia lives.'[557] The

---

[549] Hunt and Edgar, *Select Papyri*, 3
[550] Bernard P. Grenfell and Arthur S. Hunt, eds., *The Oxyrhynchus Papyri: Part II* (London: Egypt Exploration Fund, 1899), 235-36
[551] Llewelyn, *New Documents*, 3
[552] Hunt and Edgar, *Select Papyri*, 11
[553] Llewelyn, *New Documents*, 1; Yiftach-Firanko, 'Judaean Desert Marriage Documents,' in Katzoff and Schaps, *Law in the Documents of the Judaean Desert*, 75-76
[554] Llewelyn, *New Documents*, 8
[555] Llewelyn, *New Documents*, 15
[556] Hunt and Edgar, *Select Papyri*, 3
[557] Hunt and Edgar, *Select Papyri*, 7

document further states: 'If Apollonia chooses of her own will to separate from Philiscus, Philiscus shall repay her the bare dowry.'[558]

P.Oxy.II.265 (81-95 BCE Oxyrhynchus) line 13 has: 'in the case of a divorce the dowry is to be repaid by Dionysius [the husband].'[559]

Laudation Turiae (ca. 18-2 BCE Rome) is a Latin inscription from a tomb and seems to be a husband's eulogy to his wife of forty-one years.[560] Horsley describes it as: 'the most impressive personal statement of the depth of the marriage-bond known to me in the later Graeco-Roman world.'[561] The husband declares: 'Uncommon are marriages which lasted so long, brought to an end by death, not broken apart by divorce.'[562] It is clear from the inscription they had been childless and she had offered to grant her husband a divorce so he could remarry and have children.

BGU IV. 1103 (13 BCE Alexandria) is a divorce deed:

> Zois and Antipater agree that they have separated from each other, severing the union which they had formed on the basis of an agreement made through the same tribunal in Hathur of the current 17th year of Caesar ... and hereafter it shall be lawful for Zois to marry another and for Antipater to marry another woman.[563]

It acknowledged that the husband had returned the dowry and it was agreed there were no further claims against him for it.[564]

BGU IV. 1104 (8 BCE Alexandria) is an annulment of a marriage contract where the widow, Dionysarion, acknowledges to her mother-in-law the return of the dowry and that she has no further claim on her husband's estate.[565]

---

[558] Hunt and Edgar, *Select Papyri*, 7

[559] Grenfell and Hunt, *The Oxyrhynchus Papyri: Part II*, 235-36

[560] The marriage might have been for thirty-one years: G. H. R. Horsley, ed., *New Documents Illustrating Early Christianity*, Vol 3 (North Ryde: Macquarie University, 1983), 35

[561] Horsley, *New Documents*, 35

[562] Horsley, *New Documents*, 35

[563] Hunt and Edgar, *Select Papyri*, 23

[564] Hunt and Edgar, *Select Papyri*, 23

[565] Mary Lefkowitz F. and Maureen B. Fant, *Women's Life in Greece and Rome: A Source Book in Translation*

P.Oxy.II.267 (36 CE) records the fact that the husband acknowledges receipt of the dowry and that he agrees to return it unconditionally on a specific date (Oct 27 CE 36), and goes on to discuss arrangements 'If we separate from each other.'[566]

P.Ryl. 154 (66 CE Bacchias) acknowledges the dowry from his bride's father and that previously the couple had lived together as man and wife without a written contract and outlines financial arrangements should there be a divorce.[567]

P.Oxy.II.266 (96 CE) references a couple who had been married just over a year but had divorced, the document acknowledges they have no other claims on each other.[568]

8.4.4 Summary: The Graeco-Roman Documents

None of these extant papyri demonstrate that a neoplatonic concept of marriage had been incorporated into the marriage practices of the Graeco-Roman world; instead marriage practice appears consonant with that employed in biblical marital imagery notwithstanding the adoption of a dowry system rather than a *mohar*.

8.5 Summary: The Documents of the Second Temple Period

Collins states:

> The pragmatic, contractual character of marriage in second temple Judaism is most evident in the ready availability of divorce. We have no way of calculating the actual frequency of divorce, but both the literary evidence and the papyri accept it as routine.... To judge by the evidence of the papyri, the contracts worked well for the protection of women in situations of divorce and widowhood.[569]

(Bristol: Bristol Classical, 1982; Repr. London: Bloomsbury, 2013), 91; Ann Ellis Hanson, 'The Widow Babatha and the Poor Orphan Boy,' in Katzoff and Schaps, *Law in the Documents of the Judaean Desert*, 97

[566] Grenfell and Hunt, *The Oxyrhynchus Papyri: Part II*, 243–44

[567] Hunt and Edgar, *Select Papyri*, 14–16

[568] Grenfell and Hunt, *The Oxyrhynchus Papyri: Part II*, 238

[569] Collins, 'Marriage, Divorce, and Family,' in Perdue et al., *Families in Ancient Israel*, 149

The survey in this chapter appears to confirm such. The 'scanty evidence' of a neoplatonic marriage model that Satlow sees in the literature of the period (§7.1) is just that. Even in Alexandria where the Hellenistic influence was at its height (§7.6.1), marriage practice, as evidenced above, fails to demonstrate such a model. Metaphor theory requires a source domain rooted in the experience of its intended audience, thus it is suggested that a neoplatonic mundane marriage cannot be used in New Testament marital imagery, and that this presents a challenge to the perception that such forms the basis of its mundane marriage teaching.

Chapter 9: Marital Imagery in the New Testament

9.1 Introduction

In chapter 6 we saw how the target domain of the marital imagery employed in the Old Testament (the divine marriage of Yahweh and Israel) closely mirrored both mundane marriage as evidenced in the Old Testament narratives, and its mundane marital legislation. Chapter 7 considered the emergence in Second Temple literature of the concept of a neoplatonic archetype for mundane marriage based on the marriage of Adam and Eve and there was some limited evidence of such. But chapter 8 demonstrated that the concept of a neoplatonic model had not impacted marriage practice in the New Testament world, which remained largely consistent with Jewish marriage practice in ancient Israel.

The aim of this chapter is to explore the key features of New Testament marital imagery to identify the source domain and the associated cross-mapping. It will be seen that the Gospel writers in particular draw (as in the Old Testament), not on the primal couple, but, as expected, on contemporary Jewish marriage practice underpinned by the conceptual domain of Genesis 2:24. Although both Old Testament and New Testament marital imagery share this same basis, the focus of the latter will be seen to be different. The root metaphor in the Old Testament marital imagery was *Yahweh: The Husband of Israel.* Thus the Old Testament narratives exploited the consequent analogies and portrayed the turbulent nature of Israel's relationship with Yahweh as a difficult marriage, a divorce, a separation, and reconciliation (represented by two exiles and a return), with the promise of a better future.

But the imagery in the Gospels and Apocalypse is based on the root metaphor *Jesus: The Bridegroom of the Church.* This gives rise to a different set of analogies (as set out in §1.4.1):

MAP 2 *Jesus: The Bridegroom of the Church* (New conceptual domain 'B' is created)

CONCEPTUAL DOMAIN Gen 2:24		NEW TARGET DOMAIN (B) Jesus: The Bridegroom of the Church
A woman becomes the wife of a man in a metaphoric one-flesh union formed by means of a volitional covenant.	ROOT METAPHOR 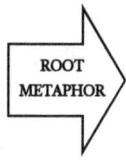	Men and women are invited to become what they were not: members of the covenant community that is the metaphoric bride of Christ.
• Betrothal • Wedding feast • Invitations to guests • Groom prepares a place for his bride • Groom pays a *mohar* for his bride • Groom promises to care for his bride • Bride waits for groom • Groom comes for his bride • Groom takes his bride to his own home	CNTA 	• Betrothal • Wedding feast • Invitations to guests • Jesus prepares a place for the church • Jesus pays a *mohar* for the church • Christ cares for the church • The church waits for Jesus • Jesus comes for the church • Jesus takes the church to his own home

CNTA = Consequent New Testament Analogies

The source domain remains the same, but contemporary mundane marriage practices are exploited in the Gospels and Apocalypse for aspects of the betrothal period that will illustrate Jesus' ministry. Thus Jesus is portrayed early in his public ministry as a 'bridegroom' (νυμφίος), suggesting that he was standing in the very place of Yahweh, but unlike Yahweh, he is not directly referenced as a husband (§6.10.3).[570]

---

[570] Carr and Conway discuss this aspect of New Testament imagery (i.e. the continuity between the Old Testament marital imagery and that of the New) and state: 'the early Christian imagery often celebrates the

Although the Pauline corpus employs the same imagery as the Gospels and the Apocalypse at several points (1 Cor 6:19–20; 2 Cor 11:2; Eph 5:22–33; 2 Tim 2:10–13), the focus is not on contemporary marital practices that illustrate the betrothal period of the imagery; instead Paul goes directly to Genesis 2:24 and exploits that in his marital and corporate body imagery. The New Testament writers will be seen to utilise this marital and body imagery to show how the Old Testament promises of a better future for Israel are to be achieved in the consummation of a divine marriage at the eschaton. Thus the concept of an inchoate marriage in the New Testament is consistent with the imagery of the Apocalypse.[571]

The examples considered in this chapter are intended to be illustrative, not exhaustive; for example, Tait includes Galatians 4 in his consideration of Pauline marital imagery; McWhirter sees many allusions to Song in her monograph (though these are disputed by others); and Smolarz includes a consideration of Romans 9:25–29 in his publication—but these examples do not add materially to this study.[572]

---

bride's betrothal and anticipates the wedding consummation. This orientation toward the promise of a restored marriage in the future began with Second and Third Isaiah': Carr and Conway, 'The Divine Human Marriage,' in Nissinen and Uro, *Sacred Marriages*, 295; there is further discussion in: Smolarz, *Covenant and Metaphor*, 181-85

[571] Beale commenting on Rev 21-9-10 says: 'The bride is also called the Lamb's "wife," since betrothal was much more closely related to marriage in biblical culture'; and on Rev 22:17: '"The bride" has been used previously only in reference to the church's future, consummated marriage to Christ at his final return (19:7-9; 21:ff., 9ff.). Application of it here to the present church suggests that what has been prophesied has begun already in their midst (as in 2 Cor 11:2 and Eph 5:25-27). The relationship between the "already" and the "not yet" is that between a woman's engagement and her marriage ceremony. This is best understood by remembering that in the Old Testament betrothal was conceived of as an inchoate state of marriage': Beale, *Revelation*, 1063, 1148; *contra* Smolarz who sees that the divine marriage has already been accomplished: Smolarz, *Covenant and Metaphor*, 222-27, 372. The marital imagery employed in the New Testament appears to support Beale's analysis.

[572] Michael Tait, *Jesus, the Divine Bridegroom, in Mark 2:18–22: Mark's Christology Upgraded* AB 185 (Rome: Pontificio Istituto Biblico, 2012), 228-30; McWhirter, *The Bridegroom Messiah*, 79-105; Foster disputes McWhirter's analysis of Song: in Paul Foster, 'The Bridegroom Messiah and the People of God: Marriage in the Fourth Gospel,' *Expository Times* 118 11 Ag (2007), 564-65; Smolarz, *Covenant and Metaphor*, 214-19

9.2 Marital Imagery in the Gospels

Carr and Conway claim: 'The New Testament ... features a significant focus on images of divine-human marriage.'[573] Long states:

> Like any other teacher of the Second Temple Period, Jesus intentionally alluded to traditions drawn from the Hebrew Bible in order to describe a new situation. Jesus claims that his ministry is an on-going wedding celebration that signals the end of the Exile and the restoration of Israel to her position as the Lord's beloved wife.[574]

There appears to be extensive evidence that the New Testament writers perceived Jesus' role to be that of a bridegroom who in effect had stepped into the role that Yahweh had occupied in the Old Testament marital imagery. As referenced in §2.2, the treatment of New Testament marital imagery in the literature is sparse. Chavasse sees intertextual links between Psalm 45:3–5 and Matthew 21:5, and so Jesus' entry to Jerusalem can be seen as a bridegroom coming to claim his bride;[575] and a reference to Psalm 45 in Hebrews 1:8 implies that Jesus is the promised bridegroom.[576] Chavasse sees other allusions to marital imagery, including the parable of the vine in John 15 which he suggests is based on Psalm 128 which portrays the vine ('a normal metaphor for Israel') as a wife;[577] and both Long and Chavasse point out that an 'adulterous generation' (Matt 12:39; 16:4; Mark 8:38) assumes marital imagery.[578]

I will suggest, however, that the analysis below demonstrates a more obvious imagery and a systematic exploitation of contemporary marital practice to populate the target domain of the imagery.

---

[573] Carr and Conway, 'The Divine Human Marriage,' in Nissinen and Uro, *Sacred Marriages*, 294
[574] Long, *Jesus the Bridegroom*, 2
[575] Chavasse, *The Bride of Christ*, 57
[576] Chavasse, *The Bride of Christ*, 85
[577] Chavasse, *The Bride of Christ*, 61–62
[578] Long, *Jesus the Bridegroom*, 201–02; Chavasse, *The Bride of Christ*, 53

9.2.1 The Wedding at Cana

When asked to make up the shortfall of wine (John 2:1–11) Jesus is said to declare that 'My hour is not yet come'; Jesus is nonetheless recorded as performing the miracle and when the wine is produced the master of the feast comments on its quality and assumes it is the bridegroom who has made the provision (vv. 9–10). Pitre suggests that this was in accord with the Jewish wedding tradition where it was the bridegroom's responsibility to provide the wine (as inferred in v. 9).[579] It follows that Mary had been, in effect, asking Jesus to act as if he was on that day the bridegroom—such an analysis would explain his enigmatic reply to her.

Pitre further suggests Mary's reference to the lack of wine is an echo of Isaiah 24:7, 9, 11—Isaiah subsequently describing a future restoration of Israel when Yahweh will ensure wine will be in abundance (Isa 25:6–8).[580] Thus Pitre sees that the writer of the fourth Gospel, in recounting such an extravagant supply of wine, is employing contemporary Jewish marriage traditions to portray Jesus as the divine bridegroom self-consciously taking the role occupied by Yahweh in the Old Testament imagery.

9.2.2 The Bridegroom Introduced

In John 3:22–30 Jesus is introduced as the bridegroom and the Baptist describes his joy at hearing the 'bridegroom's voice' which Pitre sees as a reference to Jeremiah 33:10–11, 14–17, and that the Gospel writer is using marital imagery to identify Jesus as the promised messianic king;[581] he maintains, based on rabbinic sources, that when the Baptist describes himself as the 'friend of the bridegroom' he is in effect comparing his role to that of the Best Man in a Jewish wedding, whose duty was to lead the bride to the bridegroom when the time for the wedding had arrived.[582]

---

[579] Brant Pitre, *Jesus the Bridegroom,* 35–39; also: McWhirter, *The Bridegroom Messiah,* 57

[580] Pitre, *Jesus the Bridegroom,* 39–45; also Amos 9:11–13

[581] McWhirter, in connection with the 'bridegroom's voice,' also references: Jer 7:32–34; 16:9; 25:10; Song 8:13 and Ps 45: McWhirter, *The Bridegroom Messiah,* 5-6, 18–19, 50–56

[582] Pitre, *Jesus the Bridegroom,* 31–34; the Mishnah states: 'By friend is meant a man's groomsman' (*m. Sanh:* 3.5).

9.2.3 The Woman from Samaria

There are clear connections in John 4:5–29 with previous meetings at a well that resulted in marriage (Isaac and Rebekah, Gen 24:14–16; Jacob and Rachel, Gen 29:1–20; Moses and Zipporah, Exod 2:15–17, 21), McWhirter pointing out many detailed parallels.[583] Pitre makes a comparison between the Samaritan woman and Gomer, the former serving, like the latter, as a symbol for her people.[584] Like McWhirter, he sees the five husbands that the Samaritan woman had had represent the five false (male) gods of the Samaritans (2 Kgs 17:28–31), and that 'the one you now have is not your husband' they consider a reference to the Samaritan's syncretistic worship of Yahweh (2 Kgs 17:29–41).[585] Pitre sees the 'gift' of v. 10 as parallel to the gifts given at the well to Rebekah (Gen 24:22–27) and that it is the equivalent of the bridegroom's *mohar*;[586] the 'living water' is a possible reference (among other potential meanings) to the ritual bath a Jewish bride took before her wedding (referred to as 'living water' in *Jos. Asen.*14:12–17); with Carmichael, and McWhirter, he sees that John is making a link with Song 4:12, 15 ('A garden locked is my sister, my bride, a spring locked, a fountain sealed ... a garden fountain, a well of living water').[587]

Thus Carmichael, McWhirter, and Pitre see that the Gospel writer is portraying Jesus as offering the woman, and through her, the Samaritan people (divorced Israel), in this traditional Jewish setting for betrothals, redemption in a new marriage. McWhirter comments:

> there is no need to postulate symbolism in John 4:18. John is simply making a comparison. The Samaritan woman with her six men is like

---

[583] McWhirter, *The Bridegroom Messiah*, 59–78; Carmichael comments: 'The evangelist is using Old Testament tradition with consummate effect': Calum M. Carmichael, 'Marriage and the Samaritan Woman,' *NTS* 26 (1980), 337

[584] Pitre, *Jesus the Bridegroom*, 65–68

[585] Pitre, *Jesus the Bridegroom*, 66–68; McWhirter, *The Bridegroom Messiah*, 69–72. There are seven gods referenced in the Old Testament pericope but two are female—Josephus refers to the five gods of Samaria in *Ant.* 9.288.

[586] Pitre, Jesus the Bridegroom, 69–70

[587] Pitre, *Jesus the Bridegroom*, 73–75; Carmichael, 'Marriage,' 336; McWhirter, *The Bridegroom Messiah*, 107

a Samaritan people with their six religions ... [her] worship of [the] Father in spirit and in truth makes her "marital history" obsolete.[588]

Pitre points out that the woman must have had multiple divorces and remarriages;[589] nonetheless he sees that:

> through this encounter with Jesus the non-Jewish peoples of the world begin to be "betrothed"—so to speak—to the one who is both Bridegroom Messiah and Savior of the world.[590]

9.2.4 The Sons of the Bride Chamber

The Gospel writers record the disciples' question and Jesus' response about fasting in Matthew 9:15, Luke 5:34, and Mark 2:19-20, which has:

> And Jesus said to them, "Can the wedding guests fast while the bridegroom is with them? As long as they have the bridegroom with them, they cannot fast. The days will come when the bridegroom is taken away from them, and then they will fast in that day."

Pitre points out that 'wedding guests' is actually υἱοὶ τοῦ νυμφῶνος ('sons of the bride chamber') and, based on rabbinic sources (*b. Sukkah* 25b–26a), describes them as special friends of the bridegroom excused from religious duties for the wedding week celebration;[591] this implies Jesus' whole public ministry can be seen as his week as the bridegroom preparing for his wedding, supporting Long's claim that 'Jesus refers to himself as the bridegroom and his own ministry as a wedding banquet.'[592]

---

[588] The sixth religion McWhirter sees as being the worship of Yahweh whom they 'do not know': McWhirter, *The Bridegroom Messiah*, 71-72

[589] Pitre, *Jesus the Bridegroom*, 64

[590] Pitre, *Jesus the Bridegroom*, 69; similarly: Carmichael, 'Marriage,' 341-42

[591] Pitre, *Jesus the Bridegroom*, 85-89

[592] Long cites Mark 2:18-22 (cf. Luke 5:34 / Matt 9:14-15): Long, *Jesus the Bridegroom*, 194; similarly Zimmermann: 'die Erdenzeit Jesu mit seinen Jüngern als Verlobung oder Vorhochzeit der eschatologischen Hochzeit aufgefasst werden, wie sie in Mt 25,1-13, Apk 19-21 und 2 Kor 11 dann explizit erhofft wird' [so Jesus's time on earth with his disciples could be understood as an 'engagement' or 'pre-wedding' preparing for the eschatological wedding as it is portrayed in Matt 25:1-13, Rev 19-21, and 2 Cor 11], translation by Dora James: Zimmermann, *Geschlechtermetaphorik Und Gotteseverhaltnis*, 286-87, 295; also: Chavasse, *The Bride of Christ*, 53-55

9.2.5 The Ten Virgins

Pitre references this parable (Matt 25:1–13), and citing 1 Macc 9:37, 39 states: 'ancient Jewish weddings climaxed with the *arrival* of the bridegroom at the wedding feast, when he came to take a bride to himself,' suggesting that the parable portrays Jesus' unexpected arrival as the bridegroom at his own wedding.[593] Like Pitre, Long believes the bridesmaids were a feature of contemporary weddings and that 'Jesus stands on traditions drawn from the Hebrew Bible';[594] Long comments:

> There is no need to see the use of a marriage metaphor as a sign of an allegorizing Gospel writer since it was very much part of Second Temple Period Judaism. Jesus created the parables himself out of existing traditions.[595]

9.2.6 The Wedding Banquet

Long makes a detailed analysis of the parable in Matthew 22:1–14, and as in Matt 25:1–13, sees an extended metaphor and not an allegory.[596] He points out that in Matthew 22 Jesus is the king not the bridegroom and the parable 'develops the eschatological banquet (Isa 25:6–8) by combining it with a Marriage metaphor'; thus Long sees the parable as describing Jesus' own ministry.[597]

---

[593] Pitre, *Jesus the Bridegroom*, 118–21; 1 Macc 9:37; 39 has: '[37].... The family of Jambri are celebrating a great wedding, and are conducting the bride, the daughter of one of the great nobles of Canaan, from Nadabath with a large escort ... [39] They looked out and saw a tumultuous procession with a great amount of baggage; and the bridegroom came out with his friends and his brothers to meet them with tambourines and musicians and many weapons'; translation from: Michael D. Coogan, Marc Z. Brettler, Carol A. Newsom, and Pherme Perkins, eds., *The New Oxford Annotated Apocrypha: New Revised Standard Version* (Oxford: Oxford University Press, 2010)
[594] Long, *Jesus the Bridegroom*, 220
[595] Long, *Jesus the Bridegroom*, 219–21, 243; similarly: Pitre, *Jesus the Bridegroom*, 119–21; Zimmermann *contra* Pitre sees that the bridesmaids were a feature of contemporary Greek (i.e. not Jewish) weddings: Zimmermann, 'Das Hochzeitsritual im Jungfrauengleichnis,' 64; similarly Donfried: 'what is related in the text does not describe normal Jewish practice': Karl P. Donfried, 'The Allegory of the Ten Virgins (Matt 25:1-13) as a Summary of Matthean Theology,' *JBL* 93 (1974), 417
[596] Long, *Jesus the Bridegroom*, 209–26; *contra* Syreeni who sees an allegory: Kari Syreeni, 'From the Bridegroom's Time to the Wedding of the Lamb,' in Nissinen and Uro, *Sacred Marriages*, 348–50
[597] Long, *Jesus the Bridegroom*, 217–18

9.2.7 The Last Supper

Pitre sees intertextual links between John 2:4 ('My hour has not yet come') and Matthew 26:45, Mark 14:41-42, John 12:27; and John 13:1 ('Now before the Feast of the Passover, when Jesus knew that his hour had come to depart out of this world to the Father ... '); and points out that John 13:1 ties 'his hour' to the beginning of the Last Supper.[598] Furthermore, in the Gospels (e.g. Luke 22:20) and 1 Corinthians 11:25, the Last Supper is linked to the new (marriage) covenant referenced in Jeremiah 31:31-33, and is seen by Pitre as Jesus' wedding banquet, the twelve disciples representing the 'bride of God—the people of Israel.'[599]

9.2.8 The Bridegroom Prepares a Place

Pitre argues that John 14:1-3 reflects the Jewish bridegroom's responsibility to provide a home for his bride and that Jesus' promise to return reflected the Jewish bridegroom taking his bride to the home he had prepared.[600]

9.2.9 The Cross

Pitre points out that Jewish bridegrooms wore a seamless robe and a crown on their marriage day (Exod 28:31-32 cf. Isa 61:10; Song 3:11; *m. Soṭah* 9:14) as Jesus wore on the day of his crucifixion (Matt 27:27-29; John 19:23).[601]

9.3 Marital Imagery in the Apocalypse

Syreeni states: 'The approaching marriage feast of the Lamb and his bride ... accounts for much of the symbolism of the book of Revelation' and Smolarz believes, 'the scope of the metaphor in the book is far more wide ranging than has usually been acknowledged by New Testament scholars.'[602] However, in

---

[598] Pitre, *Jesus the Bridegroom*, 46-48.

[599] Pitre, *Jesus the Bridegroom*, 49-51; also: Chavasse, *The Bride of Christ*, 60-64; James D. G. Dunn, *Jesus Remembered: Christianity in the Making Volume 1* (Grand Rapids, MI: Eerdmans, 2003), 427.

[600] Pitre, *Jesus the Bridegroom*, 117-18; Satlow states: 'In Greece, Rome, and Jerusalem, a wedding normally began with the procession of the bride from her father's house to her future husband's residence, sometimes joined by the groom himself': Satlow, *Jewish Marriage*, 170.

[601] Pitre, *Jesus the Bridegroom*, 102-07; also: Satlow, *Jewish Marriage*, 172.

[602] Syreeni, 'From the Bridegroom's Time,' in Nissinen and Uro, *Sacred Marriages*, 364; although Smolarz sees the use of the divine marriage metaphor to be explicit in Rev 19, 21, 22, he posits its presence elsewhere:

the Apocalypse the focus is on the eschatological consummation of the divine marriage and there is only limited evidence of its author drawing on contemporary marital practices to form his imagery. Nonetheless, Pitre suggests the Ἀποκάλυψις of Revelation 1:1 is a reflection of the ancient Jewish custom of the bridegroom lifting the veil covering his bride's face.[603] Zimmermann points out that the 'crown' in Revelation 2:10; 3:11 is a possible reference to the bridal crown of Judaic and Hellenistic wedding rituals.[604]

Fekkes points out that Revelation 21:3 is a:

> covenant promise which is ultimately patterned after Near Eastern marriage contracts, "and they shall be his people[s] and God himself shall be with them [and be their God]."[605]

Smolarz posits that the idea of inheritance in the imagery (e.g. Rev 21:7) recalls the *mohar* payment.[606]

It is widely accepted that marriages in ancient Israel were not matrilocal but patrilocal, that is, the bride usually went to live with her groom's extended family.[607] However, Zimmermann points out the marriage ceremony/consummation can be at the home of the groom or the bride, and comments:

Smolarz, *Covenant and Metaphor*, 228; as does: Zimmermann, 'Nuptial Imagery,' 153. In this present study the bridegroom is considered to be Jesus (Rev 19:7 the 'Lamb'), and the bride to be God's people; similarly Beale, who comments that Jesus is referenced as the 'Lamb' twenty seven times and that: 'The bride is a metaphor for the saints': Beale, *Revelation*, 352, 1045; Zimmermann so identifies the bridegroom but debates the identity of the bride without coming to a firm conclusion: Zimmermann, 'Nuptial Imagery,' 167, 174; Smolarz states: 'the two motifs of Yahweh being Zion's (Jerusalem's) builder as well as the husband of Jerusalem (people represented by the city) are connected.... The former refers to Yahweh dwelling with his people, while the latter signifies his intimate covenant union with them. [The] Old Testament context instantly solves the problem of identifying the constituents of the city/bride: they are the people of God themselves': Smolarz, *Covenant and Metaphor*, 262–63

[603] Pitre, *Jesus the Bridegroom*, 123

[604] Zimmermann also cross references Ezek 16:12: Zimmermann, 'Nuptial Imagery,' 154–56

[605] Jan Fekkes III, "'His Bride Has Prepared Herself'': Revelation 19–21 and Isaian Nuptial Imagery,' *JBL* 109/2 (1990), 283. The square brackets reflect MS discrepancies, the specific ANE documents referenced are an Aramaic papyri from Elephantine (Cowley, 15) and Mur 20 from the JDD collection—Mur 20 line 3 has: 'Yo]u shall be my wife according to the law of Mo[ses.'

[606] Smolarz, *Covenant and Metaphor*, 265

[607] Block, 'Marriage and Family,' in Campbell, *Marriage and Family*, 58

> It is above all the statement in Rev 22:17 that a bride summons her bridegroom to come that is interesting. As the donor field of this metaphor we can look at two situations within the Judaic marriage ritual. On the one hand, the bride could here summon the bridegroom to come to the house of her parents in order to accompany her to his house and thereby to bring the actual wedding to its commencement.... On the other hand the background could be a summons of the bride to the bridegroom to come to her in her bridal chamber.[608]

9.4 Marital Imagery in the Pauline Corpus

Chavasse comments:

> When we come to the Nuptial Idea in St. Paul's Epistles, we find all the subtlety, fluidity, and development that we should expect;... But the startling change which St. Paul introduces into the Idea is that ... he invariably finds its type in Genesis.[609]

Chavasse is referencing Paul's exploitation of Genesis 2:24. He further suggests that the Pauline marital imagery is less focused than Old Testament marital imagery on redemption, although he notes its presence.[610]

9.4.1 Ephesians 5:31–32

> "Therefore a man shall leave his father and mother and hold fast to his wife, and the two shall become one flesh." This mystery is profound, and I am saying that it refers to Christ and the church. (Eph 5:31–32)

The pericope can be analysed as: 'A' refers to 'B,' or in metaphor terms A 'is' B, where 'A' is Genesis 2:24, and 'B' is the relationship of Christ and the church—thus the two conceptual domains are brought together by the Ephesians author. In other words, the pericope articulates the structure map of the

---

[608] Zimmermann, 'Nuptial Imagery,' 175–76
[609] Chavasse, *The Bride of Christ*, 66
[610] Chavasse, *The Bride of Christ*, 80–82; he cites 1 Cor 6:11, 20; 7:23; 2 Cor 5:19; Eph 5:25–26.

marital imagery employed in the Gospels and the Apocalypse where the root metaphor is *Jesus: The Bridegroom of the Church* (MAP 2).

The specific identification of Genesis 2:24 (quoted here, as elsewhere in the New Testament, from the Septuagint) as the source domain of the imagery, which the analysis of §9.2 has shown to be contemporary mundane marriage, reinforces the claim of this study that in both the Jewish and Christian Scriptures Genesis 2:24 is understood to reference mundane marriage and is the source domain for their marital imagery. Verses 31–32 of Ephesians 5 are further considered in §9.4.8 in the context of the wider pericope of Ephesians 5:22–33.

9.4.2 Romans 7:1–6

> Or do you not know, brothers—for I am speaking to those who know the law—that the law is binding on a person only as long as he lives? Thus a married woman is bound by law to her husband while he lives, but if her husband dies she is released from the law of marriage. Accordingly, she will be called an adulteress if she lives with another man while her husband is alive. But if her husband dies, she is free from that law, and if she marries another man she is not an adulteress. Likewise, my brothers, you also have died to the law through the body of Christ, so that you may belong to another, to him who has been raised from the dead, in order that we may bear fruit for God. For while we were living in the flesh, our sinful passions, aroused by the law, were at work in our members to bear fruit for death. But now we are released from the law, having died to that which held us captive, so that we serve not under the old written code but in the new life of the Spirit. (Rom 7:1–6)

Little succinctly analyses the exegetical problems of this pericope and the various approaches to it. She cites Dodd: 'What, then, is the application of the illustration, or metaphor, or allegory, or whatever it is?'[611]

---

[611] J. A. Little, 'Paul's Use of Analogy: A Structural Analysis of Romans 7:1-6,' *CBQ* 46 (1984), 85; C. H. Dodd, *The Epistle to the Romans* (New York, NY: Harper, 1932), 101

Little herself treats it as an analogy and sees the success of such as depending:

> upon the existence of similarities between things which are otherwise dissimilar.... If the dissimilarities are more prominent, the suggestion cannot be avoided that the analogy has somehow failed.[612]

However, it is suggested in this present study, that Paul is employing marital imagery, and, unlike an analogy, the success of a metaphor is not based on the similarity of the two things being compared, but on the new, perhaps previously unconsidered connections that can be made.

Here in Romans 7:1–6, as in Old Testament marital imagery, mundane marriage is the source domain which is cross-mapped to illustrate a spiritual concept, but in this case there is some difficulty identifying who constitute the marriage partners in the target domain. Various possibilities have been suggested: the wife as the church and the husband as the law; the wife as a believer and the husband as the law; the wife is the symbolic new self and the husband is the old self.[613] It seems the majority position is that in the target domain the husband is the law and the people of God represent the wife.[614]

However, there are at least four problems with this view: Israel saw the law as their 'marriage-ring';[615] they were married, not to the law, but to Yahweh, so this postulated use of the imagery would somewhat confusingly suggest they were married to the symbol of their marriage. Secondly, in biblical marital imagery, the source and target domains both have marriage partners who have an independent volitional personhood, the inanimate 'marriage law' in the target domain cannot fulfil that role. A third problem with this interpretation is that vv. 2–3 (with their reference to the marriage law) introduce a redundant

---

[612] Little, 'Paul's Use of Analogy,' 84

[613] See analysis in: Little, 'Paul's Use of Analogy,' 86

[614] Dunn comments: 'having died to that in/by which we were confined/restrained ... obviously refers to the law [the Torah] (as most recognize), not to the "old man" [of Rom 6:6]' and references others, who *contra* to himself, see the reference to marriage as being 'to "a general principle of all law"': James D. G. Dunn, *Romans 1–8*, in WBC 38A, ed. Bruce M. Metzger (Nashville, TN: Thomas Nelson, 1988), 359, 365; such include Käsemann: 'the husband in the illustration is not the Torah.... The only point of comparison is that death dissolves the obligations valid throughout life': Ernst Käsemann, *Commentary on Romans* (Grand Rapids, MI: Eerdmans, 1980), 187; similarly: I. A. Muirhead, 'The Bride of Christ,' *SJT* 5 (1952), 180; but Little points out that any such analysis makes the analogy redundant: Little, 'Paul's Use of Analogy,' 85–86

[615] Thus: Cohen, 'The Song of Songs,' in Finkelstein, *The Samuel Friedland Lectures*, 12

layer into the argument, as v. 1 makes clear a man is no longer bound to the law once he dies. A fourth problem is that the deliverance declared in v. 24 is not from the law but from the 'body of death.'

Thus it is suggested Wright is correct in seeing that it was not the law that was the first husband, rather it was the law (i.e. the 'law of marriage' v. 2) that had 'bound the woman *to* the "first husband."' Wright goes on to identify (*contra* Dunn) that the first husband was the 'old self' of Romans 6:6.[616]

Romans 7:4 has:

> Likewise, my brothers, you also have died to the law through the body of Christ, so that you may belong to another, to him who has been raised from the dead, in order that we may bear fruit for God.

Wright's explanation is:

> "You" in the first half of 7:4 is the "former husband"; "you" in the second half is the "wife." Or if we prefer, "you" in the first half is the "old human being" of 6:6—the "old Adam," or perhaps better "the person 'in Adam.'" "You" in the second half, at least when the "re-marriage" has occurred, is the person "in Christ."[617]

However, this has its own problems as marital imagery. It has been suggested in this present study that mundane marriage is the source domain of the biblical marriage metaphor, and its volitional contractual union of two people who previously had an independent existence informs the μεταφέρω to the target of the imagery—Yahweh's covenant with Israel at Sinai or Christ's new covenant with redeemed humanity. Wright sees the wife in the second half of the verse as 'the person "in Christ,"' but who are the two independent entities before the 'remarriage'? In other words who is the wife of the first husband ('the person "in Adam"')? And what was the basis of that 'marriage' union? A further problem is that in Wright's analysis the wife in the target domain of the imagery is seemingly the individual 'person "in Christ"'; but nowhere else in

---

[616] N. T. Wright, 'The Letter to the Romans,' in *The New Interpreter's Bible (Vol. X) Acts Introduction to Epistolary Literature Romans 1 Corinthians*, ed. Leander E. Keck (Nashville, TN: Abingdon, 2002), 539, 559
[617] Wright, 'The Letter to the Romans,' in Keck, *NIB: Romans*, 559

the target domain of biblical marital imagery is the wife an individual, rather it is a corporate entity (e.g. Israel or the church).

Sanders comments:

> We should pay special attention to the degree to which Sin is treated by Paul as an enemy power ... Paul believed in the triumph of Christ over Sin – whether it takes the form of a demon, Satan, or another evil power.[618]

Thus Sanders sees that when Paul speaks of sin he is not necessarily referencing sins, but that Paul also has a concept of an entity Sanders calls *Sin*—an understanding the Genesis author seems to share when in Genesis 4:7 he references sin as a crouching animal (§1.1.3). Wright expresses something similar when he says the *body of sin* can be 'seen as the entity that "sin" has made its own.'[619] Also Dunn:

> translations tend to individualize *sarx* ... and to lose sight of *sarx* as denoting a corporate or national identity. In so doing they also lose sight of the important theological point that humankind as *sarx* in this sense is equally vulnerable to manipulation by national demagogery of all kinds.[620]

Wright, when commenting on Romans 7:24, sees that when Paul speaks in the first person singular he is apparently speaking for all Adamic humanity (including Israel), the same entity as the 'body of death':

> Israel too is "in Adam," ... the "I" finds itself unable to escape from "this body of death," referring perhaps both to its own "fleshy" state but also to the solidarity of sin, of Adamic humanity, with which it is unavoidably bound up (cf. 6:6).[621]

With his reference to Romans 6:6 Wright seems to be linking the *body of death* and *Adamic humanity* to the 'old self' and the 'body of sin' of that

---

[618] E.P. Sanders, *Paul: A Brief Insight* (New York, NY: Oxford University Press, 1991; Repr. New York, NY: Sterling, 2009), 57, 59

[619] Wright, 'The Letter to the Romans,' in Keck, *NIB: Romans*, 539

[620] Dunn, *Theology of Paul*, 70

[621] Wright, 'The Letter to the Romans,' in Keck, *NIB: Romans*, 571

verse.[622] It follows that Dunn, Sanders, and Wright all appear to understand that Paul had a concept that humanity is somehow being manipulated by an entity, one that Sanders and Wright describe as 'sin,' and Dunn as 'demagogery.' It has been seen, as above, that Wright believes that the binding agent is the *law of marriage* referenced in Romans 7:2, but he does not clearly articulate the two entities that are bound by such before the release declared in vv. 24–25.

Thus it is suggested that Holland's analysis is the most successful (and consonant with cross-mapping principles) when he posits that the two parties that Dunn, Sanders, and Wright variously articulate, are the 'wife' and the 'husband' in the target domain of marital imagery: that is, corporate unredeemed humanity in Adam, and *Sin* respectively.[623] Thus *Sin* binds Adamic humanity (the metaphoric wife) in a marriage covenant to himself by means of the 'law of marriage' (v. 2) that Wright sees as being key to the passage—it is a 'marriage' that is the precise antithesis of the pervasive Old Testament imagery of a marriage between God and his people.

Holland's exegesis is consistent with the marital imagery posited in §6.12, where Adam can be seen in Eden to have broken the covenant with God. Thus Adam (and humanity whom he represented) was 'divorced' by God, the divorce represented by Adam's expulsion from Eden. Adam had, in effect, entered into a new 'marriage' covenant with Satan.

If, as has been argued in this present study, Paul is to be understood in light of his Jewish roots (§1.4.4; §3.4) how probable is this new imagery? Chavasse comments (§9.4) that Paul's employment of the marital imagery is 'startling,' and pericopae such as Romans 6 and 7 might be the cause of Peter's comment that Paul is sometimes hard to understand (2 Peter 3:16). But the imagery in Romans is not as innovative as it might appear, in that it seems Paul is

---

[622] It might be wondered why Paul did not describe such as the 'body of Adam' (a term Holland claims the rabbis were familiar with: Holland, *Romans*, 187)—but the relationship of humankind to Adam is, in effect, a consanguineous, non-covenantal, non-volitional, one-flesh union and this would not be compatible with Paul's imagery whereby unredeemed humanity is portrayed as being in a covenantal metaphoric marital union with Sin—the antithesis of the body of Christ.

[623] Holland, *Romans*, 185–93, 226–35, 245–46

following Jeremiah, who similarly sees that the target domain in the marital imagery is governed by concepts in the source domain that restrict the options for humanity. In Jeremiah's case it was Israel (Jer 3:1–8) who is locked out of a relationship with God by the Pentateuchal marriage law, for Paul it is fallen humanity.

Another potential difficulty with this posited imagery is that Wright sees (as above) that 'Israel too is "in Adam"'—so how could she have been taken in a marriage by Yahweh if she was already married to Sin? However, the Bible's marital imagery is based on metaphoric concepts that at their heart have a false literalism. In other words, there is no marriage to Sin, and there is no marriage to Yahweh, they are rather concepts that illustrate a truth. This allows great flexibility in the imagery—the target domain is not bound to all aspects of the mundane marriage source domain. In the target domain Yahweh/Christ is portrayed as marrying a city (e.g. Isa 54; Rev 21) and a temple (e.g. Ezek 44–48); and Ezekiel 23 portrays Yahweh as married to two sisters, even though such was forbidden in the Pentateuch.

If the above analysis is correct, the root metaphor Paul employs in his imagery comes, as in all the marital imagery of the Jewish and Christian Scriptures, from the source domain: Genesis 2:24, but it now populates a new target domain: *Sin: The Husband of Unredeemed Humanity.*

The new situation (divorced from God married to Satan) was portrayed in §1.4.2 diagrammatically like this:

MAP 3 *Sin: The Husband of Unredeemed Humanity* (New conceptual domain 'C' is created)

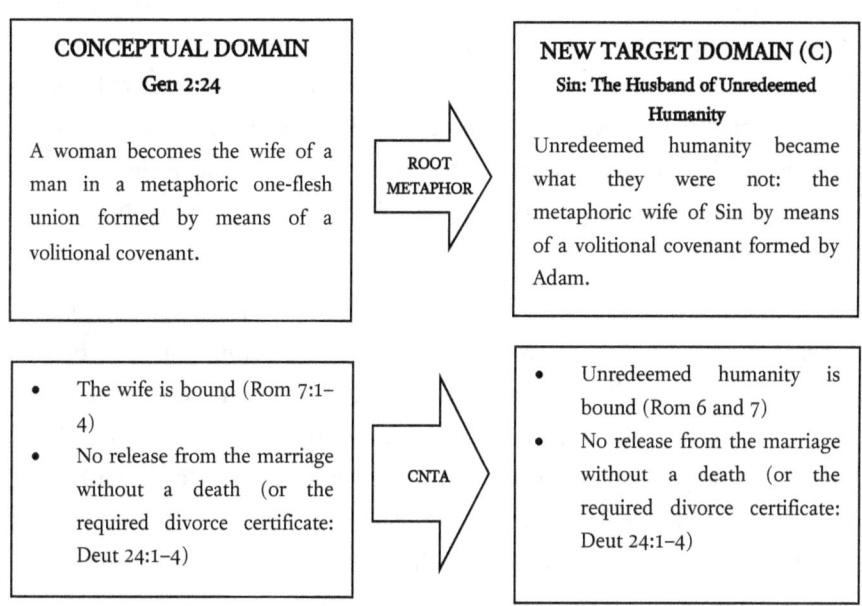

CNTA = Consequent New Testament Analogies

This identification of the imagery by Holland solves the problem of how we can be 'set free' (Rom 6:7) or, as the Greek suggests, 'justified' (δεδικαίωται) from sin by death: as Holland sees it, it is the death of Christ in the place of his people that has severed the relationship with the old husband ('Sin,' i.e. Satan) and thus the 'wife' is 'justified' in taking a new husband.

Notwithstanding the difficulties posed when analysing the target domain of Paul's imagery, the source domain of the cross-mapping in Romans 7 is clear.[624] As commented above, Paul's employment of mundane marriage in his imagery can be seen to be following Jeremiah, in that he, like Jeremiah, understands that mundane marriage legislation in some way controls, or at least limits the available actions in the target domain of his imagery. Thus

---

[624] A similar complexity in the target domain of the marital imagery in the Old Testament prophetic corpus is commented on in §6.13.

Jeremiah uses Deuteronomy 24:1–4 to explain why Israel could not go back to Yahweh having been divorced by him (§6.9.3). Although a mundane wife is able to separate from her husband, she cannot remarry without the decree of divorce referenced there. But such can only be issued by the husband—if he refuses to issue the certificate she is not free to remarry, so is in effect bound to him until his (or her) death, as Paul outlines in Romans 7:1–3. Based on this teaching Paul perceives that the wife in the target domain (in this case, according to Holland, fallen humanity 'married' to Satan) is similarly bound to her husband.[625]

Holland posits that the way out of the impasse, which Paul describes in Romans 7:24: 'Wretched man that I am! Who will deliver me from this body of death?' (i.e. corporate unredeemed humanity), is found in the substitutionary death of Christ in the place of his people trapped in the 'body of death' (the 'wife' in the target domain). The marriage in the imagery is now terminated— the 'wife' is now: 'free from that law [the law of marriage], and if she marries another man she is not an adulteress' (Rom 7:3)—and so can be taken as the bride of Christ. It is a persuasive analysis by Holland.[626]

9.4.3 First Corinthians 6:15–16: The Body of Christ

> Do you not know that your bodies are members of Christ?... For, as it is written, "The two will become one flesh." (1 Cor 6:15–16)

Paul is clearly referencing Genesis 2:24. But here it seems he is cross-mapping that source domain on to Christian believers in what Masson would describe, not as mapping from a source to a target, but as a forced equivalence mapping of two existing conceptual domains.[627] Thus the metaphoric one-flesh/one-body union of Genesis 2:24 (as discussed in §1.4.3 and §1.4.4), embracing the Hebraic concept of *flesh* as kinship (or as Dunn expresses it *flesh* as 'a

---

[625] Elon points out that this is not a situation confined to a wife in ancient Israel but applies to many today in Israel and Jewish Diaspora communities—such a wife: 'becomes an agunah (tied), unable to remarry as long as the death of her husband has not been proven': Aviad Hacohen and Menachem Elon, *The Tears of the Oppressed: An Examination of the Agunah Problem: Background and Halakhic Sources*, ed. Blu Greenberg (Jersey City, NJ: KTAV, 2004), vii–viii

[626] Holland, *Romans*, 226–50

[627] Masson, *Without Metaphor*, 59–68, 186

corporate or national identity'[628]), is cross-mapped with all believers (i.e. the church) generating a third conceptual domain: that all believers are seen to form one new covenantal body, the 'body of Christ'—the logic being that this new corporate identity replaces the corporate body of Israel that Paul had previously expressed confidence in (Phil 3:3–5)—in effect, a new Israel.

It has been suggested (§1.4.3) that this cross-mapping can be represented diagrammatically thus:

MAP 4 The Corporate *Body of Christ* (New conceptual domain 'D' is created)

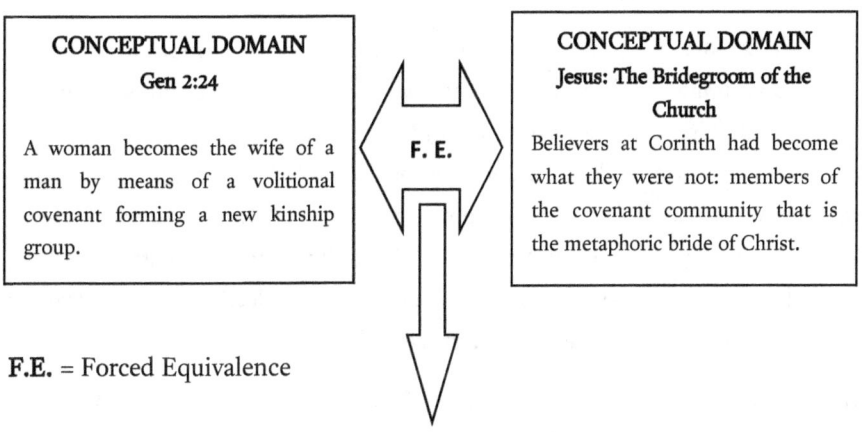

F.E. = Forced Equivalence

---

[628] Dunn, *Theology of Paul*, 70

This body imagery cross-mapping is a logical consequence of the Ephesians 5:31–32 marital imagery—if all believers are in a metaphoric one-flesh union with Christ, it follows that all believers are in a metaphoric one-flesh union with each other: thus Christian believers are (metaphoric) 'brothers' and frequently referred to as such in the New Testament (e.g. Rom 14:10). Paul thus gives the church the same cohesive 'horizontal' identity that Israel demonstrated in 2 Samuel 5:1: 'Then all the tribes of Israel came to David at Hebron and said, "Behold, we are your bone and flesh."'

Paul's cross-mapping in the body imagery is not marital imagery, notwithstanding the fact that the imagery has its source domain in the volitional, metaphoric one-flesh union of Genesis 2:24. Chavasse points out the inter-related nature of the two concepts of the body imagery and the marital imagery when he states: 'She is only the Body of Christ because she is primarily the Mystical Bride of Christ.'[629] Tait similarly comments: 'It is thus perfectly conceivable that the image of the bride is indeed the root image for which that of the [corporate] body derives.'[630]

This forced equivalence cross-mapping allows Paul, to employ Masson's terminology, 'to make logical moves otherwise unavailable'; thus Paul employs this new corporate entity extensively in the corpus not only to represent the church as Jesus' body (e.g. 1 Cor 12:12; Eph 1:22–23; 2:14–16; 3:6; Col 1:18, 24), but to represent the individual members of that body, in their ministries, as forming a functioning entity (e.g. Rom 12:4–8; 1 Cor 12:14–31; Eph 4:15–16). Therefore, uniquely in the Jewish or Christian Scriptures, Paul uses Gen 2:24 in a forced equivalence cross-mapping to generate a functioning corporate body imagery.

---

[629] Chavasse, *The Bride of Christ*, 71

[630] Tait, *Jesus*, 238; the connection between the two is also pointed out in: Holland, *Romans*, 401; Carr and Conway, 'The Divine Human Marriage,' in Nissinen and Uro, *Sacred Marriages*, 300. It is possible Paul was influenced by the body concept in Plato's *Republic*: Plato, 'Republic Book 5,' n. <http://www.perseus.tufts.edu/hopper/text?doc=Perseus%3Atext%3A1999.01.0168%3Abook%3D5%3Apage%3D462> [Accessed: 4/18/2014]; see also for possible origins: J. Paul Sampley, *And the Two Shall Become One Flesh: A Study of Traditions in Ephesians 5:21–33*, SNTSMS 16 (Cambridge: Cambridge University Press, 1971), 61–66

Metaphoric concepts, as discussed in chapter 1, mean that it is not necessary to see a mystical or ontological aspect to the New Testament use of the corporate body language, but as Huber suggests, they can elucidate one's perception of a posited reality:

> Conceptual metaphor theory suggests that much of metaphor's persuasive power lies beneath the surface of a text, because a text's metaphorical mappings prompt the audience to understand particular concepts in interpretive ways. For example, by employing the A CITY IS A WOMAN mapping, a text encourages an audience to envision a collective as an individual entity, which then acts as an individual.[631]

9.4.4 First Corinthians 6:15–16: The Body of a Prostitute

> Do you not know that your bodies are members of Christ? Shall I then take the members of Christ and make them members of a prostitute? Never! Or do you not know that he who is joined to a prostitute becomes one body with her? For, as it is written, 'The two will become one flesh.' (1 Cor 6:15–16)

Commenting on this passage Loader says:

> Sexual intercourse leads to people becoming "one flesh".... Again we have to draw on Gen 2:24. I make myself a member of a prostitute by having sexual intercourse with her.[632]

Thus Loader believes, as outlined in §1.4.4, that one act of sexual intercourse with a prostitute creates a new reality and precludes a believer from communion with Christ, as the two realities created by sexual intercourse are 'mutually exclusive.'[633] It has been suggested that this literal approach fails to identify Paul's imagery.

Deming speculates why it is sex with a prostitute rather than any other illicit sexual relationship that causes the problem and suggests that the pericope is

---

[631] Huber, *Like a Bride*, 180
[632] Loader, *The New Testament on Sexuality*, 170, 172
[633] Loader, *The New Testament on Sexuality*, 177; similarly: Son, 'Implications,' 108

connected with the immorality of 1 Corinthians 5:1 and that the step-mother was perhaps selling her services as a prostitute.[634] But Rosner challenges that view. He describes the pericope as 'difficult' and suggests the issue is one of religious allegiance and the offence 'amounts to apostasy' and that 1 Corinthians 6:16 is used by Paul to 'introduce the notion of a believer's nuptial union with Christ'; but then he fails to follow through with the metaphoric theme of apostasy, describing the offence as a literal sexual liaison with a temple prostitute.[635]

However, it has been seen that the Old Testament marital imagery consistently portrayed Israel's apostasy from her 'husband' Yahweh, not as adultery, but as prostitution (§6.3), thus when Holland follows through with that metaphoric theme he offers a more satisfactory exegesis. He sees that Paul is using the corporate body metaphor and is addressing the church which has members (i.e. believers, employing μέλη as in Eph 5:30) and its counterpart is another corporate body that also has members (i.e. unbelievers), a 'prostitute,' citing in support, 1 Tim 1:20; Rev 2:20–22; and Rev 17:1–7.[636]

Thus it is suggested Paul is cross-mapping Genesis 2:24 in the same way as in his body of Christ imagery, but cross-mapping with a different marital conceptual domain—unredeemed humanity 'married' to Satan, thus generating the corporate body imagery of a 'prostitute.' Paul warns that members of the church family when exhibiting behaviour that is not consistent with New Testament teaching (including, for example, sexual immorality) means they are identifying with the wrong family, becoming 'one flesh' with a 'prostitute'— that is, exchanging (metaphoric) membership of one corporate body for the membership of another.

---

[634] Will Deming, 'The Unity of 1 Corinthians 5–6,' *JBL* 115 (1992), 304

[635] Brian S. Rosner, 'Temple Prostitution in 1 Corinthians 6:12–20,' *NovT* 40 (1998), 341–43; however, Baugh challenges the concept of cult prostitution in New Testament times, including at Corinth: S. M. Baugh, 'Cult Prostitution in New Testament Ephesus: A Reappraisal,' *Journal of the Evangelical Theological Society* 42.3 (1999), 443–60; also Winter, 'The size of the Roman temple of Aphrodite on the Acrocorinth ruled out ... temple prostitution': Bruce W. Winter, *After Paul Left Corinth: The Influence of Secular Ethics and Social Change* (Grand Rapids, MI: Eerdmans, 2001), 88

[636] Holland, *Contours*, 124–39

Huber (as referenced in §1.4.4) endorses such a concept when commenting on the imagery of Revelation 17–21:

> the images of harlot and bride depict two possible forms of existence for the Christian community. The community can live in idolatry, as a prostitute, or the community can live in faithfulness to God, as a bride.[637]

The diagrammatic representation of Paul's imagery, as in §1.4.4, was:

MAP 5 The Corporate *Body of a Prostitute* (New conceptual domain 'E' is created)

CONCEPTUAL DOMAIN Gen 2:24		CONCEPTUAL DOMAIN Sin: The Husband of Unredeemed Humanity
A woman becomes the wife of a man by means of a volitional covenant forming a new kinship group.	F. E.	Unredeemed humanity becomes the metaphoric wife of 'Sin' by means of a volitional covenant formed by Adam.

F.E. = Forced Equivalence

NEW CONCEPTUAL DOMAIN (E)
A New 'Horizontal' Identity:
The Body of a Prostitute
(The Body of Sin)
Or do you not know that he who is joined to a prostitute becomes one body with her? For, as it is written, "The two will become one flesh."
(1 Cor 6:16)

---

[637] Huber, *Like a Bride*, 32; similarly Beale, pointing out the parallel between Rev 17:1–3 and Rev 21:9–10 states: 'Just as Babylon symbolizes socio-economic and religious culture arrayed in antagonism to God, so the bride, portrayed as the new Jerusalem, represents the redeemed community': Beale, *Revelation*, 1064

Although Holland does not reference metaphor theory, I believe that his exegesis nonetheless correctly identifies the imagery. It is an exegesis that has many advantages—not least it means the imagery employed is consistent with the imagery of the 'prostitute' in the Old Testament and the Apocalypse, and consistent with the use of the corporate body metaphor employed elsewhere in the Pauline corpus. Furthermore, it does not see that one act of sexual intercourse with a literal prostitute changes an ontological reality—Loader, although understanding that this is the teaching of the pericope, acknowledges the conceptual difficulties of such.[638]

The literal interpretation of this Corinthians pericope has led to the concept that Genesis 2:24 speaks of a one-flesh union, formed by sexual intercourse, that has an ill-defined ontological and/or mystical dimension. However, the Hebrew Bible understanding is that the Genesis 2:24 one-flesh union refers to a union of kinship formed by a volitional covenant (§1.2). The consensus view that Paul is speaking of a literal prostitute, in effect, sees that this short pericope in 1 Corinthians 6 has redefined the Hebrew Bible one-flesh union of Genesis 2:24, the nature of mundane marriage, and given sexual intercourse an ontological dimension—all significant departures from ancient Israel's understanding of marriage and their own Scriptures. However, if the analysis above is correct, the pericope does not change the Hebrew Bible's understanding of coitus, mundane marriage, or Genesis 2:24. Thus this study suggests it is the Hebrew Bible's metaphoric, covenantal, kinship concept of the Genesis 2:24 one-flesh union that is cross-mapped in the body of Christ imagery, and in the body of a prostitute imagery.

9.4.5 First Corinthians 6:19–20: Bought With a Price

> Or do you not know that your body is a temple of the Holy Spirit within you, whom you have from God? You are not your own, for you were bought with a price. So glorify God in your body. (1 Cor 6:19–20)

---

[638] Loader describes sexual intercourse as creating a 'permanent bond'; but then when commenting on what he sees as the sexual act with a prostitute in 1 Cor 6 he speculates as to whether or not that particular new ontological reality is 'reversible,' and states 'presumably it is': Loader, *The New Testament on Sexuality*, 175–77, 269

It appears that in v. 19 Paul is addressing the whole church at Corinth employing σῶμα (body) as in v. 16 with a corporate meaning: the Greek has 'your [plural] body [singular] is a temple'—it is the church collectively that is the temple of the Holy Spirit, the body of Christ raised to replace the Jerusalem temple (John 2:19).[639]

Carr and Conway observe that the pericope could be a reference to a slave price or a bride-price, but conclude: 'in the context of 1 Corinthians 6, Paul's reasoning suggests he has a marriage exchange in mind.'[640] Chavasse suggests Jesus is the divine husband paying the redemption money he believes is referenced in Hosea 3:2-3 (§6.6).[641] If this analysis is correct it would mean Paul is using the same structure map as the Gospels and the Apocalypse (*Jesus: The Bridegroom of the Church*) and cross-mapping the mundane marriage practice of the bridegroom paying a *mohar* for his bride, to the concept in the target map of the imagery that Christ's death on the cross was the *mohar* for his bride, the church.

9.4.6 Second Corinthians 11:2: Betrothed to Christ

Second Corinthians 11:2 states: 'I feel a divine jealousy for you, for I betrothed you to one husband, to present you as a pure virgin to Christ.' Paul is again using the structure map employed by the Gospels and the Apocalypse and writes to the Corinthians portraying them as the bride and himself as the bride's father who had betrothed her. In mundane marriage in ancient Israel during the betrothal period, when the daughter lived in the parental home, the father, having received the *mohar* for a virgin daughter, would have to accept some responsibility for such, as is implied by Deuteronomy 22:13-21.[642]

---

[639] Both Gehring and Grosheide suggest it is possible that σῶμα is a corporate reference to the church in v. 19 even though both see that σῶμα in v. 16 references a literal prostitute: Gehring, *The Biblical "One Flesh,"* 266-67; Grosheide, *Commentary*, 148-52

[640] Carr and Conway, 'The Divine Human Marriage,' in Nissinen and Uro, *Sacred Marriages*, 298; similarly Holland, *Contours*, 112-21; *contra* 1 Cor 7:22-23 which implies slave redemption.

[641] Chavasse, *The Bride of Christ*, 64-65

[642] Epstein, speaking of rabbinic concepts, suggests: 'The non-virgin, in the spirit of Biblical legislation, was not entitled to any mohar': Epstein, *The Jewish Marriage Contract*, 72; on the duty of parents: Mace, *Hebrew Marriage*, 182-83

Instone-Brewer points out that the future remarriage promised Israel in the Old Testament is:

> described as though it were the first marriage of a virgin bride, as though the new united nation was a completely new individual without the murky past of either of her component nations.[643]

Instone-Brewer believes (as this present study posits) that this remarriage promise is embraced in the New Testament imagery.[644] The concept of a virgin bride is consonant with this Corinthians pericope, and thus the problem in the imagery of remarrying the first husband *contra* Deuteronomy 24, is circumvented.

9.4.7 Second Timothy 2:10–13: The Betrothal Period

When Paul speaks of the elect awaiting their 'eternal glory' in 2 Timothy 2:10 it might be interpreted as speaking of a betrothal period, although not specifically articulated as such:

> Therefore I endure everything for the sake of the elect, that they also may obtain the salvation that is in Christ Jesus with eternal glory. The saying is trustworthy, for: If we have died with him, we will also live with him; if we endure, we will also reign with him; if we deny him, he also will deny us; if we are faithless, he remains faithful—for he cannot deny himself. (2 Tim 2:10–13)

If such is the case Paul is again using the structure map based on *Jesus: The Bridegroom of the Church* and is implying that Jesus as the bridegroom would only breach the betrothal agreement if the bride actively sought it by 'denying him'; but if she had merely lost faith that he would fulfil his promise to come for her he would nonetheless be true to that promise. This is consistent with the asymmetrical gender-based mundane marriage covenant in ancient Israel, in that the wife could choose to leave the relationship and the husband treat such as a divorce of him (Exod 21:10–11); but he could only initiate a divorce based on her 'indecency' as outlined in Deuteronomy 24:1–4 (also Matt 5:32;

---

[643] Instone-Brewer, *Divorce and Remarriage*, 53
[644] Instone-Brewer, *Divorce and Remarriage*, 53

Matt 19:9); thus Joseph is described as a 'just man' when he looked to initiate a divorce against Mary for her presumed sexual unfaithfulness in their betrothal period (Matt 1:18–19).

9.4.8 Ephesians 5:22–33

This pericope is the longest sustained teaching on marriage in either the Jewish or Christian Scriptures. It is suggested that in light of the analysis above it is now possible to see that it consists of a juxtaposition of the two different but related models: Christ as head of the church, his metaphoric body; and Christ as saviour of the church, his metaphoric bride. Farla describes the chain of reasoning as complicated, and although his commentary is not persuasive, his structural analysis of the pericope forms the basis of the analysis below.[645]

> Wives, submit to your own husbands, as to the Lord. For the husband is the head of the wife even as Christ is the head of the church, his body, and is himself its Saviour. Now as the church submits to Christ, so also wives should submit in everything to their husbands. (Eph 5:22–24)

The metaphoric corporate body of Christ imagery is used analogically to suggest a husband has similar headship of his wife to that of Christ over the church and thus the analogy reinforces the household codes (e.g. Col 3:18–4:1; 1 Pet 2:13–3:7)—marital imagery *per se* is not employed.

> Husbands, love your wives, as Christ loved the church and gave himself up for her, that he might sanctify her, having cleansed her by the washing of water with the word, so that he might present the church to himself in splendour, without spot or wrinkle or any such thing, that she might be holy and without blemish. (Eph 5:25–27)

Here the metaphoric marital imagery is used analogically to suggest a husband has a similar responsibility to love his wife as Christ does the church, utilising in the imagery bridal baths and bridal purity from Jewish traditions of

---

[645] Piet J. Farla, '"The Two Shall Become One Flesh": Gen 1.27 and 2.24 in the New Testament Marriage Texts,' in *Intertextuality in Biblical Writings: Essays in Honour of Bas van Iersel*, ed. S. Draisma (Kampen: Kok Pharos, 1989), 72–75

mundane marriage.[646] Verse 25 is a clear example of articulated reverse cross-domain mapping of the marital imagery.[647]

The pericope continues:

> In the same way husbands should love their wives as their own bodies. He who loves his wife loves himself. For no one ever hated his own flesh, but nourishes and cherishes it, just as Christ does the church, because we are members of his body. (Eph 5:28–30)

Farla (*contra* Sampley) argues persuasively that at v. 28 the author is reverting to the corporate body image and setting up another analogy between that and mundane marriage and applying its lessons to the husband.[648] It is a structural analysis that gives the pericope up to this point a clear A B A structure whereby the Ephesians author is seen to move from: corporate body imagery to emphasise headship; marital imagery to illustrate the sacrificial love a husband should have for his wife; and back to corporate body imagery to illustrate a husband's responsibility to nourish his wife as he might his own body—this latter duty appears to be a reflection of a husband's responsibility as outlined in Exodus 21:10–11.

But rather than seeing an analogy in v. 28, that is, husbands should love their wives *as if they were* their own bodies;[649] Farla would have v. 28 say that husbands should love their wives *because* they are their own bodies—and thus he appears to see that the pericope teaches some sort of literal one-flesh union in mundane marriage: 'the love of a husband for his wife is actually love for

---

[646] O'Brien sees v. 26 a reference to Ezek 16:8–14 and the prenuptial Jewish bathing customs (not baptism): Peter T. O'Brien, *The Letter to the Ephesians* (Grand Rapids, MI: Eerdmans, 1999), 422–24; *contra* Schnackenburg: 'The author is clearly thinking of Baptism': Rudolf Schnackenburg, *The Epistle to the Ephesians,* trans. Helen Heron (Edinburgh: T&T Clark, 1991), 249; Batey equates the bridal bath to baptism: Batey, *New Testament Nuptial Imagery,* 28; similarly Sampley sees a reference to Ezek 16, baptism, and the bridal bath; he comments on v. 27 and the purity required of a bride and allusions to Song: Sampley, *And the Two,* 41–51, 131, 139

[647] However, it is suggested in this present study that the use of this analogy does not necessarily imply that Christ in this Ephesians pericope is deemed to be the husband of the church, *contra*: Smolarz, *Covenant and Metaphor,* 222–27

[648] Sampley states: 'Verse 30 must be taken as the conclusion of the entire comparison between Christ and the church and husband and wife': Sampley, *And the Two,* 145

[649] Barth sees οὕτως ... καὶ of Eph 5:28 means 'in the same manner': Markus Barth, *Ephesians 4–6: A New Translation with Introduction and Commentary by Markus Barth,* AB 34A. (Garden City, NY: Doubleday, 1974), 629–30; similarly: Schnackenburg, *Ephesians,* 252

himself, for his wife is his own body – it is just as with Christ and the Church.'⁶⁵⁰

> "Therefore a man shall leave his father and mother and hold fast to his wife, and the two shall become one flesh." This mystery is profound, and I am saying that it refers to Christ and the church. However, let each one of you love his wife as himself, and let the wife see that she respects her husband. (Eph 5:31–33)⁶⁵¹

These verses, containing the closing comments of the pericope, have generated much academic debate. Farla points out that, although the 'clear consensus' on v. 32 is that the profound mystery (and the Gen 2:24 quotation) has 'a meaning related to Christ and the Church,' he argues against such.⁶⁵² Farla sees that the mystery is that the husband and wife mirror, not the Christ/church union as in the marital imagery, but the one-flesh union as in the corporate body of Christ imagery—'it explains why Christ loves the church: because it is His own body ... the ideal of mutual love between husband and wife in marriage is founded on God's plan of creation.'⁶⁵³ Thus Farla sees a primal couple marriage model. However, Schnackenburg points out that:

---

⁶⁵⁰ Farla, 'The Two,' in Draisma, *Intertextuality*, 73; *contra* O'Brien: 'Nowhere in the context is the wife regarded as the husband's body as the church is Christ's body': O'Brien, *Letter*, 414–15

⁶⁵¹ Barth analyses in some detail the textual variants of v. 30 where some MSS have as an ending: 'from his flesh and from his bones'; he further analyses the quotation of Gen 2:24 from the LXX in v. 31—but none of his comments appear to be materially significant for this study: Barth, *Ephesians 4–6*, 720–25

⁶⁵² Farla, 'The Two,' in Draisma, *Intertextuality*, 74; O'Brien analyses various views on the nature of the 'mystery': O'Brien, *Letter*, 430–35

⁶⁵³ Farla, 'The Two,' in Draisma, *Intertextuality*, 73, 75. Others have made arguments similar to Farla, thus Batey: 'The church is not considered to be the wife of Christ; it is his Body': Batey, *Nuptial Imagery*, 31; Miletic apparently comes to a similar conclusion but via a different route—he sees that Eph 5:31 is (in effect) cross-mapping the Christ/church union with Adam and Eve as he equates Gen 2:24 with the primal couple: Stephen Francis Miletic, *"One Flesh": Eph. 5.22–24, 5.31: Marriage and the New Creation* (Rome: Analecta Biblica, 1988), 114–15; similarly Moritz, 'the writer undoubtedly alludes to or implies human one flesh union on the basis of the narrator's aside in Gen 2:24': Thorsten Moritz, *A Profound Mystery: The Use of the Old Testament in Ephesians* (Leiden: Brill, 1996), 143; Lincoln similarly has: 'It is surely because of the notion of Gen. 2:24 that the act of marriage makes husband and wife one flesh that the writer can make this comparison of the wives to their husband's bodies': Andrew T. Lincoln, 'The Use of the Old Testament in Ephesians,' *JSNew Testament* 14 (1982), 31

> it would contradict the structure of the whole paraclesis on marriage if the relationship between husband and wife were now interpreted according to the order of Creation and not as hitherto according to the model of Christ and the Church.... The "great mystery" ... [lies] not in marriage as such but in the relationship between Christ and the Church.[654]

In other words Schnackenburg sees, consonant with the analysis of the pericope in this present study, that the (reverse cross-mapped) model for mundane marriage is not the primal couple, but the Christ/church relationship. Such an analysis is in accord with the marital imagery employed by the Gospels and the Apocalypse, and that of the Pauline corpus elsewhere (1 Cor 6:19–20; 2 Cor 11:2; 2 Tim 2:10–13).

Thus it is argued in this present study that the pericope alternates between the Pauline corpus marital and body imagery and uses both as models for mundane marriage, and the marriage relationship that the imagery is analogically cross-mapped with throughout the pericope is the metaphoric one-flesh relationship described in Genesis 2:24 as quoted in v. 31—not the one-flesh relationship of the primal couple described in Genesis 2:23. The analogies employed in the pericope emphasise the ongoing commitment for the husband to nourish and cherish his wife, reflecting the Exodus triad of care, rather than suggesting an ontological dimension to mundane marriage that might have been the case if the cross-mapping had been with the understanding of a primal couple model based on the one-flesh union of Genesis 2:23.

But the mystery now revealed, it is suggested, lies (*contra* Farla), not in a new mundane marriage teaching or even, as per Schnackenburg et al., in the Christ/church union (there is no mystery in the marital imagery of the pericope *per se*—it is the marital imagery of the Old Testament); the mystery lies in the identity of the 'members of his body' referenced in v. 30.

---

[654] Schnackenburg, *Ephesians*, 254-55; similarly Barth: 'in Eph 5, [the Christ-church union] is the sole basis upon which all statements of marriage are founded': Barth, *Ephesians 4–6*, 737

Sampley sees that a key focus of Ephesians is the incorporation of Gentile and Jew into the one body—the body of Christ.[655] He points out that the author is developing this theme from Ephesians 2:11–22;[656] verses 15–16 state:

> That he might create in himself one new man in place of the two, so making peace, and might reconcile us both to God in one body through the cross, thereby killing the hostility. (Eph 2:15–16)

Ephesians 2:17 references Isaiah 57:19 and a future hope for Israel; and Ephesians 2:18 has: 'For through him we both have access in one Spirit to the Father.' Sampley suggests:

> When a substantive like μυστήριον is used six times in such crucial places as it is in Ephesians, there is considerable probability of some lines of continuity of meaning between the uses in the different contexts.[657]

Thus for Sampley the μυστήριον of Ephesians 5:32 is the incorporation of Gentile and Jew into the one body;[658] he comments: 'The recipients of Ephesians are urged to recognise that they, together with Jews, share in God's cosmic purposes.'[659] As has been seen (§1.6), Israel's hope was in the conceptual domain of Genesis 2:23 in that they came *from* Abraham—just as Eve came *from* Adam. Here Paul appears to say that the Gentile hope lies in the conceptual domain of Genesis 2:24, in that they can become what they were not *into* a one-flesh union with Christ.

---

[655] Sampley, *And the Two*, 92–94
[656] Sampley, *And the Two*, 161–62
[657] Sampley, *And the Two*, 91; the mystery is referenced in: Eph 1:9; 3:3, 4, 6, 9; 5:32; 6:19.
[658] Sampley, *And the Two*, 90–96; similarly Lincoln: 'In the other five references in Ephesians ... "mystery" involves ... the coming together in Christ of Jews and Gentiles in the one Church.... Is it not most likely that ... here in 5:32 the writer has this same Christ-event in view': Lincoln, 'The Use of the Old Testament,' 32–33; however Barth, accepting that *mystery* elsewhere in the letter is a reference to the Jew/Gentile union in Christ favours the view that *mystery* in Eph 5:32 'indicates that the Scripture passage quoted ... is to be understood in an allegorical or typological way': Barth, *Ephesians 4–6*, 641–44; similarly Coppens specifically rejects *mystery* as a reference to the Jew/Gentile union in Eph 5:32 and states: 'In Eph 5:32 the mystery concerns the relations of Christ with the Church': Joseph Coppens, '"Mystery" in the Theology of Saint Paul and its Parallels at Qumran,' in *Paul and Qumran: Studies in New Testament Exegesis*, ed. Jerome Murphy-O'Connor (London: Chapman, 1968), 142, 150
[659] Sampley, *And the Two*, 162

In other words, Ephesians 5:31–32 links the Christ/church relationship and the inclusion of the Gentiles with the marital affinity relationship of Genesis 2:24, whereby a non-consanguineous couple on marriage can be counted as being in one family. Galatians 3:16 states:

> 'Now the promises were made to Abraham and to his offspring. It does not say, "And to offsprings," referring to many, but referring to one, "And to your offspring," who is Christ.'

It is clear Paul sees that the promise to Abraham is fulfilled in Christ, thus when the believing community becomes the bride of Christ they, by means of the Genesis 2:24 affinity union, become a member of Christ's family. Paul continues in Galatians 3:29, 'And if you are Christ's, then you are Abraham's offspring, heirs according to promise.' This, it is argued in this present study, is how the promise to Abraham's offspring is reconciled with the Old Testament promises to include the Gentiles, and is the profound mystery referenced in Ephesians 5:32. This argument is further strengthened when it is considered that in Romans 9:22–29 the inclusion of the Gentiles is linked to the promised 'remarriage' in the marital imagery as foretold by Hosea: 'Those who were not my people I will call "my people"'—an imagery the New Testament sees as being fulfilled in the marriage of Christ and the church at the eschaton.

It follows from this analysis that the pericope can be seen to be bringing together the two metaphoric images which, as Chavasse and Tait suggest, belong together: the one-flesh corporate body imagery and the one-flesh marital imagery, and in so doing portray Jew and Gentile together forming one body (with Christ as the head) and one bride (with Christ as the bridegroom) in a marriage to be consummated at the eschaton where they will become one flesh with their 'husband'—Carmichael pointing out that Christ in effect 'marries' his own body as did Adam with Eve, fulfilling, he believes, that Edenic ideal.[660] Thus, it is suggested in this present study, that the author of

---

[660] Carmichael, 'Marriage,' 341–42

Ephesians sees a *sensus plenior* in Genesis 2:24 foreshadowing redemptive history and the inclusion of the Gentiles.[661]

9.5 A Second Divorce

Instone-Brewer draws attention to the fact that Origen saw that the destruction of Jerusalem in 70 CE was in effect God's divorce of Jerusalem:

> Now, keeping in mind what we said above in regard to the passage from Isaiah about the bill of divorcement we will say that the mother of the people separated herself from Christ, her husband, without having received the bill of divorcement, but afterwards when there was found in her an unseemly thing, and she did not find favour in his sight, the bill of divorcement was written out for her;... And a sign that she has received the bill of divorcement is this, that Jerusalem was destroyed along with what they called the sanctuary of the things in it which were believed to be holy, and with the altar of burnt offerings, and all the worship associated with it.[662]

It is suggested in this present study that if the destruction of Jerusalem can, in light of New Testament marital imagery, be treated as a divorce, it is a divorce of Judah—the remnant of national Israel, with Jesus' comment as recorded in Matthew 23 (also Luke 13:34-35) being a reference to such:

> O Jerusalem, Jerusalem, the city that kills the prophets and stones those who are sent to it! How often would I have gathered your children together as a hen gathers her brood under her wings, and you would not! See, your house is left to you desolate. For I tell you, you will not see me again, until you say, 'Blessed is he who comes in the name of the Lord.' (Matt 23:37-39)

---

[661] Accepting that *sensus plenior* differs from typology in that the meaning is in the words rather than the people or the event.

[662] Origen, *Commentary on Matthew,* translated by John Patrick from Ante-Nicene Fathers, Vol. 9 (Buffalo, NY: Christian Literature Publishing Co, 1896). Revised and edited for New Advent by Kevin Knight <http://www.newadvent.org/fathers/1016.htm>, 14-19; Instone-Brewer, *Divorce and Remarriage,* 246-47

Thus it might be that Matthew understood that Malachi 2:10–16 was referencing such a potential divorce (as posited in §6.9.4), Malachi promising Elijah as a final messenger (Mal 3:1; 4:5–6) before its enactment, whom Matthew sees as being represented by John the Baptist, despite the latter's claim otherwise (Matt 11:10–14 cf. John 1:21):[663]

> Behold, I will send you Elijah the prophet before the great and awesome day of the LORD comes. And he will turn the hearts of fathers to their children and the hearts of children to their fathers, lest I come and strike the land with a decree of utter destruction. (Mal 4:5-6)

9.6 Adam and Eve as Types in the New Testament

It has been pointed out (§2.3) that many scholars see that the New Testament employs Adam and Eve as archetypes for mundane marriage. But Romans 5:14 specifically states that Adam is a type (τύπος) 'of the one who was to come.'[664] Similarly 1 Corinthians 15:21–22, 45–49; v. 47 states: 'The first man was from the earth … the second man is from heaven.'

2 Corinthians 11:2–3 has:

> I feel a divine jealousy for you, for I betrothed you to one husband, to present you as a pure virgin to Christ. But I am afraid that as the serpent deceived Eve by his cunning, your thoughts will be led astray from a sincere and pure devotion to Christ. (2 Cor 11:2–3)

Here Paul employs marital imagery, but then expands on the metaphor and compares the Corinthian church to Eve in her waywardness, thus implying that Christ could be compared to Adam. It is possible to see parallels between the events in Eden and the cross: Pitre and Chavasse see that Eve coming from Adam's side when he was in a deep sleep prefigured Christ's death and

---

[663] A possible explanation to the anomaly is that the Baptist denied being in any literal sense Elijah, while the 'he is Elijah' of Matt 11:14 is a metaphoric expression; Luke similarly links John the Baptist with the Malachi promise of a final messenger and cites Jesus as declaring Jerusalem's destruction: Luke 7:27; 13:34–35.

[664] This employment of τύπος is similar to 1 Cor 10:11 which, when referring to the desert experience of the Israelites, has: 'Now these things happened to them as an example [τυπικῶς], but they were written down for our instruction.'

resurrection, and that the primal couple typologically prefigure the marriage of Christ and the Church.[665] Furthermore, Gehring sees many distinct parallels between the Genesis account of Eden and the new heaven and earth.[666]

But, if the analysis of this chapter is correct, Adam and Eve's marriage is not referenced in the marital imagery as an archetype, paradigm, or model for mundane marriage, the Pauline corpus confining itself to drawing a parallel between Adam's headship of Eve and a man's headship of a 'woman' (γυνή)—possibly, but not necessarily, a wife (1 Tim 2:13-14; 1 Cor 11:7-10).

9.7 Summary: Marital Imagery in the New Testament

The aim of this chapter was to explore the key features of New Testament marital imagery to identify the source domain and the associated cross-mapping. It was posited (§9.1) that it would be demonstrated that the New Testament writers draw not on the primal couple, but on mundane marriage underpinned by the concepts of Genesis 2:24—that is, a volitional, conditional, metaphoric one-flesh union. It was further posited that a new root metaphor is introduced: rather than *Yahweh: The Husband of Israel*, the Gospels and the Apocalypse employ the root metaphor: *Jesus: The Bridegroom of the Church*. It is suggested that the above analysis confirms this.

It has been seen that the New Testament writers demonstrate, as does the Hebrew Bible, great flexibility in their use of the imagery to suit their own ends. Thus the betrothal practices of contemporary mundane marriage are extensively exploited to illustrate the ministry of Jesus. It is clear that the primal couple can play no part in such imagery—there was no betrothal in Eden. The Pauline corpus further demonstrates originality in that it develops a body of Christ imagery, and a marital and body imagery based on unredeemed humanity's relationship with sin. Ephesians 5:22-33 brings the bride of Christ/body of Christ imagery together to portray the inclusion of the Gentiles in the eschatological marriage, seeing such as the *sensus plenior* of Genesis

---

[665] Pitre, *Jesus the Bridegroom*, 111; Chavasse, *The Bride of Christ*, 79
[666] Gehring, *The Biblical "One Flesh,"* 300-309

2:24. Thus Paul claims that the Gentiles, who do not belong to the consanguineous one-flesh family of Israel, can now become what they were not, in a metaphoric one-flesh union, as the bride and body of Christ.

Furthermore, there is no requirement for consistency in the target domain even when the imagery is employed by the same (apparent) author: so the 'bride' can represent both the lost and the saved (Rom 6 and 7), and be both a woman and a city (Rev 19 and 21). But despite this flexibility in the target domain in New Testament marital imagery, just as in the Hebrew Bible, the consistent source map of the imagery is Genesis 2:24 and the contemporary Jewish marital practices that that conceptual domain underpinned.

9.8 New Testament Marital Imagery and Traditional Teaching

The published material that explores Old Testament marital imagery considered in chapter 6 is marked by an analysis of metaphor theory, and an examination of the imagery in light of that in order to understand it in its context. In contrast, few New Testament scholars appear to have engaged with metaphor theory and this, it seems, has led to a failure by many to identify aspects of the marital and body imagery employed by the New Testament writers. And no published work this study is aware of has commented on what the New Testament writers appear to allude to (e.g. John 4), and to articulate (e.g. Eph 5:31–32): that is, it is the Old Testament understanding of marriage outlined in Genesis 2:24 that is cross-mapped in the imagery, not the marriage of Genesis 2:23, and that each marriage has their own mutually exclusive principles.

It seems that the traditional teaching of the church, supported by the understanding of many scholars, has wrongly identified Genesis 2:24 as being a literal, or at least a mystical, restatement of the one-flesh union of the primal couple which has given rise to the concept, articulated by Son (and specifically endorsed by Gehring and shared by Loader) that 'husband/wife = Christ/church = Adam/Eve';[667] each is believed to be an ontological union

---

[667] Son, 'Implications,' 110, 114; Gehring, *The Biblical "One Flesh,"* 312

formed by God (or each union is seen as specifically endorsed by God)—and perceived to be a union based on sexual intercourse.[668]

This belief that marriage (and specifically sexual intercourse) forms an ontological union is the prism through which key New Testament passages on marriage, divorce, and remarriage are understood. But this present study suggests Son's equation, and therefore the subsequent logic, is flawed, in that it fails to consider that the husband/wife relationship, like the Christ/church relationship (at least until the eschaton), is a metaphoric, covenantal, kinship, one-flesh union, and therefore unlike the one-flesh union of Adam and Eve.

In this chapter, I have argued that the New Testament cross-maps the same source and target domains as does the Old Testament in its marital imagery: the covenantal one-flesh marriage of Genesis 2:24 and the divine marriage respectively; with the Pauline corpus developing a new marriage imagery with the root metaphor *Sin: The Husband of Unredeemed Humanity*; and new metaphoric corporate body imagery by cross-mapping Genesis 2:24—first with all believers (the body of Christ), and then with all unbelievers (the body of a prostitute). The primal couple do not figure in the imagery.

9.9 Some Implications for New Testament Exegesis

The analysis of the Old Testament imagery in chapter 6 posited that Adam's expulsion from Eden can be described as a divorce (§6.12), and that Israel's expulsion from the Promised Land amounted to the same thing (§6.9). The analysis of the New Testament imagery in this chapter has suggested that the destruction of Jerusalem in 70 CE can be portrayed as Christ's divorce of Judah (§9.5). But that same imagery portrays the eschatological marriage as a marriage open to all—Jew (Israel and Judah) and Gentile (§9.4.8). As the Gentiles are perceived to share the same fate of all humanity in ('divorced') Adam (Rom 5:12), it can be seen that all the parties in the proposed eschatological marriage are divorcees. Thus it appears that divorce and

---

[668] Loader: 'sexual intercourse actually changes people by creating a new reality ... something almost magical ... occurs in sexual intercourse, especially initial intercourse': Loader, *The New Testament on Sexuality*, 176, 291

remarriage is central to the marital imagery of both the Jewish and Christian Scriptures.

It follows that the Bible's marital imagery presents at least three problems to any exegesis of New Testament divorce and remarriage teaching that sees the primal couple as the mundane marriage model, a model that leads to an understanding that New Testament teaching forbids divorce and/or remarriage.

Firstly, a primal couple marriage model cannot serve as the source domain for an imagery that embraces betrothal, divorce, and remarriage—it does not have the characteristics required for the cross-mapping.

Secondly, as New Testament marital imagery embraces divorce and remarriage in its target domain, it would mean the New Testament writers employed an imagery that embraced concepts they repudiated in their own mundane marriage teaching.

Thirdly, metaphors rely on the utilisation of a source domain known to its intended audience. Thus Westbrook's comment when speaking of Old Testament marital imagery (as cited in §5.1), I would suggest, applies equally to New Testament marital imagery:

> If God's relationship with Israel is to be explained by a metaphor drawing upon the everyday life of the audience, then that metaphor, to be effective, must reflect accurately the reality known to the audience. If the narrator were to invent the legal rules on which the metaphor is based, it would cease to be a valid metaphor.[669]

The literary and documentary evidence suggests that a primal couple marriage model was not part of the cultural world of the implied readership of the New Testament. In contrast, it seems clear that divorce and remarriage was an integral part of both first century Jewish culture, and of New Testament marital imagery. Thus it is argued in this study that any exegesis of New Testament teaching on mundane marriage should seek one that is consonant with the marital imagery it employs, and only if one cannot be found should

---

[669] Westbrook, 'Adultery in Ancient Near Eastern Law,' 577

the attempt be abandoned in favour of another. This premise is reinforced when the extensive nature of New Testament marital imagery is contrasted with the brevity of its mundane marriage teaching, a brevity that has apparently obfuscated its meaning for subsequent exegetes; and the fact that the New Testament itself identifies Genesis 2:24 and mundane marriage as the source domain of its imagery, and articulates a reverse cross-mapping of the imagery to teach about mundane marriage in Ephesians 5.

The task of chapter 10 is to seek such an exegesis of the New Testament pericopae that address, in particular, mundane divorce and remarriage teaching.

Chapter 10: Divorce and Remarriage in the New Testament

10.1 Introduction

The apparent consensus among New Testament scholars and the church is that the one-flesh marriage of the primal couple is introduced (or restored) in New Testament teaching as the model for human marriage (§2.3). Based on this various church groupings have adopted teaching that, in summary, forbids: divorce (the Church of Rome);[670] remarriage after divorce while the divorced partner lives (the Church of England);[671] remarriage after divorce for the 'innocent party,' and remarriage after desertion if the deserting partner is not a believer (many independent churches).[672] These views, and their different permutations, will be referred to in this chapter as the traditional teaching.

However, the primal couple model employed by scholars and the church, and the divorce and remarriage restrictions consequently embraced by various church groupings, are not reflected in the legislation or marital practices of the Old Testament, or in its marital imagery (chapters 5 & 6). Although there is some limited evidence of discussion of a primal couple model in the Second Temple literature (chapter 7), the extant papyri from the period (a period that embraces the New Testament era) demonstrate that such a model was not adopted in practice (chapter 8).

---

[670] Catechism 1615: '[There is an] unequivocal insistence on the indissolubility of the marriage bond': Peter J. Kreeft, *Catholic Christianity: A Complete Catechism of Catholic Beliefs Based on the Catechism of the Catholic Church* (San Francisco, CA: Ignatius Press, 2001), 362

[671] 'The Church of England agreed in 2002 that divorced people could remarry in church under certain circumstances. However, because the Church views marriage to be lifelong, there is no automatic right to do so and it is left to the discretion of the Priest': Church of England, 'As Someone Who is Divorced, Can I Marry in Church,' n.p. [cited 12 September 2015]. Online: <https://www.churchofengland.org/our-views/marriage,-family-and-sexuality-issues/divorce.aspx>. The impact of the Church of England teaching on the UK monarchy can be seen in the 1936 abdication of Edward VIII because of his decision to marry a divorcee, and the refusal of the Church to marry Prince Charles and the divorced Mrs Parker-Bowles while her ex-husband was still alive, hence their civil ceremony in 2005.

[672] See analysis in: Wayne H. House, ed., *Divorce and Remarriage: Four Christian Views* (Downers Grove, IL: InterVarsity, 1990); William A. Heth, 'Jesus on Divorce: How My Mind Was Changed,' *SBJT* 6.1 (Spring 2002), 4–12; Paul E. Engle and Mark L. Strauss, eds., *Remarriage after Divorce in Today's Church: 3 Views* (Grand Rapids, MI: Zondervan, 2006)

Chapter 9 demonstrated that the source and target domains of New Testament imagery were congruent, both being based on the Old Testament understanding of the volitional, conditional, covenantal marital union of Genesis 2:24. It might be argued that this does not negate the possibility that the New Testament writers adopted a primal couple model as the basis for their mundane marriage teaching (i.e. utilised a source domain rooted in Gen 2:23); but this would mean that they were repudiating in their teaching the marriage model they employed in their imagery: a model of marriage familiar to contemporary society—one that the Bridegroom Messiah is portrayed in the Gospels as fulfilling in some detail, and which climaxes in the Apocalypse when he is seen to take the elect, including it seems the elect of 'divorced' Israel, into a new 'marriage.'

The aim of this chapter is to demonstrate that an exegesis of New Testament mundane marriage teaching, with special reference to divorce and remarriage, can be found that is consonant with its marital imagery. There is a large volume of published material that articulates various combinations of the traditional views regarding New Testament marriage and divorce teaching but it is beyond the scope of this chapter to address that corpus. Various commentators will be cited on a particular verse or pericope to support an exegesis that is consonant with the marital imagery, but this is not meant to imply that they agree with the position taken in this study, or that they might not dissent from such a consonant exegesis on another verse or pericope.

10.2 Marriage in the New Testament

The only two New Testament pericopae containing systematic teaching specifically on marriage are Ephesians 5:22–33 (considered in §9.4.8); and 1 Corinthians 7, where vv. 1–5 and vv. 32–35 speak of the mutual obligations of marriage, the rest of 1 Corinthians 7 (excepting vv. 17–24) being given over to singleness, separation, and divorce. Furthermore, unlike the Old Testament, the New Testament does not contain narrative accounts from which it is possible to make deductions about contemporary Jewish practice, thus a picture of the New Testament understanding of marriage, outside the two pericopae mentioned, has to be gleaned from scattered references considered below.

Matthew 19:3–9 and Mark 10:2–12 both affirm the aetiology of mundane marriage as being based on Genesis 2:24. Although it is widely perceived that this is a reference to the primal couple it has been argued that Genesis 2:24 is a metaphoric restatement of that union and thus underpins a separate conceptual domain (§1.2). Although in §9.4.8 it was seen that Ephesians 5:22–33 used the Christ/church union to model mundane marriage, there is no evidence in the JDD, or in New Testament teaching, that each mundane marriage itself was considered to have a heavenly dimension. Jesus' answer as recorded in Matthew 22:23–30 in reply to the Sadducees' question about marriage militates against such: 'For in the resurrection they neither marry nor are given in marriage' (v. 30). Nor is there any evidence that mundane marriage was considered to be a union witnessed before God, or that any controlling function was exercised by the temple, synagogue, or state—the JDD suggesting there was continuity with the Old Testament institution: a mutual, volitional agreement enacted between families.[673]

There is only one mention of betrothal in mundane marriage (Matt 1:18) and none to mundane marriage payments, however, both are referenced in the JDD (§8.3.5). Ephesians 5:22–33 reverse cross-maps the marital and body imagery on to mundane marriage to teach that a husband should love his wife (also Col 3:19) and nourish her, and 1 Timothy 5:8 states that he should provide for his family (which would include his wife), these references perhaps reflecting his responsibility for the Exodus 21:10 triad. The wife in the Ephesians pericope is expected to submit to him (also 1 Pet 3:1), reflecting the household codes in Colossians 3:18–4:1. Titus 2:3–4 encourages older women to train wives to love their husbands; 1 Peter 3:7 encourages husbands to live with their wives 'in an understanding way' and marriage partners are expected to give each other conjugal rights and to 'please' each other in 1 Corinthians 7:1–7, 33–34.

---

[673] However, Rome had marriage laws for Roman citizens, see: Treggiari, 'Marriage and Family in Roman Society,' in Campbell, *Marriage and Family*, 141–75

These references, it is suggested, do not imply that marital practices in the New Testament were any different from the marital practices of ancient Israel as portrayed in the Old Testament legislation and narratives, and as evidenced in the JDD. Some things are articulated that do not feature specifically in the Old Testament, for example, the requirement of husbands and wives to love each other (Col 3:19; Titus 2:3–4). But there is little evidence of a primal couple aetiology, in that: sexual intercourse is not stated to be valid only for procreation; there does not appear to be a link between celibacy and holiness, notwithstanding the fact that Paul in 1 Corinthians 7:5 suggests abstinence for a time to devote time to prayer is acceptable; nor is there a concept that God ordains each marriage—or that each marriage has an ontological dimension, excepting that mundane marriage illustrates the relationship of Christ and the church.

It is possible however, to see that the New Testament quotations of Genesis 2:24 from the Septuagint (which has 'the two shall become one flesh,' rather than the Hebrew Bible's 'and they shall become one flesh') emphasises monogamy.[674] And that the phrase, 'Therefore an overseer must be above reproach, the husband of one wife' in 1 Timothy 3:2 (also Titus 1:6) possibly excludes polygyny, at least for overseers. But it is suggested such teaching on its own does not necessarily indicate a Genesis 2:23 primal couple model, as polygyny is not intrinsic to Genesis 2:24, although the understanding in ancient Israel of the aetiology of that marriage did not exclude it.

Thus New Testament teaching does not appear to be incompatible with a model of marriage found in Genesis 2:24. However, the primal couple model which is employed by scholars and the church seems to have stemmed from 1 Corinthians 6:15–16 (§9.4.4), and the New Testament pericopae that deal with divorce and separation. These are considered below.

---

[674] Thus: David Instone-Brewer, 'Jesus' Old Testament Basis for Monogamy,' in *The Old Testament in the New Testament: Essays in Honour of J. L. North*, ed. Steve Moyise (Sheffield: Sheffield Academic, 2000); Loader considers the Septuagint translation of Genesis 2:24 including the addition of 'the two': Loader, *The Septuagint*, 39–42

10.3 Divorce and Remarriage in the Gospels

10.3.1 Matthew 19:3–9 and Mark 10:2–12

The structural analysis by Instone-Brewer (as below) will be followed.[675]

Matthew 19	Mark 10
Question	*Question*
And Pharisees came up to him and tested him by asking, "Is it lawful to divorce one's wife for any cause?" (19:3)	And Pharisees came up and in order to test him asked, "Is it lawful for a man to divorce his wife?" (10:2)
Digression	*Moses's teaching*
He answered, "Have you not read that he who created them from the beginning made them male and female, and said, 'Therefore a man shall leave his father and his mother and hold fast to his wife, and the two shall become one flesh'? So they are no longer two but one flesh. What therefore God has joined together, let not man separate." (19:4–6)	He answered them, "What did Moses command you?" They said, "Moses allowed a man to write a certificate of divorce and to send her away." And Jesus said to them, "Because of your hardness of heart he wrote you this commandment." (10:3–5)
Moses's teaching	*Digression*
They said to him, "Why then did Moses command one to give a	"But from the beginning of creation, 'God made them male and female.' 'Therefore a man shall leave his father and mother and hold fast to his wife, and the two shall become one flesh.' So they are no longer two but

---

[675] David Instone-Brewer, 'Jesus' Old Testament Basis for Monogamy,' in *The Old Testament in the New Testament: Essays in Honour of J. L. North,* ed. Steve Moyise (Sheffield, England: Sheffield Academic, 2000), 92–93. ESV Collins (2002) in Matt 19:5 and Mark 10:8, for reasons that are not clear, cites the Gen 2:24 quotation as 'and they shall become one flesh'; this present study will follow NA28 which has: καὶ ἔσονται οἱ δύο εἰς σάρκα μίαν ('and the two shall become one flesh'). Textual variations in the Gospel pericopae are considered by both Gehring, and Parker, but none are considered significant for this study: Gehring, *The Biblical "One Flesh,"* 203–11; David M. Parker, 'The Early Traditions of Jesus' Sayings on Divorce Theology,' *Theology* 96 (1993), 372–83.

certificate of divorce and to send her away?" He said to them, "Because of your hardness of heart Moses allowed you to divorce your wives, but from the beginning it was not so." (19:7–8) *Answering the Question* "And I say to you: whoever divorces his wife, except for sexual immorality, and marries another, commits adultery." (19:9).	one flesh. What therefore God has joined together, let not man separate." (10:6–9) *Answering the Question* And in the house the disciples asked him again about this matter. And he said to them, "Whoever divorces his wife and marries another commits adultery against her, and if she divorces her husband and marries another, she commits adultery." (10:10–12)

10.3.2 The Question

Instone-Brewer et al. see that the 'any cause' of Matthew 19:3 is a reference to the rabbinic debate about the meaning of עֶרְוַת דָּבָר in Deuteronomy 24:1.[676] He persuasively argues that the contemporary debate and the precise phrases used therein were so well known (the Hillelites saw that Deut 24:1 meant divorce by the husband was legitimate for 'any cause' and indecency, but the Shammaites understood that divorce was legitimate for indecency only), that any contemporary audience would automatically in their minds insert the words missing from Mark in his abbreviated account—that is, they would be assumed.[677]

---

[676] The Septuagint gives ἄσχημον πρᾶγμα as the translation of עֶרְוַת דָּבָר of Deut 24:1 (BGT: BibleWorks Greek LXX/BNT); Tomson translates the Septuagint as 'an unworthy deed' and compares it with the ἀσχημοσύνη πράγματος 'shameful deeds' of Deut 23:15; Peter J. Tomson, *Paul and the Jewish Law: Halakha in the Letters of the Apostle to the Gentiles* (Minneapolis, MN: Fortress, 1990), 122; Matt 5:32 and 19:9 use πορνεία which ESV translates as 'indecency.'

[677] Instone-Brewer, *Divorce and Remarriage,* 134–36; similarly: Craig S. Keener, *And Marries Another: Divorce and Remarriage in the Teaching of the New Testament* (Peabody, MA: Hendrickson, 1991), 38–40; Craig A. Blomberg, 'Marriage, Divorce, Remarriage, and Celibacy: An Exegesis of Matthew 19:3–12,' *TJ* 11NS (1990), 164; Evald Lövestam, 'Divorce and Remarriage in the New Testament,' in *The Jewish Law Annual* Vol. 4, ed. B.S.

10.3.3 The Digression

Blomberg and Clark see the reference to Genesis 1:27 in Matthew 19:4 means that the Mosaic concession to men's hardness of heart no longer applies.[678] But neither Blomberg nor Clark see that divorce is now excluded, and Jesus, notwithstanding the reference, appeals to Genesis 2:24 for the aetiology of mundane marriage, not the primal couple of Genesis 1:27, or their union in Genesis 2:23. Furthermore, Blomberg, commenting on Matthew 19 believes that 'only the institution [of marriage] is grounded in creation'—that is, not each individual marriage; and claims that sex itself does not create a marriage, but sex and 'commitment,' thus he believes that infidelity itself does not terminate it, but that the 'volitional commitment ... can be rescinded.'[679]

10.3.4 Moses's Teaching

Kaye points out that Genesis 2:24 in its original context did not prohibit divorce as provision for such was contained in the Pentateuch.[680] Gehring states: 'Jesus is not playing the Edenic ideal off against the Mosaic instruction';[681] and Allison concurs: 'it is doubtful that the First Gospel allows any contradiction between Moses and Jesus.'[682] Smith surveys the literature on the pericope and states: 'It [is] most plausible that Matthew was conscientiously composing his gospel with a view to presenting Jesus in agreement with the Torah.'[683] Sprinkle comments:

Jackson (Leiden: Brill, 1981), 48–49; for an explanation of the basis of Hillelite argument: David Instone-Brewer, *Techniques and Assumptions in Jewish Exegesis before 70 CE* (TSAJ 30; Tübingen: Mohr Siebeck, 1992), 136–38; Blomberg sees that 'lawful' in the pericopae embraces any combination of the oral or written Torah: Blomberg, 'Marriage,' 165

[678] Clark, *Putting Asunder*, 89; Blomberg: 'Now in the age of the new covenant, therefore, Christians may no longer appeal to hard-heartedness as grounds for dissolving a marriage': Blomberg, 'Marriage,' 171. See §10.5 for comments on 'from the beginning' in Matt 19:8 and Mark 10:6.

[679] Blomberg, 'Marriage,' 167–68

[680] Kaye, 'One Flesh,' 49–50

[681] Gehring, *The Biblical "One Flesh,"* 232

[682] D. C. Allison, 'Divorce, Celibacy and Joseph (Matthew 1.18–25 and 19:1–12),' *JSNew Testament* 49 (1993), 5; also Bockmuehl draws attention to Joseph's situation (Matt 1:19) and sees that Matthew could not be denying the divorce provisions of Deut 24: Markus N. A. Bockmuehl, 'Matthew 5.32; 19.9 in the Light of Pre-Rabbinic Halakhah,' *NTS* Vol. 35 (1989), 294

[683] Don T. Smith, 'The Matthean Exception Clauses in the Light of Matthew's Theology and Community,' *StudBib* 17 (1989), 80

> Note that Jesus does not deny the validity of Old Testament teaching on marriage and divorce. Indeed, he denied that he came to "abolish the law".... Instead he reinforces the OT's authority on this topic by pointing to Gen 2:24.[684]

Moo in his analysis states:

> Both the Matthean pericopae give teaching on divorce closely similar to the Mosaic provisions. This being the case, the "hardness of heart" to which Jesus attributes the Mosaic teaching is not done away with in the new age of the Kingdom; indeed, the case of "serious sexual sin" (πορνεία) which justifies divorce is a prominent example of just that.[685]

None of these commentators see that Jesus's comment and affirmation of the aetiology of marriage recorded in Genesis 2:24 revokes the Mosaic divorce provision. It is suggested in this present study that the view that Jesus in some way replaces or amends the Deuteronomic teaching does not take sufficient account of the fact that Jesus is recorded as explaining and applying the Deuteronomic teaching in Matthew 19, or of the teaching of Matthew 5:31-32.

10.3.5 Other Gospel Divorce and Remarriage Teaching

> It was also said, "Whoever divorces his wife, let him give her a certificate of divorce." But I say to you that everyone who divorces his wife, except on the ground of sexual immorality, makes her commit adultery. And whoever marries a divorced woman commits adultery. (Matt 5:31-32)

> Everyone who divorces his wife and marries another commits adultery, and he who marries a woman divorced from her husband commits adultery. (Luke 16:8)[686]

---

[684] Sprinkle, 'Old Testament Perspectives,' 548

[685] D. J. Moo, 'Jesus and the Authority of the Mosaic Law,' *JSNew Testament* 6, 20 (January 1984), 20; also France: 'Our society cannot avoid the sad realities which resulted in the concessive legislation of Deut 24:1-4 ... but if it is to be true to Jesus' understanding ... it must not allow failure to become the norm': R. T. France, *The Gospel of Matthew*, NICNT (Grand Rapids, MI: Eerdmans, 2007), 721

[686] ἀπολύων in Luke 16:18 has been debated but is seen in Mur 115 to be referencing divorce: J. A. Fitzmyer, 'The

The teaching of Matthew 5:27–48 is in the form of an antithesis: 'You have heard that it was said.... But I say to you.' Daube comments that Jesus was here using a rabbinic form of argument: 'these declarations, "Ye have heard—But I say unto you", are intended to prove Jesus the Law's upholder, not destroyer.'[687] According to MacArthur, the first part of the antithesis is a 'self-righteous externalism typified by the scribes and Pharisees,' the second points to the true meaning of the law, a 'heart righteousness.'[688] But in Matthew 5:31–32 the 'heart righteousness' in v. 32 is not a renunciation of the Mosaic provision, but a clarification of it. The heart righteousness Jesus proclaimed, it is suggested, is his repudiation of the *any cause* Hillelite divorce and the affirmation of the more strict Shammaite interpretation of the Deuteronomy 24 pericope.

If the arguments in §10.3.4 and §10.3.6 (as below) are accepted, and that it was rabbinic practice to abbreviate such discussion, then there is no contradiction in the divorce teaching of Matthew 5:31–32 and Luke 16:18 and the longer pericopae in Matthew 19 and Mark 10.[689]

10.3.6 Answering the Question

Matthew 5:32: has 'except on the grounds of sexual immorality' (παρεκτὸς λόγου πορνείας); Matthew 19:9: 'except for sexual immorality' (μὴ ἐπὶ πορνείᾳ). Blomberg argues that they cannot be translated as 'even in the case of' and that both amount to a genuine exception clause.[690]

All the Gospel divorce pericopae record Jesus as saying that a subsequent marriage can give rise to adultery and Instone-Brewer contends persuasively that any such adultery is consequent only on remarriage after an invalid divorce.[691] He suggests: 'The solution [to the problem of Gospel

---

Matthean Divorce Texts and Some New Palestinian Evidence,' *TS* 37 (1976), 212–13

[687] David Daube, *The New Testament and Rabbinic Judaism* (Peabody, MA: Hendrickson, 1956), 60

[688] John MacArthur, *Matthew 1–7,* MacArthur New Testament Commentary (Chicago, IL: Moody Bible Institute, 1985), 299

[689] For rabbinic practice of abbreviation: Instone-Brewer, *Divorce and Remarriage,* 161–67

[690] Blomberg, 'Marriage,' 175

[691] Instone-Brewer, *Divorce and Remarriage,* 149; Blomberg states: 'It is better ... to recognize a metaphorical meaning for adultery in Matt 5:32a ... Jesus has indisputably used the verb μοιχεύω to refer to other than actual sexual relations ... if this is the most likely interpretation of 5:32, it should probably be considered for 19:9 as

harmonisation] that almost all commentators have found is to assume that the divorce was invalid.'[692] He gives this analysis:

1.   A man who marries an invalidly divorced woman commits adultery (Luke 16:18; Matt 5:32).

2.   A man who invalidly divorces his wife causes her to commit adultery (Matt 5:32; variants of Matt 19:9).

3.   A man who invalidly divorces his wife and marries another commits adultery (Mark 10:11; Matt 19:9; Luke 16:18).

4.   A woman who invalidly divorces her husband and marries another commits adultery (Mark 10:12).[693]

Instone-Brewer points out that the assumption of an invalid divorce fits all the four scenarios;[694] and argues (with others) that Matthew's account clarifies the ambiguity of Deuteronomy 24:1 and in effect endorses the Shammaite position and that divorce is permitted, not commanded, in the situation described.[695] Blomberg concurs and believes that the exception references divorce and

---

well': Blomberg, 'Marriage,' 174–75; similarly Keener: 'I would consider Jesus' claim of "adultery" ... to be hyperbolic': Craig S. Keener, 'Remarriage for Adultery or Desertion,' in *Remarriage after Divorce in Today's Church: 3 Views*, ed. Paul E. Engle and Mark L. Strauss (Grand Rapids, MI: Zondervan, 2006), 92. Thus they argue the 'adultery' consequent on a marriage after an invalid divorce should not be taken literally, but rather to mean 'unfaithfulness'; similarly Instone-Brewer suggests this 'adultery' could be a rhetorical expression: David Instone-Brewer, 'What God Has Joined Together,' n.p. [cited 30 September 2014]. Online: <http://www.baylor.edu/ifl/christianreflection/MarriageArticleInstoneBrewer.pdf>; Fitzmyer suggests that Matt 5:32 relates the divorce itself to adultery (i.e. a form of unfaithfulness) not the divorce with remarriage: Fitzmyer, 'The Matthean Divorce Texts,' 203, 207

[692] Instone-Brewer, *Divorce and Remarriage*, 149

[693] Instone-Brewer, *Divorce and Remarriage*, 150

[694] Instone-Brewer, *Divorce and Remarriage*, 152; similarly Keener: '*If the divorce is valid so is the remarriage*,' but suggests only the innocent partner can be remarried: Keener, *And Marries Another*, 44, 49

[695] Instone-Brewer, *Divorce and Remarriage*, 110–17, 133–36; also: Lehmann, 'Gen 2:24 as the Basis for Divorce,' 266; Tomson, *Paul and the Jewish Law*, 115; Smith, 'The Matthean Exception Clauses,' 60–61; France suggests in his 2002 commentary on Mark that the one-flesh union of mundane marriage is 'indissoluble': France, *The Gospel of Mark*, 392–94; but on Matt 5:27–30 in 2007 he appears to endorse Instone-Brewer's position that a divorce and the right to remarry are inseparable and that adultery on a subsequent marriage is only occasioned if the divorce was invalid—for France a valid divorce is when there has been *porneia*, which he suggests reflects Deut 24 and covers various kinds of 'sexual irregularity': France, *Matthew*, 210–12

remarriage, thus both are possible after πορνεία.⁶⁹⁶ Although a concept widely held is that only the 'innocent' party of a divorce is free to remarry Instone-Brewer counters this: 'The right to remarry after divorce was the fundamental right that was communicated by the Jewish divorce certificate.'⁶⁹⁷ Murray comments:

> it is difficult to discover any biblical ground on the basis of which to conclude that the remarriage of the guilty divorcee is to be considered in itself an act of adultery and as constituting an adulterous relation.⁶⁹⁸

10.3.7 Answering the Question: πορνεία

πορνεία is used in Acts 15:20 to denote incestuous marriages forbidden in Leviticus 18 and 20 but Malina claims that 'most, if not all, exegetes' believe πορνεία in Matthew 5:32 and Matthew 19:9 relates to illicit sexual intercourse.⁶⁹⁹ Blomberg suggests it possibly includes, 'incest, homosexuality, prostitution, molestation, or indecent exposure';⁷⁰⁰ furthermore, Blomberg, along with Smith, posits that it is an intentional imitation of the Shammaite reading of Deuteronomy 24:1.⁷⁰¹

---

⁶⁹⁶ Blomberg, 'Marriage,' 177–79, 181; also: Instone-Brewer, *Divorce and Remarriage*, 155–56; Thomas R. Edgar, 'Divorce & Remarriage for Adultery or Desertion,' in *Divorce and Remarriage: Four Christian Views*, ed. Wayne H. House (Downers Grove, IL: InterVarsity, 1990), 155–62; *contra*: Cornes, *Divorce and Remarriage*, 216–19

⁶⁹⁷ Instone-Brewer, *Divorce and Remarriage*, 211–12; *contra* Köstenberger (endorsing Keener): 'a clear distinction should be drawn between the guilty and innocent party ... the innocent party should be treated as if single or unmarried, the guilty party as divorced': Andreas J. Köstenberger, 'Marriage and Family in the New Testament,' in Campbell *Marriage and Family*, 264; Heth gives an account of the 'majority view' as freeing only the innocent party to remarry: Heth, 'Jesus on Divorce,' 12

⁶⁹⁸ Murray, *Divorce*, 100

⁶⁹⁹ Bruce Malina, 'Does Porneia Mean Fornication,' *NovT* 14 (January 1972), 10; Lövestam sees it as 'sexual unfaithfulness': Lövestam, 'Divorce and Remarriage,' in *The Jewish Law Annual* (Jackson), 58; Smith makes the persuasive point that incestuous sexual relationships shocked even the Gentiles at Corinth (1 Cor 5:1) so a specific exclusion in the Gospels seems unlikely: Smith, 'The Matthean Exception Clauses,' 80–81; *contra* Jensen who argues that *porneia* in the New Testament has a wide range of meanings and attempts to allocate a specific meaning to its various appearances, seeing that incestuous relationships is the meaning in the divorce pericopae: Joseph Jensen, 'Does Porneia Mean Fornication? A Critique of Bruce Malina,' *NovT* 20 (July 1978), 180

⁷⁰⁰ Blomberg, 'Marriage,' 177–78

⁷⁰¹ Blomberg, 'Marriage,' 178; Smith, 'The Matthean Exception Clauses,' 81; also: Instone-Brewer, *Divorce and Remarriage*, 156–59

Instone-Brewer suggests that the λόγου πορνείας in Matthew 5:32 is the reverse of the natural order, and thus reflects the Shammaite argument that he sees as being reproduced in *m. Git* 9:10, which he cites as:

> The School of Shammai says: A man should not divorce his wife except he found in her a matter of indecency (דבר ערוה), as it is said: *For he finds in her an indecent matter* (ערות דבר).[702]

This interpretation sees that Jesus is affirming the Shammaite understanding of Deuteronomy 24:1–4 and endorsing this restricted basis for any husband validly initiating a divorce.[703] This is consonant with the understanding of marriage that the JDD seem to demonstrate, and gives continuity between the Old and New Testament. Furthermore, it means the congruence between Scripture's mundane marriage teaching and its marital imagery is maintained.

10.3.8 Other Grounds for Divorce

The Christian community consensus (with the exception of the Roman Catholic Church) appears to be that divorce is allowed for sexual unfaithfulness (but not necessarily remarriage) and Matthew either reported the conversation with the Pharisees more fully than Mark, or added the exception clauses believing that such could be assumed.[704] Instone-Brewer comments that most see that this Gospel teaching means Jesus only recognized this one basis for divorce, but he argues that Jesus was answering the question asked and giving his interpretation of the contentious of עֶרְוַת דָּבָר in Deuteronomy 24:1; it does not necessarily mean that there were no other grounds.[705] Blomberg points out:

---

[702] Instone-Brewer, *Divorce and Remarriage*, 159, 185–86

[703] It was pointed out in §5.11.1.1 that if a husband under Old Testament legislation could divorce his wife at will (as Hillel's followers claimed Deut 24 taught) there would appear to be no point trying to divorce a wife by suggesting she was not a virgin on marriage and risk the penalties involved (Deut 22:13–19); the more relaxed Hillelite position (divorce for 'any matter') Instone-Brewer describes as 'invented': Instone-Brewer, *Divorce and Remarriage*, 110

[704] See analysis in: Heth, 'Jesus on Divorce,' 4–5

[705] Instone-Brewer, *Divorce and Remarriage*, 156

> The polemical context, the specific nature of the Pharisees' question, and the form of pronouncements in controversy stories in general all have suggested that v. 9 might be more a proverbial maximum than a legal absolute ... [how could Paul] feel free to introduce a second exception to Jesus' prohibition of divorce unless he realized that pronouncements like Matt 19:9 were not absolutes.[706]

Sprinkle states: 'Without giving full weight to Old Testament teaching, readers of the New Testament treatment of divorce are too quick to absolutize the words of Jesus' and argues for a covenantal basis for marriage and believes such principles can be applied to divorce in the New Testament even if not specifically articulated.[707] Hugenberger suggests, referencing Matthew 5:17–20 and the work of Dodd and Charlesworth, that:

> In recent years ... there has been a fresh appreciation for the Jewish background of the teachings of Jesus of Nazareth and his radical dependence on the Old Testament in keeping with his own disavowal of originality.[708]

Heth says he was caught 'off guard' by his own failure to take these factors sufficiently into account (and specifically retracts some of his earlier teaching);[709] and quotes with approval Blomberg's comments on Jesus's discourse with the Pharisees:

> Few try to make the pronouncements in various other controversy or pronouncement stories absolute (cf., e.g., Matt 19:21, 9:15, and esp. 13:57, a particularly interesting parallel because of its similar exception

---

[706] Blomberg, 'Marriage,' 186–87

[707] He states: 'Only two of these things (sexual immorality and abandonment) are (arguably) explicit grounds for divorce in the NT. If the covenant principle is behind these applications, however, we might be justified in concluding that the two examples in the New Testament are not intended to be exhaustive but that other grounds are likewise applicable under the new covenant': Sprinkle, 'Old Testament Perspectives,' 547, 549

[708] Hugenberger, *Marriage as a Covenant*, 149

[709] Heth, 'Jesus on Divorce,' 15; he cites his indebtedness to Instone-Brewer's work: William A. Heth, 'Remarriage for Adultery or Desertion,' in *Remarriage after Divorce in Today's Church*, 96

clause ...) so one should be equally wary of elevating 19:9 (or Mark 10:11–12) into an exceptionless absolute.[710]

Few commentators point out that the Gospel divorce pericopae (except for Mark 10:12) only address men and it is often presumed by those that hold the traditional views that gender reciprocity in New Testament divorce teaching can be assumed, thus Murray: 'surely it is necessary to believe ... the same rights and liberties are granted to the woman.'[711] However, in light of the social milieu of the time and the millennia of history behind Jewish contemporary marital practices it is suggested that such an assumption is ill-founded. The question posed in the longer pericopae was about a husband's grounds for divorce and Jesus specifically in his answer makes it clear he is addressing that issue. Mark 10:12 has Jesus say: 'and if she [the wife] divorces her husband and marries another man, she commits adultery.' The fact that wives are now addressed separately underlines the fact that they had not been included in the immediately preceding comments—furthermore, it is difficult to make sense of Jesus's words as recorded if a wife could not initiate a divorce.[712] This Markan statement comprises the entire divorce teaching in the Gospels from a wife's perspective. There are two possible interpretations:

• The statement by Jesus in Mark 10:12 stands as it is written. In effect Jesus removes any Old Testament teaching about divorces initiated by the wife; whatever their previous position, divorce for them is now forbidden.

• A general principle was being articulated (as in Matt 19:6 and Mark 10:11), but the accepted grounds for divorce for wives, apparently taught in

---

[710] Heth, 'Jesus on Divorce,' 15; citing: Blomberg, 'Marriage,' 162; also Köstenberger: 'it is much more likely that he [Jesus] did not elaborate on points at which he agreed with the commonly held view in his day'—and quotes Instone-Brewer with approval on this point, however, he distances himself from Instone-Brewer in his belief that Exod 21:10–11 can be assumed as divorce grounds in the New Testament: Köstenberger and Jones, *God, Marriage, and Family*, 242, 355

[711] Murray, *Divorce*, 98

[712] Although it is possible, as some believe, that Jesus was referring to non-Jewish divorce, for example Brody: 'but [Mark 10:12] is plausibly explained as reflecting Mark's Gentile milieu, and the familiarity of his readership with Roman law, in which husband and wife were on equal footing with regard to divorce': Brody, 'Evidence for Divorce by Jewish Women,' 231. But it has to be considered how probable this is when the context is an answer to the Pharisees about the Pentateuch's teaching, and Ilan argues that the context of the conversation suggests Jesus was confining his comments to Jewish divorces: Ilan, 'On a Newly Published Divorce Bill,' 201–02

Exodus 21, and evidenced in the extant archaeological data, were retained even though not, in this context, specifically mentioned.

It seems unreasonable to believe that Jesus's audience would have assumed in Mark 10:12 that a husband's exception clause 'except for sexual immorality' was now to be a wife's (only) grounds for divorce (if Markan priority is accepted, found not in Matthew, but in Deuteronomy 24);[713] it would mean that in the one sentence recorded in Mark 10, the New Testament audience are to assume an implicit inclusion of the husband's exception clause in a wife's grounds for divorce, and assume a simultaneous implicit exclusion of her own grounds for divorce as outlined in Exodus 21. It is an exegesis that relies on a presumption that Jesus's audience would make two assumptions, both of which involve a remarkable *volte face* in first century ethics in Jewish Palestine.[714] Furthermore, it would mean that Jesus's teaching as recorded by Mark was not congruent with Mark's own marital imagery, or with the marital imagery of the rest of the New Testament.[715]

The assumption of gender reciprocity in New Testament divorce teaching by many that hold the traditional views, in effect, curtails a wife's freedom of action. Under the Old Testament economy (as it has been argued in this study) a wife already had divorce grounds that were more broadly based than those of her husband. Furthermore, the logic of the Exodus pericope that granted such (Exod 21:10–11) is that a wife could insist on a monogamous relationship as a condition of staying in the marriage—some of the ANE, Elephantine, and Graeco-Roman marriage documents articulate such (§4.37; §8.2.2; §8.4.3).

Gender-based asymmetry in marriage and divorce practice is widely evidenced in the ANE (§4.4); in Old Testament teaching (Exod 21:10–11; Deut 24:1–4); in Old Testament marital imagery (§6.7); in the extant papyri (§8.3.5–§8.3.7; §8.4.2); in New Testament marital imagery (§9.4.7); in specific New Testament

---

[713] For Markan priority see: Blomberg, 'Marriage,' 163 n. 8

[714] Instone-Brewer states: 'a wife could not gain a divorce by claiming her husband had been unfaithful': Instone-Brewer, *Divorce and Remarriage*, 99

[715] In that Mark's marital imagery, as elsewhere in the New Testament, was rooted in contemporary marital practices that were based on the understanding of marriage evidenced in ancient Israel, where a husband had a duty to provide for his bride, and any repudiation of him by her was to be based on the failure of such.

marriage teaching (e.g. Eph 5:25–29); and in specific New Testament divorce teaching (Matt 5:31–32; 19:3–9)—thus it seems reasonable, if any assumptions are to be made, that Mark considered that these gender-based divorce grounds remained in place.

Thus it is argued that Mark 10:12, in articulating a general principle for wives (as was done for husbands in Matt 19:6 and Mark 10:11), in effect acknowledges the existence of wife-initiated divorces as evidenced in contemporary Jewish society. However, in this exchange with the Pharisees these grounds for initiating a divorce for a wife were not outlined, probably because that was not the question asked—the teaching of Exodus 21 was not in dispute.[716]

The alternative interpretation would mean that Mark records Jesus as repudiating that historical teaching leaving a wife with no means of divorce, a position that it will be seen would appear to contradict the teaching of 1 Corinthians 7—and furthermore, not be congruent with the marital imagery that the New Testament writers, including Mark, employ.

10.3.9 Summary: Divorce and Remarriage in the Gospels

Instone-Brewer argues that without Matthew's additions to Mark, the Pharisees' question makes no sense, and that the Matthean comment would have been self-evident to any contemporary Jew.[717] Although there is much debate about the validity of using rabbinic sources to interpret the New Testament, many commentators accept the fact that Jesus was addressing the Hillel/Shammai debate.[718] It appears that those who hold to the traditional views of marriage and divorce have seen that one brief polemical exchange

---

[716] Instone-Brewer states: 'There are no records of disputes among the rabbis about any of the grounds for divorce based on Exodus 21:10–11 except in matters of detail.... From at least the beginning of the first century it was recognized that the obligations of Exodus 21:10–11 could form the basis of a claim for divorce': Instone-Brewer, *Divorce and Remarriage*, 102

[717] Instone-Brewer, *Divorce and Remarriage*, 187

[718] Neusner is sceptical: Jacob Neusner, *Rabbinic Literature and the New Testament: What We Cannot Show, We Do Not Know* (Eugene, OR: Wipf and Stock, 1994); yet Ilan states: 'The historical value of rabbinic sources has been vigorously debated in recent scholarship.... However ... even the greatest skeptics, draw the line somewhere': Ilan, *Jewish Women in Greco-Roman Palestine*, 33

recorded in the Gospels overturns Old Testament teaching and millennia of marital practice.

For these reasons it is argued in this study that the most reasonable assumption is that the asymmetrical divorce grounds based on the covenant that formed the marriage remained—a woman was free to leave her husband based on his neglect of her, but a husband had the more restricted divorce grounds, as clarified in the Matthean pericopae. Such is the situation evidenced in the extant contemporary marriage documents, and is mirrored in the Old Testament imagery. Thus Yahweh would not desert his people unless they were unfaithful to him, but Israel was not compelled to remain in the relationship with him. Similarly in the New Testament imagery—Jesus will not fail to come for his bride unless she denies him, but the church, it seems, has the same choice as Israel had.

10.4 Separation, Divorce, and Remarriage in First Corinthians 7

10.4.1 Introduction

Instone-Brewer comments on 1 Corinthians 7:

> Comparisons with Jewish marriage and divorce papyri show that the lifestyle and morals that Paul wishes the Corinthians to adopt are based primarily on the Jewish interpretation of the Old Testament. This is illustrated from both Greek Jewish papyri, which show a Judaism thoroughly embedded in the Graeco-Roman world, and Aramaic papyri, which use concepts very closely aligned to Paul's.[719]

It has been seen that several scholars believe that the adoption of Greek legal terms in a Jewish marriage contract need not mean an assimilation of a Hellenistic understanding of marriage (§8.3.4).

Instone-Brewer further comments on 1 Corinthians 7:

---

[719] Instone-Brewer, '1 Corinthians 7 in the Light of the Jewish Papyri,' 225

> [Paul's] emphasis throughout is that marriage is a binding commitment, and should not be treated lightly, as it was in Graeco-Roman law ... he only allowed divorce on certain biblical grounds.[720]

Thus it is suggested in this present study, even though Paul is addressing a church in the Graeco-Roman world, that the exegetical frame of reference for the teaching of the chapter should be the Jewish understanding of marriage as demonstrated in the legislation, narratives, and marital imagery of the Jewish Scriptures, supplemented by the Jewish understanding of contemporary marriage demonstrated in the JDD. Furthermore, it is expected that the teaching of the chapter will be congruent with the marriage teaching and marital imagery elsewhere in the Pauline corpus, and that of the Gospels and Apocalypse.

10.4.2 Separation and Divorce

In the first verses of the chapter the mutual obligations of marriage are addressed, with Daube et al. seeing a link to the obligations of Exodus 21:10 in 1 Corinthians 7:3-5.[721] After a comment regarding the single and widows, Paul addresses the issue of separation and divorce in vv. 10–16. Lövestam believes that Paul pre-supposes that the wife as well as the husband has the right to divorce 'which was the case in the Graeco-Roman world.'[722] It has been suggested (§5.12) that although a Jewish wife, unlike her husband, could not unilaterally divorce, she could nonetheless initiate a divorce. However, in the Graeco-Roman world it does appear divorce rights were fully mutual and this was the background to the situation Paul was addressing.[723] Instone-Brewer

---

[720] David Instone-Brewer, '1 Corinthians 7 in the Light of the Graeco-Roman Marriage and Divorce Papyri,' *TynBul* 52.1 (2001), 116

[721] 'An ancient law in Exodus [21:10] provides that ... a man ... may not "diminish" ... [a first wife's] due. Paul no doubt uses the verb in the same sense when he admonishes married couples to fulfil their mutual obligations and not to "defraud" one another': Daube, *The New Testament and Rabbinic Judaism*, 365; similarly: Instone-Brewer, *Divorce and Remarriage*, 193; elsewhere Instone-Brewer comments: 'This reference to Exod 21:10–11 in 1 Cor 7:3–5 has not been widely recognised' but cites other publications that have: Instone-Brewer, '1 Corinthians 7 in the Light of the Jewish Papyri,' 233 n. 29

[722] Lövestam, 'Divorce and Remarriage,' in Jackson, *The Jewish Law Annual*, 47

[723] Thus: Instone-Brewer, '1 Corinthians 7 in the Light of the Graeco-Roman Papyri,' 105; Treggiari, 'Marriage and Family,' in Campbell, *Marriage and Family*, 156

argues that although translations use 'separate' and 'divorce' throughout this passage he believes:

> There may be no significance in their use other than stylistic variation.... There were more than fifty words used for "divorce" in Greek marriage and divorce contracts, and it was common to use several in a single document.[724]

1 Corinthians 7:10-11 has:

> To the married I give this charge (not I, but the Lord): the wife should not separate from her husband (but if she does, she should remain unmarried or else be reconciled to her husband), and the husband should not divorce his wife.

It appears these verses contain the general principle: neither partner should initiate a separation/divorce—if they have, they should seek reconciliation. In the next verses (vv. 12–14) Paul presses home his general principle of no separation, even for 'mixed' marriages:

> To the rest I say (I, not the Lord) that if any brother has a wife who is an unbeliever, and she consents to live with him, he should not divorce her. If any woman has a husband who is an unbeliever, and he consents to live with her, she should not divorce him. For the unbelieving husband is made holy because of his wife, and the unbelieving wife is made holy because of her husband. Otherwise your children would be unclean, but as it is, they are holy.

This might have seemed a surprising position for Paul to take, when the teaching in Israel (Deut 23:2) was that, 'No one born of a forbidden union may enter the assembly of the LORD. Even to the tenth generation, none of his descendants may enter the assembly of the LORD'—and Ezra's instruction to the men of Judah had been to separate from their non-Jewish wives (Ezra 10:11). Satlow believes (as commented in §5.11.2) that Ezra had the concept

---

[724] Instone-Brewer, *Divorce and Remarriage,* 198–99. He has a more detailed consideration of this point and provides a list of Greek terms for divorce: Instone-Brewer, '1 Corinthians 7 in the Light of the Graeco-Roman Papyri,' 105–108, 117

that all Jewish men had holy seed: 'The mingling of this [Jewish male] holy seed with the impurity of Gentile women … was seen as a true abomination' and that the children of mixed marriages were considered 'unclean'—so the issue for Ezra it seems was about race, not faith.[725]

It is suggested in this present study that this was the background to Paul's comments—he is saying that those Old Testament principles do not come through to the Christian faith community—children of mixed-faith marriages in the church are 'holy' (v. 14), that is, not 'unclean'; contra Sampley who sees that the children of these marriages 'are set apart for and belong to God.'[726]

In v. 15 Paul articulates a qualification to his general principle: 'But if the unbelieving partner separates, let it be so. In such cases the brother or sister is not enslaved. God has called you to peace.' Thus the pericope follows the same format as Matt 19:3-9—in other words, when Paul gave the general principle (vv. 10-14), he was not contradicting any Gospel divorce provisions, or the teaching of Exodus 21:10-11 and Deuteronomy 24:1-4, where it is clear a wife or a husband (with no reference to their personal faith) can initiate a divorce. Paul acknowledges that the reconciliation he suggests in v. 11 might not be possible, and in such a situation he recommends: 'let it be so.'

Thus it is suggested that the qualification is addressing desertion in any marriage—not just the 'mixed' marriages to which vv. 12-14 refer.[727] The fact that Paul references mixed marriages in v. 15 is most likely to be incidental—he had just been speaking about them, and he will have realised such marriages are particularly vulnerable—some separations might already have occurred.

Blomberg states:

> desertion was Paul's primary concern; that it was an unbeliever wanting to leave is "accidental" in the technical sense of that term....

---

[725] Satlow, *Jewish Marriage*, 137, 260. It seems the *Yebamot* in the Mishnah has a similar perspective—it records extensive discussions about the definition of an acceptable Jewish wife, but her personal faith is never mentioned.

[726] Sampley, 'The First Letter,' in Keck, *NIB: Romans*, 877

[727] Instone-Brewer suggests the same: Instone-Brewer, *Divorce and Remarriage,* 199-201

Once again, in an age and culture in which divorce almost universally carried with it provisions for remarriage, Paul would have had specifically to exclude this possibility in v. 15 if he had expected anyone to understand that he was actually forbidding all remarriage.[728]

Heth supports this line of argument and sees desertion as a legitimate ground for divorce for non-mixed marriages because: '[it] is an abdication of the mutual physical, financial, emotional, and spiritual support that is pledged to one another as covenant partners (cf. Exod 21:10–11; 1 Cor 7:3–5; Eph 5:25–32).'[729] Similarly Edgar: 'although not specifically stated, desertion even by a believer may be grounds for divorce and remarriage.'[730]

Although Scripture is against mixed-faith marriages in the community of God's people (e.g. Deut 7:1–4; 1 Cor 7:39; 2 Cor 6:14) there does not appear to be a concept that such a marriage is in some way not valid as a marriage. When Jesus was asked about divorce he is recorded as referencing the Edenic situation, not any ethnic or faith community to find its *raison d'etre*—marriage it seems was intended for all people, not made valid by the personal faith of one or both spouses. Thus it is suggested Paul was addressing vulnerability not validity, *contra* various confessional positions today, including the Church of Rome (§10.1).[731]

While both mixed marriages and non-mixed marriages are valid marriages, it might be considered that the expectations of the latter would be greater and any separation/divorce in the marriage of two believers would be based on biblical grounds. Nonetheless, it appears that Paul does teach in v. 15 that if a marriage partner has been abandoned by their spouse, whatever the personal faith of either of them, they can take that to be a divorce and are free to remarry.[732]

---

[728] Blomberg, 'Marriage,' 188; also Instone-Brewer, '1 Corinthians 7 in the Light of the Jewish Papyri,' 242
[729] Heth, 'Remarriage for Adultery or Desertion,' in Engle and Strauss, *Remarriage after Divorce in Today's Church*, 77–78
[730] Edgar, 'Divorce & Remarriage,' in House, *Divorce and Remarriage*, 191
[731] Canon 1086 states: 'A marriage between two persons, one of whom has been baptized in the Catholic Church or received into it and has not defected from it by a formal act and the other of whom is not baptized, is invalid': Vatican, 'Code of Canon Law,' <http://www.vatican.va/archive/ENG1104/_P3Y.HTM> [Accessed: 11/14/2014]
[732] However, this study does not address any legal issues surrounding divorce and remarriage for any marriage

10.4.3 Not Enslaved

Instone-Brewer comments on v. 15:

> The only freedom that makes any sense in this context is the freedom to remarry. We do not have to rely on a process of elimination to decide what this phrase means, because the language that Paul used would have been very plain to any first-century reader. We find similar phraseology in a large number of ancient divorce certificates ... all Jewish divorce certificates and most Greco-Roman ones contained the words "you are free to marry any man you wish," or something very similar. These words were so important that the rabbis concluded that they were the only words that were essential in a Jewish divorce certificate. These words can be found in Jewish divorce certificates in rabbinic sources from the first-century CE and back to the Aramaic contracts from the Elephantine community of the fifth century BCE.[733]

At the time of writing this present study, in Israel, and in Jewish law where applicable in the Diaspora, if a couple decide to divorce and the husband refuses to release his wife by issuing a divorce certificate she is *agunah*.[734] This means although separated and to all intents and purposes divorced, she is still 'bound' ('chained') to her husband, 'unable to remarry as long as the death of her husband has not been proven'—or until she receives her certificate.[735] It seems, in light of the archaeological evidence, and the historical Jewish understanding of *agunah*, that Paul's 'not enslaved' ('not bound') can only mean 'not *agunah*'—that is free to remarry;[736] Instone-Brewer pointing out that

---

registered under the civil law of a nation.

[733] Instone-Brewer, *Divorce and Remarriage*, 202

[734] Hacohen, *The Tears of the Oppressed*, vii-viii; in August 2013 the FBI investigated a New Jersey rabbi believed to be using torture to compel husbands to issue the certificate of divorce for their estranged wives and a court case followed in February 2015: Will Pavia, 'Rabbi Accused of Torturing Husbands to Grant Divorce,' *The Times, London* (19 February 2015), 33

[735] Hacohen, *The Tears of the Oppressed*, viii

[736] Paul applies his 'not enslaved' to 'brother or sister,' that is, husband or wife, although under the Old Testament economy only the wife was bound if she did not receive the certificate—Paul it seems is emphasising the thrust of his teaching in the chapter that in the New Testament era neither partner is bound in the case of desertion.

the background to the use of δουλόω is to be found in Exodus 21:10-11, the divorce deeds of the day (he cites Mur 19), and rabbinic traditions—the Mishnah has: 'writs of divorce and writs of emancipation are alike' (*m. Git.* 1:4).[737]

It is of interest to note that in the posited imagery of Romans 6-7 (§9.4.2) it was seen that in the target domain of the imagery Christ's death had freed the elect from the body of sin to enable them to become the bride of Christ, thus Satan's bride was no longer 'bound'—and it appears that Paul is saying here that now the mundane wife is also no longer to be bound. Thus Paul, in this teaching, a marriage teaching new to Scripture, is synchronising mundane marriage with the new situation in the target domain of the imagery. Certainly there is no concept of *agunah* taught in the Christian church, despite the repetition of the requirement for a certificate from the husband in Matthew 5:31. If it is thought that any freedom articulated by Paul applies only to those in mixed marriages it would mean that with his 'not enslaved' Paul was actually introducing a new form of enslavement for a deserted husband—one that is based on the profession of faith of an absent partner; under the Old Testament economy he had no need of a certificate and would have always been free to remarry.

10.4.4 For God Has Called You to Peace

Instone-Brewer suggests Paul's comment is based on rabbinic traditions (citing *m. Git.* 5:8), where a solution was found to an issue that was not based on a strict interpretation of the law, but instead, for the 'sake of peace.'[738] It seems Paul's argument is that if the woman had been deserted, her husband was clearly not providing her with her entitlement, and although she had not received her certificate as outlined in Deuteronomy 24:1-4, she could, for the sake of peace, consider herself divorced and free to remarry of her own volition.[739] It appears in v. 15 that Paul is saying for the Christian community

---

[737] Instone-Brewer, '1 Corinthians 7 in the Light of the Jewish Papyri,' 238-42; Danby, *The Mishnah*, 307

[738] Instone-Brewer, *Divorce and Remarriage*, 203

[739] Bacchiocchi states: 'In Paul's day, there was no provision for a wife to be legally separated from her husband without being divorced'—if correct this supports the argument that if a wife did separate she could consider the separation a divorce: Samuele Bacchiocchi, *The Marriage Covenant: A Biblical Study on Marriage, Divorce, and*

there is no need for a wife to have a certificate of divorce from her previous husband in order to remarry, thus freeing that community from the *agunah* problem that impacts Jewish communities across the world today.[740] Furthermore, Paul seems to be saying that the husband could assume that a deserting wife was in effect divorcing him, so he should release her without evidence of sexual impurity—such teaching is consonant with Exodus 21:10–11.

10.4.5 Remarriage after Widowhood or Divorce

> A wife is bound to her husband as long as he lives. But if her husband dies, she is free to be married to whom she wishes, only in the Lord. Yet in my judgment she is happier if she remains as she is. And I think that I too have the Spirit of God. (1 Cor 7:39–40)

Instone-Brewer argues:

> Paul's quotation [is] from a standard Jewish divorce certificate. According to the Mishnah, which is confirmed by a surviving papyrus certificate, first century divorce certificates contained a line stating: "You are free to marry any Jewish man you wish" ... for Paul and for his contemporary Jews, it was more obvious that a divorcée could marry anyone she wished than that a widow had this freedom.... Many commentators have ... concluded [erroneously] that Paul thought a marriage could end only with death.[741]

Paul's comment does appear to mirror Mur 19 (assumed to be 72 CE):[742]

1. On the first of Marheshwan, the year six, at Masada

2. I divorce and repudiate of my own free will, today I

3. Joseph, son of Naqsan, from [...]ah, living at Masada, you

---

Remarriage (Berrien Springs, MI: Biblical Perspectives, 2001), 192

[740] As noted in: Hacohen and Elon, *The Tears of the Oppressed*.

[741] Instone-Brewer, *Divorce and Remarriage*, 208–09; also: Instone-Brewer, '1 Corinthians 7 in the Light of the Jewish Papyri,' 238–39

[742] Satlow dates Mur 19 as possibly 111 CE: Satlow, *Jewish Marriage*, 352

4. Miriam, daughter of Jonathan [fro]m Hanablata, living

5. At Masada, who was my wife up to this time, so that you

6. Are free on your part to go and become the wife of any

7. Jewish man that you wish ...

Thus Paul, as Instone-Brewer argues, appears to be freeing widows in the Christian church from the levirate obligation to marry her deceased husband's brother (Deut 25:5–10). Paul merely stipulates that any subsequent marriage should be 'in the Lord'—reflecting Mur 19, only now in a Christian context. If it is thought that Paul was outlining a principle of life-long marriage that allowed no exceptions it would mean Paul was contradicting the Matthean pericopae and his own earlier statement in v. 15.

10.4.6 Summary: Separation, Divorce, and Remarriage in First Corinthians 7

As anticipated in §10.4.1, Paul's teaching is congruent with both the marital imagery and mundane marriage teaching found elsewhere in both the Jewish and Christian Scriptures.

He teaches, as Edgar and Heth suggest (as above), that desertion by either partner is grounds for divorce. It has been seen that a wife was free to initiate a divorce from her husband if she believed she was not being provided for (Exod 21:10–11)—thus any desertion by her would indicate such, and would amount to a divorce. If a husband deserted his wife he would obviously be failing in his duties, and the wife would be free to consider it a divorce. Paul did not rescind Exodus 21:10–11, and the understanding of the chapter suggested in this study is fully compatible with that Pentateuchal teaching.

But it is argued that no new grounds for *initiating* a divorce are given in 1 Corinthians 7 to either the husband or the wife. Although the chapter expresses the ideal of mutual commitment (vv. 3–5, 33–34), these commitments are not coextensive with the grounds for divorce. In other words, only the failure to fulfil certain specific (asymmetrical) expectations are given as grounds for initiating a divorce in Scripture. Thus there is no such thing as 'the Pauline privilege' in the chapter—Paul was merely articulating the logic of the Scriptural position.[743] If he was looking to convey the concept that grounds for initiating a divorce were now to be based on a wider range of marital expectations, it might be thought he would have endeavoured to express it as clearly as possible, as from this study's perspective, the understanding of divorce in the Old Testament (Deut 24:1–4, Exod 21:10–11), as well as in contemporary Judaism (evidenced in the JDD), and the teaching in Matthew (Matt 5:32, 19:9), is that the grounds for initiating a divorce were different for men and women.

Furthermore, the concept of fully mutual grounds for divorce is not congruent with the Bible's marital imagery. For example, although Deuteronomy 10:12 states that Israel had a duty to love their God, Ackerman points out that: 'Deuteronomy never describes the people ... as actually offering Yahweh this love.'[744] Indeed, I am not aware of the Hebrew Bible speaking of Israel's love for Yahweh anywhere, except for Jeremiah 2:2, which apparently references the desert wanderings of Israel and portrays them as a 'honeymoon' period after their 'marriage' at Sinai (§6.4). But Yahweh's divorce of Israel was not for their failure to meet any expectations which he may have had for them in terms of wider covenant obedience, nor for their lack of any demonstrated love for him, but for the sole reason that they had forsaken him and behaved as 'prostitutes.' It has been suggested a similar concept is found in the New Testament imagery, where Christ will only breach his betrothal promise if believers 'deny' him—not because of a lack of sufficient love for him (§9.4.7).

In the Conclusion of this study the relevance of its posited asymmetrical divorce grounds will be briefly considered when, in much of the developed world today, there is greater social and economic parity between marriage partners.

---

[743] Many of the traditional views see that Paul added to the Gospel divorce rights a further exception for those being deserted by an unbeliever—for analysis: Engle and Strauss, *Remarriage after Divorce*. William A. Heth, 'Jesus on Divorce: How My Mind Was Changed,' *SBJT* 6.1 (Spring 2002): 4-12; Wayne H. House, ed., *Divorce and Remarriage: Four Christian Views* (Downers Grove, IL: InterVarsity, 1990)

[744] Ackerman, 'The Personal is Political,' 445.

10.5 Adam and Eve

In §6.12 it was pointed out that it is possible that Adam represented God's people, or more specifically (as Postell believes), Israel—Exodus 4:22 describing Israel as God's firstborn son and Luke 3:38 referring to Adam as the son of God.

On the creation of Eve it can be seen that her relationship with Adam reflected Adam's relationship with God—Adam now represented God, and Eve represented God's people. Thus (as referenced in §9.6), Romans 5:12-21 and 1 Corinthians 15:21-22, 45-49 compares Adam with Christ, and 2 Corinthians 11:2-3 compares Eve to the church, suggesting they should be considered as types, as Romans 5:14 states of Adam. If this analysis is correct, the miraculous primal couple's heterosexual literal one-flesh relationship was seen, at least by the New Testament writers, to portray the relationship of God and his people. Thus it might be seen that at the eschaton the final relationship of Christ and the church is a typological fulfilment of the primal couple's union: Genesis 2:21-23 portrays Eve as being formed from the body of Adam and then becoming his wife—at the marriage supper of the Lamb the body of Christ becomes the bride of Christ: a miraculous, permanent, unconditional union formed by God.[745] But this study suggests that the miraculous Edenic marriage did not form the aetiology of mundane marriage: there is no evidence of such in the Old Testament legislation, narratives, or marital imagery, or in the New Testament marital imagery.

Furthermore, the New Testament marriage teaching pericopae of Ephesians 5:22-33 and 1 Corinthians 7, and the other scattered New Testament references to marriage considered in §10.2 above, are consistent in that none reference an Edenic model—although the Pauline corpus draws a parallel between Adam's headship of Eve and a man's headship of a 'woman' (γυνή) in 1 Timothy 2:13-14 and 1 Corinthians 11:7-10. It appears that the sole basis for

---

[745] Carmichael when commenting on Jesus offering 'marriage' to the woman from Samaria in John 4 states that: 'the marital aspect of the narrative is the original story of creation. It provides the unique model of the single process whereby a woman was both created and married to a man at the same time.... The Samaritan woman is led in the direction of being both re-created and re-married through a union with Jesus': Carmichael, 'Marriage,' 341

a miraculous primal couple marriage model in the Gospels rests on the comment by Jesus as recorded in Matthew 19:4-8 and Mark 10:5-6, the Matthew account giving:

> He answered, "Have you not read that he who created them from the beginning made them male and female.... Because of your hardness of heart Moses allowed you to divorce your wives, but from the beginning it was not so." (Matt 19:4-8)

Verse 4 is an apparent reference to the primal couple of Genesis 1:27 and v. 8 implies that divorce was never God's intention. But there is no unanimity on what Jesus meant (§10.3.3)—it could be a reference to what might have been had Adam and Eve not transgressed. Instone-Brewer argues that with the reference to the 'beginning' that:

> It might be supposed that the force of the argument lay in the fact that this is how it was done "in the beginning". However the emphasis was more likely to be on "creation", which was an act of God. In other words, if God did something one way, we should follow his example.[746]

Instone-Brewer points out that this is a form of argument employed by Hillel and Shammai and seen in CD 4.21.[747] This present study suggests that such an argument implies an understanding of the primal couple as being formed by an act of God from which lessons can be learned, and not that the Gospel writer believes that such a marriage is to be replicated in some way in every subsequent mundane marriage. And rather than reference Genesis 2:23 Jesus is specifically recorded as saying that mundane marriage was to be based on the post-fall Genesis 2:24 aetiology of the Mosaic era. Furthermore, many commentators (§10.3.4) see that the pericope cannot mean that Jesus was prescribing a return to a pre-fall Edenic model for mundane marriage, as he

---

[746] Instone-Brewer, 'Jesus' Basis for Monogamy,' in Moyise, *The Old Testament in the New Testament*, 86-87

[747] Instone-Brewer, 'Jesus' Basis for Monogamy,' in Moyise, *The Old Testament in the New Testament*, 97. Lehmann sees the 'in the beginning' as a reference to pre-Sinai Noahide Jews who were: 'closer to fulfilling the divine command than post-Sinai Jews': Manfred R. Lehmann, 'Gen 2:24 as the Basis for Divorce in Halakhah and New Testament,' *ZAW* 72 no. 3 (1960), 266

clarifies and applies the Mosaic Deuteronomy 24:1–4 teaching for the New Testament era in line with the contemporary Shammaite understanding.

10.6 Summary: Divorce and Remarriage in the New Testament

This chapter has looked to find an exegesis of the New Testament's divorce and remarriage teaching that is congruent with its own marital imagery. It has been suggested that divorce (and remarriage) in the New Testament was permitted for a breach of the marriage covenant, that is, for a failure by either partner to do what they had agreed: for the husband to provide for his wife; for the wife not to be sexually impure. It has been seen that many published scholars support the exegesis at various points even though it appears none have looked to find congruence with the marital imagery.

If the analysis of this chapter is correct, it demonstrates such congruence, in that there is no mundane marriage teaching in the New Testament that would imply in its imagery that a divorced bridegroom could not take a divorced bride in a new marriage, as appears to happen at the marriage supper of the Lamb. Furthermore, the imagery is consonant with Old Testament teaching and marital imagery, and the understanding of contemporary New Testament Jewish marriage practice.

It is now possible to give example references for the key analogies for the cross-mapping chart posited in §1.4.1. The betrothal practices in the source domain are to be found in Old Testament teaching and evidenced in contemporary marital practices rather than in specific New Testament teaching.

MAP 2 *Jesus: The Bridegroom of the Church* (New conceptual domain 'B' is created)

CONCEPTUAL DOMAIN Gen 2:24		NEW TARGET DOMAIN (B) Jesus: The Bridegroom of the Church
A woman becomes the wife of a man in a metaphoric one-flesh union formed by means of a volitional covenant.	 ROOT METAPHOR	Men and women are invited to become what they were not: members of the covenant community that is the metaphoric bride of Christ. (Matt 22:1–14)
• Betrothal (Matt 1:18) • Wedding feast (§9.2.6) • Invitations to guests (§9.2.3) • Groom prepares a place for his bride (§9.2.8) • Groom pays a *mohar* for his bride (§8.3.5) • Groom promises to care for his bride (§8.3.6) • Bride waits for groom (§9.2.8) • Groom comes for his bride (§9.3) • Groom takes his bride to his own home (§9.3)	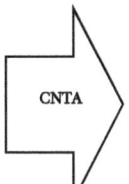 CNTA	• Betrothal (2 Cor 11:2) • Wedding feast (Matt 22:1–14) • Invitations to guests (John 4:5–29) • Jesus prepares a place for the church (John 14:1–3) • Jesus pays a *mohar* for the church (1 Cor 6:19–20) • Christ cares for the church (Eph 5:22–29) • The church waits for Jesus (2 Tim 2:10–13) • Jesus comes for the church (Matt 25:1–13) • Jesus takes the church to his own home (Rev 21:1–4)

CNTA = Consequent New Testament Analogies

Therefore it can be seen that New Testament marriage teaching is consistent with its own marital imagery, and as metaphoric principles would suggest, that imagery is based on a source domain rooted in the understanding of marriage in contemporary Jewish society. Furthermore, the aetiology of New Testament mundane marriage has been seen to be specifically stated in Matthew 19:3–9 and Mark 10:2–12 to be based on the conceptual domain of Genesis 2:24, a conceptual domain which forms the basis of both Old Testament marriage and its marital imagery.

Genesis 2:24 is consistently cross-mapped in both the Jewish and Christian Scriptures to underpin their marital imagery. The New Testament develops this concept to define the people of God: it is all who by means of a volitional covenant come into a metaphoric one-flesh/one-body relationship with their God—the New Testament portraying Jesus as the Bridegroom Messiah, inviting all (Jew and Gentile) into such a union. Thus each mundane marriage based on Genesis 2:24, in effect, becomes a picture of the gospel offer that the New Testament writers articulate.

Conclusion

As stated in the Introduction, the aim of this study was to investigate the possibility that the metaphoric marital imagery employed in the Jewish and Christian Scriptures may provide paradigmatic and hermeneutic guidelines for a better understanding of New Testament divorce and remarriage teaching. Such a study does not seem to have been attempted previously; and no published study appears to have challenged the widely assumed primal couple marriage model; or explored how the conceptual domains of Genesis 2:23 and Genesis 2:24 differ and the significance of that difference; or examined New Testament marital imagery in light of either traditional metaphor theory or the more recent developments in structure-mapping theory; or how, in light of that structure-mapping theory, Genesis 2:24 with its metaphoric, covenantal concepts, is cross-mapped in both the Jewish and Christian Scriptures.

Wenham articulates the consensus view of the church and New Testament scholars: '[Gen 2:24] is a comment by the narrator applying the principles of the first marriage to every marriage.'[748]

However, it has been seen that the four principles of Genesis 2:24 outlined in this present study are mutually exclusive to the principles underlying Genesis 2:23 and the first marriage described there, and it seems clear that it is the principles of Genesis 2:24, not those of Genesis 2:23, which underpin subsequent marriages:

Genesis 2:23	Genesis 2:24
1. A miraculous man and woman.	1. A naturally born man and woman.
2. Remain as they are.	2. Become what they were not.
3. In a literal one-flesh union.	3. In a metaphoric one-flesh union.
4. Without need of a covenant.	4. By a volitional, conditional covenant.

It is suggested that the exploration of the Bible's marital imagery has demonstrated that it is the principles of Genesis 2:24, not those of Genesis

---

[748] Wenham, *Genesis*, 70

2:23, which are cross-mapped in the marital imagery, and in the related corporate body imagery. Thus Genesis 2:24 has been shown to have been cross-mapped in the marital imagery to create three new conceptual domains:

MAP 1   *Yahweh: The Husband of Israel* (All Old Testament imagery)

MAP 2   *Jesus: The Bridegroom of the Church* (Gospels, Paul, and Apocalypse)

MAP 3   *Sin: The Husband of Unredeemed Humanity* (Rom 6 and 7)

And in the body imagery of the New Testament, the Genesis 2:24 conceptual domain has been seen to be employed twice in a forced equivalence cross-mapping of the two conceptual domains formed by the New Testament marital imagery, to create its corporate body imagery:

MAP 4   *The Body of Christ* (1 Cor 6:15–16)

MAP 5   *The Body of a Prostitute* (1 Cor 6:15–16)

Thus the conceptual domain of Genesis 2:24 is cross-mapped in five different ways in the Jewish and Christian Scriptures as represented in the five cross-mapping structure maps (Appendix A: Maps 1–5): three times in the marital imagery and twice in the body imagery.

It is further suggested that chapter 10 of this study has demonstrated that an exegesis of the divorce and remarriage pericopae of the New Testament can be found that is compatible with both its own marital imagery and that of the Jewish Scriptures. This is a conclusion that is congruent with metaphoric principles which would expect the marital practices of a nation's culture to be consonant with the metaphoric imagery of the Scriptures produced by that culture.

It might be wondered why there is such a diverse understanding in Christendom of New Testament divorce and remarriage teaching if, as suggested in this study, an exegesis is possible that harmonises the Gospel teaching with that in the Pauline corpus, and harmonises both with the understanding of marriage as demonstrated in the Old Testament legislation and narratives. Instone-Brewer suggests that the post-apostolic church struggled to make sense of the Gospels' divorce and remarriage teaching because of the destruction of Jerusalem in 70 CE—the subsequent loss of

Jewish culture within the church meant that the background to the debate recorded in Matthew 19 and Mark 10 was lost.[749] Hays comments: 'Christian tradition early on lost its vital connection with the Jewish interpretative matrix.'[750] Blomberg, although not commenting on the loss of any distinctive Jewish understanding, cautions against valuing the patristic views on New Testament teaching on marriage and divorce. He points out that they took no uniform position and relied on a textual version of Matthew 19:9 that appeared to exclude any option for remarriage and further points out 'the general tendencies toward asceticism in sexual matters in early Greek and Latin Christianity.'[751]

Although this study has challenged Loader's assertion that the New Testament writers employed Genesis 2:24 with a Greek understanding of σάρξ, it suggests that Witte is correct to see that the early post-apostolic church's teaching on marriage and divorce was a synthesis of Greek philosophy, Roman law, and biblical teaching.[752] Witte points out that Clement of Alexandria was:

> particularly well-schooled in Platonism, and he worked hard to show that Christianity was a form of philosophy that was consonant with this ancient Greek philosophy.[753]

It was posited in chapter 8 that these neoplatonic ideas introduced the concept of Adam and Eve's marriage as an archetype. Sly comments:

> Primarily, all Philo's allegorical interpretation of the story is a development of that pattern ... Adam is the prototype of man as husband, Eve the prototype of woman as wife.[754]

---

[749] Instone-Brewer, *Divorce and Remarriage*, 238–39

[750] Hays, *Conversion of the Imagination*, 43. For an overview of the history of divorce and remarriage teaching in the Christian West see: Instone-Brewer, *Divorce and Remarriage*, 238–67; also: Witte *From Sacrament to Contract*.

[751] Blomberg, 'Marriage,' 180–81; Parker has an analysis of the textual variations in the relevant pericopae: Parker, 'The Early Traditions,' 372–83

[752] Loader sees that the Septuagint had a significant influence on the understanding of the New Testament writers on sexual matters: William R. G. Loader, *The Septuagint, Sexuality, and the New Testament: Case Studies on the Impact of the LXX on Philo and the New Testament* (Grand Rapids, MI: Eerdmans, 2004)

[753] Witte, *From Sacrament to Contract*, 55

The distinctive teaching that is thought to be derived from a primal couple model (§5.1) soon followed. As early as *The Shepherd of Hermas* (variously dated between 90 CE and 150 CE) the perception seems to have been that there was no remarriage after divorce:

> The husband should put her away, and remain by himself. But if he put his wife away and marry another, he also commits adultery.[755]

But Witte believes it was Augustine of Hippo who had the greatest influence on Western Christendom's perception of marriage—in his *Of the Good of Marriage* (401 CE) Augustine states:

> [Marriage is] a certain sacrament, that it is not made void even by separation itself, since, so long as her husband lives, even by whom she has been left, she commits adultery, in case she be married to another: and he who has left her, is the cause of this evil.

And that: 'marriage and continence [celibacy] are two goods, whereof the second is better.' And:

> But a marriage once for all entered upon in the City of our God, where, even from the first union of the two, the man and the woman, marriage bears a certain sacramental character, can no way be dissolved but by the death of one of them.[756]

The idea that marriage was a sacrament that conveyed grace developed in the Middle Ages, but such teaching was not formalised by the Church of Rome until the Council of Trent in 1563. From which time the marriage was to be conducted by a priest and the ceremony to involve a couple who were consenting baptised adults and such: 'spiritually transformed their relationship—removing the sin of sexual intercourse' creating an indissoluble

---

[754] Sly, *Philo's Perception of Women*, 95

[755] Hermas, *The Shepherd of Hermas Vol. 2*, ed. Alexander Roberts, James Donaldson, and A. Cleveland Coxe, trans. F. Crombie (Buffalo, NY: Christian Literature Publishing Co., 1885), Commandment 4, Chapter 1 <http://www.newadvent.org/fathers/02012.htm> [Accessed: 11/3/2014]

[756] Philip Schaff, ed., *On the Good of Marriage*, Vol. 3 of *Nicene and Post-Nicene Fathers* (Buffalo, NY: Christian Literature Publishing Co., 1887), §6; §7; §17 <http://www.newadvent.org/fathers/1309.htm> [Accessed: 11/11/2014]

union.[757] The Reformers, as they looked afresh at the text of Scripture, were united in rejecting marriage as a sacrament as defined by the Church of Rome but failed to reach a consensus on divorce and remarriage, as is reflected in the situation today (§10.1).[758]

This study has not attempted to consider the applicability of its posited New Testament mundane divorce teaching for a Christian community today, or any pastoral consequences of such. It has been suggested that the New Testament teaches, and the JDD evidences, narrower grounds for divorce for husbands than wives. Thus, although Exodus 21:10–11 and 1 Corinthians 7 indicate a wife can leave her husband if he has not provided for her needs, and that a husband can treat his wife's abandonment of him as a *de facto* divorce initiated by her, it seems from Deuteronomy 24:1 and Jesus's endorsement of it recorded in Matthew, that the husband can only legitimately initiate a divorce of his wife based on her sexual impurity. The effect of this teaching is to give the wife emotional and financial security within the marriage. However, such asymmetry might not be thought to be applicable today, especially in the developed world, where a woman is perhaps more able to achieve financial self-sufficiency than in the ANE or the Graeco-Roman world of the Second Temple period.

Instone-Brewer believes 1 Corinthians 7 gives gender equality in divorce grounds.[759] Such a position does remove the potential anomaly of the restricted grounds of divorce for the husband—he references Origen who points out that such teaching means a wife might have committed any number of atrocities, for example, murdering the couple's infant child, but if she had not committed any sexual indecency her husband was forbidden a divorce.[760]

---

[757] Witte, *From Sacrament to Contract*, 77–112; Kreeft, *Catholic Christianity*, 363–68

[758] Witte, *From Sacrament to Contract*, 130; Witte gives a detailed account of Calvin's position and that of his contemporaries in Geneva in: John Witte Jr. and Robert M. Kingdon, 'Sex, Marriage and Family in John Calvin's Geneva: Courtship, Engagement, and Marriage' in *Religion, Marriage, and Family Vol.1*, ed. Don S. Browning and John Witte Jr. (Grand Rapids, MI: Eerdmans, 2005)

[759] Instone-Brewer, *Divorce and Remarriage*, 195–97

[760] Instone-Brewer, *Divorce and Remarriage*, 248; Origen, *Commentary on Matthew*, §14.24.

The understanding of biblical divorce teaching posited in this present study is that a divorce can be legitimately initiated by either spouse when the other fails to fulfil their own specific covenantal responsibilities. However, 1 Corinthians 7:3–5 states that the sexual relationship (one of the triad of obligations in Exod 21:10) is a duty of both husband and wife, and in vv. 33–34 Paul appears to also expect both husband and wife to be 'anxious' to please each other, furthermore Titus 2:3–4 explains that wives are to love their husbands. Thus, although not (as this study understands it) strictly according to the explicit teaching of the New Testament, it might be an acceptable pragmatic solution to the potential problem of asymmetrical divorce grounds, to allow a husband to initiate a divorce on the more broadly based grounds of the failure by his wife to fulfil her responsibilities in the marriage as articulated in the New Testament.[761] This might be seen to be an acceptable pastoral solution in line with the principles outlined in §10.4.4 and Paul's comment: 'God has called you to peace' (1 Cor 7:15). The equity of such a solution is perhaps underpinned by the fact that, as mentioned above, in the twenty-first century developed world a divorced wife is potentially less disadvantaged than in biblical times.

Furthermore, apart from not addressing the pastoral implications of divorce, this present study has not considered the wider implications of the Bible's cross-mapping of Genesis 2:24 in its imagery, focusing rather on the issue of divorce and remarriage. In particular, the way in which the Pauline corpus employs the metaphoric one-flesh union of Genesis 2:24 to both delineate the people of God and underpin the offer of the gospel to the Gentiles is a specific area probably worthy of further consideration.

On metaphoric theology in general Long comments:

> Within religion and theology Ian Ramsey ... Paul Ricouer ... Sallie Macfague ... Janet Soskice ... Peter Macky and Marjo Korpel are a few who acknowledge the vital cognitive function of nonliteral language,

---

[761] Instone-Brewer addresses some of these issues: David Instone-Brewer, *Divorce and Remarriage in the Church* (Carlisle: Paternoster, 2003; Repr. Milton Keynes, 2011), 69–80.

> particularly metaphor and its importance in understanding the world and the other world.[762]

And Neusner in his consideration of the significance of social metaphors saw that:

> the ways in which a religious system defines its own society, in particular the modes of thought and processes of imagination that yield one picture of the social entity and not some other – that is not a routine enquiry.[763]

These statements seem to be borne out by the fact that to date there appears to be no analysis of New Testament marital or corporate body imagery in light of metaphor theory published in English.

Finally, in the process of exploring the marital imagery of the Jewish and Christian Scriptures, it has been seen it is possible to posit that Adam's expulsion from Eden is a divorce from God;[764] his new relationship (and thus mankind's relationship) with Satan is a marriage;[765] Israel's exodus from the 'idols of Egypt' (Ezek 20:8) and the covenant giving at Sinai is a divorce and remarriage respectively;[766] Israel's Assyrian exile (in contrast to Judah's Babylonian exile) is a divorce;[767] Jesus's encounter with the woman from Samaria is a remarriage offer to divorced Israel;[768] Christ's death on the cross is to release the elect from their marriage to Satan;[769] and the destruction of Jerusalem represents Christ's divorce of the Israelite cult (Origen, ca. 250).

Despite this, there does not appear to be any systematic study that has explored how the marital imagery of the Pentateuch was developed by the Old Testament Jewish prophets and exploited by the New Testament authors to

---

[762] Gary Alan Long, 'Dead or Alive? Literality and God-Metaphors in the Hebrew Bible,' *AAR* 62 No.2 (Summer 1994), 510

[763] Neusner, *Judaism and its Social Metaphors*, 13

[764] Postell, *Adam as Israel*

[765] Holland, *Romans: The Divine Marriage*

[766] Lunn, 'Let My people Go!'

[767] Instone-Brewer, *Divorce and Remarriage in the Bible*

[768] McWhirter, *The Bridegroom Messiah*

[769] Holland, *Romans: The Divine Marriage*

produce what appears to be a biblical marital metanarrative—embracing an exodus from Egypt culminating in a marriage at Sinai, and an inchoate marriage forming the background to a new exodus and the marriage supper of the Lamb.[770] It is a metanarrative that portrays the proposed marriage at the eschaton as a remarriage after divorce for both bride and groom, where the groom takes his own body in a new marital union to re-instate the Edenic bliss of the primal couple.[771]

---

[770] Long states: 'Jesus combined the image of an eschatological banquet with the marriage metaphor to describe the end of the Exile as a new Exodus': Long, *Jesus the Bridegroom*, 7

[771] Calum M. Carmichael, 'Marriage and the Samaritan Woman,' *New Testament Studies* 26 (1980), 332–46

Appendix A: Cross-Domain Mapping Diagrams

MAP 1 *Yahweh: The Husband of Israel* (New conceptual domain 'A' is created)

| CONCEPTUAL DOMAIN
Gen 2:24
A woman becomes the wife of a man in a metaphoric one-flesh union formed by means of a volitional covenant. | NEW TARGET DOMAIN (A)
Yahweh: The Husband of Israel
Israel becomes what they were not in a metaphoric marital union with Yahweh formed by means of a volitional covenant.
(Jer 31:31–32) |

ROOT METAPHOR

- Marital obligations for the husband
  (Exod 21:7–11)
- Adultery forbidden
  (Exod 20:14)
- Divorce certificate required
  (Deut 24:1–4)
- Remarriage to first husband forbidden
  (Deut 24:1–4)

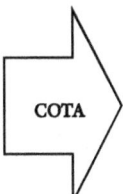

COTA

- Marital obligations for Yahweh
  (Ps 132:13–16)
- Adultery forbidden
  (Ezek 23:1–9)
- Divorce certificate required
  (Jer 3:6–8)
- Remarriage to Yahweh forbidden
  (Jer 3:6–8)
- But a future betrothal followed by a remarriage is promised (Hos 2:19–20; Isa 54:4-8)

COTA = Consequent Old Testament Analogies

274

MAP 2 *Jesus: The Bridegroom of the Church* (New conceptual domain 'B' is created)

CONCEPTUAL DOMAIN Gen 2:24		NEW TARGET DOMAIN (B) Jesus: The Bridegroom of the Church
A woman becomes the wife of a man in a metaphoric one-flesh union formed by means of a volitional covenant.	ROOT METAPHOR →	Men and women are invited to become what they were not: members of the covenant community that is the metaphoric bride of Christ.
• Betrothal (Matt 1:18) • Wedding feast (§9.2.6) • Invitations to guests (§9.2.3) • Groom prepares a place for his bride (§9.2.8) • Groom pays a *mohar* for his bride (§8.3.5) • Groom promises to care for his bride (§8.3.6) • Bride waits for groom (§9.2.8) • Groom comes for his bride (§9.3) • Groom takes his bride to his own home (§9.3)	CNTA →	• Betrothal (2 Cor 11:2) • Wedding feast (Matt 22:1–14) • Invitations to guests (John 4:5–29) • Jesus prepares a place for the church (John 14:1–3) • Jesus pays a *mohar* for the church (1 Cor 6:19–20) • Christ cares for the church (Eph 5:22–29) • The church waits for Jesus (2 Tim 2:10–13) • Jesus comes for the church (Matt 25:1–13) • Jesus takes the church to his own home (Rev 21:1–4)

CNTA = Consequent New Testament Analogies

MAP 3 *Sin: The Husband of Unredeemed Humanity* (New conceptual domain 'C' is created)

CONCEPTUAL DOMAIN Gen 2:24		NEW TARGET DOMAIN (C) Sin: The Husband of Unredeemed Humanity
A woman becomes the wife of a man in a metaphoric one-flesh union formed by means of a volitional covenant.	ROOT METAPHOR 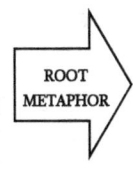	Unredeemed humanity became what they were not: the metaphoric wife of Sin by means of a volitional covenant formed by Adam.

• The wife is bound (Rom 7:1–4) • No release from the marriage without a death (or the required divorce certificate: Deut 24:1–4)	CNTA 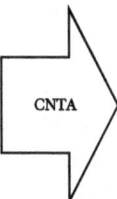	• Unredeemed humanity is bound (Rom 6 and 7) • No release from the marriage without a death (or the required divorce certificate: Deut 24:1–4)

CNTA = Consequent New Testament Analogies

MAP 4 The Corporate *Body of Christ* (New conceptual domain 'D' is created)

CONCEPTUAL DOMAIN
Gen 2:24

A woman becomes the wife of a man by means of a volitional covenant forming a new kinship group.

⟨ F. E. ⟩

CONCEPTUAL DOMAIN
Jesus: The Bridegroom of the Church

Believers at Corinth had become what they were not: members of the covenant community that is the metaphoric bride of Christ.

F.E. = Forced Equivalence

NEW CONCEPTUAL DOMAIN (D)
A New 'Horizontal' Identity: The Body of Christ

Do you not know that your bodies are members of Christ?... For, as it is written, "The two will become one flesh." (1 Cor 6:15–16)

For just as the body is one and has many members, and all the members of the body, though many, are one body, so it is with Christ. (1 Cor 12:12)

MAP 5 The Corporate *Body of a Prostitute* (New conceptual domain 'E' is created)

CONCEPTUAL DOMAIN Gen 2:24	CONCEPTUAL DOMAIN Sin: The Husband of Unredeemed Humanity
A woman becomes the wife of a man by means of a volitional covenant forming a new kinship group.	Unredeemed humanity becomes the metaphoric wife of 'Sin' by means of a volitional covenant formed by Adam.

F. E.

F.E. = Forced Equivalence

NEW CONCEPTUAL DOMAIN (E)
A New 'Horizontal' Identity:
The Body of a Prostitute
(The Body of Sin)

Or do you not know that he who is joined to a prostitute becomes one body with her? For, as it is written, "The two will become one flesh." (1 Cor 6:16)

MAP 6 Structure Map of First Corinthians 6:15–16

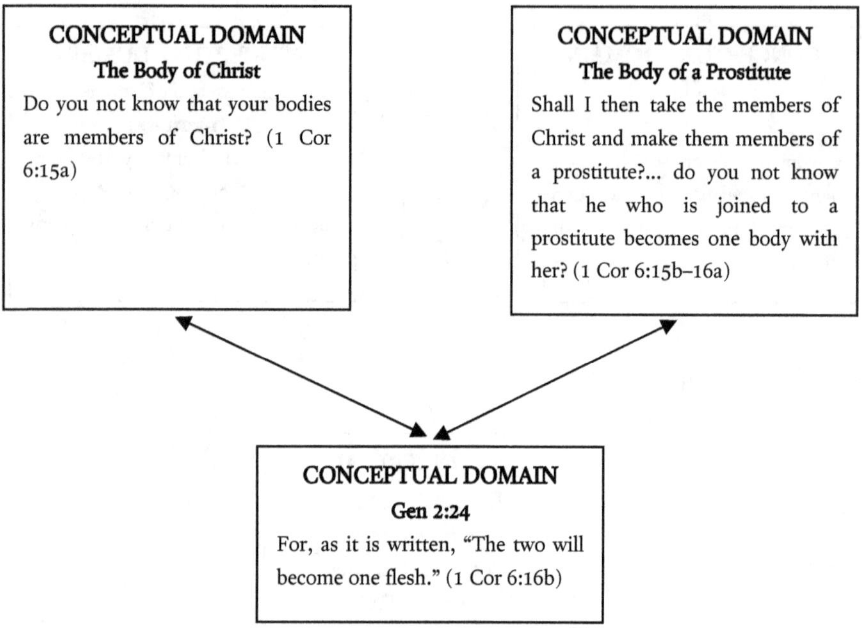

CONCEPTUAL DOMAIN
The Body of Christ
Do you not know that your bodies are members of Christ? (1 Cor 6:15a)

CONCEPTUAL DOMAIN
The Body of a Prostitute
Shall I then take the members of Christ and make them members of a prostitute?... do you not know that he who is joined to a prostitute becomes one body with her? (1 Cor 6:15b–16a)

CONCEPTUAL DOMAIN
Gen 2:24
For, as it is written, "The two will become one flesh." (1 Cor 6:16b)

Appendix B: Judaean Desert Documents Chart

SBL reference	Former sigla	Date of origin	Language	Discovered	First published	Location
Marriage:						
Mur 20	DJD II 20	117 CE	Aramaic	1952	1961	Murabba'at
Mur 21	DJD II 21	Early 2nd CE	Aramaic	1952	1961	Murabba'at
Mur 115	DJD II 115	124 CE	Greek	1952	1961	Murabba'at
Mur 116	DJD II 116	Early 2nd CE	Greek	1952	1961	Murabba'at
XḤev/Se 69	P.Ḥev 69	130 CE	Greek	1952	1994	Naḥal Ḥever
5/6Ḥev 10	P.Yadin10 (Babatha's *Ketubah*)	125-128 CE	Aramaic	1961	1994	Naḥal Ḥever
5/6Ḥev 18	P.Yadin18	128 CE	Greek	1961	1989	Naḥal Ḥever
5/6Ḥev 37	XḤev/Se gr 65	131 CE	Greek	1961	1989	Naḥal Ḥever
Divorce:						
Mur 19	DJD 19	72 CE	Aramaic	1952	1961	Murabba'at
XḤev/Se 13	Se'elim13	130 CE	Aramaic	1952	1995	Naḥal Ḥever

Appendix C: Judaean Desert Documents Translations
Mur 20

1   The Document

'[An] Aramaic marriage contract, concluded in Hardona, 5km from Jerusalem'; possibly dating from 117 CE—or as early as 51 CE or 65 CE[772] It was found in the Wadi Murabba'at in 1952.

2   First Published

Pierre Benoit, Jozef T. Milik, and Roland De Vaux, *Discoveries in the Judaean Desert II: Les Grottes de Murabba'at* (Oxford: Oxford University Press, 1961)

3   Translation of the Text

1. [On] the seventh of Adar, the year ele[ven at Haradona, Yehuda son of Yo ...

2   Son of] Manasseh, of the sons of Eliashib [living at Haradona, said to ... daughter of ...

3. Yo]u shall be my wife according to the law of Mo[ses ... and me I shall feed and clothe you, from today for]

4. Always, from my property and upon [me is the duty of/I am giving you the *mohar* of your virginity ...]

5. Of good coinage, the sum of [200] zuzin ... [

6. And] it shall be valid. And if you are divorced from me I will return the money of your *kethubah* and all that you have brought to my house.

7. I]f you go to the house of eternity [before me, sons which you have by me will inherit your *kethubah* ...

---

[772] Thus Cotton, who furthers states: 'Milik assumed that "year 11" refers to the era of the province of Arabia, thus yielding the year 116/7. Since Judaea did not have its own a provincial era, "year 11" is likely to refer to a regnal year of an emperor. Claudius or Nero could easily fit the lacuna, i.e. 51 CE or 65 CE': Cotton, 'The Languages of the Documents,' 224

8. According to] the law. And if there shall be daughters which you shall have by me, they shall live in my house and shall be maintained from my goods.

9. Until marriage. Or if I [go] to the house [of eternity before you, you will dwell ...]

10. And you will be nourished and clothed [all the days, in the house of our children throughout the time of]

11. Your widowhood, af[ter me (my death) and until your death/you cannot be prevented from living in my house. All the goods that I have and that

12. I shall acquire are guarantees and sure[ties for your *kethuba* ...]

13. An in favour of your heirs against every [counter-claim ... And at whatever time you ask it of me, I will renew]

14. For you the document as long as I am alive

Translation:

Léonie J. Archer, *Her Price is Beyond Rubies: The Jewish Woman in Graeco-Roman Palestine,* Journal for the Study of the Old Testament Supplement 60 (Sheffield, England: Sheffield Academic, 1990), 291–92

Mur 21

1 The Document

A marriage contract written in Aramaic found in the Wadi Murabba'at in 1952 dating from the early 2nd century.

2 First Published

Pierre Benoit, Jozef T. Milik, and Roland De Vaux, *Discoveries in the Judaean Desert II: Les Grottes de Murabba'at* (Oxford: Oxford University Press, 1961)

3 Translation of Text

1. [On the twenty first of the month] ... the year ... [Menahem son of ...

2. took as wife Le']uton, daughter of [...

3. ... [*hb* Le'uth[on/Le'uth[on has given as dowry

4.

5. ...] guarant[ee from all th[at he possesses ...]

6. [On the twen[ty the fir]st ... Menahem, son of ... living at ... said to Le'uthon

7. Daughter of ... a living at] 'Ain [... you shall] be [my wife]

8.

9. ... I]f I di[vorce you ...]

10. I will return [to you the money of] your [*ke*]*thubah* and everything that is [yours that is with] me And if [there be] child[ren (daughters) by me]

11. According to the law, th[ey a]re to live [in] my house and [be] nourished fr[om my possessions ... until]

12. To marriage [and even a]fter [me (my death) wi]th you until their marriage. [I]f you [go] to [the House of eternity] bef[ore me]

13. The sons which you [shall have] by me [will inherit] the money of your *kethubah* and [all] of you[rs that is with me and that is written] above

14. Inside and out[side. I]f I go to that hou[se] be[fore you, you are to dwell]

15. And be nourished [from my possession] all the days in the house o[f our sons]s, the house of your widow[hood until]

16. Your death [and] your [*keth*]*ubah* ... is yours [...]

17. And I Menahem [son of ...], which is on the part of Le'[u]th[o]n [...

18. And I Le'uth[on daughter of ...] that which [is written] above.

19. And at (any) [ti]me that you [ask me I will replace for you the doc[ument]

20. [As long as] I am alive ...

Translation:

Léonie J. Archer, *Her Price is Beyond Rubies: The Jewish Woman in Graeco-Roman Palestine,* Journal for the Study of the Old Testament Supplement 60. Sheffield (Sheffield, England: Academic, 1990), 292–94

Mur 115

1 The Document

A marriage document written in Greek dating from 124 CE found in Wadi Murabba'at in 1951.[773]

2 First Published

Pierre Benoit, Jozef T. Milik, and Roland De Vaux, *Discoveries in the Judaean Desert II: Les Grottes de Murabba'at* (Oxford: Oxford University Press, 1961)

3 Translation of Text

1. In the seventh year of the emperor Trajan Hadrian Caesar Augustus, under the consuls Manius Acilius Glabrio and Bellicius Torquatas, the fourteenth before the Calends of November

2. Which is the fifteenth of Dystros at Bethbassi ... of the toparchy of the Herodion. It has been agreed and concluded by Eleaios son of Simon of the village of Galoda which is under Aqraba

3. Living in the village of Betharda which is under Gophna, with regard to Salome daughter of John Galgoula, who was once married to the same Eleaios. Then it previously happened that the same Eleaios

4. Son of Simon did divorce and repudiate Salome daughter of John Galgoula [...] for the sake of communal life (?), now the same Eleaios son of Simon is agreed

5. To be reconciled again and retake the same Salome daughter of John Galgoula as legitimate wife with a 'dowry' of 200 *denars*, which make 50 tyrian shekels, amount which

6. The same Eleaios son of Simon and recognized (acknowledged) having being counted (to him?) [...] the above written at 200 denars ... as dowry on the part of Salome's daughter of John Galgoula ...

---

[773] Cotton comments: 'This is a contract of remarriage between Elaios son of Shim'on who came 'from the village of Galoda of Akrabatta, but [was] an inhabitant of Batharda of Gophna' – both in Samaria – and his former wife Salome daughter of Yohanan Galgoula': Cotton, 'The Languages of the Documents,' 229

285

7. [...] Salome daughter of John Galgoula against (?) the same son of Simon her husband (?) ...

8. And against (?) his goods. If [...] and of the children which she has and which she may have

9. By him, sons and daughters that [...] that she may have by him, they will be nourished and clothed with the help of

10. The goods that the same Eleaios [...] If at the same Eleaios son of Simon happens to die before the same

11. Salome or if she [... it will nourish and clothe Sa]lome with the help of the goods [...] the above

12. Mentioned 200 *denars* of that which concerns the dowry. If Salome daughter of John Galgoula happens to die before the same Eleaios , the sons

13. Which she may have by him ... will inherit [...] death [...] besides their share

14. Of the paternal inheritance ... [with their half-] brothers. If ... (prior?) claim(?)

15.

16. Right of execution belong to the same Salome daughter of John Galgoula and to any other who will act [in her place]/who presents himself for her [in lieu of her] ... Salome (right) on

17. Eleaios son of Simon her husband and on (all) his goods, those which he has and those which he may acquire ... (execution) in whatever form.

18. That the executor should choose; this contract being valid [...] presented legally [...]

19.

20. (repeat of opening formula, very fragmentary)

21.

22.

Translation:

Léonie J. Archer, *Her Price is Beyond Rubies: The Jewish Woman in Graeco-Roman Palestine,* Journal for the Study of the Old Testament Supplement 60 (Sheffield, England: Sheffield Academic, 1990), 295–96

Mur 116

1 The Document

Portion of a marriage contract written in Greek found in 1952 in the Wadi Murabba'at dating from the first half of second Century CE.[774]

2 First Published

Pierre Benoit, Jozef T. Milik, and Roland De Vaux, *Discoveries in the Judaean Desert II: Les Grottes de Murabba'at* (Oxford: Oxford University Press, 1961)

3 Translation of Text

1.

2.

3.

4. ... if she (?) nourishes the daughters and gives them in marriage ... [If Salome before Aurelios]

5. Happens to die sons which she will have by hi[m ...] will inherit

6. The dowry and those written above [...

7. [They will have moreover divide] all the inheritance of the fortune of Aurelios

8. With the (half) brothers which they may (?) have. If Aurelios before Salo-

9. me happens to die Salome will be nourished and clothed from the

10. Fortune of Aurelios all the time that she wishes to remain a widow ... But if she wishes

11. To leave after his death or if she sends in her place ...

12. ... [she will recover the *kethubah* of] 2000(!) *denars*

13. ...

---

[774] Cotton, 'The Languages of the Documents,' 229

Translation:

Léonie J. Archer, *Her Price is Beyond Rubies: The Jewish Woman in Graeco-Roman Palestine,* Journal for the Study of the Old Testament Supplement 60 (Sheffield, England: Sheffield Academic, 1990), 297

XḤev/Se 69 (Ḥev 69)

1 The Document

A cancelled marriage contract in Greek dating from 130 CE found in August 1952 and believed to be from the Naḥal Ḥever caves, Cotton states: 'The date of cancellation of our contract is unknown, except that it was after 130 CE.'[775]

2 First Published

Hannah Cotton, 'A Cancelled Marriage Contract from the Judaean Desert,' *Journal of Roman Studies* Vol. 84 (1994), 64–86

3 Translation of Text

1. In the fourteenth year of the Emperor T[rajan Hadrian Caesar Augustus, in the consul-

2. ship of Marcus Flavius Aper and Quintus Fabius [Catullinus

3. in Aristoboulias of the Zephine. Sela.e[ ] gave in marriage[her daughter (?) Selampious

4. through Bork.. 'Agla, her guardian for this matter[

5. to 'Aqabas son of Meir from the village of Iaqim [of the Zephene ... she bringing

6. to him on account of bridal gift of the dowry(?) in si[lver and gold ... all appraised in money value as five

7. hundred denarii which are the equivalent of [one hundred and twenty five] staters, [and the groom acknowledges

8. to have received and to hold from her[...

9. five hundred denarii forthwith by hand [

---

[775] 'The document [XḤev/Se 69] published for the first time here is among the few Greek papyri which together with Aramaic and Nabataean papyri were brought to the Rockefeller Museum in Jerusalem ... in August 1952 by Bedouin, who claimed to have found them in Wadi Seiyal, whence the designation *P.Se'elim*; nevertheless they are now generally believed to come from the Caves of Naḥal Ḥever': Cotton, 'A Cancelled Marriage Contract,' 66, 76

10. wedded (wife) so that Selampious is nourished and cloth[ed ... upon the security of all his posse-

11. ssions both those which he has now and those which he will acquire. And in the event of the death of[

12. [ ] the male children or if heirs

13. [ ] the daughters will be nourished and clothed[

14. [ ] and if he who is mentioned before[

15. [ ] five hundred denarii [

16.

Translation:

Hannah Cotton, 'A Cancelled Marriage Contract from the Judaean Desert,' *Journal of Roman Studies* Vol. 84 (1994), 68

5/6Ḥev 10 (P.Yadin 10)

1 The Document

A marriage contract written in Aramaic found in 1961 in the Cave of Letters.[776] It dates from between 125 and 128 CE.[777]

2 First Published

Yigael Yadin, Jonas C. Greenfield and Ada Yardeni, 'Babatha's Ketubba,' *Israel Exploration Journal* 44 (1994), 75-101

3 Translation of Text

1. [On] the [thi]rd of Adar in the consulship of[

2. [...] ... [...]

3. [...] you [...]

4. [... from 'Ei]n Ged[i ... that you will be to me (**or:** Be to me)]

5. as a wif[e (**or:** in wife[hood]) according to the la]w of Moses and the J[u]daeans. And I will [feed] you and cl[othe] you (**or:** and I will re[mit] to you, pursuant to your *mo*[*har*]), and pursuant to your *ketubba*, I will bring you into (my house).

6. And you have a binding claim on me (for) silver (in the amount of) four hundred denarii (*zuzin*), which equal one hundred T[y]rian (tetradrachms), whatever

7. she (!=you) may wish to take and to ... from the *dowry*, together with the rightful allocation of your food, and your clothing and your *bed*,

8. the (fitting) sustenance of a free (=married) woman. Or (**or:** which is) the sale value of silver (in the amount of) [f]our hundred de[n]arii (*zuzin*) which are (equal to) one hundred tetradrachms (= *sil'in*).

---

[776] 'The document published here (P.Yadin 10) was discovered by the expedition led by Yigael Yadin to the Cave of the letters in Naḥal Ḥever as part of the second campaign in the Judaean desert, which took place in the spring of 1961': Yigael Yadin, Jonas C. Greenfield, and Ada Yardeni, 'Babatha's *Ketubba*,' *IEJ* 44 (1994), 75

[777] 'By 128 CE, but perhaps as early as 125 CE, Judah had taken Babatha as a second wife': Satlow, *Jewish Marriage*, 98

9. Whatever you wish *to* take and to ... [... from (the) *dow*]*ry* together with the right(ful allocation of your[food], and your *bed*

10. and your clothing as (is fitting) for a free (=married) woman. And if you are taken captive, I will redeem you, from my "house" and estate,

11. [and I will rest]ore you as a wife, [and (the amount due on)] your *ketubba* will remain as a binding claim on me as (**or**: according to) ... [...] ... [...]

12-13. [*and if you should go to your eternal home before me, male children that you may have from me shall inherit the sum of your ketubah, over and above the share with her brothers;*]

14. fe[m]ale c[hild]ren [sh]all reside, and (continue to) be provided for from my "house" and from [my properties until]the time are m[arrie]d to husbands. And if

15. >and if< I should go to my eternal h[ome] before you, you will [re]side, and (continue to) be provided for from my "house" and from my properties,

16. [until the t]ime that my [heir]s will agree to give you the silver of your *ketubba*. And whenever [you] tell me,

17. [I will exchange] for [you *this document, as is fitting. And all the properties that I possess and that I will acquire are guaranteed and pledged.*]

18. [*to* (payment of) your ketubba. And I Yehudah, son of, ʾElʿazar, it is bind]ing on me, I,[myself, all that is] written [above],

19. [...] (due) to babathaʾ (*vacat*) [da]ughter of Shimʿon, (incumbent) upon Yehudah, son of ʾElʿazar.

Translation:

Yigael Yadin et al., eds., *The Documents from the Bar Kokhba Period in the Cave of Letters: Hebrew, Aramaic and Nabatean-Aramaic Papyri* (Jerusalem: Israel Exploration Society, 2002), 127[778]

---

[778] There is an earlier translation in: Yadin, Greenfield, and Yardeni, 'Babatha's *Ketubba,*' 79

5/6Hev 18 (P.Yadin 18)

1   The Document

'a marriage document [written in Greek] from 128 CE from Ma'oza in the province Arabia, published for the first time in 1987.'[779] It was found in 1961 in the Cave of Letters.

2   First Published

Naphtali Lewis, Ranon Katzoff and Jonas C. Greenfield, 'Papyrus Yadin 18,' *IEJ* 37 (1987), 229–50

3   Translation of Text

In the consulship of Publius Metilius Nepos for the second time and Marcus Annius Libos on the nones of April, and by the compute of the new province of Arabia year twenty-third, month of Xandikos fifteenth, in Maoza, Zoara district, Judah some of the Eleazar, also known as Khthousion, has given over Shelamzion, his very own daughter, a virgin, to Judah, surnamed Cimber, son of Ananias of Somalas, both of the village 'En Gedi in Judaea residing here, for Shelamzion to be a wedded wife to Judah Cimber for the partnership of marriage according to the laws, she bringing to him on account of bridal gift feminine adornment in silver and gold and clothing appraised by mutual agreement, as they both say, to be worth 200 denarii of silver which appraised value the bridegroom Judah called Cimber acknowledged that he has received from her by hand forthwith from Judah her father and owes Shelamzion his wife together with another three hundred denarii which he promised to give her in addition to the sum of her aforestated bridal gift, all accounted toward her dowry, pursuant to his undertaking of feeding and clothing both her and the children to come in accordance with Greek custom upon the said Judah Cimber's good faith and peril [and security of] all his possessions, both those which he now possesses in his said home village and here and all those which he may in addition validly acquire everywhere, in whatever manner his wife Shelamzion may choose, or whoever acts through her or for her may choose, to pursue the execution. Judah called Cimber shall redeem this contract for his

---

[779] Yiftach-Firanko, 'Judaean Desert Marriage Documents,' in Katzoff and Schaps, *Law in the Documents*, 67

wife Shelamzion, whenever she may demand it of him, in silver secured in due form, at his own expense interposing no objection. If not, he shall pay to her all the aforesaid denarii twofold, she having the right of execution both from Judah Cimber her husband and upon the possessions lawfully his in whatever manner Shelamzion or whoever acts through her or for her may choose to pursue the execution. In good faith the formal question was asked and it was agreed in reply that this is thus rightly done.

[Witness statements follow]

Translation:

Naphtali Lewis, Ranon Katzoff and Jonas C. Greenfield, 'Papyrus Yadin 18,' *IEJ* 37 (1987), 233

5/6Ḥev 37 (XḤev/Se gr 65/P.Yadin 37)

1 The Document

A marriage contract written in Greek found in the Cave of Letters in 1961 dated 7 August 131 CE. [780]

2 First Published

Naphtali Lewis, Yigael Yadin and Jonas C. Greenfield, *The Documents from the Bar Kokhba period in the Cave of Letters: Greek papyri* (Jerusalem: Israel Exploration Society, 1989)

3 Translation of Text

In the consulship of Sergius Octavius Laenas Pontianus and Marcus Antonius Rufinus, the seventh of August, and according to the computation of the new province of Arabia year twenty-six, on the nineteenth of month Loos, in Maḥoza in the district of Zo'ar of the administrative region of Petra, metropolis of Arabia, Yeshuʻa son of Menaḥem, domiciled in the village of Soffathe ... in the district of the city of Livias of the administrative region of P[eraia] acknowledged of his own free will(?) that he has taken Salome also called Komaïse ... a woman from Maḥoza, for them to ... and for Yeshuʻa to live with her as also before this time ... to the said Komaïse as her dowry ninety-six denarii of silver, and the bridegroom, the said Yeshuʻa, acknowledged that he has received from her on the present day feminine adornment in silver and gold and clothing and other feminine articles equivalent in appraised value to the [stated sum of] money, with his undertaking to feed and clothe both her and her children to come in accordance with Greek custom and Greek manners upon the said Yeshuʻa's good faith and on peril of all his possessions, both those which he possesses in his home village of Soffathe ... and those which he may in addition acquire, she having the right of execution both from the said Yeshuʻa and upon all(?) his validly held possessions everywhere, in whatever manner the said Komaïse or whoever acts through her or for her may choose to carry out the execution, regarding this being thus rightly done the formal

---

[780] However, Cotton comments that the document was not discovered in a controlled archaeological excavation: Cotton, 'The Archive of Salome Komaïse,' 172, 204

question having in good faith been asked and acknowledged in reply. I, X, son of Menaḥem, guardian of the said Komaïse, have agreed(?) ...

Translation:

Hannah M. Cotton, 'The Archive of Salome Komaïse Daughter of Levi: Another Archive from the "Cave of Letters,"' *ZPE* 105 (1995), 204–06

Mur 19

1 The Document

A divorce certificate written in Aramaic found in 1952 at Wadi Murabba'at dating from 72 C. E.

2 First Published

Pierre Benoit, Jozef T. Milik, and Roland De Vaux, *Discoveries in the Judaean Desert II: Les Grottes de Murabba'at* (Oxford: Oxford University Press, 1961)

3 Translation of Text

1. On the first of Marheshwan, the year six, at Masada

2. I divorce and repudiate of my own free will, today I

3. Joseph, son of Naqsan, from [...]ah, living at Masada, you

4. Miriam, daughter of Jonathan [fro]m Hanablata, living

5. At Masada, who was my wife up to this time, so that you

6. Are free on your part to go and become the wife of any

7. Jewish man that you wish. And here on my part is the bill of repudiation

8. And the writ of divorce. Now I give back [the dow]ry.[781] And all the ruined,

9. And damaged (goods) and ... [they will be restored] as is my duty by this/ so let it be determined

10. And I will pay (them) fourfold. And at any ti[me] that you ask it of me, I will replace for you

11. The document as long as I am alive witnesses ...

Translation:

---

[781] Ilan does not restore the word dowry in her translation of the text: Ilan, 'On a Newly Published Divorce Bill,' 199

Léonie J. Archer, *Her Price is Beyond Rubies: The Jewish Woman in Graeco-Roman Palestine,* Journal for the Study of the Old Testament Supplement 60 (Sheffield, England: Sheffield Academic, 1990), 298–99

XḤev/Se 13 (P. Se'elim 13)

1   The Document

Opinions differ: a divorce certificate issued by the husband, a divorce certificate issued by the wife, or a renunciation of claims written in the aftermath of a divorce. Written in Aramaic it is thought to date from 135 CE and was found in 1952 (?) but not published until much later.[782]

2   First Published

Ada Yardeni, *Naḥal Se'elim Documents (Hebrew)* (Ben-Gurion: University of the Negev Press & the Israel Exploration Society, 1995)

Hannah M. Cotton and Ada Yardeni, 'Aramaic, Hebrew and Greek Documentary Texts from Naḥal Ḥever and Other Sites: With an Appendix Containing Alleged Qumran Texts The Seiyâl Collection II' in *Discoveries in the Judaean Desert*, ed. Emmanuel Tov (Oxford: Oxford University Press, 1997)

3   Translation of Text

As per Schremer:[783]

1. On the twentieth of Sivan, third year of Israel's freedom.
2. In the name of Shim'on bar Kosibah, the Nasi of Israel
3. ... I do not have —
4. I, Shelamzion, daughter of Yehoseph Qebshan
5. of Ein Gedi — with you, Eleazar son of Hananiah —
6. who have been my husband before this time, and who have said:
7. "this is to you from me a bill of divorce and release

---

[782] Ilan states: 'In 1956 ... Milik also claimed he possessed and would eventually publish another ancient Jewish bill of divorce.... The Dominican Fathers in Jerusalem had procured the document from bedouins, who claimed to have found it, along with a large group of other documents, in Naḥal Se'elim': Ilan, 'On a Newly Published Divorce Bill,' 196

[783] Adiel Schremer, 'Divorce in Papyrus Se'elim 13 Once Again: A Reply to Tal Ilan,' *HTR* Vol. 91, No. 2 (April 1998), 201–02

8. without reservation" — I do not have with you,

9. Eleazar, anything I wish for. And I confirm — I,

10. Shelamzion — all that is written [above].

11. Shelamzion, daughter of Yehoseph, by herself lent the [hand] writing [of]

12. Mattat son of Shim'on Mamre.

13. [...] son of Shim'on, witness.

14. Masbala, son of Shim'on, witness

As per Ilan:[784]

1. On the twentieth of Sivan, year three of Israel's freedom

2. In the name of Simon bar Kosibah, the Nasi of Israel

3. ... I do not have ...

4. I, Shelamzion, daughter of Joseph Qebshan

5. of Ein Gedi, with you, Eleazar son of Hananiah

6. who had been the husband before this time, that

7. this is from me to you a bill of divorce and release.

8. I do not have with you. ..

9. Eleazar anything (I wish for?), as is my duty and remains upon me.

10. I Shelamzion (accept) all that is written (in this document)

11. Shelamzion present, lent her hand writing(?)

12. Mattat son of Simon by her order

13. ... son of Simon, witness

14. Masbala, son of Simon, witness

---

[784] Ilan, 'On a Newly Published Divorce Bill,' 199–200

Judaean Desert Documents Select Bibliography

Archer, Léonie J., *Her Price is Beyond Rubies: The Jewish Woman in Graeco-Roman Palestine,* Journal for the Study of the Old Testament Supplement 60 (Sheffield: Sheffield Academic, 1990)

Benoit, Pierre, Jozef T. Milik, and Roland De Vaux, *Discoveries in the Judaean Desert II: Les Grottes de Murabba'at* (Oxford: Oxford University Press, 1961)

Brody, Robert, 'Evidence for Divorce by Jewish Women,' *Journal of Jewish Studies* L, No. 2 (Autumn 1999), 230–34

Cotton, Hannah M, and Ada Yardeni, *Aramaic, Hebrew and Greek Documentary Texts from Naḥal Ḥever and Other Sites: With an Appendix Containing Alleged Qumran Texts, The Seiyâl Collection II* in, *Discoveries in the Judaean Desert* XXVII, ed. Emmanuel Tov (Oxford: Oxford University Press, 1997)

Cotton, Hannah M., 'A Cancelled Marriage Contract from the Judaean Desert,' *Journal of Roman Studies* Vol. 84 (1994), 64–86

—— 'The Archive of Salome Komaïse Daughter of Levi: Another Archive from the "Cave of Letters",' *Zeitschrift für Papyrologie und Epigraphik* 105 (1995), 171–208

—— 'The Languages of the Legal and Administrative Documents from the Judaean Desert,' *Zeitschrift für Papyrologie und Epigraphik* 118 (1997), 219–31

—— 'The Rabbis and the Documents' in *Jews in a Graeco-Roman World,* ed. Martin Goodman (Oxford: Oxford University Press, 1998), 167–80

Cotton, Hannah M., and Elisha Qimron, 'XḤev/Se ar 13 of 134 or 135 C.E: A Wife's Renunciation of Claims,' *Journal of Jewish Studies* 49 (1998), 108–18

De Vaux, Roland, Jozef T. Milik, and Pierre Benoit, *Les Grottes de Muraba'at,* Discoveries in the Judaean Desert II (Oxford: Oxford University Press, 1961)

Freund, Richard A., *Secrets of the Cave of Letters* (New York, NY: Humanity Books, 2004)

Friedman, Mordechai A., 'Babatha's *Ketubba*: Some Preliminary Observations,' *Israel Exploration Journal* 46 (1996), 55–76

Geiger, Joseph, 'A Note on PYadin 18,' *Zeitschrift für Papyrologie und Epigraphik* 93 (1992), 67–68

Ilan, Tal, 'A Correction: On a Newly Published Divorce Bill from the Judaean Desert,' *Harvard Theological Review* Vol. 90, No. 2 (April 1997), 225

—— *Integrating Women into Second Temple History* (Peabody, MA: Hendrickson, 2001)

—— 'On a Newly Published Divorce Bill from the Judaean Desert,' *Harvard Theological Review* Vol. 89, No. 2 (April 1996), 195–202

—— 'Premarital Cohabitation in Ancient Judea: The Evidence of the Babatha Archive and the Mishnah (Ketubbot 1.4),' *Harvard Theological Review* 86 No. 3 (1993), 247–64

—— 'The Provocative Approach Once Again: A Response to Adiel Schremer,' *Harvard Theological Review* Vol. 91, No. 2 (April 1998), 203–04

Instone-Brewer, David, '1 Corinthians 7 in the Light of the Jewish Greek and Aramaic Marriage and Divorce Papyri,' *Tyndale Bulletin* 52.2 (2001), 225–44

—— 'Jewish Women Divorcing Their Husbands in Early Judaism: The Background to Papyrus Se'elim 13,' *Harvard Theological Review* 92:3 (July 1999), 349 57

—— 'Marriage & Divorce Papyri of the Ancient Greek, Roman and Jewish World,' <http://www.tyndalearchive.com/Brewer/MarriagePapyri/> [Accessed: 4/15/2009]

Katzoff, Ranon, 'On Yadin 37 = Hever 65,' in *Law in the Documents of the Judaean Desert*, ed. Ranon Katzoff and David Schaps (Leiden: Brill, 2005), 133–144

—— 'Papyrus Yadin 18 Again: A Rejoinder,' *Jewish Quarterly Review* 82 (1991), 171–176

—— 'Polygamy in Yadin,' *Zeitschrift für Papyrologie und Epigraphik* 109 (1995), 128–132

Lewis, Naphtali, Ranon Katzoff, and Jonas C. Greenfield, 'Papyrus Yadin 18,' *Israel Exploration Journal* 37 (1987), 229–50

Lewis, Naphtali, Yigael Yadin, and Jonas C. Greenfield, eds., *Documents from the Bar Kokhba Period in the Cave of Letters: Greek Papyri* (Jerusalem: Israel Exploration Society, 1989)

Milik, Jozef T., 'Le travail d'edition des manuscript du Desert de Juda,' *Vetus Testamentum Supplements* 4 (1956), 15–35

Piattelli, Daniela, 'The Marriage Contract and Bill of Divorce in Ancient Hebrew Law,' in *The Jewish Law Annual* Vol. 4, ed. B.S. Jackson (Leiden: Brill, 1981), 66–78

Safrai, Ze'ev, 'Halakhic Observance in the Judaean Desert,' in *Law in the Documents of the Judaean Desert,* ed. Ranon Katzoff and David Schaps (Leiden: Brill, 2005), 205–36

Satlow, Michael L., 'Marriage Payments and Succession Strategies in the Documents from the Judaean Desert,' in *Law in the Documents of the Judaean Desert,* ed. Ranon Katzoff and David Schaps (Leiden: Brill, 2005), 51–65

—— 'Reconsidering the Rabbinic ketubah Payment,' in Shaye J.D. Cohen, ed., *The Jewish Family in Antiquity* (Atlanta, GA: Brown Judaic Studies, 1993), 133–51

Schremer, Adiel, 'Divorce in Papyrus Se'elim 13 Once Again: A Reply to Tal Ilan,' *Harvard Theological Review* Vol. 91, No. 2 (April 1998), 193–202

Yadin, Yigael, 'Expedition D: "The Cave of Letters",' *Israel Exploration Journal* 12 (1962), 235–248

Yadin, Yigael, Jonas C. Greenfield, Ada Yardeni, and Baruch A. Levine, eds., *The Documents from the Bar Kokhba Period in the Cave of Letters: Hebrew, Aramaic and Nabatean-Aramaic Papyri* (Jerusalem: Israel Exploration Society, 2002)

Yadin, Yigael, Jonas C. Greenfield, and Ada Yardeni, 'Babatha's Ketubba,' *Israel Exploration Journal* 44 (1994), 75–101

Yardeni, Ada, *Naḥal Se'elim Documents (Hebrew)* (Israel: Ben-Gurion University of the Negev Press & the Israel Exploration Society, 1995)

Yiftach-Firanko, Uri, 'Judaean Desert Marriage Documents and *Ekdosis* in the Greek Law of the Roman Period,' in *Law in the Documents of the Judaean Desert,* ed. Ranon Katzoff and David Schaps (Leiden: Brill, 2005), 67–84

Abbreviations

Bible Versions

ESV	English Standard Version
ISV	International Standard Version
KJV	King James Version
LXX	Septuagint
MT	Masoretic Text
NA28	Nestle-Aland Greek New Testament 28th Edition
NASB	New American Standard Bible
NIV	New International Version
NT	New Testament
OT	Old Testament
RSV	Revised Standard Version

Primary Sources

The Ancient Near East

ANE	Ancient Near East
LE	The Laws of Eshnunna
LH	The Laws of Hammurabi
HL	The Hittite Laws
MAL	The Middle Assyrian Law

The Apocrypha

1 Macc	1 Maccabees
Sir	Sirach/Ecclesiasticus
Tob	Tobit
Wis	Wisdom of Solomon

Bible Books

Gen	Genesis
Exod	Exodus
Lev	Leviticus
Num	Numbers
Deut	Deuteronomy
Josh	Joshua
Judg	Judges
1–2 Sam	1–2 Samuel
1–2 Kgs	1–2 Kings
1–2 Chr	1–2 Chronicles
Neh	Nehemiah
Ps	Psalm
Prov	Proverbs
Song	Song of Songs
Isa	Isaiah
Jer	Jeremiah
Lam	Lamentations
Ezek	Ezekiel
Dan	Daniel
Hos	Hosea
Mic	Micah
Nah	Nahum
Zeph	Zephaniah
Mal	Malachi

Matt	Matthew	**Papyri: Other**	
Rom	Romans	P.Amst.40	Amsterdam University
1–2 Cor	1–2 Corinthians		
Eph	Ephesians	BGU (various)	Berlin Griechische Urkunden
Phil	Philippians	P.Eleph1	Elephantine
Col	Colossians	P.Oxy. (various)	Oxyrhynchus
1–2 Tim	1–2 Timothy	P.Ups.Frid.2	Uppsala University
Heb	Hebrews	P.Ryl.	Rylands Library
1 Pet	1 Peter		
Rev	Revelation		

Josephus

Ag. Ap.	Against Apian
Ant.	Jewish Antiquities
Life	The Life

Papyri: Judaean Desert Documents

JDD	Judaean Desert Documents
5/6Ḥev 10	Naḥal Ḥever
5/6Ḥev 18	Naḥal Ḥever
5/6Ḥev 37	Naḥal Ḥever
Mur 19	Murabba'at
Mur 20	Murabba'at
Mur 21	Murabba'at
Mur 115	Murabba'at
Mur 116	Murabba'at
XḤev/Se 13	Naḥal Ḥever
XḤev/Se 69	Naḥal Ḥever

Philo

Agr.	De agricultura
Cher.	Cherubim
Leg.	Legum allegoriae
Sacr.	De sacrificiis Abelis et Caini
Spec. Law	De specialibus legibus

The Pseudepigrapha

2 Bar.	2 Baruch (Syriac Apocalypse)
1 En.	1 Enoch (Ethiopic Apocalypse)
Jos. Asen	Joseph and Aseneth
Jub.	Jubilees
Ps.-Jonathan	Pseudo Jonathan
Ps.-Phoc.	Pseudo-Phocylides
Sib. Or.	Sibylline Oracles
T. Iss.	Testament of Issachar
T. Reu.	Testament of Reuben

Qumran

4Q159	4Q Ordinances
4Q416 III	4Q Instruction
4Q416 IV	4Q Instruction
4QMMT 4Q	*Miqsat Ma'aśê ha-Torah* (Some of the Torah Observations)
CD	Cairo Damascus Document

Rabbinic Works

b. Sukkah	Babylonian Talmud Sukkah
m. Git.	Mishnah Gittin
m. Ket	Mishnah Ketubbot
m. Sanh	Mishnah Sanhedrin
m. Sotah	Mishnah Sotah
m. Yebam	Mishnah Yebamot
t. Ketub.	Tosefta Ketubbot

Secondary Sources

AAR	American Academy of Religion
Bib	Biblica
BibInt	Biblical Interpretation
BR	Biblical Research
BSac	Bibliotheca sacra
BT	The Bible Translator
CBQ	Catholic Biblical Quarterly
Colloq	Colloquium
CTR	Criswell Theological Review
ErIsr	Eretz-Israel
EvQ	Evangelical Quarterly
ExpTim	Expository Times
HTR	Harvard Theological Review
HUCA	Hebrew Union College Annual
IEJ	Israel Exploration Journal
JAOS	Journal of the American Oriental Society
JATS	Journal of the Adventist Theological Society
JBL	Journal of Biblical Literature
JCS	Journal of Cuneiform Studies
JETS	Journal of the Evangelical Theological Society
JJS	Journal of Jewish Studies
JNES	Journal of Near Eastern Studies
JQR	Jewish Quarterly Review
JRS	Journal of Roman Studies
JSNT	Journal for the Study of the New Testament
JSOT	Journal for the Study of the Old Testament
Maarav	A Journal for the Study of the Northwest Semitic Languages and Literatures
NovT	Novum Testamentum
NTS	New Testament Studies

PAAJR	Proceedings of the American Academy of Jewish Research	TynBul	Tyndale Bulletin
RevQ	Revue de Qumran	VT	Vetus Testamentum
RB	Revue biblique	VTSup	Vetus Testamentum Supplements
SBJT	Southern Baptist Journal of Theology	WTJ	Westminster Theological Journal
SJT	Scottish Journal of Theology	ZPE	Zeitschrift für Papyrologie und Epigraphik
StudBib	Studia Biblica		
Th	Theology		
TJ	Trinity Journal		
TS	Theological Studies		

Bibliography

Abma, Richtsje, *Bonds of Love: Methodic Studies of Prophetic Texts with Marriage Imagery (Isaiah 50:1-3 and 54:1-10, Hosea 1-3, Jeremiah 2-3)* (Assen: Van Gorcum, 1999)

Ackerman, Susan, 'The Personal is Political: Covenantal and Affectionate Love (*'āhēb, 'ahăbâ*) in the Hebrew Bible', *Vetus Testamentum* 52 (October 2002), 437–58

Adler, Elaine J., 'The Background for the Metaphor of Covenant as Marriage in the Hebrew Bible' (Ph.D diss., University of California, Berkeley, 1989)

Allison, D. C., 'Divorce, Celibacy and Joseph (Matthew 1.18-25 and 19:1–12)', *Journal for the Study of the New Testament* 49 (1993), 3–10

Anderson, Gary, 'Celibacy or Consummation in the Garden? Reflections on Early Jewish and Christian Interpretations of the Garden of Eden,' *Harvard Theological Review* 82/2 (1989), 121–48

Archer, Léonie J., *Her Price is Beyond Rubies: The Jewish Woman in Graeco-Roman Palestine,* Journal for the Study of the Old Testament Supplement 60 (Sheffield: Sheffield Academic, 1990)

Bacchiocchi, Samuele, *The Marriage Covenant: A Biblical Study on Marriage, Divorce, and Remarriage* (Berrien Springs, MI: Biblical Perspectives, 2001)

Balla, Ibolya, 'Ben Sira / Sirach,' in *The Pseudepigrapha on Sexuality: Attitudes towards Sexuality in Apocalypses, Testaments, Legends, Wisdom, and Related Literature,* ed. William R. G. Loader (Grand Rapids, MI: Eerdmans, 2011), 362–97

Barth, Markus, *Ephesians 4–6: A New Translation with Introduction and Commentary by Markus Barth,* Anchor Bible 34A (Garden City, NY: Doubleday, 1974)

Batey, Richard A., *New Testament Nuptial Imagery* (Leiden: Brill, 1971)

Baugh, S. M., 'Cult Prostitution in New Testament Ephesus: A Reappraisal,' *Journal of the Evangelical Theological Society* 42.3 (1999), 443–60

——— 'Marriage and Family in Ancient Greek Society,' in *Marriage and Family in the Biblical World,* ed. Ken M. Campbell (Downers Grove, IL: InterVarsity, 2003), 105–31

Baumann, Gerlinde, *Love and Violence: Marriage as Metaphor for the Relationship between YHWH and Israel in the Prophetic Books,* trans. Linda M. Maloney (Stuttgart: Verlag Katholisches Biblewerk, 2000; repr. Collegeville, MN: Liturgical Press, 2003)

Beale, G. K., 'Positive Answer to the Question: Did Jesus and His Followers Preach the Right Doctrine from the Wrong Texts? An Examination of the Presuppositions of Jesus' and the Apostles' Exegetical Method,' in G. K. Beale, ed., *The Right Doctrine from the Wrong Texts* (Grand Rapids, MI: Baker Books, 1994), 387–404

——— *The Book of Revelation,* Howard I. Marshall and Donald A. Hagner, eds., New International Greek Testament Commentary (Grand Rapids, MI: Eerdmans, 1999)

Beckwith, Roger T., 'The Unity and Diversity of God's Covenants,' *Tyndale Bulletin* 38 (1987), 38–118

Ben-Barak, Zafrira, 'The Legal Background to the Restoration of Michal to David,' *Telling Queen Michal's Story: An Experiment in Comparative Interpretation,* Journal for the Study of the Old Testament Supplement 119, ed. David J. A. Clines and Tamara C. Eskenazi (Sheffield: Sheffield Academic, 1991), 74–93

Benoit, Pierre, Jozef T. Milik, and Roland De Vaux, *Discoveries in the Judaean Desert II: Les Grottes de Murabba'at* (Oxford: Oxford University Press, 1961)

Bickerman, Elias Joseph, 'Two Legal Interpretations of the Septuagint,' in *Studies in Jewish and Christian History (Ancient Judaism and Early Christianity),* ed. Amram Tropper (Leiden: Brill, 1976), 201–04

Bird, Phyllis, 'To Play the Harlot: An Enquiry into Old Testament Metaphor,' in *Gender Difference in Ancient Israel,* ed. Peggy L. Day (Minneapolis, MN: Fortress, 1989), 75–94

Black, Max, 'How Metaphors Work: A Reply to Donald Davidson,' in *On Metaphor,* ed. Sheldon Sacks (Chicago, IL: University of Chicago, 1978), 181–92

——— *Models and Metaphors: Studies in Language and Philosophy* (Ithaca, NY: Cornell University, 1962)

Blenkinsopp, John, 'The Family in First Temple Israel,' in *Families in Ancient Israel,* ed. Leo G. Perdue, Joseph Blenkinsopp, John J. Collins, and Carol Meyers (Louisville, KY: Westminster John Knox, 1997), 48–103

Block, Daniel I., 'Marriage and Family in Ancient Israel,' in *Marriage and Family in the Biblical World,* ed. Ken M. Campbell (Downers Grove, IL: InterVarsity, 2003), 33–102

Blomberg, Craig A., 'Marriage, Divorce, Remarriage, and Celibacy: An Exegesis of Matthew 19:3–12,' *Trinity Journal* 11NS (1990), 161–96

Bockmuehl, Markus N. A., 'Matthew 5.32; 19.9 in the Light of Pre-Rabbinic Halakhah,' *New Testament Studies* Vol. 35 (1989), 291–95

Brettler, Marc Zvi, *God is King: Understanding an Israelite Metaphor* (Sheffield: Sheffield Academic, 1989)

――― 'Incompatible Metaphors for Yhwh in Isaiah 40-66,' *Journal for the Study of the Old Testament* 78 (1998), 97–120

Brody, Robert, 'Evidence for Divorce by Jewish Women,' *Journal of Jewish Studies* L, No. 2 (Autumn 1999), 230–34

Caird, George B., *The Language and Imagery of the Bible* (London: Duckworth, 1980)

Carmichael, Calum M., 'Marriage and the Samaritan Woman,' *New Testament Studies* 26 (1980), 332–46

Carmichael, D. B., 'David Daube on the Eucharist and the Passover Seder,' *Journal for the Study of the New Testament* 42 (1997), 45–67

Carr, David M., and Colleen M. Conway, 'The Divine Human Marriage Matrix and Constructions of Gender and Bodies in the Christian Bible,' in *Sacred Marriages: The Divine-Human Sexual Metaphor from Sumer to Early Christianity,* ed. Marti Nissinen and Risto Uro (Winona Lake, IN: Eisenbraums, 2008), 275–303

Chapman, David, 'Marriage and Family in Second Temple Judaism,' in *Marriage and Family in the Biblical World,* ed. Ken M. Campbell (Downers Grove, IL: InterVarsity, 2003), 183–239

Charlesworth, James H., *The Historical Jesus* (Nashville, TN: Abingdon, 2008)

Charlesworth, James H., ed., *The Old Testament Pseudepigrapha: Vol. 2, Expansions of the 'Old Testament' and Legends, Wisdom and Philosophical Literature, Prayers, Psalms, and Odes, Fragments of Lost Judeo-Hellenistic Works* (Garden City, NY: Doubleday, 1985)

Chavasse, Claude, *The Bride of Christ: An Enquiry into the Nuptial Element in Early Christianity* (London: Faber&Faber, 1940)

Clark, Stephen, *Putting Asunder: Divorce and Remarriage in Biblical and Pastoral Perspective* (Bridgend: Bryntirion Press, 1999)

Cohen, Gerson, 'The Song of Songs and the Jewish Religious Mentality,' in *The Samuel Friedland Lectures 1960,* ed. Louis Finkelstein (New York, NY: Jewish Theological Seminary of America, 1966), 1–21

Collins, John C., *Genesis 1–4: A Linguistic, Literary, and Theological Commentary* (Phillipsburg, NJ: Presbyterian and Reformed, 2006)

Collins, John J., 'Marriage, Divorce, and Family in Second Temple Judaism,' in *Families in Ancient Israel,* ed. Leo G. Perdue, Joseph Blenkinsopp, John J. Collins, and Carol Meyers (Louisville, KY: Westminster John Knox, 1997), 104–62

────── 'Sibylline Oracles: A New Translation and Introduction,' in *The Old Testament Pseudepigrapha: Vol. 1, Apocalyptic Literature and Testaments*, ed. James H. Charlesworth (Garden City, NY: Doubleday, 1983), 317–472

Coogan, Michael D., Marc Z. Brettler, Carol A. Newsom, and Pherme Perkins, eds., *The New Oxford Annotated Apocrypha: New Revised Standard Version* (Oxford: Oxford University Press, 2010)

Coppens, Joseph, '"Mystery" in the Theology of Saint Paul and its Parallels at Qumran,' in *Paul and Qumran: Studies in New Testament Exegesis,* ed. Jerome Murphy-O'Connor (London: Chapman, 1968), 132–58

Cornes, Andrew, *Divorce and Remarriage: Biblical Principles & Pastoral Practice* (London: Hodder&Stoughton, 1993)

Cotton, Hannah M., 'A Cancelled Marriage Contract from the Judaean Desert,' *Journal of Roman Studies* Vol. 84 (1994), 64–86

────── 'The Archive of Salome Komaïse Daughter of Levi: Another Archive from the "Cave of Letters",' *Zeitschrift für Papyrologie und Epigraphik* 105 (1995), 171–208

────── 'The Languages of the Legal and Administrative Documents from the Judaean Desert,' *Zeitschrift für Papyrologie und Epigraphik* 118 (1997), 219–31

────── 'The Rabbis and the Documents,' in *Jews in a Graeco-Roman World,* ed. Martin Goodman (Oxford: Oxford University Press, 1998), 167–80

Cotton, Hannah M., and Elisha Qimron, 'XḤev/Se ar 13 of 134 or 135 C.E: A Wife's Renunciation of Claims,' *Journal of Jewish Studies* 49 (1998), 108–18

Cotton, Hannah M., and Werner Eck., 'Roman Officials in Judaea and Arabia and Civil Jurisdiction,' in, *Law in the Documents of the Judaean Desert,* ed. Ranon Katzoff and David Schaps (Leiden: Brill, 2005), 23–44

Cowley, A. E., ed., *Aramaic Papyri of the Fifth Century B.C.* (Oxford: Oxford University Press, 1923)

Danby, Herbert, ed., *The Mishnah,* trans. Herbert Danby (Oxford: Oxford University Press, 1933)

Daube, David, *The New Testament and Rabbinic Judaism* (Peabody, MA: Hendrickson, 1956)

Davidson, Donald, 'What Metaphors Mean,' in *On Metaphor*, ed. Sheldon Sacks (Chicago, IL: University of Chicago, 1978), 29–45

Davidson, Richard M., *The Flame of Yahweh: Sexuality in the Old Testament* (Peabody, MA: Hendrickson, 2007)

Davies, W. W., *The Codes of Hammurabi and Moses,* (Stilwell: Digireads.com, 2006)

Day, Peggy L., 'The Bitch Had It Coming To Her: Rhetoric and Interpretation in Ezekiel 16,' *Biblical Interpretation* 8 (2000), 231–53

———. 'Yahweh's Broken Marriages as Metaphoric Vehicle in the Hebrew Bible Prophets,' in *Sacred Marriages: The Divine-Human Sexual Metaphor from Sumer to Early Christianity,* ed. Marti Nissinen and Risto Uro (Winona Lake, IN: Eisenbraums, 2008), 219–41

Deasley, Alex R. G., *Marriage and Divorce in the Bible and the Church* (Kansas City, MS: Beacon Hill, 2000)

De Vaux, Roland, *Ancient Israel: Its Life and Institutions* (London: Darton, Longman & Todd, 1961)

Deming, Will, 'The Unity of 1 Corinthians 5–6,' *Journal of Biblical Literature* 115 (1992), 289–312

Dodd, C. H., *According to the Scriptures* (London: Nisbet, 1952)

———. *The Epistle to the Romans* (New York, NY: Harper, 1932)

Donfried, Karl, 'The Allegory of the Ten Virgins (Matt 25:1–13) as a Summary of Matthean Theology,' *Journal of Biblical Literature* 93 (1974), 415–28

Dumbrell, William J., *Covenant and Creation: An Old Testament Covenant Theology* (Milton Keynes: Paternoster, 2013)

Dunn, James D. G., *Jesus Remembered: Christianity in the Making Volume 1* (Grand Rapids, MI: Eerdmans, 2003)

———. *Romans 1–8* in Word Biblical Commentary 38A, ed. Bruce M. Metzger (Nashville, TN: Thomas Nelson, 1988)

———. *The Theology of Paul the Apostle* (Edinburgh: T&T Clark, 1998)

Edgar, Thomas R., 'Divorce & Remarriage for Adultery or Desertion,' in *Divorce and Remarriage: Four Christian Views,* ed. Wayne H. House (Downers Grove, IL: InterVarsity, 1990), 151–96

Eilberg-Schwartz, Howard, *God's Phallus and Other Problems for Men and Monotheism* (Boston, MA: Beacon, 1994)

Elliot, Elisabeth, *Let Me be a Woman* (London: Tyndale, 1976)

———. *The Mark of a Man* (Grand Rapids, MI: Revell, 1981)

Engle, Paul E. and Mark L. Strauss, eds., *Remarriage after Divorce in Today's Church: 3 Views* (Grand Rapids, MI: Zondervan, 2006)

Epstein, Louis M., *Marriage Laws in the Bible and the Talmud,* Harvard Semitic Series 12, 1942 (Reprinted by New York, NY: Johnson Reprint Company, 1968)

———. *Sex Laws and Customs in Judaism* (Jersey City, NY: Ktav, 1967)

———. 'The Institution of Concubinage among the Jews,' *Proceedings of the American Academy of Jewish Research* 6 (1934–1935), 153–58

———. *The Jewish Marriage Contract: A Study in the Status of the Woman in Jewish Law* (New York, NY: Jewish Theological Seminary, 1927; repr. Clark, NJ: Lawbook Exchange, 2004)

Evans, Craig A., *Ancient Texts for New Testament Studies* (Peabody, MA: Hendrickson, 2005)

———. *Mark 8:27–16:20,* Word Biblical Commentary 34B (Nashville, TN: Nelson, 2001)

Fairbairn, Patrick, *The Typology of Scripture: Viewed in Connection with the Whole Series of the Divine Dispensations* (New York, NY: Funk & Wagnalls, 1900)

Farla, Piet J., '"The Two Shall Become One Flesh": Gen 1.27 and 2.24 in the New Testament Marriage Texts,' in *Intertextuality in Biblical Writings: Essays in Honour of Bas van Iersel,* ed. S. Draisma (Kampen: Kok Pharos, 1989), 67–82

Fauconnier, Gilles, and Mark Turner, 'Rethinking Metaphor,' in *The Cambridge Handbook of Metaphor and Thought,* ed. Raymond W. Gibbs Jr. (Cambridge: Cambridge University Press, 2008), 53–66

Fekkes III, Jan, '"His Bride Has Prepared Herself": Revelation 19-21 and Isaian Nuptial Imagery,' *Journal of Biblical Literature* 109/2 (1990), 269–87

Fitzmyer, J. A., 'Divorce Among First-Century Palestinian Jews,' *Eretz-Israel* 14 (1978), 103–10

———. 'The Matthean Divorce Texts and Some New Palestinian Evidence,' *Theological Studies* 37 (1976), 197–226

Foster, Paul, 'The Bridegroom Messiah and the People of God: Marriage in the Fourth Gospel,' *Expository Times* 118 11 Ag (2007), 564–65

Foulkes, Francis, 'The Acts of God: A Study of the Basis of Typology in the Old Testament,' in *The Right Doctrine from the Wrong Texts,* ed. G. K. Beale (Grand Rapids, MI: Baker, 1994), 342–371

France, R. T., 'The Formula-Quotations of Matthew 2 and the Problem of Communication,' in *The Right Doctrine from the Wrong Texts,* ed. G. K. Beale (Grand Rapids, MI: Baker, 1994), 114–34

———. *The Gospel of Mark: New International Greek Testament Commentary* (Grand Rapids, MI: Eerdmans, 2002)

———. *The Gospel of Matthew: New International Commentary on the New Testament* (Grand Rapids, MI: Eerdmans, 2007)

Frey, Jörg, Jan Rohls, and Ruben Zimmermann, eds., *Metaphorik Und Christologie, Theologische Bibliothek Tapelmann* (Berlin: Walter de Gruyter, 2003)

Friedman, Mordechai A., *Jewish Marriage in Palestine: The Ketubba Traditions,* A Cairo Geniza Study Vol 1 (Tel Aviv: The Jewish Theological Seminary of America, 1981)

———. 'Termination of the Marriage upon the Wife's Request: A Palestinian *Ketubba* Stipulation,' *Proceedings of the American Academy of Jewish Research* 37 (1969), 29–55

Futato, Mark D., 'Because It Had Rained: A Study of Gen 2:5–7 with Implications for Gen 2:4–25 and Gen 1:1–23,' *Westminster Theological Journal* 60 (1998), 1–21

Gafni, Isaiah M., 'The Institution of Marriage in Rabbinic Times,' in *The Jewish Family: Metaphor and Memory,* ed. David Kraemer (Oxford: Oxford University Press, 1989), 13–30

Galambush, Julie, *Jerusalem in the Book of Ezekiel: The City as Yahweh's Wife,* The Society of Biblical Literature Dissertation Series 130 (Atlanta, GA: Scholars, 1992)

Gane, Roy, 'Old Testament Principles Relevant to Divorce and Remarriage,' *Journal of the Adventist Theological Society* 12 (2 2001), 35–61

Gehring, René, *The Biblical "One Flesh" Theology of Marriage as Constituted in Genesis 2:24* (Eugene, OR: Wipf and Stock, 2013)

Geller, Markham. J., 'New Sources for the Origin of the Rabbinic *Ketubah,*' *Hebrew Union College Annual* 49 (1978), 227–45

———. 'The Elephantine Papyri and Hosea 2, 3: Evidence for the Form of the Early Jewish Divorce Writ,' *Journal for the Study of Judaism in the Persian, Hellenistic, and Roman Periods* 8 (1977), 139–48

Gentner, Dedre, and Brian Bowdle, 'Metaphor as Structure-Mapping,' in *The Cambridge Handbook of Metaphor and Thought,* ed. Raymond W. Gibbs Jr. (Cambridge: Cambridge University Press, 2008), 109–28

Gerhart, Mary, and Allan Melvin Russell, *Metaphoric Process: The Creation of Scientific and Religious Understanding* (Fort Worth, TX: Texas Christian University, 1984)

———. *New Maps for Old: Explorations in Science and Religion* (London: Continuum, 2001)

Gibbs, Raymond W. Jr., ed., *The Cambridge Handbook of Metaphor and Thought* (Cambridge: Cambridge University Press, 2008)

Gilchrest, Eric, 'For the Wages of Sin is … Banishment: An Unexplored Substitutionary Motif in Leviticus 16 and the Ritual Aspect of the Scapegoat,' *Evangelical Quarterly* 85.1 (2013), 36–51

Glazier-McDonald, Beth, 'Intermarriage, Divorce and the *Bat-'él Nékar*: Insights into Mal. 2:10–16.' *Journal of Biblical Literature* 106 (1987), 603–11

Glucksberg, Sam, 'How Metaphors Create Categories – Quickly,' in *The Cambridge Handbook of Metaphor and Thought,* ed. Raymond W. Gibbs Jr. (Cambridge: Cambridge University Press, 2008), 67–83

Grabbe, Lester L., *Introduction to Second Temple Judaism: History and Religion of the Jews in the Time of Nehemiah, the Maccabees, Hillel, and Jesus* (London: T&T Clark, 2010)

Greengus, Samuel, 'Filling Gaps: Laws Found in Babylonia and in the Mishnah but Absent in the Hebrew Bible,' *A Journal for the Study of the Northwest Semitic Languages and Literatures* 7 (1991), 149–71

———. *Laws in the Bible and in Early Rabbinic Collections: The Legal Legacy of the Ancient Near East* (Eugene, OR: Cascade, 2011)

———. 'Old Babylonian Marriage Ceremonies and Rites,' *Journal of Cuneiform Studies* 20/2 (1966), 55–72

———. 'The Old Babylonian Marriage Contract,' *Journal of the American Oriental Society* 89 (1969), 505–32

Grenfell, Bernard and Arthur S. Hunt, eds., *The Oxyrhynchus Papyri: Part II* (London: Egypt Exploration Fund, 1899)

Grosheide, F. W., *Commentary on The First Epistle to the Corinthians: The English Text with Introduction, Exposition and Notes* (Grand Rapids, MI: Eerdmans, 1953)

Grosz, Katarzyna, 'Bride Wealth and Dowry in Nuzi,' in *Images of Women in Antiquity*, ed. Avril Cameron and Amélie Kuhrt (Detroit, MI: Wayne State University, 1983), 193–206

Hacohen, Aviad, and Menachem Elon, in Blu Greenberg, ed., *The Tears of the Oppressed: An Examination of the Agunah Problem: Background and Halakhic Sources* (Jersey City, NJ: KTAV, 2004)

Haley, John W., *Alleged Discrepancies of the Bible* (New Kensington, PA: Whittaker, 1992)

Hamer, Colin, *Being a Christian Husband: A Biblical Perspective* (Darlington: Evangelical Press, 2005)

———. *Divorce and the Bible: A Systematic Exegesis to Challenge the Traditional Views* (Bloomington, IN: Author House, 2006)

Hays, Richard B., *Echoes of Scripture in the Letters of Paul* (New Haven, CT: Yale University Press, 1989)

———. *The Conversion of the Imagination* (Grand Rapids, MI: Eerdmans, 2005)

Hengel, Martin, *The 'Hellenization' of Judaea in the First Century after Christ*, trans. John Bowden (London: SCM, 1989)

Hermas, *The Shepherd of Hermas*, in Alexander Roberts, James Donaldson, and A. Cleveland Coxe, eds., *From Ante-Nicene Fathers* Vol. 2, trans. F. Crombie (Buffalo, NY: Christian Literature Publishing Co., 1885) <http://www.newadvent.org/fathers/02012.htm> > [Accessed: 11/3/2014]

Heth, William A., 'Jesus on Divorce: How My Mind Was Changed,' *Southern Baptist Journal of Theology* 6.1 (Spring 2002), 4–29

———. 'Remarriage for Adultery or Desertion,' in *Remarriage after Divorce in Today's Church: 3 Views,* ed. Paul E. Engle and Mark L. Strauss (Grand Rapids, MI: Zondervan, 2006), 59–83

Holland, Tom, *Contours of Pauline Theology* (Fearn: Christian Focus, 2004)

———. *Romans: The Divine Marriage* (Eugene, OR: Wipf and Stock, 2011)

Holtz, Shalom E., '"To Go and Marry Any Man That You Please", A Study of the Formulaic Antecedents of the Rabbinic Writ of Divorce,' *Journal of Near Eastern Studies* 4:20 (October 1960), 241–58

Horsley, G. H. R. and S. Llewelyn, eds., *New Documents Illustrating Early Christianity: New Documents Illustrating Early Christianity* Vol. 3 (North Ryde: Macquarie University, 1983)

House, Wayne H., ed., *Divorce and Remarriage: Four Christian Views* (Downers Grove, IL: InterVarsity, 1990)

Huber, Lynn R., *Like a Bride Adorned: Reading Metaphor in John's Apocalypse,* Emory Studies in Early Christianity (New York, NY: T&T Clark, 2007)

Hugenberger, Gordon, *Marriage as a Covenant: Biblical Law and Ethics as Developed from Malachi* (Grand Rapids, MI: Baker, 1994)

Hunt, Arthur S., and C. C. Edgar, *Select Papyri With an English Translation* (London: Heinemann, 1932)

Hvidberg, Flemming F., *Weeping and Laughter in the Old Testament: A Study of Canaanite-Israelite* (Leiden: Brill, 1962)

Ilan, Tal, 'A Correction: On a Newly Published Divorce Bill from the Judaean Desert,' *Harvard Theological Review* Vol. 90, No. 2 (April 1997), 225

———. *Integrating Women into Second Temple History* (Peabody, MA: Hendrickson, 2001)

———. *Jewish Women in Greco-Roman Palestine: An Inquiry into Image and Status* (Peabody, MA: Hendrickson, 1995)

———. 'On a Newly Published Divorce Bill from the Judaean Desert,' *Harvard Theological Review* Vol. 89, No. 2 (April 1996), 195–202

———. 'The Provocative Approach Once Again: A Response to Adiel Schremer,' *Harvard Theological Review* Vol. 91, No. 2 (April 1998), 203–04

Instone-Brewer, David, '1 Corinthians 7 in the Light of the Graeco-Roman Marriage and Divorce Papyri,' *Tyndale Bulletin* 52.1 (2001), 101–16

———. '1 Corinthians 7 in the Light of the Jewish Greek and Aramaic Marriage and Divorce Papyri,' *Tyndale Bulletin* 52.2 (2001), 225–44

———. 'Deuteronomy 24:1-4 and the Origin of the Jewish Divorce Certificate,' *Journal of Jewish Studies* 49 (1998), 230–42

———. *Divorce and Remarriage in the Bible: The Social and Literary Context* (Grand Rapids, MI: Eerdmans, 2002)

———. *Divorce and Remarriage in the Church* (Carlisle: Paternoster, 2003; repr. Milton Keynes: Paternoster, 2011)

———. 'How Do We Read Malachi in the Light Of God's Divorce? Interview with Dr. Instone-Brewer on Divorce in Cases of Abuse and Neglect in the Old Testament,' <https://www.youtube.com/watch?v=zNtvV7NAaFs> [Accessed 1/25/2015]

———. 'Jesus' Old Testament Basis for Monogamy,' in *The Old Testament in the New Testament: Essays in Honour of J. L. North*, ed. Steve Moyise (Sheffield: Sheffield Academic, 2000), 75–105

———. 'Jewish Women Divorcing Their Husbands in Early Judaism: The Background to Papyrus Se'elim 13,' *Harvard Theological Review* 92:3 (July 1999), 349–57

———. 'Nomological Exegesis in Qumran "Divorce" Texts,' *Revue de Qumran* 18 (1998), 561–79

———. *Techniques and Assumptions in Jewish Exegesis before 70 CE* Texte und Studien zum antiken Judentum 30 (Tübingen: Mohr Siebeck, 1992)

———. 'Three Weddings and a Divorce: God's Covenant with Israel, Judah and the Church,' *Tyndale Bulletin* 47.1 (1996), 1–25

———. 'What God Has Joined Together,' <http://www.baylor.edu/ifl/christianreflection/MarriageArticleInstoneBrewer.pdf> [Accessed 9/30/2014]

Isaksson, Abel, *Marriage and Ministry in the New Temple* (Gleerup: Lund, 1965)

Jensen, Joseph, 'Does *Porneia* Mean Fornication? A Critique of Bruce Malina,' *Novum Testamentum* 20 (July 1978), 161–84

Johnson, M. D., 'Life of Adam and Eve: A New Translation and Introduction,' in *The Old Testament Pseudepigrapha Vol. 2: Expansions of the 'Old Testament' and Legends, Wisdom and Philosophical Literature, Prayers, Psalms, and Odes, Fragments of Lost*

Judeo-Hellenistic Works, ed. James H. Charlesworth (Garden City, NY: Doubleday, 1985), 249–95

Josephus, Flavius, *Josephus: The Complete Works,* trans. William Whiston (Nashville, TN: Thomas Nelson, 1998)

Kaiser, Walter C. Jr., 'Divorce in Malachi 2:10-16,' *Criswell Theological Review* 2 (1987), 73–84

———. 'The Single Intent of Scripture,' in *The Right Doctrine from the Wrong Texts,* ed. G. K. Beale (Grand Rapids, MI: Baker, 1994), 55–69

———. *Toward Old Testament Ethics* (Grand Rapids, MI: Zondervan, 1983)

Kamionkowski, Tamar S., 'Gender Reversal in Ezekiel 16,' in *Prophets and Daniel: A Feminist Companion to the Bible (Second Series),* ed. Athalya Brenner (London: Sheffield Academic, 2001), 170–85

Katzoff, Ranon, 'On Yadin 37 = Hever 65,' in *Law in the Documents of the Judaean Desert,* ed. Ranon Katzoff and David Schaps (Leiden: Brill, 2005), 133–144

———. 'Papyrus Yadin 18 Again: A Rejoinder,' *Jewish Quarterly Review* 82 (1991), 171–176

Katzoff, Ranon and David Schaps, eds., *Law in the Documents of the Judaean Desert* (Leiden: Brill, 2005)

Kaye, Bruce, '"One Flesh" and Marriage,' *Colloquium* 2 (May 1990), 46–57

Keener, Craig S., *And Marries Another: Divorce and Remarriage in the Teaching of the New Testament* (Peabody, MA: Hendrickson, 1991)

———. 'Remarriage for Adultery or Desertion: Responses,' in *Remarriage after Divorce in Today's Church: 3 Views,* ed. Paul E. Engle and Mark L. Strauss (Grand Rapids, MI: Zondervan, 2006), 85–95

Kelle, Brad E., *Hosea 2: Metaphor and Rhetoric in Historical Perspective* (Atlanta, GA: Society of Biblical Literature, 2005)

Kennedy, George A., *New Testament Interpretation through Rhetorical Criticism* (Chapel Hill, NC: University of North Carolina, 1984)

Knight, George W., 'Husbands and Wives as Analogues of Christ and the Church: Ephesians 5:21-33 Colossians 3:18-19,' in *Recovering Biblical Manhood and Womanhood: A Response to Evangelical Feminism,* ed. John Piper and Wayne A. Grudem (Wheaton, IL: Crossway, 2012), 165–78

Korpel, Marjo Christina Annette, *A Rift In the Clouds: Ugaritic and Hebrew Descriptions of the Divine* (Munster: Ugarit-Verlag, 1990)

Kreeft, Peter J., *Catholic Christianity: A Complete Catechism of Catholic Beliefs Based on the Catechism of the Catholic Church* (San Francisco, CA: Ignatius, 2001)

Käsemann, Ernst, *Commentary on Romans* (Grand Rapids, MI: Eerdmans, 1980)

Köstenberger, Andreas J., 'Marriage and Family in the New Testament,' in *Marriage and Family in the Biblical World,* ed. Ken M. Campbell (Downers Grove, IL: InterVarsity, 2003), 240–84

Köstenberger, Andreas J., and David J. Jones, *God, Marriage, and Family: Rebuilding the Biblical Foundation* (Wheaton, IL: Crossway, 2004)

Lakoff, George, and Mark Johnson, *Metaphors We Live By* (Chicago, IL: University of Chicago, 1980)

Laney, Carl J., 'Deuteronomy 24:1–4 and the Issue of Divorce,' *Bibliotheca sacra* 149 (1992), 3–15

Lefkowitz, Mary F., and Maureen B. Fant, *Women's Life in Greece and Rome: A Source Book in Translation* (Bristol: Bristol Classical, 1982; repr. London: Bloomsbury, 2013)

Lehmann, Manfred R., 'Gen 2:24 as the Basis for Divorce in Halakhah and New Testament,' *Zeitschrift für die alttestamentliche Wissenschaft* 72 no. 3 (1960), 263–67

Leith, Mary Joan Winn, 'Verse and Reverse: The Transformation of the Woman, Israel, in Hosea 1–3,' in *Gender Difference in Ancient Israel,* ed. Peggy L. Day (Minneapolis, MN: Fortress, 1989), 95–108

Lemos, T. M., *Marriage Gifts and Social Change in Ancient Palestine: 1200 BCE to 200 CE* (New York, NY: Cambridge University Press, 2010)

Lewis, Naphtali, Ranon Katzoff, and Jonas C. Greenfield, 'Papyrus Yadin 18,' *Israel Exploration Journal* 37 (1987), 229–50

Lincoln, Andrew T., 'The Use of the Old Testament in Ephesians,' *Journal for the Study of the New Testament* 14 (1982), 16–57

Lindars, Barnabas, 'The Place of the Old Testament in the Formation of New Testament Theology: Prolegomena,' in *The Right Doctrine from the Wrong Texts,* ed. G. K. Beale (Grand Rapids, MI: Baker, 1994), 137–45

Lipiński, Edward, 'Divorce in the Light of an Ancient Near Eastern Tradition,' in *The Jewish Law Annual* Vol. 4, ed. B.S. Jackson (Leiden: Brill, 1981), 9–27

Little, J. A., 'Paul's Use of Analogy: A Structural Analysis of Romans 7:1-6,' *Catholic Biblical Quarterly* 46 (1984), 82–90

Loader, William R. G., 'Did Adultery Mandate Divorce? A Reassessment of Jesus' Divorce Logia,' *New Testament Studies* 61.1 (2015), 67–78

———. *Making Sense of Sex: Attitudes towards Sexuality in Early Jewish and Christian Literature* (Grand Rapids, MI: Eerdmans, 2013)

———. *Philo, Josephus, and the Testaments on Sexuality: Attitudes Towards Sexuality in the Writings of Philo and Josephus and in the Testaments of the Twelve Patriarchs* (Grand Rapids, MI: Eerdmans, 2011)

———. *The New Testament on Sexuality* (Grand Rapids, MI: Eerdmans, 2012)

———. *The Septuagint, Sexuality, and the New Testament: Case Studies on the Impact of the LXX on Philo and the New Testament* (Grand Rapids, MI: Eerdmans, 2004)

Long, Gary Alan, 'Dead or Alive? Literality and God-Metaphors in the Hebrew Bible,' *American Academy of Religion* 62 No.2 (Summer 1994), 209–37

Long, Phillip J., *Jesus the Bridegroom: The Origin of the Eschatological Feast as a Wedding Banquet in the Synoptic Gospels* (Eugene, OR: Pickwick, 2013)

Luck, William F., *Divorce & Re-Marriage: Recovering the Biblical View* (Richardson, TX: Biblical Studies, 2009)

Lunn, Nicholas, 'Let My people Go! The Exodus as Israel's Metaphorical Divorce from Egypt,' *Evangelical Quarterly* LXXXVI No. 3 (July 2014), 239–51

Lövestam, Evald, 'Divorce and Remarriage in the New Testament,' in *The Jewish Law Annual* Vol. 4, ed. B. S. Jackson (Leiden: Brill, 1981), 47–65

MacArthur, John, *Matthew 1–7*, The MacArthur New Testament Commentary (Chicago, IL: Moody Bible Institute, 1985)

———. *The Divorce Dilemma: God's Last Word on Lasting Commitment* (Leominster: Day One, 2009)

Mace, David. R., *Hebrew Marriage: A Sociological Study* (London: Epworth, 1953)

MacKay, John L., *Hosea: A Mentor Commentary* (Fearn: Christian Focus, 2012)

Macky, Peter, *The Centrality of Metaphors to Biblical Thought: A Method for Interpreting the Bible* (Lewiston, NY: Edwin Mellen, 1990)

Malina, Bruce, 'Does *Porneia* Mean Fornication,' *Novum Testamentum* 14 (January 1972), 10–17

Masson, Robert, *Without Metaphor, No Saving God: Theology after Cognitive Linguistics,* Studies in Philosophical Theology 54 (Leuven: Peeters, 2014)

Matthews, Victor H., 'Marriage and Family in the Ancient Near East,' in *Marriage and Family in the Biblical World,* ed. Ken M. Campbell (Downers Grove, IL: InterVarsity, 2003), 1–32

Matthews, Victor H., and Don C. Benjamin, *Old Testament Parallels: Laws from the Ancient Near East* (Mahwah, NJ: Paulist Press, 2006)

McCarthy, Dennis J., 'Covenant in the Old Testament: The Present State of Enquiry,' *Catholic Biblical Quarterly* 27 (1965), 217–240

———. *Old Testament Covenant: A Survey of Current Opinions* (Stuttgart: Verlag Katholisches Biblewerk, 1967; repr. Oxford: Blackwell, 1972)

———. *Treaty and Covenant: A Study in Form in the Ancient Oriental Documents and in the Old Testament,* Analecta biblica 21 (Rome: Biblical Institute, 1963)

McFague, Sallie, *Metaphorical Theology: Models of God in Religious Language* (Philadelphia: Fortress, 1982)

McWhirter, Jocelyn, *The Bridegroom Messiah and the People of God: Marriage in the Fourth Gospel,* Society for New Testament Studies Monograph Series (Cambridge: Cambridge University Press, 2006)

Meyers, Carol, *Discovering Eve: Ancient Israelite Women in Context* (New York, NY: Oxford University Press, 1988)

———. 'The Family in Early Israel,' in *Families in Ancient Israel,* ed. Leo G. Perdue, Joseph Blenkinsopp, John J. Collins, and Carol Meyers (Louisville, KY: Westminster John Knox, 1997), 1–47

Mieroop, Marc Van De, *A History of the Ancient Near East ca. 3000–323 BC,* 2nd ed. (Malden, MA: Blackwell, 2007)

Miletic, Stephen Francis, *"One Flesh": Eph. 5.22–24, 5.31: Marriage and the New Creation* (Rome: Analacta Biblica, 1988)

Milik, Jozef T., 'Le travail d'edition des manuscript du Desert de Juda,' *Vetus Testamentum Supplements* 4 (1956), 15–35

Moo, D. J., 'Jesus and the Authority of the Mosaic Law,' *Journal for the Study of the New Testament* 6, 20 (January 1984), 3–49

Moritz, Thorsten, *A Profound Mystery: The Use of the Old Testament in Ephesians* (Leiden: Brill, 1996)

Moughtin-Mumby, Sharon, *Sexual and Marital Metaphors in Hosea, Jeremiah, Isaiah, and Ezekiel* (Oxford: Oxford University Press, 2008)

Muirhead, I. A., 'The Bride of Christ,' *Scottish Journal of Theology* 5 (1952), 175–87

Murray, John, *Divorce* (Phillipsburg, NJ: Presbyterian and Reformed, 1961)

Neufeld, E., *Ancient Hebrew Marriage Laws: With Special References to General Semitic Laws and Customs* (London: Longmans, Green & Co, 1944)

Neusner, Jacob, *Judaism and its Social Metaphors: Israel in the History of Jewish Thought* (Cambridge: Cambridge University Press, 1989)

———. *Rabbinic Literature and the New Testament: What We Cannot Show, We Do Not Know* (Eugene, OR: Wipf and Stock, 1994)

Neusner, Jacob, and William S. Green, *Dictionary of Judaism in the Biblical Period: 450 B.C.E. to 600 C.E.* 1996 (Reprinted by Peabody, MA: Hendrickson, 1999)

Neusner, Jacob, ed., *The Mishnah: A New Translation* (New Haven, CT: Yale University, 1988)

Newsom, Carol A., 'Introduction to the Apocryphal/Deuterocanonical Books,' in *The New Oxford Annotated Apocrypha: New Revised Standard Version*, ed. Michael Coogan, D. Marc, Z. Brettler, Carol A. Newsom, and Pheme Perkins (Oxford: Oxford University Press, 2010), 3–9

Noam, Vered, 'Divorce in Qumran in Light of Early Halakah,' *Journal of Jewish Studies* LVI, No. 2 (Autumn 2005), 206–23

O'Brien, Julia M., *Challenging Prophetic Metaphor: Theology and Ideology in the Prophets* (Louisville, KY: Westminster John Knox Press, 2008)

———. 'Judah as Wife and Husband: Deconstructing Gender in Malachi,' *Journal of Biblical Literature* 115 (1996), 241–50

O'Brien, Peter T., *The Letter to the Ephesians* (Grand Rapids, MI: Eerdmans, 1999)

Ogden, Graham S., 'The Use of Figurative Language in Malachi 2.10–16,' *The Bible Translator* 39 (1988), 223–30

Origen, *Commentary on Matthew*, translated by John Patrick from Ante-Nicene Fathers, Vol. 9 (Buffalo, NY: Christian Literature Publishing Co, 1896). Revised and edited for New Advent by Kevin Knight <http://www.newadvent.org/fathers/1016.htm>

Parker, David M., 'The Early Traditions of Jesus' Sayings on Divorce Theology,' *Theology* 96 (1993), 372–83

Patai, Raphael, *Sex and Family in the Bible and the Middle East* (Garden City, NY: Doubleday, 1959)

Patterson, Richard D., 'Metaphors of Marriage as Expressions of Divine-Human Relations,' *Journal of the Evangelical Theological Society* 5 (December 2008), 689–702

Paul, Shalom M., 'Exod 21.10: A Threefold Maintenance Clause,' *Journal of Near Eastern Studies* 28 (January 1969), 48–53

Pavia, Will, 'Rabbi Accused of Torturing Husbands to Grant Divorce,' *The Times, London* (19 February 2015), 33

Perdue, Leo G., 'The Household, Old Testament Theology, and Contemporary Hermeneutics,' in *Families in Ancient Israel*, ed. Leo G. Perdue, Joseph Blenkinsopp, John J. Collins, and Carol Meyers (Louisville, KY: Westminster John Knox, 1997), 223–57

———. 'The Israelite and Early Jewish Family: Summary and Conclusions,' in *Families in Ancient Israel*, ed. Leo G. Perdue, Joseph Blenkinsopp, John J. Collins, and Carol Meyers (Louisville, KY: Westminster John Knox, 1997), 163–222

Petersen, David L., *Zechariah 9–14 and Malachi* (Louisville, KY: Westminster John Knox, 1995)

Phillips, Anthony, 'Another Look at Adultery,' *Journal for the Study of the Old Testament* 20 (1981), 3–25

Philo, *The Works of Philo*, trans. C. D. Yonge (Peabody, MA: Hendrickson, 1993)

Pitre, Brant, *Jesus the Bridegroom: The Greatest Love Story Ever Told* (New York, NY: Crown, 2014)

Plato, 'Republic Book 5' <http://www.perseus.tufts.edu/hopper/text?doc=Perseus%3Atext%3A1999.01.0168%3Abook%3D5%3Apage%3D462> [Accessed: 4/18/2014]

Porten, Bezalel, *Archives from Elephantine: The Life of an Ancient Jewish Military Colony* (Berkeley, CA: University of California, 1968)

Postell, Seth D., *Adam as Israel: Genesis 1–3 as the Introduction to the Torah and Tanakh* (Eugene, OR: Pickwick, 2011)

Poythress, Vern S., *Science and Hermeneutics*, in *Foundations of Contemporary Interpretation: Implications of Scientific Method for Biblical Interpretation* Vol. 5, ed. Moisés Silva (Grand Rapids, MI: Zondervan, 1996)

Pressler, Carolyn, 'Wives and Daughters, Bond and Free: Views of Women in the Slave Laws of Exodus 21:2–11,' in *Gender and Law in the Hebrew Bible and the Ancient Near East*, ed. Victor H. Matthews, Bernard M. Levinson, and Tikva Frymer-Kensky (Sheffield: Sheffield Academic, 1998; repr. London: T&T Clark, 2004), 147–72

Pritchard, James B., ed., *Ancient Near Eastern Texts Relating to the Old Testament (With Supplement)* 3d ed. (Princeton, NJ: Princeton University Press, 1969)

—— *The Ancient Near East: An Anthology of Texts and Pictures* (Princeton, NJ: Princeton University Press, 2011)

Rabello, Alfredo Mordechai, 'Divorce of Jews in the Roman Empire,' in *The Jewish Law Annual* Vol. 4, ed. B.S. Jackson (Leiden: Brill, 1981), 79–102

Rabinowitz, Jacob J., 'Marriage Contracts in Ancient Egypt in the Light of Jewish Sources,' *Harvard Theological Review* 46. No. 2 (April 1953), 91–97

Richards, I. A., *The Philosophy of Rhetoric* (New York, NY: Oxford University Press, 1936)

Ricoeur, Paul, *The Rule of Metaphor: The Creation of Meaning in Language*, trans. Robert Czerny (Paris: Editions du Seuil, 1975; repr. London: Routledge, 2003)

Robinson, A. T., *The Body: A Study in Pauline Theology*, Studies in Biblical Theology 5 (London: SCM, 1952)

Rosner, Brian S., 'Temple Prostitution in 1 Corinthians 6:12–20,' *Novum Testamentum* 40 (1998), 336–51

Roth, Martha, *Babylonian Marriage Agreements: 7th–3rd Centuries B.C.*, Alter Orient und Altes Testament (Kevelaer: Butzon & Bercker, 1989)

Safrai, Ze'ev, 'Halakhic Observance in the Judaean Desert,' in *Law in the Documents of the Judaean Desert*, ed. Ranon Katzoff and David Schaps (Leiden: Brill, 2005), 205–36

Sailhamer, John H., *The Pentateuch as Narrative* (Grand Rapids, MI: Zondervan, 1992)

Sampley, J. Paul, *And the Two Shall Become One Flesh: A Study of Traditions in Ephesians 5:21–33,* Society for New Testament Studies Monograph Series 16 (Cambridge: Cambridge University Press, 1971)

———. 'The First Letter to the Corinthians,' in *Acts Introduction to Epistolary Literature Romans 1 Corinthians,* Vol. X of *The New Interpreter's Bible: A Commentary in Twelve Volumes,* ed. Leander E. Keck (Nashville, TN: Abingdon, 2002), 771–1003

Sanders, E.P., *Jesus and Judaism* (London: SCM, 1985)

———. *Paul: A Brief Insight* (New York, NY: Oxford University Press, 1991; repr. New York, NY: Sterling, 2009)

Satlow, Michael L., *Creating Judaism: History, Tradition, Practice* (New York, NY: Columbia University Press, 2006)

———. *Jewish Marriage in Antiquity* (Princeton, NJ: Princeton University Press, 2001)

———. 'Marriage Payments and Succession Strategies in the Documents from the Judaean Desert,' in *Law in the Documents of the Judaean Desert,* ed. Ranon Katzoff and David Schaps (Leiden: Brill, 2005), 51–65

———. 'Reconsidering the Rabbinic *Ketubah* Payment,' in *The Jewish Family in Antiquity,* ed. Shaye J.D. Cohen (Atlanta, GA: Brown Judaic Studies, 1993), 133–51

———. 'Rhetoric and Assumptions: Romans and Rabbis on Sex,' in *Jews in a Graeco-Roman World,* ed. Martin Goodman (Oxford: Oxford University Press, 1998), 135–44

———. *Tasting the Dish: Rabbinic Rhetorics of Sexuality* (Atlanta, GA: Brown Judaic Studies, 1995)

Schaff, Philip, ed., *On the Good of Marriage,* Vol. 3 of Nicene and Post-Nicene Fathers (Buffalo, NY: Christian Literature Publishing Co., 1887) <http://www.newadvent.org/fathers/1309.htm> [Accessed: 11/11/2014]

Schnackenburg, Rudolf, *The Epistle to the Ephesians,* trans. Helen Heron (Edinburgh: T&T Clark, 1991)

Selms, Adrianus van, *Marriage and Family Life in Ugaritic Literature* (London: Luzac, 1954)

Sherwood, Yvonne, *The Prostitute and the Prophet: Reading Hosea in the Late Twentieth Century* (Sheffield: Sheffield Academic, 1996; repr. London: T&T Clark, 2004)

Skinner, John, *A Critical and Exegetical Commentary on Genesis,* International Critical Commentary (Edinburgh: T&T Clark, 1930)

Skinner, Quentin, 'Meaning and Understanding in the History of Ideas,' *History and Theory* 8:1 (1969), 3–53

Sly, Dorothy, *Philo's Perception of Women,* Brown Judaic Studies 209 (Atlanta, GA: Scholars, 1990)

Smith, Don T., 'The Matthean Exception Clauses in the Light of Matthew's Theology and Community,' *Studia Biblica* 17 (1989), 55–82

Smolarz, Sebastian R., *Covenant and the Metaphor of Divine Marriage in Biblical Thought: A Study with Special Reference to the Book of Revelation* (Eugene, OR: Wipf and Stock, 2011)

Sohn, Seock-Tae, '"I Will Be Your God and You Will Be My People": The Origin and Background of the Covenant Formula,' in *Ki Baruch Hu: Ancient Near Eastern, Biblical, and Judaic Studies in Honor of Baruch A. Levin,* ed. Robert Chazan, William W. Hallo, and Lawrence H. Schiffman (Winona Lake, IN: Eisenbrauns, 1999), 355–72

———. *YHWH, The Husband of Israel* (Eugene, OR: Wipf and Stock, 2002)

Sommer, Benjamin D., *A Prophet Reads Scripture: Allusion in Isaiah 40–66* (Stanford, CA: Stanford University Press, 1998)

Son, Aaron S., 'Implications of Paul's "One Flesh" Concept for His Understanding of the Nature of Man,' *Biblical Research* 11 (2001), 107–22

Sousan, André, 'The Woman in the Garden of Eden: A Rhetorical-Critical Study of Genesis 2:4b–3:24,' (Ph.D. diss. Graduate School of Vanderbilt University, 2006)

Sprinkle, Joe M., 'Old Testament Perspectives on Divorce and Remarriage,' *Journal of the Evangelical Theological Society* 40 (Dec 1997), 529–50

Stienstra, Nelly, *YHWH is the Husband of His People: Analysis of a Biblical Metaphor with Special Reference to Translation* (Kampen: Kok Pharos, 1996)

Syreeni, Kari, 'From the Bridegroom's Time to the Wedding of the Lamb,' in Marti Nissinen and Risto Uro, eds., *Sacred Marriages: The Divine-Human Sexual Metaphor from Sumer to Early Christianity* (Winona Lake, IN: Eisenbrauns, 2008), 343–69

Tait, Michael, *Jesus, the Divine Bridegroom, in Mark 2:18–22: Mark's Christology Upgraded,* Analecta Biblica 185 (Rome: Pontificio Istituto Biblico, 2012)

Taylor, Richard A., and Ray E. Clendenen, *Haggai Malachi,* The New American Commentary: An Exegetical and Theological Exegesis of Holy Scripture Vol 21A (Nashville, TN: Broadman & Holman, 2004)

Thiselton, Anthony C., *The Hermeneutics of Doctrine* (Grand Rapids, MI: Eerdmans, 2007)

Tomson, Peter J., *Paul and the Jewish Law: Halakha in the Letters of the Apostle to the Gentiles* (Minneapolis, MN: Fortress, 1990)

Torrey, C. C., 'The Prophecy of "Malachi",' *Journal of Biblical Literature* 17 (1 1898), 1–15

Tosato, Angelo, 'On Genesis 2:24,' *Catholic Biblical Quarterly* 52 no. 3 (1990), 389–409

Treggiari, Susan, 'Marriage and Family in Roman Society,' in *Marriage and Family in the Biblical World,* ed. Ken M. Campbell (Downers Grove, IL: InterVarsity, 2003), 132–82

Van de Mieroop, Marc, *A History of the Ancient Near East ca 3000–323 BC,* 2d ed. (Malden, MA: Blackwell, 2007)

Vanhoozer, Kevin J., *Is There Meaning in this Text?* (Grand Rapids, MI: Zondervan, 1998)

Vatican, 'Code of Canon Law,' <http://www.vatican.va/archive/ENG1104/_P3Y.HTM> [Accessed: 11/14/2014]

Vermes, Geza, 'Sectarian Matrimonial Halakhah in the Damascus Rule,' *Journal of Jewish Studies* 25 (1974), 197–202

———. *The Complete Dead Sea Scrolls in English* (London: Pelican, 1962; repr. London: Penguin, 1998)

Walton, John H., *Ancient Israelite Literature in Its Cultural Context: A Survey of Parallels Between Biblical and Ancient Near Eastern Texts* (Grand Rapids, MI: Zondervan, 1989)

———. *Ancient Near Eastern Thought and the Old Testament: Introducing the Conceptual World of the Hebrew Bible* (Nottingham: Apollos, 2007)

Warren, Andrew, 'Did Moses Permit Divorce? Modal wĕqāṭal as Key to New Testament Readings of Deuteronomy 24:1-4,' *Tyndale Bulletin* 49 (1998), 39–56

Wasserstein, A., 'A Marriage Contract from the Province of Arabia Nova: Notes on Papyrus Yadin 18,' *Jewish Quarterly Review* 80 No.1/2 (Jul–Oct 1989), 93–130

Weems, Renita, *Battered Love: Marriage, Sex, and Violence in the Hebrew Prophets* (Minneapolis, MN: Augsburg Fortress, 1995)

Weiss, David H., 'The Use of קנה in Connection with Marriage,' *Harvard Theological Review* Vol. 57, No. 3 (July 1964), 244–48

Wenham, Gordon J., *Genesis 1–15,* (Nashville, TN: Word, 1987)

———. 'No Remarriage After Divorce,' in Paul E. Engle and Mark L. Strauss, eds., *Remarriage after Divorce in Today's Church: 3 Views* (Grand Rapids, MI: Zondervan, 2006), 19–42

Westbrook, Raymond, 'Adultery in Ancient Near Eastern Law,' *Revue Biblique* 97 (1990), 542–80

———. *Old Babylonian Marriage Law* (Yale University, CT: University Microfilms International, 1984)

———. 'The Female Slave,' in *Gender and Law in the Hebrew Bible and the Ancient Near East.* ed. Victor H. Matthews, Bernard M. Levinson, and Tikva Frymer-Kensky (Sheffield: Sheffield Academic, 1998; repr. London: T&T Clark, 2004), 214–38

———. 'The Prohibition on the Restoration of Marriage in Deuteronomy 24:1–4,' in *Scripta Hierosolymitana: Studies in Bible: 31,* ed. Sarah Japhet (Jerusalem: Magnes, 1986), 387–405

White, Ellen, 'Michal the Misinterpreted,' *Journal for the Study of the Old Testament* 31 (2007), 451–64

Winter, Bruce W., *After Paul Left Corinth: The Influence of Secular Ethics and Social Change* (Grand Rapids, MI: Eerdmans, 2001)

Wintermute, O. S., 'Jubilees: A New Translation and Introduction,' in *The Old Testament Pseudepigrapha Vol. 2: Expansions of the 'Old Testament' and Legends, Wisdom and Philosophical Literature, Prayers, Psalms, and Odes, Fragments of Lost Judeo-Hellenistic Works,* ed. James H. Charlesworth (Garden City, NY: Doubleday, 1985), 35–51

Witte, John Jr., *From Sacrament to Contract: Marriage, Religion, and Law in the Western Tradition,* 2nd ed. (Louisville, KY: Westminster John Knox, 2012)

Witte, John Jr., and Robert M. Kingdon, *Sex, Marriage and Family in John Calvin's Geneva: Courtship, Engagement, and Marriage.* Religion, Marriage, and Family Vol. 1 (Grand Rapids, MI: Eerdmans, 2005)

Wolff, Hans Walter, *Hosea,* trans. Paul D. Hanson (Philadelphia: Fortress, 1974)

Wright, Christopher J. H., *God's People in God's Land* (Grand Rapids, MI: Eerdmans, 1990; repr. Carlisle: Paternoster, 1997)

Wright, N. T., 'The Letter to the Romans,' in *Acts Introduction to Epistolary Literature Romans 1 Corinthians* Vol. X of *The New Interpreter's Bible: A Commentary in Twelve Volumes,* ed. Leander E. Keck (Nashville, TN: Abingdon, 2002), 393–770

Yadin, Yigael, Jonas C. Greenfield, Ada Yardeni, and Baruch A. Levine, eds., *The Documents from the Bar Kokhba Period in the Cave of Letters: Hebrew, Aramaic and Nabatean-Aramaic Papyri* (Jerusalem: Israel Exploration Society, 2002)

Yamauchi, Edwin M., 'Cultural Aspects of Marriage in the Ancient World,' *Bibliotheca sacra* 135 (1978), 241–52

Yardeni, Ada. *Naḥal Se'elim Documents (Hebrew)* (Israel: Ben-Gurion University of the Negev Press & the Israel Exploration Society, 1995)

Yiftach-Firanko, Uri, 'Judaean Desert Marriage Documents and *Ekdosis* in the Greek Law of the Roman Period,' in *Law in the Documents of the Judaean Desert,* ed. Ranon Katzoff and David Schaps (Leiden: Brill, 2005), 67–84

———. *Marriage and Marital Arrangements: a History of the Greek Marriage Document in Egypt, 4th century BCE–4th century CE* (Munich: Münchener Beiträge 93, 2003)

Zakovitch, Yair, 'The Woman's Rights in the Biblical Law of Divorce,' in *The Jewish Law Annual* Vol. 4, ed. B.S. Jackson (Leiden: Brill, 1981), 28–46

Zehnder, Markus, 'A Fresh Look at Malachi II 13–16,' *Vetus Testamentum* 53 (2003), 224–59

Zimmermann, Ruben, 'Das Hochzeitsritual im Jungfrauengleichnis: Sozialgeschichtliche Hintergrunde zu Mt 25.1–13,' *New Testament Studies* 48 (2002), 48–70

———. *Geschlechtermetaphorik Und Gotteseverhaltnis* (Tübingen: Mohr Siebeck, 2001)

———. 'Nuptial Imagery in the Revelation of John,' *Biblica* 84 (2003), 153–83

———. 'The Love Triangle of Lady Wisdom: Sacred Marriage in Jewish Wisdom Literature,' in *Sacred Marriages: The Divine-Human Sexual Metaphor from Sumer to Early Christianity,* ed. Marti Nissinen and Risto Uro (Winona Lake, IN: Eisenbraums, 2008), 243–58